LAW AND ECONOMICS

A Collection of Essays and Cases

Series Editor

Jenny B. Wahl
Carleton College

Series Contents

Economic Analysis of Contract Law, Antitrust Law, and Safety Regulations

Edited with an introduction by

Jenny B. Wahl

Carleton College

Routledge
Taylor & Francis Group
New York London

First published by Garland Publishing, Inc.

This edition published 2012 by Routledge

Routledge
Taylor & Francis Group
711 Third Avenue
New York, NY 10017

Routledge
Taylor & Francis Group
2 Park Square, Milton Park
Abingdon, Oxon OX14 4RN

Library of Congress Cataloging-in-Publication Data

Economic analysis of contract law, antitrust law, and safety regulations/ edited with an introduction by Jenny B. Wahl.
p. cm. — (Law and economics ; 2)
Includes bibliographical references.
ISBN 0-8153-3086-3 (alk. paper)
1. Contracts—Economic aspects—United States. 2. Antitrust law—Economic aspects—United States. 3. Safety regulations—Economic aspects—United States. I. Wahl, Jenny Bourne. II. Series: Law and economics (New York, N.Y.) ; 2.
KF801.E24 1998
346.7302—dc21 98-48287
CIP

Contents

Introduction

The introduction to volume I explains how voluntary exchange can lead to an efficient allocation of resources. This volume focuses on two means by which people formalize their voluntary transactions: contracts and firms. It also looks at how regulation can help — or hinder — the process of voluntary exchange by its effect on the behavior of producers (particularly through antitrust laws) and consumers (especially through their reactions to safety regulations).

Contracts

As we have seen, the law can play an important role in helping a society achieve certain goals. In particular, legal rules can assist people as they seek to improve their well-being. One means by which people attempt to make themselves better off is to engage in voluntary transactions with others — trading their tree-trimming skills for wages they can then spend on groceries, shelter, and entertainment, for example. Often, people use contracts to arrange such transactions. Economic analysis proves useful in two ways: understanding why people choose certain contractual forms, and determining what remedies for breach of contract will lead to efficient outcomes.

Uncertainty frequently gives rise to contracts. Aside from instantaneous exchanges, transactions contain an element of time and, therefore, uncertainty. Suppose I agree to trim your black walnut tree for $300, payable when the job is completed. All sorts of circumstances might intervene. I might accidentally cut off my arm on the job (mistaking one limb for another) and end up at the hospital for weeks. A violent storm could uproot the tree and send it across town, eliminating the need for a trim. You might find someone willing to trim the tree for $100 before I begin work. I could receive a tempting job offer from the U.S. Forest Service and become too busy to finish your trimming. Although we might address some of these contingencies in our contract, we may also leave some gaps. Legal rules help determine what contingencies must be addressed, which agreements will be enforced, and how gaps will be treated.

Contract Formation

Before considering how the law shapes contracts, let's examine why contracts exist.

Efficiency considerations often underlie contractual arrangements. You hire me to trim your tree because I have a better sense of balance and more expertise at cutting wood. This frees you up to do things you excel at — playing basketball, say. By entering into contracts, we both feel better off. I put my talents toward trimming trees, you hone your shooting skills. You are willing to pay me for tree-trimming, and I gladly buy tickets to your games.

One important way that contracts can improve efficiency is by shifting risk toward those most able to bear it. You'll pay me to trim your tree in part because you don't want to risk severing your arm or breaking your kneecap. I in turn buy disability insurance from a company that can spread risks over lots of people like me. Yet the very possibility of shifting risk carries with it certain problems that may prevent contracts from forming. In particular, asymmetries in information plague contract formation.

George Akerlof's famous "lemons" article points out one sort of information problem: adverse selection. Akerlof illustrates this concept with the used-car market. Car owners know a lot about the performance and reliability of their cars. Suppose potential buyers of used cars cannot, however, distinguish good cars from "lemons." Used cars will sell for a single price, then, and only "lemons" will be for sale. Depending upon the distribution of quality in used cars, buyers and sellers may not come to a mutually agreeable price. In this example, sellers have information and buyers do not. In other potential markets, the opposite may be true. Consider the market for health insurance. Suppose individuals have good information about their own health and habits but insurance companies cannot distinguish fit from enfeebled or foolhardy persons. Companies therefore charge the same price to everyone. If all policies cost a monthly premium of $100, only those who expected monthly medical bills of $100 or more would buy insurance. Insurance companies would quickly go bankrupt — indeed, might never open their doors for business.[1]

A second sort of information problem is moral hazard. Again using the insurance market as an example, moral hazard refers to the incentive people have to change behavior once they are insured. If I had no car insurance, I would carefully park my vehicle in a lighted area and keep it locked. If I am fully insured, however, I might well be more lax because someone else will pay for losses.

Market mechanisms often can help solve adverse selection and moral hazard problems. Insurance companies cope with adverse selection by separating people into different risk classes. They categorize people by age, sex, health history or driving records, certain habits (smoking, for instance), and the like. Co-payments and deductibles help minimize moral hazard problems. Car sellers use warranties to send signals about the quality of their products and reduce adverse selection problems. Laws that encourage private exchange and private solutions to information problems can often enhance allocative efficiency.

Yet sometimes regulations substitute for market mechanisms because lawmakers want to shield people from fraud, deceptive practices, and sharp dealing. Such laws may promote effective disclosure of pertinent information. But, in some cases, regulations might actually lead to inefficiency. For example, some states require sellers of used cars to issue warranties. Why might this be inefficient? Because no one will be able to buy cheap used cars. Those willing to take the risk of an unwarranted "lemon"

— perhaps because they have mechanical expertise and can evaluate cars as well as sellers — can no longer do so; some of these folks may not be able to afford used cars as a result. They would have been better off with cheap, unwarranted used cars than with no cars at all.[2]

The articles by Cheung and Umbeck analyze formation of contracts in two activities: Chinese tenant farming and California gold mining. Both examine the conditions that make contracts worthwhile, the means by which people overcome asymmetries in information, and the ways parties balance reduced risk against the transaction costs of addressing contingencies.

Remedies for Breach

Although contracts sometimes specify ways of settling disputes or damages to be paid in the event of breach, most contracts contain gaps. When parties fail to live up to a contractual agreement and the contract does not provide a solution, the law fills in these gaps.[3] Generally, courts have three remedies: damages, specific performance, and discharge.

The included article by Posner and Rosenfield offers an economic way of thinking about the remedies that courts choose in breach-of-contract cases. They suggest that a court promotes efficiency if it allocates risks and estimates losses as the parties would have, had they done so themselves. By mimicking the market, courts will also encourage similarly situated parties to save court costs in the future by addressing contingencies within the contract.

But what is "mimicking the market"? Posner and Rosenfield contend that people would logically assign a risk to the party who could bear it at least cost. The answers to two questions help determine which party that is: Who can more cheaply assess a loss associated with a particular risk? Who can more cheaply insure against the risk? The first question has two subparts: because an expected loss depends on the probability of the risk occurring as well as the size of a loss should it occur, one needs to ask who can more cheaply estimate each element.

Let's return to the tree-trimmer example. Suppose I cut off my arm midway through the job. You sue me because your tree did not get a full trim and therefore damaged your roof. I cannot perform my part of the bargain.[4] Should the court discharge the contract or make me pay damages? To answer this, use the Posner-Rosenfield method. I can likely assess the probability of my mishap more easily than you. I can probably also more cheaply estimate the loss from my non-performance — perhaps the extra cost entailed by having to hire another trimmer quickly. Most compelling, I can probably insure against the loss more cheaply — by having reciprocal arrangements with others in the business, carrying third-party insurance, or including a risk premium in my price for every customer. All these answers point in one direction: I should pay you damages. If we had addressed this contingency in the contract, undoubtedly we would have agreed that I should bear the risk associated with cutting off my arm. By making me liable for damages, the court does the same.

If damages are the appropriate remedy for a given situation, what size damages will promote efficiency? Typically, expectation damages – the amount of money that would put the plaintiff in the same position as he or she would have been had the contract been performed.[5] Expectation damages encourage defendants to choose the efficient course of action. Suppose I consider not trimming your tree because I have found a lucrative alternative job. If I have to pay you expectation damages, you are indifferent as to whether I finish trimming your tree. If my alternative job still seems attractive, I will take it, pay you damages, and have something left over. If it does not, I will complete your tree trimming. I alone bear the costs and reap the benefits of my actions, so I will make the efficient choice.

Efficient damages must avoid compensating plaintiffs for overreliance, however. Suppose you schedule an elaborate garden party with certain festivities that require a trimmed tree. I know nothing about your party, I have no reason to expect that you will hold such an event, and I do not trim your tree in time. Although efficiency probably requires me to pay you something, expectation damages likely would not include costs associated with canceling or moving the party. You are in a better position than I to have made alternative festive arrangements. *Hadley* v. *Baxendale* is the archetypal overreliance case.

Courts do not always impose liability and damages in breach-of-contract cases. In some circumstances they discharge the contract instead. *Sherwood* v. *Walker* and *Williams* v. *Walker-Thomas* are illustrative cases. In *Sherwood*, mutual mistake constituted the basis for discharge. Both parties apparently thought the object for sale was a barren cow, good only for butchering. After the sale, the cow was found to be pregnant. Breeders sell for far more than beef cattle so the appellate court rescinded the contract. Yet economists generally prefer the trial court decision, which upheld the sale. Because the seller should have had better knowledge about his wares than the buyer, efficiency considerations would imply that the sale go through at the agreed-upon price. Not only would this place the risk of mis-classifying the cow on the least-cost risk bearer, it would give sellers incentives to price their cattle accurately.

Evidence of unconscionability — the failure to give contractual partners a meaningful choice — can also persuade judges to rescind a contract. In *Williams*, dicta by Judge Skelly Wright indicate that a trial court could reasonably call a rent-to-own contract unconscionable because it allowed the defendant to repossess all rented items — even the ones paid off — if the plaintiff defaulted on one item. Yet an economist might suggest that the collateralization offered by the repossession clause actually made efficiency-improving trades possible. Calling such a contract unconscionable could shut off opportunities for poor people to acquire household furnishings and durable goods. Richard Epstein's article suggests that duress, fraud, and incompetence arguments obviate the need for unconscionability as a protective device.

Applications: The Family and the Labor Market

Some of the more provocative contract articles focus on family issues: marriage and children. Although Jane Austen would be comfortable with the notion of marriage as a contract, many modern-day believers in love matches might not. Yet Margaret Brinig's article offers empirical evidence of American marriage as a contractual arrangement, even in this century. If marriage-as-a-contract strikes you as an unconventional topic, how about baby sales? Elisabeth Landes and Richard Posner tackle this possibility, suggesting that market pricing might do a better job at finding homes for babies than adoption agencies. Mark Ramseyer extends the analysis to investigate the market for children in early modern Japan.

The labor market provides more traditional applications of the economics of contract law. The case of *Paris* v. *Stepney Borough* raises an important contractual issue — who should be responsible for worker safety, the employer or the employee? Here, the Posner and Rosenfield article offers a useful framework for analysis.[6] The articles by Fishback and Kantor and by Lehn look at a different question: if the legal context changes, what else happens in employment markets? Fishback and Kantor point out that the early-twentieth-century move to workers' and unemployment compensation schemes might have seemed to put more money in workers' pockets, but wages could have adjusted to erase any potential gains. In essence, they evaluate whether instituting insurance schemes actually shifted the cost of risk. Lehn examines the effect that the repeal of baseball's reserve clause has had upon contract choice and player disability rates. Using a situation of low transaction costs, he finds that different initial property rights led to a different efficient result because owners could diversify risks more easily than players.

The Firm, Regulation, and Antitrust

The study of firms has long been a part of law and economics. In his (other) famous law and economics article, Ronald Coase portrays the firm as a nexus of implicit contracts, a substitute for external contractual arrangements. As he notes, firms can do away with the costs of negotiation by integrating various aspects of the process that transforms inputs to output. Instead of contracting with outside suppliers for minerals, say, a firm could acquire its own mining operation. Rather than relying on transport services for distribution, a firm could purchase its own trucking fleet.

But what if firms acquire substantial market power? Monopolies could forestall Pareto-improving exchanges because they want to get a larger piece of the pie — and they have the power to do so. As a society, we must consider if, when, and how we should regulate monopolies. Mere control over different facets of the production process may not mean monopoly power exists. Vertical integration may be desirable from an efficiency viewpoint because, as Coase shows, a firm can reduce transaction costs — often without gaining power in any particular input or output market. Horizontal integration — where a firm does control a larger share of a given market — may also lead to greater efficiency if economies of scale exist. That is, bigger may be better for society, because costs are lower (and output higher) under monopoly than under competition. But unfettered horizontal integration could arguably also lead to higher prices and a less-than-efficient amount of output. Asymmetric information or other market irregularities may also justify regulatory intervention.

The literature on industrial organization, regulation, and antitrust is vast; the articles included here merely touch upon some of the important topics. George Stigler's well-known work suggests that industries often seek out regulation in order to exclude new firms. Regulation may therefore actually help create monopoly power. Stigler teamed up with Claire Friedland to write another well-known article examining whether regulation really makes a difference in the behavior of an industry. In a fascinating paper, Peter Swan determines that Judge Learned Hand had correctly decided that Alcoa's monopoly over virgin aluminum gave it indirect control over the output of recycled material. Swan's work contains a nice discussion of game theory, an economic tool increasingly used to analyze legal developments.[7] Gallick and Sisk argue that regulation, by its reduction of search costs for consumers, can increase the number and variety of taxi trips.

Regulation and Safety

Just as lawmakers have used regulation to try influencing the number of firms and the level of prices charged in an industry, so have they passed regulations in attempts to affect the safety of products and services. (Volume III looks at an alternative to *ex ante* safety regulation: *ex post* products liability litigation.) Two included articles (by Kip Viscusi and by Steven Peterson, George Hoffer, and Edward Millner) contain a common theme: we might be able to make products less dangerous in certain respects, but we cannot dictate how people use them. Special caps on aspirin bottles may seem safer, but not if people leave them off or put bottles where children can easily reach them. Air bags may simply increase driver aggressiveness. (In a pathbreaking earlier article too long for inclusion here, Sam Peltzman finds that mandatory seatbelt use actually increased the incidence of pedestrian injuries — because drivers with seatbelts drive less carefully.[8]) The Mitchell and Maloney article argues that regulation did little to promote airline safety. Why? Because the market already "regulated" safety via stock-price effects.

NOTES

[1] These figures assume that policyholders are risk-neutral. Risk-averse people may buy $100 policies even if their expected bills fall short of $100. Such folks will pay a premium to avoid income variability.
[2] See the related discussion below on *Williams* v. *Walker-Thomas*.
[3] Because individual parties to a lawsuit do not bear all the costs of running a court system, people tend to leave an inefficiently large number of gaps in contracts.
[4] Some commentators (Thomas Ulen in particular) advocate more extensive use of specific performance remedies.
[5] Certainly, expectation damages can be hard to calculate. They can also exclude two significant costs — the promisee's litigation costs and the costs of the breach on third parties.
[6] See also the article by Viscusi included in volume III.
[7] See also Cooter and Ulen (1997), cited in volume I.
[8] Peltzman (1975).

Further Reading

Contracts

Arrow, Kenneth. *Essays in the Theory of Risk Bearing* (1971).

Ayres, Ian, and Robert Gertner. "Filling Gaps in Incomplete Contracts: An Economic Theory of Default Rules." 99 *Yale Law Journal* 87 (1989).

Barton, John. "The Economic Basis of Damages for Breach of Contract." 1 *Journal of Legal Studies* 277 (1972).

Bebchuk, Lucien, and Steven Shavell. "Information and the Scope of Liability for Breach of Contract: The Rule of *Hadley* v. *Baxendale*." 7 *Journal of Law, Economics, and Organization* 286 (1991).

Chisholm, Darlene. "Profit Sharing vs. Fixed-Payment Contracts." 13 *Journal of Law, Economics, and Organization* 169 (1997).

Epstein, Richard. "Beyond Foreseeability: Consequential Damages in the Law of Contracts." 18 *Journal of Legal Studies* 105 (1989).

Farber, Daniel. "Contract Law and Modern Economic Theory." 78 *Northwestern University Law Review* 303 (1983).

Grossman, Sanford, and Oliver Hart. "An Analysis of the Principal-Agent Problem." 51 *Econometrica* 7 (1983).

Joskow, Paul. "Commercial Impossibility, The Uranium Market, and the Westinghouse Case." 6 *Journal of Legal Studies* 119 (1977).

Kessler, Friedrich. "Contracts of Adhesion: Some Thoughts about Freedom of Contract." 43 *Columbia Law Review* 629 (1943).

Klein, Benjamin, and Keith Leffler. "The Role of Market Forces in Assuring Contractual Performance." 89 *Journal of Political Economy* 615 (1981).

Kornhauser, Lewis. "Contract Remedies." 51 *University of Colorado Law Review* 683 (1986).

Kronman, Anthony, and Richard Posner, eds. *Economics of Contract Law* (1979).

Kronman, Anthony. "Specific Performance." 45 *University of Chicago Law Review* 351 (1978).

Polinsky, A. Mitchell. "Risk Sharing Through Breach of Contract Remedies." 12 *Journal of Legal Studies* 427 (1983).

Ross, Stephen. "The Economic Theory of Agency." 63 *American Economic Review* 134 (1973).

Ulen, Thomas. "The Efficiency of Specific Performance: Toward a Unified Theory of Contract Remedies." 83 *Michigan Law Review* 358 (1984).

Vlatas, Anthony. "Economic Analysis of Implied Warranty of Fitness in Commercial Losses." 94 *Columbia Law Review* 658 (1994)

Economics of the Family

Becker, Gary. *A Treatise on the Family* (1991).

Pritchard, J. Robert. "A Market for Babies?" 34 *University of Toronto Law Journal* 341 (1984).

Shavell, Steven. "Economic Analysis of Altruism and Deferred Gifts." 20 *Journal of Legal Studies* 401 (1991).

Wahl, Jenny. "American Fertility Decline in the Nineteenth Century: Tradeoff of Quantity and Quality?" In Goldin and Rockoff, eds., *Strategic Factors in Nineteenth Century American Economic Growth* (1991).

Wahl, Jenny. "New Results on the Decline in Household Fertility in the United States from 1750 to 1900." In Gallman and Engerman, eds., *Long Term Factors in American Economic Growth* (1986).

Weitzman, Lenore. "The Economics of Divorce: Social and Economic Consequences." 28 *UCLA Law Review* 1181 (1981).

Zelder, Martin. "The Economic Analysis of The Effect of No-Fault Divorce Law on the Divorce Rate." 16 *Harvard Journal of Law and Public Policy* 24 (1993).

Employment Law

Ashenfelter, Orley, and Ronald Oaxaca. "The Economics of Discrimination: Economists Enter the Courtroom." 77 *American Economic Review* 321 (1987).

Becker, Gary. *The Economics of Discrimination* (1971).

Cohen, Wayne. "An Economic Analysis of The Issues Surrounding AIDS in the Workplace." 41 *American University Law Review* 1199 (1992).

Fishback, Price, and Shawn Kantor. "Did Workers Pay for the Passage of Workers' Compensation Laws?" 109 *Quarterly Journal of Economics* 713 (1995).
Landes, William. "The Economics of Fair Employment Laws." 76 *Journal of Political Economy* 507 (1968).
Posner, Richard. "Economic Analysis of Sex Discrimination Law." 56 *University of Chicago Law Review* 1311 (1989).
Spence, Michael. "Job Market Signaling." 87 *Quarterly Journal of Economics* 355 (1973).
Viscusi, W. Kip. *Risk by Choice* (1983).
Worrall, John, ed. *Safety and the Work Force* (1983).

The Firm, Regulation, Antitrust, Corporate Law

Alchian, Armen, and Harold Demsetz. "Production, Information Costs, and Economic Organization." 62 *American Economic Review* 777 (1972).
Bailey, Elizabeth, and Jeffrey Williams. "Sources of Economic Rent in the Deregulated Airline Industry." 31 *Journal of Law and Economics* 173 (1988).
Baumol, William, and Janusz Ordover. "Use of Antitrust to Subvert Competition." 28 *Journal of Law and Economics* 247 (1985).
Berle, Adolf, and Gardiner Means. *The Modern Corporation and Private Property* (1932).
Blackstone, Erwin, and Joseph Fuhr. "Hospitals, Mergers, and Antitrust: An Economic Analysis." 14 *Journal of Health Policy* 383 (1989).
Boltuck, Richard. "An Economic Analysis of Dumping." 21 *Journal of World Trade Law* 45 (1987).
Bork, Robert. *The Antitrust Paradox* (1978).
Coase, Ronald. *The Firm, the Market, and the Law* (1988).
Darby, Michael, and Edi Karni. "Free Competition and the Optimal Amount of Fraud." 16 *Journal of Law and Economics* 67 (1973).
Demsetz, Harold. "Why Regulate Utilities?" 11 *Journal of Law and Economics* 55 (1968).
Demsetz, Harold. "Economics as a Guide to Antitrust Regulation." 19 *Journal of Law and Economics* 371 (1976).
Easterbrook, Frank, and Daniel Fischel. *The Economic Structure of Corporate Law* (1989).
Easterbrook, Frank, William Landes, and Richard Posner. "Contribution among Antitrust Defendants: A Legal and Economic Analysis." 23 *Journal of Law and Economics* 331 (1980).
Gellhorn, Ernest. *Antitrust Law and Economics* (1976).
Grady, Mark. "Toward a Positive Theory of Antitrust." 30 *Economic Inquiry* (1992).
Hopenhayn, Hugo, and Susanne Lohmann. "Fire-Alarm Signals and Political Oversight of Regulatory Agencies." 12 *Journal of Law, Economics, and Organization* 196 (1996).
Jensen, Michael, and William Meckling. "The Theory of the Firm: Managerial Behavior, Agency Costs, and Ownership Structure." 3 *Journal of Financial Economics* 305 (1976).
Kahai, Simran, David Kaserman, and John Mayo. "Is the 'Dominant' Firm Dominant?" 39 *Journal of Law and Economics* 499 (1996).
Moore, Thomas. "The Purpose of Licensing." 4 *Journal of Law and Economics* 93 (1962).
Ogus, Anthony, and Cento Veljanovski, eds. *Readings in the Economics of Law and Regulation* (1984).
Posner, Richard. "Theories of Economic Regulation." 5 *Bell Journal of Economics* 335 (1974).
Posner, Richard. "The Rule of Reason and the Economic Approach: Reflections on the *Sylvania* Decision." 45 *University of Chicago Law Review* (1977).
Posner, Richard. *Antitrust Law* (1981).
Posner, Richard. "Antitrust and Economic Efficiency." 28 *Journal of Law and Economics* 245 (1985).
Posner, Richard, and Frank Easterbrook. *Antitrust Cases* (1981).
Posner, Richard, and William Landes. "Market Power in Antitrust Cases." 94 *Harvard Law Review* 937 (1981).
Posner, Richard, and Kenneth Scott. *Economics of Corporation Law and Securities Regulation* (1980).
Rottenberg, Simon. "The Economics of Occupational Licensing." In *Aspects of Labor Economics* (1962).
Round, David, and John Siegfried. "Can Economists Agree?" 39 *Antitrust Bulletin* 753 (1994).
Scherer, F.E. *Industrial Market Structure and Economic Performance* (1980).
Telser, Lester. "Why Should Manufacturers Want Fair Trade?" 3 *Journal of Law and Economics* 86 (1961).
Ulen, Thomas. "The Coasean Firm." 18 *Journal of Corporation Law* 301 (1993).
Viscusi, W. Kip, John Vernon, and Joseph Harrington. *Economics of Regulation and Antitrust* (1992).
Williamson, Oliver. "The Economics of Antitrust: Transactions Cost Consideration."122 *University of Pennsylvania Law Review* (1974).
Wollenberg, Keith. "Economic Analysis of Tie In Sales." 39 Stanford Law Review 737 (1987).

Regulation and Safety

Arnold, Richard, and Henry Grabowki. "Auto Safety Regulation: An Analysis of Market Failure." 12 *Bell Journal of Economics* 27 (1981).

Crandell, Robert, Theodore Keeler, and Lester Lave. "The Cost of Auto Safety and Emissions Regulation to the Consumer." 72 *American Economic Review* 324 (1982).

Jarrell, Gregg, and Sam Peltzman. "Impact of Product Recalls on the Wealth of Sellers." 93 *Journal of Political Economy* 512 (1985).

Peltzman, Sam. "The Benefits and Costs of New Drug Regulation." In Landau, ed., *Regulating New Drugs* (1973).

Peltzman, Sam. "Effects of Auto Safety Regulation." 83 *Journal of Political Economy* 677 (1975).

Peltzman, Sam. "Toward a More General Theory of Regulation." 19 *Journal of Law and Economics* 211 (1976).

Shavell, Steven. "Liability for Harm vs. Regulation of Safety." 13 *Journal of Legal Studies* 357 (1984).

Shavell, Steven. "A Model of the Optimal Use of Liability and Safety Regulation." 15 *Rand Journal of Economics* 271 (1984).

Viscusi, W. Kip. *Risk by Choice: Regulating Health and Safety in the Workplace* (1983).

Williams, Alan, Paul Zador, Sandra Harris, and Ronald Korpf. "Effect of Raising the Legal Minimum Drinking Age in Fatal Crashes." 12 *Journal of Legal Studies* 169 (1983).

Wittman, Donald. "Prior Regulation vs. Post Liability." 6 *Journal of Legal Studies* 193 (1977).

Economic Analysis of Contract Law, Antitrust Law, and Safety Regulations

THE MARKET FOR "LEMONS": QUALITY UNCERTAINTY AND THE MARKET MECHANISM *

George A. Akerlof

I. Introduction

This paper relates quality and uncertainty. The existence of goods of many grades poses interesting and important problems for the theory of markets. On the one hand, the interaction of quality differences and uncertainty may explain important institutions of the labor market. On the other hand, this paper presents a struggling attempt to give structure to the statement: "Business in underdeveloped countries is difficult"; in particular, a structure is given for determining the economic costs of dishonesty. Additional applications of the theory include comments on the structure of money markets, on the notion of "insurability," on the liquidity of durables, and on brand-name goods.

There are many markets in which buyers use some market statistic to judge the quality of prospective purchases. In this case there is incentive for sellers to market poor quality merchandise, since the returns for good quality accrue mainly to the entire group whose statistic is affected rather than to the individual seller. As a result there tends to be a reduction in the average quality of goods and also in the size of the market. It should also be perceived that in these markets social and private returns differ, and therefore, in some cases, governmental intervention may increase the welfare of all parties. Or private institutions may arise to take advantage of the potential increases in welfare which can accrue to all parties. By nature, however, these institutions are nonatomistic, and therefore concentrations of power — with ill consequences of their own — can develop.

* The author would especially like to thank Thomas Rothenberg for invaluable comments and inspiration. In addition he is indebted to Roy Radner, Albert Fishlow, Bernard Saffran, William D. Nordhaus, Giorgio La Malfa, Charles C. Holt, John Letiche, and the referee for help and suggestions. He would also like to thank the Indian Statistical Institute and the Ford Foundation for financial support.

The automobile market is used as a finger exercise to illustrate and develop these thoughts. It should be emphasized that this market is chosen for its concreteness and ease in understanding rather than for its importance or realism.

II. The Model with Automobiles as an Example

A. The Automobiles Market

The example of used cars captures the essence of the problem. From time to time one hears either mention of or surprise at the large price difference between new cars and those which have just left the showroom. The usual lunch table justification for this phenomenon is the pure joy of owning a "new" car. We offer a different explanation. Suppose (for the sake of clarity rather than reality) that there are just four kinds of cars. There are new cars and used cars. There are good cars and bad cars (which in America are known as "lemons"). A new car may be a good car or a lemon, and of course the same is true of used cars.

The individuals in this market buy a new automobile without knowing whether the car they buy will be good or a lemon. But they do know that with probability q it is a good car and with probability $(1-q)$ it is a lemon; by assumption, q is the proportion of good cars produced and $(1-q)$ is the proportion of lemons.

After owning a specific car, however, for a length of time, the car owner can form a good idea of the quality of this machine; i.e., the owner assigns a new probability to the event that his car is a lemon. This estimate is more accurate than the original estimate. An asymmetry in available information has developed: for the sellers now have more knowledge about the quality of a car than the buyers. But good cars and bad cars must still sell at the same price — since it is impossible for a buyer to tell the difference between a good car and a bad car. It is apparent that a used car cannot have the same valuation as a new car — if it did have the same valuation, it would clearly be advantageous to trade a lemon at the price of new car, and buy another new car, at a higher probability q of being good and a lower probability of being bad. Thus the owner of a good machine must be locked in. Not only is it true that he cannot receive the true value of his car, but he cannot even obtain the expected value of a new car.

Gresham's law has made a modified reappearance. For most cars traded will be the "lemons," and good cars may not be traded at all. The "bad" cars tend to drive out the good (in much the same way that bad money drives out the good). But the analogy with Gresham's law is not quite complete: bad cars drive out the good because they sell at the same price as good cars; similarly, bad money drives out good because the exchange rate is even. But the bad cars sell at the same price as good cars since it is impossible for a buyer to tell the difference between a good and a bad car; only the seller knows. In Gresham's law, however, presumably both buyer and seller can tell the difference between good and bad money. So the analogy is instructive, but not complete.

B. Asymmetrical Information

It has been seen that the good cars may be driven out of the market by the lemons. But in a more continuous case with different grades of goods, even worse pathologies can exist. For it is quite possible to have the bad driving out the not-so-bad driving out the medium driving out the not-so-good driving out the good in such a sequence of events that no market exists at all.

One can assume that the demand for used automobiles depends most strongly upon two variables — the price of the automobile p and the average quality of used cars traded, μ, or $Q^d = D(p, \mu)$. Both the supply of used cars and also the average quality μ will depend upon the price, or $\mu = \mu\ (p)$ and $S = S(p)$. And in equilibrium the supply must equal the demand for the given average quality, or $S(p) = D(p, \mu(p))$. As the price falls, normally the quality will also fall. And it is quite possible that no goods will be traded at any price level.

Such an example can be derived from utility theory. Assume that there are just two groups of traders: groups one and two. Give group one a utility function

$$U_1 = M + \sum_{i=1}^{n} x_i$$

where M is the consumption of goods other than automobiles, x_i is the quality of the ith automobile, and n is the number of automobiles.

Similarly, let

$$U_2 = M + \sum_{i=1}^{n} 3/2 x_i$$

where M, x_i, and n are defined as before.

Three comments should be made about these utility functions: (1) without linear utility (say with logarithmic utility) one gets needlessly mired in algebraic complication. (2) The use of linear utility allows a focus on the effects of asymmetry of information; with a concave utility function we would have to deal jointly with the usual risk-variance effects of uncertainty and the special effects we wish to discuss here. (3) U_1 and U_2 have the odd characteristic that the addition of a second car, or indeed a kth car, adds the same amount of utility as the first. Again realism is sacrificed to avoid a diversion from the proper focus.

To continue, it is assumed (1) that both type one traders and type two traders are von Neumann-Morgenstern maximizers of expected utility; (2) that group one has N cars with uniformly distributed quality x, $0 \leqq x \leqq 2$, and group two has no cars; (3) that the price of "other goods" M is unity.

Denote the income (including that derived from the sale of automobiles) of all type one traders as Y_1 and the income of all type two traders as Y_2. The demand for used cars will be the sum of the demands by both groups. When one ignores indivisibilities, the demand for automobiles by type one traders will be

$$D_1 = Y_1/p \qquad \mu/p > 1$$
$$D_1 = 0 \qquad \mu/p < 1.$$

And the supply of cars offered by type one traders is

$$S_1 = pN/2 \qquad p \leqq 2 \tag{1}$$

with average quality

$$\mu = p/2. \tag{2}$$

(To derive (1) and (2), the uniform distribution of automobile quality is used.)

Similarly the demand of type two traders is

$$D_2 = Y_2/p \qquad 3\mu/2 > p$$
$$D_2 = 0 \qquad 3\mu/2 < p$$

and

$$S_2 = 0.$$

Thus total demand $D(p, \mu)$ is

$$D(p, \mu) = (Y_2 + Y_1)/p \qquad \text{if } p < \mu$$
$$D(p, \mu) = Y_2/p \qquad \text{if } \mu < p < 3\mu/2$$
$$D(p, \mu) = 0 \qquad \text{if } p > 3\mu/2.$$

However, with price p, average quality is $p/2$ and therefore at no price will any trade take place at all: in spite of the fact that *at any given price* between 0 and 3 there are traders of type one who are willing to sell their automobiles at a price which traders of type two are willing to pay.

C. Symmetric Information

The foregoing is contrasted with the case of symmetric information. Suppose that the quality of all cars is uniformly distributed, $0 \leqq x \leqq 2$. Then the demand curves and supply curves can be written as follows:

Supply

$$S(p) = N \qquad p > 1$$
$$S(p) = 0 \qquad p < 1.$$

And the demand curves are

$$D(p) = (Y_2 + Y_1)/p \qquad p < 1$$
$$D(p) = (Y_2/p) \qquad 1 < p < 3/2$$
$$D(p) = 0 \qquad p > 3/2.$$

In equilibrium

(3) $p = 1$ if $Y_2 < N$

(4) $p = Y_2/N$ if $2Y_2/3 < N < Y_2$

(5) $p = 3/2$ if $N < 2Y_2/3$.

If $N < Y_2$ there is a gain in utility over the case of asymmetrical information of $N/2$. (If $N > Y_2$, in which case the income of type two traders is insufficient to buy all N automobiles, there is a gain in utility of $Y_2/2$ units.)

Finally, it should be mentioned that in this example, if traders of groups one and two have the same probabilistic estimates about the quality of individual automobiles — though these estimates may vary from automobile to automobile — (3), (4), and (5) will still describe equilibrium with one slight change: p will then represent the expected price of one quality unit.

III. Examples and Applications

A. Insurance

It is a well-known fact that people over 65 have great difficulty in buying medical insurance. The natural question arises: why doesn't the price rise to match the risk?

Our answer is that as the price level rises the people who insure themselves will be those who are increasingly certain that they will need the insurance; for error in medical check-ups, doctors' sympathy with older patients, and so on make it much easier for the applicant to assess the risks involved than the insurance company. The result is that the average medical condition of insurance applicants deteriorates as the price level rises — with the result that no insurance sales may take place at any price.[1] This is strictly analogous to our automobiles case, where the average quality of used cars supplied fell with a corresponding fall in the price level. This agrees with the explanation in insurance textbooks:

> Generally speaking policies are not available at ages materially greater than sixty-five. . . . The term premiums are too high for any but the most pessimistic (which is to say the least healthy) insureds to find attractive. Thus there is a severe problem of adverse selection at these ages.[2]

The statistics do not contradict this conclusion. While demands for health insurance rise with age, a 1956 national sample survey of 2,809 families with 8,898 persons shows that hospital insurance coverage drops from 63 per cent of those aged 45 to 54, to 31 per cent for those over 65. And surprisingly, this survey also finds average medical expenses for males aged 55 to 64 of $88, while males over 65 pay an average of $77.[3] While noninsured expenditure rises from $66 to $80 in these age groups, insured expenditure declines from $105 to $70. The conclusion is tempting that insurance companies are particularly wary of giving medical insurance to older people.

The principle of "adverse selection" is potentially present in all lines of insurance. The following statement appears in an insurance textbook written at the Wharton School:

> There is potential adverse selection in the fact that healthy term insurance policy holders may decide to terminate their coverage when they become older and premiums mount. This action could leave an insurer with an undue proportion of below average risks and claims might be higher than anticipated. Adverse selection "appears (or at least is possible) whenever the individual or group insured has freedom to buy or not to buy, to choose the amount or plan of insurance, and to persist or to discontinue as a policy holder."[4]

Group insurance, which is the most common form of medical insurance in the United States, picks out the healthy, for generally

1. Arrow's fine article, "Uncertainty and Medical Care" (*American Economic Review*, Vol. 53, 1963), does not make this point explicitly. He emphasizes "moral hazard" rather than "adverse selection." In its strict sense, the presence of "moral hazard" is equally disadvantageous for both governmental and private programs; in its broader sense, which includes "adverse selection," "moral hazard" gives a decided advantage to government insurance programs.

2. O. D. Dickerson, *Health Insurance* (Homewood, Ill.: Irwin, 1959), p. 333.

3. O. W. Anderson (with J. J. Feldman), *Family Medical Costs and Insurance* (New York: McGraw-Hill, 1956).

4. H. S. Denenberg, R. D. Eilers, G. W. Hoffman, C. A. Kline, J. J. Melone, and H. W. Snider, *Risk and Insurance* (Englewood Cliffs, N. J.: Prentice Hall, 1964), p. 446.

adequate health is a precondition for employment. At the same time this means that medical insurance is least available to those who need it most, for the insurance companies do their own "adverse selection."

This adds one major argument in favor of medicare.[5] On a cost benefit basis medicare may pay off: for it is quite possible that every individual in the market would be willing to pay the expected cost of his medicare and buy insurance, yet no insurance company can afford to sell him a policy — for at any price it will attract too many "lemons." The welfare economics of medicare, in this view, is *exactly* analogous to the usual classroom argument for public expenditure on roads.

B. The Employment of Minorities

The Lemons Principle also casts light on the employment of minorities. Employers may refuse to hire members of minority groups for certain types of jobs. This decision may not reflect irrationality or prejudice — but profit maximization. For race may serve as a good *statistic* for the applicant's social background, quality of schooling, and general job capabilities.

Good quality schooling could serve as a substitute for this statistic; by grading students the schooling system can give a better indicator of quality than other more superficial characteristics. As T. W. Schultz writes, "The educational establishment *discovers* and cultivates potential talent. The capabilities of children and mature students can never be known until *found* and cultivated."[6] (Italics added.) An untrained worker may have valuable natural talents, but these talents must be certified by "the educational establishment" before a company can afford to use them. The certifying establishment, however, must be credible; the unreliability of slum schools decreases the economic possibilities of their students.

This lack may be particularly disadvantageous to members of

5. The following quote, again taken from an insurance textbook, shows how far the medical insurance market is from perfect competition:

> ". . . insurance companies must screen their applicants. Naturally it is true that many people will voluntarily seek adequate insurance on their own initiative. But in such lines as accident and health insurance, companies are likely to give a second look to persons who voluntarily seek insurance without being approached by an agent." (F. J. Angell, *Insurance, Principles and Practices*, New York: The Ronald Press, 1957, pp. 8–9.)

This shows that insurance is *not* a commodity for sale on the open market.

6. T. W. Schultz, *The Economic Value of Education* (New York: Columbia University Press, 1964), p. 42.

already disadvantaged minority groups. For an employer may make a rational decision not to hire any members of these groups in responsible positions — because it is difficult to distinguish those with good job qualifications from those with bad qualifications. This type of decision is clearly what George Stigler had in mind when he wrote, "in a regime of ignorance Enrico Fermi would have been a gardener, Von Neumann a checkout clerk at a drugstore." [7]

As a result, however, the rewards for work in slum schools tend to accrue to the group as a whole — in raising its average quality — rather than to the individual. Only insofar as information in addition to race is used is there any incentive for training.

An additional worry is that the Office of Economic Opportunity is going to use cost-benefit analysis to evaluate its programs. For many benefits may be external. The benefit from training minority groups may arise as much from raising the average quality of the group as from raising the quality of the individual trainee; and, likewise, the returns may be distributed over the whole group rather than to the individual.

C. The Costs of Dishonesty

The Lemons model can be used to make some comments on the costs of dishonesty. Consider a market in which goods are sold honestly or dishonestly; quality may be represented, or it may be misrepresented. The purchaser's problem, of course, is to identify quality. The presence of people in the market who are willing to offer inferior goods tends to drive the market out of existence — as in the case of our automobile "lemons." It is this possibility that represents the major costs of dishonesty — for dishonest dealings tend to drive honest dealings out of the market. There may be potential buyers of good quality products and there may be potential sellers of such products in the appropriate price range; however, the presence of people who wish to pawn bad wares as good wares tends to drive out the legitimate business. The cost of dishonesty, therefore, lies not only in the amount by which the purchaser is cheated; the cost also must include the loss incurred from driving legitimate business out of existence.

Dishonesty in business is a serious problem in underdeveloped countries. Our model gives a possible structure to this statement and delineates the nature of the "external" economies involved. In particular, in the model economy described, dishonesty, or the

7. G. J. Stigler, "Information and the Labor Market," *Journal of Political Economy*, Vol. 70 (Oct. 1962), Supplement, p. 104.

misrepresentation of the quality of automobiles, costs 1/2 unit of utility per automobile; furthermore, it reduces the size of the used car market from N to 0. We can, consequently, directly evaluate the costs of dishonesty — at least in theory.

There is considerable evidence that quality variation is greater in underdeveloped than in developed areas. For instance, the need for quality control of exports and State Trading Corporations can be taken as one indicator. In India, for example, under the Export Quality Control and Inspection Act of 1963, "about 85 per cent of Indian exports are covered under one or the other type of quality control."[8] Indian housewives must carefully glean the rice of the local bazaar to sort out stones of the same color and shape which have been intentionally added to the rice. Any comparison of the heterogeneity of quality in the street market and the canned qualities of the American supermarket suggests that quality variation is a greater problem in the East than in the West.

In one traditional pattern of development the merchants of the pre-industrial generation turn into the first entrepreneurs of the next. The best-documented case is Japan,[9] but this also may have been the pattern for Britain and America.[1] In *our* picture the important skill of the merchant is identifying the quality of merchandise; those who can identify used cars in our example and can guarantee the quality may profit by as much as the difference between type two traders' buying price and type one traders' selling price. These people are the merchants. In production these skills are equally necessary — both to be able to identify the quality of inputs and to certify the quality of outputs. And this is one (added) reason why the merchants may logically become the first entrepreneurs.

The problem, of course, is that entrepreneurship may be a scarce resource; no development text leaves entrepreneurship unemphasized. Some treat it as central.[2] Given, then, that entrepreneurship is scarce, there are two ways in which product variations impede development. First, the pay-off to trade is great for would-be entrepreneurs, and hence they are diverted from production; second, the amount of entrepreneurial time per unit output is greater, the greater are the quality variations.

8. *The Times of India*, Nov. 10, 1967, p. 1.

9. See M. J. Levy, Jr., "Contrasting Factors in the Modernization of China and Japan," in *Economic Growth: Brazil, India, Japan*, ed. S. Kuznets, *et. al.* (Durham, N. C.: Duke University Press, 1955).

1. C. P. Kindleberger, *Economic Development* (New York: McGraw-Hill, 1958), p. 86.

2. For example, see W. Arthur Lewis, *The Theory of Economic Growth* (Homewood, Ill.: Irwin, 1955), p. 196.

D. Credit Markets in Underdeveloped Countries

(1) Credit markets in underdeveloped countries often strongly reflect the operation of the Lemons Principle. In India a major fraction of industrial enterprise is controlled by managing agencies (according to a recent survey, these "managing agencies" controlled 65.7 per cent of the net worth of public limited companies and 66 per cent of total assets).[3] Here is a historian's account of the function and genesis of the "managing agency system":

> The management of the South Asian commercial scene remained the function of merchant houses, and a type of organization peculiar to South Asia known as the Managing Agency. When a new venture was promoted (such as a manufacturing plant, a plantation, or a trading venture), the promoters would approach an established managing agency. The promoters might be Indian or British, and they might have technical or financial resources or merely a concession. In any case they would turn to the agency because of its reputation, which would encourage confidence in the venture and stimulate investment.[4]

In turn, a second major feature of the Indian industrial scene has been the dominance of these managing agencies by caste (or, more accurately, communal) groups. Thus firms can usually be classified according to communal origin.[5] In this environment, in which outside investors are likely to be bilked of their holdings, either (1) firms establish a reputation for "honest" dealing, which confers upon them a monopoly rent insofar as their services are

3. *Report of the Committee on the Distribution of Income and Levels of Living*, Part I, Government of India, Planning Commission, Feb. 1964, p. 44.

4. H. Tinker, *South Asia: A Short History* (New York: Praeger, 1966), p. 134.

5. The existence of the following table (and also the small per cent of firms under mixed control) indicates the communalization of the control of firms. *Source*: M. M. Mehta, *Structure of Indian Industries* (Bombay: Popular Book Depot, 1955), p. 314.

DISTRIBUTION OF INDUSTRIAL CONTROL BY COMMUNITY

	1911	1931 (number of firms)	1951
British	281	416	382
Parsis	15	25	19
Gujratis	3	11	17
Jews	5	9	3
Muslims	—	10	3
Bengalis	8	5	20
Marwaris	—	6	96
Mixed control	28	28	79
Total	341	510	619

Also, for the cotton industry see H. Fukuzawa, "Cotton Mill Industry," in V. B. Singh, editor, *Economic History of India, 1857–1956* (Bombay: Allied Publishers, 1965).

limited in supply, or (2) the sources of finance are limited to local communal groups which can use communal — and possibly familial — ties to encourage honest dealing *within* the community. It is, in Indian economic history, extraordinarily difficult to discern whether the savings of rich landlords failed to be invested in the industrial sector (1) because of a fear to invest in ventures controlled by other communities, (2) because of inflated propensities to consume, or (3) because of low rates of return.[6] At the very least, however, it is clear that the British-owned managing agencies tended to have an equity holding whose communal origin was more heterogeneous than the Indian-controlled agency houses, and would usually include both Indian and British investors.

(2) A second example of the workings of the Lemons Principle concerns the extortionate rates which the local moneylender charges his clients. In India these high rates of interest have been the leading factor in landlessness; the so-called "Cooperative Movement" was meant to counteract this growing landlessness by setting up banks to compete with the local moneylenders.[7] While the large banks in the central cities have prime interest rates of 6, 8, and 10 per cent, the local moneylender charges 15, 25, and even 50 per cent. The answer to this seeming paradox is that credit is

6. For the mixed record of industrial profits, see D. H. Buchanan, *The Development of Capitalist Enterprise in India* (New York: Kelley, 1966, reprinted).

7. The leading authority on this is Sir Malcolm Darling. See his *Punjabi Peasant in Prosperity and Debt*. The following table may also prove instructive:

	Secured loans (per cent)	Commonest rates for — Unsecured loans (per cent)	Grain loans (per cent)
Punjab	6 to 12	12 to 24 (18 ¾ commonest)	25
United Provinces	9 to 12	24 to 37 ½	25 (50 in Oudh)
Bihar		18 ¾	50
Orissa	12 to 18 ¾	25	25
Bengal	8 to 12	9 to 18 for "respectable clients" 18 ¾ to 37 ½ (the latter common to agriculturalists)	
Central Provinces	6 to 12	15 for proprietors 24 for occupancy tenants 37 ½ for ryots with no right of transfer	25
Bombay	9 to 12	12 to 25 (18 commonest)	
Sind		36	
Madras	12	15 to 18 (in insecure tracts 24 not uncommon)	20 to 50

Source: Punjabi Peasant in Prosperity and Debt, 3rd ed. (Oxford University Press, 1932), p. 190.

granted only where the granter has (1) easy means of enforcing his contract or (2) personal knowledge of the character of the borrower. The middleman who tries to arbitrage between the rates of the moneylender and the central bank is apt to attract all the "lemons" and thereby make a loss.

This interpretation can be seen in Sir Malcolm Darling's interpretation of the village moneylender's power:

> It is only fair to remember that in the Indian village the money-lender is often the one thrifty person amongst a generally thriftless people; and that his methods of business, though demoralizing under modern conditions, suit the happy-go-lucky ways of the peasant. He is always accessible, even at night; dispenses with troublesome formalities, asks no inconvenient questions, advances promptly, and if interest is paid, does not press for repayment of principal. He keeps in close personal touch with his clients, and in many villages shares their occasions of weal or woe. *With his intimate knowledge of those around him he is able, without serious risk, to finance those who would otherwise get no loan at all.* [Italics added.] [8]

Or look at Barbara Ward's account:

> A small shopkeeper in a Hong Kong fishing village told me: "I give credit to anyone who anchors regularly in our bay; but if it is someone I don't know well, then I think twice about it unless I can find out all about him." [9]

Or, a profitable sideline of cotton ginning in Iran is the loaning of money for the next season, since the ginning companies often have a line of credit from Teheran banks at the market rate of interest. But in the first years of operation large losses are expected from unpaid debts — due to poor knowledge of the local scene.[1]

IV. Counteracting Institutions

Numerous institutions arise to counteract the effects of quality uncertainty. One obvious institution is guarantees. Most consumer durables carry guarantees to ensure the buyer of some normal expected quality. One natural result of our model is that the risk is borne by the seller rather than by the buyer.

A second example of an institution which counteracts the effects of quality uncertainty is the brand-name good. Brand names

8. Darling, *op. cit.*, p. 204.

9. B. Ward, "Cash or Credit Crops," *Economic Development and Cultural Change,* Vol. 8 (Jan. 1960), reprinted in *Peasant Society: A Reader,* ed. G. Foster *et al.* (Boston: Little Brown and Company, 1967). Quote on p. 142. In the same volume, see also G. W. Skinner, "Marketing and Social Structure in Rural China," and S. W. Mintz, "Pratik: Haitian Personal Economic Relations."

1. Personal conversation with mill manager, April 1968.

not only indicate quality but also give the consumer a means of retaliation if the quality does not meet expectations. For the consumer will then curtail future purchases. Often too, new products are associated with old brand names. This ensures the prospective consumer of the quality of the product.

Chains — such as hotel chains or restaurant chains — are similar to brand names. One observation consistent with our approach is the chain restaurant. These restaurants, at least in the United States, most often appear on interurban highways. The customers are seldom local. The reason is that these well-known chains offer a better hamburger than the *average* local restaurant; at the same time, the local customer, who knows his area, can usually choose a place he prefers.

Licensing practices also reduce quality uncertainty. For instance, there is the licensing of doctors, lawyers, and barbers. Most skilled labor carries some certification indicating the attainment of certain levels of proficiency. The high school diploma, the baccalaureate degree, the Ph.D., even the Nobel Prize, to some degree, serve this function of certification. And education and labor markets themselves have their own "brand names."

V. Conclusion

We have been discussing economic models in which "trust" is important. Informal unwritten guarantees are preconditions for trade and production. Where these guarantees are indefinite, business will suffer — as indicated by our generalized Gresham's law. This aspect of uncertainty has been explored by game theorists, as in the Prisoner's Dilemma, but usually it has not been incorporated in the more traditional Arrow-Debreu approach to uncertainty.[2] But the difficulty of distinguishing good quality from bad is inherent in the business world; this may indeed explain many economic institutions and may in fact be one of the more important aspects of uncertainty.

University of California, Berkeley
Indian Statistical Institute — Planning Unit, New Delhi

2. R. Radner, "Équilibre de Marchés à Terme et au Comptant en Cas d'Incertitude," in *Cahiers d'Econometrie*, Vol. 12 (Nov. 1967), Centre National de la Recherche Scientifique, Paris.

TRANSACTION COSTS, RISK AVERSION, AND THE CHOICE OF CONTRACTUAL ARRANGEMENTS*

STEVEN N. S. CHEUNG
University of Chicago

Every transaction involves a contract. The transactions conducted in the market place entail outright or partial transfers of property rights among individual contracting parties. The contractual arrangements through which these transfers are negotiated are several and varied.

It is common in land tenure literature to rank the relative efficiency of various lease contracts. For example, share tenancy (or sharecropping) has long been considered inefficient, as have leases with relatively short duration. These views are based on an inquiry into the resource use implied by the existing contractual arrangements. But the inquiry has been made without explicit consideration of the pertinent property right constraint and cannot account for the frequent choice of allegedly inefficient contracts. The wrong question has been asked.

Elsewhere[1] I have derived the theory of share tenancy on the condition that transaction costs, and in particular the costs of contractual negotiation and enforcement, are zero. It shows that economic efficiency is the same under various land tenure arrangements subject to the constraint of private property rights. Although transaction costs exist in the real world, the theory enables us to understand much of the farming behavior.[2] However, the presence of a variety of contractual arrangements under the *same* constraint of competition poses the question of the choice of these arrangements. In this article, I set out an approach based on non-zero transaction costs and risk

* This article is an excerpt from my manuscript, The Theory of Share Tenancy—With Special Application to Asian Agriculture and the First Phase of Taiwan Land Reform (to be published by The University of Chicago Press). For their helpful comments I am indebted to Armen A. Alchian, R. H. Coase, Harold Demsetz, Jack Hirshleifer, D. Gale Johnson, Harry G. Johnson, John McManus, Theodore W. Schultz, and George J. Stigler. Thanks for financial support are given to the Lilly Endowment grant supporting the Study of Property Rights and Behavior at the University of California at Los Angeles, and to the Ford Foundation grant for International Studies including Agricultural Economics at the University of Chicago.

[1] Steven N. S. Cheung, Private Property Rights and Sharecropping, 76 J. Pol. Econ. 1107 (1968).

[2] See Steven N. S. Cheung, The Theory of Share Tenancy, chs. 3, 7 and 8.

aversion to explain the observed contractual behavior in agriculture. The observations used are largely drawn from the Chinese experience.

If a firm can increase efficiency in production by employing productive resources of more than one resource owner, a contract to combine the resources will obtain. The formation of the contract involves partial transfers of property rights in one form or another, such as leasing, hiring or mortgaging.[3] These transfers, and the associated coordination of inputs of various factors in production, are costly events.[4] There are costs of negotiating *and* of enforcing the stipulations of the contract.

Given the state of personal wealth distribution and the portfolios of assets held as private property by resource owners, some owners will seek contractual arrangements with others in combining resources for production.[5] There is a variety of arrangements under which this is done. At least two reasons may be offered for the existence of different types of contractual arrangements. First is the existence of *natural* risk, defined here as the contribution by nature or the state of the world to the variance (or standard deviation) of the product value.[6] Given a non-zero variance for the expected output yield (the total income for the contracting parties), different contractual arrangements allow different distributions of income variances among the contracting parties. Under the postulate of risk aversion, an individual will seek to avoid risk if the cost of doing so is less than the gain from the risk averted. He may avert risk either by searching for information about the future (which may not be attainable even at infinitely high cost), by choosing less risky options when investing (which options include portfolio diversification), or by choosing among arrangements with which his burden of risk can be dispersed to other individuals—such as insurance and various contractual arrangements. A second reason for the existence of different contractual arrangements lies in the different transaction costs that are associated with them. Transaction costs differ because the physical attributes of input and output differ, because institutional arrangements differ, and be-

[3] If only *outright* transfers exist for all resources, "owner" production will exist for all firms. Contracting for outright transfers does not concern us here.

[4] See R. H. Coase, The Nature of the Firm, N.S.4 Economica 386 (1937). Reprinted in Readings in Price Theory 331 (Kenneth E. Boulding & George J. Stigler, eds. 1952).

[5] Portfolio selection is a complicated subject. The two major theses that have been advanced center on anticipated changes in the general price level and on the aversion of risk. Transaction costs may imply a third.

[6] While this concept has the advantage of treating risk as a measurable quantity that can be conveniently applied to observations, it also has some theoretical difficulties. See for example, Jack Hirshleifer, Investment Decision under Uncertainty: Choice-Theoretic Approaches, 79 Q. J. Econ. 509 (1965).

cause different sets of stipulations require varying efforts in enforcement and negotiation.[7]

Let me advance the following hypothesis: the choice of contractual arrangement is made so as to maximize the gain from risk dispersion subject to the constraint of transaction costs. In the following three sections, I shall develop this hypothesis and apply it to some observations.

I. The Choice of Contracts in Agriculture

Consider the three main forms of contracts in agriculture, namely, a fixed-rent contract (rent per acre stated in cash or in crop), a share contract and a wage contract. Under private property rights, the contracting parties are free to choose among these forms. The observed patterns of contractual choices vary from place to place. For example, share contracts were more frequent than fixed rents in Taiwan and Southeast Asia before the agrarian reforms; in China fixed rents were more frequent than share rents in the 1930's; in Japan, fixed rents predominated; and in general, wage contracts (farm hands) have been infrequent, occurring in about one to five per cent of the farming households in various localities.[8] Why do the patterns of contractual choices differ? What determines the choice of contracts?

Any contract combining resources from different owners for production involves, in addition to negotiation costs, the enforcement costs of controlling inputs and distributing output, according to the terms of the contract. Contracting on a share basis appears to involve higher transaction costs as a whole (the sum of negotiation and enforcement costs) than a fixed-rent or a wage contract. The terms in a share contract, among other things, include the rental percentage, the ratio of non-land input to land, and the types of crops to be grown.[9] These are mutually decided by the landowner and the tenant. For fixed-rent and wage contracts, however, given the market prices, one party alone is sufficient to decide how much of the other party's resources he shall employ and what crops shall be grown. And since in a share contract the sharing of output is based on the *actual* yield, efforts must be made by

[7] Transaction costs may also depend on other factors, such as the number of participants and transactions, which I shall not explore here. Changes in prices and innovations will also affect the costs of transactions. See for example, Theodore W. Schultz, Transforming Traditional Agriculture 162-174 (1964).

[8] For the case in China, see J. L. Buck, Land Utilization in China 198 (1938); for Japan, see R. P. Dore, Land Reform in Japan (1959); for other parts of Asia, see sources cited in Steven N. S. Cheung, The Theory of Share Tenancy, ch. 1 nn.10 & 14.

[9] These terms are implied by the theory in Cheung, Private Property Rights and Sharecropping, *supra* note 1. Samples of share contracts obtained from China (see next section) are consistent with this statement.

the landowner to ascertain the harvest yield. Thus negotiation and enforcement are more complex for a share contract than for a fixed-rent or a wage contract.

The ranking of transaction costs of fixed-rent and wage contracts appears uncertain. The physical attributes of land are such that the cost of enforcing the contracted amount of input is lower than in the case of labor. That is, the "shirking" of labor input, which may exist in a wage contract (also in a share contract) without either enforcing the input or checking the output, is costly to prevent.[10] But while this "shirking" problem does not appear significant for land input in a fixed-rent contract, policing (or enforcing) the maintenance of soil and other assets owned by the landlord is more costly for a fixed-rent or a share contract than for a wage contract.[11]

If we accept the above reasoning, pending empirical confirmation, and if transaction cost is the only consideration, then the minimization of transaction cost implies that share contracts will never be chosen. Why, then, are share contracts chosen?

Suppose the transaction cost is zero or the same for all forms of contract. Let us employ a behavioral postulate of risk aversion, defined here to mean that an individual, given the same expected average income, prefers a lower to a higher variance. In agriculture, variables exogenous to the production function, such as weather conditions and pests, are risk factors which are difficult to forecast and which may significantly affect the variance of the value of output. Under a fixed-rent contract, the tenant bears most, if not all, of the risk; under a wage contract, the landowner bears most, if not all, of the risk. Share tenancy may then be regarded as a device for risk sharing (or risk dispersion); that is, the variance of the output yield is distributed

[10] For the tenant's incentive to use an amount of input less than that stipulated in a share contract, see Cheung, *supra* note 1. The adoption of different forms of contractual payment for *labor* alone due to "shirking" problems and enforcement costs appears to constitute an important subject which has not been explored. For example, a piece-rate contract will be preferred to a wage contract on an hourly basis if checking output costs less than enforcing input. However, with piece rates the worker is inclined to be "sloppy" and produce products of lower quality. Thus, a piece-rate contract will be less preferable if the physical attributes of the product are such that it is relatively costly to police a specified standard. Similarly, commission payments (as in the case of insurance salesmen) are preferred to other forms when the value of output depends on the intensity of work per sale; "tipping" payments (as in the case of waitresses) are preferred to other forms when the quality of services is significant—in either case, the costs of enforcing "intensity" and "quality" of work appear to be relatively high.

[11] In horticulture, for example, the usual contracts other than owner cultivation are wage or piece-rate contracts. This may imply that in horticulture, owner management involves a lower cost of policing the orchard assets than fixed-rent contracts. On the other hand, one expects wage contracts would be infrequent when the land holding is large, for high costs of labor supervision would be incurred.

among the contracting parties. Given the postulate of risk aversion, a share contract will be mutually preferred by the landowner and the tenant.[12] However, in varying degrees, risk exists in any tenancy. Why, then, are fixed-rent and wage contracts chosen at all?

I suggest that the choice of contract should be analyzed by employing both the differences in transaction costs and the postulate of risk aversion. Given the state of risk associated with a particular output, a higher transaction cost will lead to lower returns to the productive assets. On the other hand, given the transaction cost, risk aversion implies that asset values and the variances of income are negatively related.[13] While in itself the dispersion of risk under a share contract will lead to higher values for the contracted resources, the higher associated transaction cost will lead to lower asset values. Wealth maximization (or utility maximization, depending on the relevant measurement problem) implies that the contractual arrangement chosen will be the one which yields the highest values for the contracted resources.

Given the variance of output value and the rental percentage, a share contract prescribes a specific distribution of income variances for the contracting parties. The associated state of risk dispersion may not conform to the most preferable state according to the parties' preference functions. However, since some dispersion of risk is preferred to no dispersion at all, a share contract will be chosen rather than a fixed rent or a wage contract if the higher transaction cost is at least compensated for by the gain from risk dispersion. There exist, of course, still other arrangements under which the dispersion of risk can be tailored to fit each case. But as we shall discuss in the next section, the transaction cost of an arrangement for risk dispersion more flexible than a share contract may be so high as to make it undesirable.

Evidence is available to support the applicability of this kind of analysis:

(1) Since transaction cost is assertedly higher for share than for fixed rents, there would be room for some third parties to insure the amount of crop yield. That is, if a third party (an insurance company) were to insure the expected mean yield, the contracting parties would choose a fixed-rent contract and would be willing to pay the insuring party an amount no higher

[12] This result is implied in William F. Sharpe, Capital Asset Prices: A Theory of Market Equilibrium Under Conditions of Risk, 19 J. Fin. 425 (1964); Jack Hirshleifer, *supra* note 6, and Investment Decision Under Uncertainty: Applications of the State-Preference Approach, 80 Q. J. Econ. 252 (1966). "Risk-exchange" models derived from the current state-preference and mean, variability approaches, with the aid of an Edgeworth-Bowley box, suggest that risk sharing is preferred—if we ignore transaction cost.

[13] For a theoretical treatment of asset prices and risk premiums as determined in the market place, see Sharpe, *supra* note 12.

than the saving from a lower transaction cost plus a premium for the virtually certain income now obtained as compared with the variable income in a share contract. Yet we seldom find the existence of such a crop insurance without government taking an active role. The reason, perhaps, is that the cost of handling insurance transactions may be so high as to be prohibitive: the insuring agent would have to check not only the actual crop yields but also the amount of inputs. For the French metayage (sharecropping), however, Constantia Maxwell observed:

> The usual procedure for French seigneurs was, while retaining the chateau and its immediate neighborhood for their own use, to let out their lands in *gros* to middlemen or *fermiers* (to be distinguished from *fermiers exploitants*), who paid a fixed sum to the proprietor and gathered the rents from *metayage* or from *censitaires* at their own risk for a personal profit. Some of these middlemen, like the landlords, were absentees and worked the estate through sub-agents.[14]

In this case we see the *fermiers*, a third party, interposing between landlords and tenants to provide a more certain income for the former.[15] To my knowledge, no similar arrangement existed in China, though another practice prevailed (see next section). In Japan, share tenancy has been rare; and, at the same time, a compulsory crop insurance system has been enforced.[16]

(2) In China, share tenancy is reportedly more frequent in the wheat region than in the rice region. Taking the hectare yield data of wheat and rice crops in Taiwan, we find significantly higher proportional variances for wheat than for rice. This is shown in Table 1. Due to the lack of price data, only the variances of physical output are computed, although value of output would be a more appropriate measure.

[14] Arthur Young, Travels in France During the Years 1787, 1788 and 1789 at 395 ed. n. (C. Maxwell, ed. 1929).

[15] To interpret the existence of the *fermiers* on grounds of risk aversion alone seems inconclusive. R. H. Coase has pointed out to me that the *fermiers* resembled the "farmers" in England, who served to collect taxes and postal revenues for the Crown. Coase's explanation for the existence of the English "farmers" is as follows: a collecting agent who is allowed to take the difference between what he can collect and what he has to pay the Crown has a greater incentive to maximize receipts than if the same agent is paid a wage rate for his service. This argument, I believe, is correct, and can be expressed alternatively: transaction costs differ, among other things, because different sets of stipulations require varying efforts in enforcement and negotiation; and for collection a "farming" contract involves a lower cost of enforcement than a wage contract. The *fermier* of France may therefore be viewed as a "farming" agent as well as an "insuring" agent.

[16] See Agricultural Development in Modern Japan, ch. 13 (Takekayu Ogura ed. 1963). I have been unable to discover the frequency of share contracts in Japan before the introduction of the compulsory crop insurance.

TABLE 1
Mean Yield (μ) and Proportional Variance (σ_p^2) of Wheat and Rice Hectare
Yield (kg.), Taiwan, 1901-1950

Value	Crop	Period 1901-10	1911-20	1921-30	1931-40	1941-50
μ	Wheat	880	710	759	1,058	625
	Rice	1,318	1,379	1,588	1,927	1,648
σ_p^2		291	118	357	1,180	1,158
	Rice	31	32	46	62	180

Source: Computed from data in Sino-American Joint Commission for Rural Reconstruction, Taiwan Agricultural Statistics 1901-1955 at 20, 24 (1956).

In Table 1,

$$\sigma_p^2 = \frac{\sum_{i=1}^{n} \left(\frac{X_i}{\mu} - 1 \right)^2}{n},$$

where X_i is the hectare yield in kg., and n the number of years. The higher frequency of share contracts among wheat crops appears to be a universal phenomenon.[17]

(3) According to three independent surveys conducted in China (1930-1935), share rent is generally slightly higher than fixed (crop) rent,[18] and this premium may be regarded as a return for risk bearing to the landowner.

Let us summarize. The postulate of general risk aversion or the minimization of transaction costs, taken separately, do not explain well the observed coexistence of several forms of contracts. For this reason I use both, and the choice of contracts is determined by weighing the gains from risk dispersions and the costs of contracting associated with different contracts. Two factors appear to be important in explaining different patterns of contractual choices in different localities. First, different physical attributes of crops and types of climate often result in different variances of outputs in different

[17] See for example, J. L. Buck, *supra* note 8, at 198; and James O. Bray, Farm Tenancy and Productivity in Agriculture: The Case of the United States, 4 Food Research Institute Studies 25 (Stanford Univ. 1963).

[18] See Li Fa Yuan, Tung Chi Yueh Pao II, 5 (Legislative Yuan, Statistical Monthly, 1932); Nei Cheng Pu, Nei Cheng Kung Pao II (Dep't of Int. Affairs, Public Rep. of Inst. Affairs 1932); Shih Yeh Pu, Chung Kuo Ching Chi Nien Chien G62-83 (Dep't of Real Estates, China Econ. Yearbook, 1936). Some of these findings are reproduced in Steven N. S. Cheung, The Theory of Share Tenancy, App. B.

agricultural areas. Second, different legal arrangements, such as compulsory or subsidized crop insurance, affect the variances of incomes as well as affecting transaction costs for the contracting parties. An examination of some contractual details in the next section will suggest a third factor: different market arrangements also affect the choice of contractual forms.

II. Characteristics of Fixed and Share Contracts (China, 1925-1940)

In this and the following section we analyze in some detail the observed stipulations of fixed and share contracts. This will serve not only to clarify the hypothesis that contractual arrangements are chosen to disperse risk bearing and minimize transaction cost, but also to illustrate that the contractual stipulations in sharecropping are consistent with efficient resource use.[19] I turn to some information from China, roughly from 1925 to 1940. This choice of data is based not only on the availability of information, but also on the fact that during this period in China, some 93 per cent of the farm land was held under private ownership.[20] Let me begin by translating a few sample contracts of fixed rent.

Sample (a)—fixed (crop) rent contract with definite lease duration (Shantung Province):

Tenant A now leases from landowner B [so many acres] of land at location C. We hereby stipulate, with the presence of referee D, that the annual rent per acre includes [so many catties] of millet, soybean and Indian corn. The payment in wheat will be one month after the wheat harvest, and autumn crops two months after the autumn harvest. In a famine year, rental payments shall be adjusted [downward] according to local customs. The duration of the lease is [so many years].[21]

Sample (b)—fixed (crop) rent contract with indefinite lease duration (Kiangsi Province):

[19] The prevailing inefficiency argument against sharecropping can be briefly stated as follows. Since under sharecropping a portion of every output unit is taken as rent, it is similar to an *ad valorem* excise tax—where part of every unit produced is "taxed" by the landowner (government). The distribution of output is not the same as with fixed rent or owner cultivation—where the tiller obtains the *entire* incremental product. Sharecropping, therefore, is said to result in less intensive (and less efficient) farming because the tenant's incentive to work or invest in land is reduced. This thesis, however, ignores the terms in a share contract which the participating parties must *mutually* agree to abide by when the contract is formed.

[20] See J. L. Buck, Farm Ownership and Tenancy in China (1927).

[21] Kuo Min Cheng Fu, Tung Chi Chu, Chung Kuo Tsu Tien Chih Tu Chi Tung Chi Fen Hsi 52-53 (Nat'l Gov't, Statistics Dep't, Statistical Analysis of Tenancy System in China, 1942).

. . . we contractually establish an iron-sheet [firmly fixed] rent . . . . Regardless of good or bad years, not a fraction of rent can be reduced . . . . In the event that the rental payment is reduced or delayed, the landowner is free to take back the land, together with all existing crops, and [the right] to contract a new tenant for cultivation. . . . . Furthermore, the landowner shall pay the tenant 20 copper coins for the delivery of every 100 catties of grains.[22]

Sample (c)—fixed (crop) rent contract with landowner providing non-land farming inputs (Tsinghai Province):

. . . the landowner will furnish [so many catties] of seed, together with [so many pairs] of water buffalo, [so many head] of donkeys, and all essential farming equipment. The durable assets are for use purposes only, and shall not be damaged or lost [by the tenant], . . . and they must be returned to the landowner without delay at the termination of the lease. The [aforementioned] rental rate is subject to adjustment according to local customs in a famine year.[23]

The above samples of fixed (crop) rent contracts are about as representative as I could find. They are identical to cash rent contracts in all aspects except that in the latter rental payments are stated in monetary units.[24] According to observations collected by the Department of Real Estates, covering 22 provinces in China, cash rents are generally slightly lower than crop rents.[25] This differential can be explained by landowners' sharing in the product selling cost undertaken by tenants. We may also note that with inflation occurring in 1938, due to the Sino-Japanese War beginning in 1937, 13.3 per cent of cash rents were converted into crop rents and 15.3 per cent were converted into share contracts.[26] This observation, of course, is consistent with minimizing transaction cost. Under inflation, renegotiation of cash rent contracts becomes more frequent and thus more costly.

The characteristics of fixed-rent contracts are not of special interest except for one feature. The one feature which we single out to elaborate on here is the frequent inclusion of the provision for rental reduction according to "local customs" in a "famine" year [see samples (a) and (c)], a provision which is absent under an "iron-sheet" rent [see sample (b)]. Let us call this provision an *escape clause* for the tenant, the inclusion of which in a fixed-rent contract imposes a risk burden on the landowner.

22 Pe-Yu Chang & Yin-Yuen Wang, Chung Kuo Nung Tien Wen T'i 68 (Questions of Farm Tenancy in China, 1943).

23 Nat'l Gov't, *supra* note 21, at 54-55.

24 See Nat'l Gov't, *supra* note 21, at 53-54 and Chang & Wang, *supra* note 22, at 67-70.

25 Shih Yeh Pu, Chung Kuo Ching Chi Nien Chien G62-83 (Dep't of Real Estates, China Econ. Yearbook, 1936).

26 Hsing Cheng Yuan, Ti Chuan Pien Tung No. 2 (Executive Yuan, Changes in Land Rights 1942). The data were obtained from sample contracts in 14 provinces in 1938.

We may interpret "local customs" as a set of market prices for "famine" adjustments, even though the exact magnitude of the possible reduction of rent is not stated when the contract is signed. The escape clause comes into play only in a year so "bad" that the market considers it to be a "famine." Given a sufficiently large number of fixed-rent contracts which include the escape clause, competition among landowners to keep their tenants will yield certain market rates of rental reduction which each landowner will follow. Other things being equal, the increased risk burden on the landowner associated with the inclusion of the escape clause implies that a premium will be added to the "fixed" rent over the "iron-sheet."[27]

Although shifting the risk burden by including the escape clause in a fixed-rent contract is not quite the same as the risk dispersion in a share contract, we may imagine the formation of share contracts via the escape clause. Suppose "famine" is defined as occurring when the actual harvest is reduced to a certain per cent of the expected mean yield due to natural causes. The tenant under fixed rent has the option to choose between agreeing to an "iron-sheet" contract or buying an "escape" right by paying an "insurance" premium to the landowner—such that in the event of "famine," rental payment will be reduced by a certain percentage according to a market rule.

To further the argument: there could exist in the market place not just one escape clause as observed, but a wide range of similar clauses each associated with a different level of "famine," such that the tenant could obtain any or several of them by paying different premiums to the landowner. As such, the risk burden could be dispersed between the contracting parties in an infinite number of ways each with slightly different arrangements. This hypothetical world would perhaps exist if the costs of negotiating and marketing all of the different escape clauses were zero. But with increasing transaction cost associated with additional escape clauses—in particular the cost of defining different levels of "famine" in the market place and the cost of negotiating the rental reduction for each—the incremental gains of having them may be so small that no further "custom" is developed by the market. Instead, an alternative device chosen is a share contract, under which multiple "escape" provisions for the tenant will be implicit, and within which the rental payment is no longer fixed.[28]

From the above we may deduce two implications with respect to transaction cost and risk aversion. First, we have argued that the transaction cost

[27] Unfortunately, I have been unable to find data that would confirm or refute this statement.

[28] Note that with a share contract the landowner not only shares in the possible loss in a bad year, but also the gain of a good harvest which will reduce the risk premium by a fraction.

is higher for share rent than for fixed rent, pending empirical confirmation. Observed contractual arrangements in China suggest that the transaction cost for a wide range of escape clauses is higher than for share rent. The reason is that a wide range of escape clauses would allow a greater variety of choice for risk dispersion than a share contract, and yet only one escape clause is observed as available. Thus, the range of contractual choices is constrained by transaction cost. Second, since, as noted earlier, evidence indicates that share rent is slightly higher than fixed rent due to the added risk burden imposed on the landowner, we conjecture that the landowner's income would be higher than with a share contract if an escape clause were adopted to the effect that the tenant's income variance is reduced to zero. Imaginative as it may seem, we find such an escape clause exists in the real world, disguised under the name of a wage contract.

Available data on the frequencies of escape clause adoptions under different contracts support my suggestions. A survey conducted by the University of Nanking, covering four provinces in China in 1935, reveals that the escape clause [as in contract samples (a) and (c)] was adopted in 83 per cent of the crop (fixed) rent contracts, 63 per cent of the cash (fixed) rent contract, and not at all in share contracts.[29] The higher frequency of adoption for crop rent than cash rent is what we would expect. In the event of a generally poor harvest, the market price of agricultural yield will rise, and with cash rent the tenant's income will be compensated by the rise in price more than with crop rent; hence, the escape clause will become less preferable to the tenant.

The existence of the escape clause in the market implies, other things being equal, a more frequent choice of fixed-rent contracts than of share contracts. Outside China in Southeast Asia, before the agrarian reforms, the escape clause was unpopular. However, there existed some guaranteed minimum rents or wages associated with share contracts. These guarantees could be similarly analyzed with the suggested choice-theoretic approach if more information were available. The different market practices explain, in part, the higher frequency of share contracts in Southeast Asia than in China. Indeed, the *fermiers* of the French metayage, the escape clause associated with fixed rents in China, and the minimum guarantees associated with share rents elsewhere are market practices that serve as intermediate arrangements between pure fixed rents and pure share rents. Each of them has different risk distributions and transaction costs, thus widening the range of contractual choices. Why these intermediate arrangements differ in different markets is a question which I do not seek to answer.

[29] See the University of Nanking, Ssu Hsing Chi Tsu Tien Chi Tu 65-67, Rental Systems in Four Provinces (1936).

Turning to sample contracts of share rents in China, we find that their stipulations are more complex than those of fixed rents, due to the added stipulations on tenant inputs and crops to be grown.

Sample (d)—share contract with uniform sharing percentages for all crops (Shantung Province):

> . . . tenant A agrees to cultivate [so many mows] of land for landowner B. We hereby stipulate that tenant A provides [so many head] of water buffalo, [so many bodies] of men; and every year the tenant must cultivate wheat once, Indian corn three times, and soybean twice. Fertilizer expenses are to be shared [in certain proportions]. The yields of all crops are to be shared [in certain proportions]. The lease may terminate only after the autumn harvest . . . .[30]

Sample (e)—share contract with varying sharing percentages (Honan Province):

> [Stipulations of land size and nonland inputs] . . . . We hereby stipulate that wheat yield will be split 20-80; millet, yellow bean, sesame, green bean—all will be split 30-70; cotton and sweet potatoes split 50-50 . . . ; millet straws, and bean and sesame stalks split 30-70 . . . .[31]

Sample (f)—share contract with some products unshared (Honan Province):

> . . . Tenant A . . . voluntarily agrees to furnish [so many] men, [so many head] of water buffalo and donkeys . . . and all plowing equipment . . . . We clearly stipulate that seeds of major crops are to be provided by the landowner, and seeds of minor crops by the tenant. All crop yields will be split equally, in dry and clean form . . . . But the straws go to the [tenant's] water buffalo entirely; the droppings go to the [landowner's] soil; . . . . and all fertilizer expenses are to be borne equally by both parties. All grinding equipment and living rooms are provided [by the landowner], which the tenant shall repair for his own use. These assets must be returned to the landowner at lease cancellation.[32]

In share contracts, several things should be noted. First, the explicit stipulations of tenant inputs and crop plantations are implied by economic theory. These stipulations are unnecessary for fixed rents. Evidence indicates, however, that only the actual yields are inspected, for by comparison with adjacent farms or past experience the landowner will be able to decide whether the contracted terms have been fulfilled:

> . . . the absentee landlords send their agents, or go themselves, to the fields and

[30] Nat'l Gov't, *supra* note 21 at 54.

[31] Chang & Wang, *supra* note 22 at 63.

[32] Chang & Wang, *supra* note 22 at 63-64.

estimate the yield of the crop and the share given by the tenant is based on this estimate. Such men are very expert in approximating the true yield . . . . [The tenant] commonly cheats by skilfully hiding some of the threshed grain before division takes place and also by giving the landlord inferior crops. On the other hand, the landlord or his agent often uses a large measure. When the agent collects rent the tenant has to treat the agent very well and often has to bribe him in order to keep the land for cultivation another year.[33]

Exaggerated as this quotation might be, an intramarginal tenant with specific farming knowledge (hence, with higher yields than marginal tenants) can "hide" as much as the rent imputed to his special skill and still retain his tenancy; an agent can collect enforcement cost in "bribes" from both the landowner and the tenant as much as other competing agents allow. Nonetheless, this justifies our claim that transaction cost is higher for a share contract than for fixed rent.

A second characteristic of share contracts is that the precise and at times complex delineation of resource rights between the contracting parties suggests that the sharing of investment inputs can be adjusted together with the rental percentage so as to use resources efficiently. This is consistent with a conclusion I have reached elsewhere:[34] the landowner may either require the tenant to invest more in land and charge a lower rental percentage, or the landowner may invest in land himself and charge a higher rental percentage; the investment will be made in one way or the other if it leads to a higher rental annuity.

A third characteristic of share contracts is that the rental percentage may vary among different crops in one contract [see sample (e)]. As implied by the theory of share tenancy, the rental percentage is dependent upon the cost of tenant inputs and the relative fertility of land. Since different crops usually require different intensities of tenant inputs relative to land, the sharing percentages for different crops should be expected to differ within a single contract. However, any set of different rental percentages for different crops can also be expressed in terms of a single (weighted time average) rental percentage, uniform for all crops, to yield the same present value of the rental return. It appears that the latter option of a uniform rental percentage [see contract sample (d)] would be more convenient. However, if tenancy is subject to dismissal at any moment of time in the event of poor performance, the use of one rental percentage uniform for crops harvested at different seasons would be likely to lead to disputes or renegotiation should tenancy dismissal be in effect. We usually find a uniform rental per-

[33] J. L. Buck, Chinese Farm Economy 149-150 (1930).
[34] Cheung, *supra* note 1.

centage being used in a share lease with specified duration, and that when multiple percentages are found in a lease with indefinite duration, a uniform percentage is usually used for different crops harvested in the same season [see contract sample (e)].

We may summarize the characteristics of share contracts by quoting the observation made by two writers—who were critical of tenant farming in China:

Under the system of share rent, the yields after each harvest are to be shared according to certain mutually stipulated percentages between the landowner and the tenant. With the exception of some land used for farmstead purposes, the tenant is required to cultivate almost all the assigned fields for the production of crops. Sometimes, the tenant is even required to furnish farming equipment . . . and other expenses. The landowner and the tenant mutually decide the area to be used for each crop . . . . Besides the above, the only affair of management over which the landowner exercises control is confined to permanent improvements of land assets. This last characteristic is identical with fixed-rent contracts.[35]

III. The Duration of Lease Contracts

An investigation conducted in China (1934), covering a total of 93 prefectures in 8 provinces, shows that the distribution of lease durations was as follows: 29 per cent of the tenant contracts were *indefinite* (that is, unspecified and usually terminable after every harvest), 25 per cent *annual* leases, 27 per cent from *3 to 10 years*, 8 per cent from *10 to 20 years*, and 11 per cent were *perpetual* leases.[36] Two things should be noted. First, a stipulated lease duration means only that tenancy may not be terminated as long as the contracted terms are fulfilled by each party. That the duration of the lease is specified does not prohibit mutual renegotiations within the lease duration. Second, as the frequency of short-term leases has been used to illustrate the turnover rate of tenancy, it should be pointed out that lease termination is not the same as tenancy dismissal. Available data reveal that the frequency of tenancy dismissal was not high.[37]

[35] Chang & Wang, *supra* note 22, at 49. For similar observations see Ching-Moh Chen, Chung Kuo Ko Hsing Te Ti Tsu (Land Rents of Various Provinces in China, 1936); Chi-Ming Chiao, Chung Kuo Nang Ch'un She Hui Ching Chi Hsueh ch. 9 (A Social and Economic Study of Farm Villages in China, 1938); and Chung Kuo Ke Hsueh Yan Ching Chi Yen Chiu So, Chung Kuo Ching Tai Nung Yeh Shih Tze Liao 1912-1927, at 89-95 (China Econ. Research Dep't, Source Materials of Recent Chinese Agricultural History, 1957).

[36] These precentages are computed from Shih Yeh Pu, Chung Kuo Ching Chi Nien Chien 101-104 (Dep't of Real Estates, China Econ. Yearbook, 1935). A similar investigation conducted in the same localities ten years earlier yielded a virtually identical distribution, *id.*

[37] According to a survey conducted by the Executive Yuan, *supra* note 26, covering 14 provinces in China (1937), 7.5% of the lease contracts were dismissed in that year.

In the literature of land tenure, two arguments have been commonly used in attacks upon the efficiency of lease durations of less than 10 years. One of these claims that short durations impose insecurity on the tenant and thus impair his incentive to farm. But insecurity, although undesirable to the tenant, may provide a stimulus to farming activity.[38] Another argument is that the short-term lease discourages investment in land. However, this is refuted by the fact that yields per acre on tenant farms are not lower than on owner farms; nor has any evidence been offered to show that, in China, productivity under tenancy varies with the duration of a leasing contract.[39]

The right to each privately owned resource is, by definition, transferable and exclusively delineated. Rights to resources invested in land and other assets are no exception. In the formation of a lease contract, the participating resource owners are free to accept or reject the contractual terms being negotiated. Again, the choice for the duration of the contract is no exception. Thus the relevant question here is not whether a "short-term" lease is inefficient; the relevant question is why different lease durations are chosen.

In a world uncomplicated by transaction costs and risks, in which the right to the income generated by private investment could be costlessly secured and transferred, and in which changes in contractual stipulations could be costlessly negotiated at any time, the duration of the lease becomes irrelevant and its explicit stipulation superfluous. With transaction costs included, I argue that the lease duration will be chosen so as to minimize these costs. To do so, it is convenient to separate the cost advantages for "long" and "short" lease durations.

1. *The Choice of Relatively Long Lease Duration*

A relatively long lease duration is chosen to reduce the cost of transferring (transacting) tenant assets attached to land. There exist differences in physical attributes of capital assets which involve different moving costs at lease dismissal. For example, a water buffalo owned by a tenant for grain

---

However, since inflation began in the same year, the cited percentage might be higher than that of preceding years. For the rise in prices due to the Sino-Japanese war, see Chang & Wang, *supra* note 22, at ch. 9.

38 Armen A. Alchian has argued that the desire for security leads to "long-term" contracts. But his analysis is based on a property right system which is *not* private, where the private cost of acquiring security is relatively low. See his Private Property and the Relative Cost of Tenure, The Public Stake in Union Power 350-71 (Philip Bradley ed., 1959).

39 During the period 1925-1937, surveys conducted by five organizations in China show no notable differences in acre yields or land prices that are attributable to different tenure arrangements. Among these surveys, two volumes are particularly comprehensive: Nat'l Gov't, *supra* note 21 and Land Utilization in China—Statistics—A Study of 16,786 Farms in 168 Localities and 38,256 Farm Families in Twenty-two Provinces in China, 1929-1933 (J. L. Buck ed., 1937).

grinding is easier to move at lease dismissal than an improvement in water irrigation made by him. Of course, the landowner could have invested in the water irrigation himself, or he could purchase the tenant's committed improvement outright.[40] But when assets attached to land are owned by the tenant, disputes may arise in the event of tenancy dismissal. A lease with a sufficiently long duration may become the preferred option.

However, the cost of moving the *physical* asset is not necessarily the relevant cost to consider. The tenant's property *right* to his committed investment may be transferred, either to a third party or to the landowner, at a market price. The problem is that such a price may not exist, or cannot be obtained in a short period of time, due to transaction costs. One need only point out that the depreciated value of a used asset is costly to evaluate; the landowner may choose to select his new tenant instead of allowing any party who purchases the asset to take over the lease. Also, other information problems exist in the market place. An appropriately long lease duration will thus reduce disputes and the anticipated cost of transferring the tenant's property right. This choice, however, can be made only at the expense of some cost advantage which a shorter lease duration provides.

The foregoing discussion can be supported by observations on the perpetual lease in China:

> Under perpetual leases the landowner holds ownership right to the [bottom of] land, and the tenant owns the right to the soil . . . . These two rights are separate. The occurrences of perpetual leases are confined to the following: (1) The tenant exploited [privately owned] wasteland and developed it into farm land, thus gaining a perpetual [ownership] right to the soil from the landowner. (2) Permanent improvements in land made by the tenant . . . . such as building up water-conserving devices in otherwise sandy fields . . . . (3) . . . where labor is scarce and land plentiful, the landowners attracted tenants from afar by offering the perpetual right to till [the soil] . . . . (4) The tenant had paid a lump-sum payment to obtain the perpetual right to till . . . . And (5) the peasant, when in need of money, sold the ownership right to the land bottom but retained the right to till the soil. Since ownership rights to the bottom and surface of land are separate, both the landowner and the tenant can sell their rights freely, without the consent from each other . . . .[41]

[40] Two independent surveys (China, 1921-1924 and 1935) reveal that, among tenant farms, landowners owned about 60 to 70% of the housing assets; tenants owned about 75% of the draft animals and 95% of the farming equipment. The total values of non-land assets on owner and tenant farms were roughly the same. See Nat'l Gov't, *supra* note 21, at 99-116.

[41] Chiao, *supra* note 35, at 261. For similar observations see Nat'l Gov't, *supra* note 21, at 56-58; and China Econ. Research Dep't, *supra* note 35 at 84-89.

In every case, the tenant's asset attached to land (for example, the right to the soil) is physically "permanent." With the perpetual lease and the contracted terms in effect, the landowner may not arbitrarily raise the "bottom" rent (or use other devices) to drive the tenant away. Yet such a lease duration would not be necessary if transaction costs were zero: If the "bottom" and "surface" rights were clearly delineated and costlessly enforced as private, and if these rights could be costlessly transferred, there would exist market prices for these rights at which transfers could be executed at any time.[42] Thus there would be no need for long lease durations to protect the "immobile" investments of the tenant. The same can be said for other assets attached to land.

2. *The Choice of Relatively Short Lease Duration*

The adoption of a relatively long lease duration involves forgoing some cost advantage which a shorter duration provides. When assets attached to land owned by the tenant are to be exhausted in a short period of time, or when the landowner provides all the "permanent" assets, a relatively short lease duration reduces the costs of *enforcing* the contracted terms and of *renegotiating* these terms.

When a contract is formed, the contracting parties may lack sufficient information on each other's reliability. Within a specified lease duration, the violation of the contracted terms by either party may call for increasing enforcement efforts, or for revoking the contract before its termination date through court action or other means—all to be done at some cost. The choice of a shorter lease duration, which facilitates tenancy dismissal, will reduce these costs. As noted at the beginning of this section, however, the frequency of tenancy dismissals was far less than that of short-term leases, suggesting that most terminated leases were renewed. Available data show that the frequency of lease dismissals caused by rental disputes was low.[43] I conjecture, therefore, that in China short-term leases are chosen more as a device to facilitate contractual renegotiation rather than as a device to reduce the costs of enforcing the contracted terms.

[42] I apply here the thinking in R. H. Coase, The Problem of Social Cost, 3 J. Law & Econ. 1 (1960).

[43] Legal records which cover 56 prefectures in 6 provinces (China, 1934-35) reveal a total of 124 tenancy disputes (mostly in rental payments) over a one year period. Even though the number of total tenant contracts is not available, the number of disputes brought to court appears to be so small that one suspects a substantial number of disputes were never brought to court. Over two-thirds of these recorded cases ended in tenancy dismissals, together with payment settlements. See Dep't of Real Estates, *supra* note 36, at G118-120; and *supra* note 25, at G143-144.

It is useful to distinguish two types of contractual renegotiation (revision), though at times one relates to the other. The stipulated terms in any tenure contract in essence specify two things: (a) the state of resource use, or allocation, mutually agreed upon by the contracting parties, and (b) the contracted distribution of income for the parties. To revise (a) through renegotiation for more efficient resource use may benefit *all* parties to a contract, that is, all parties may gain or lose less. However, to revise (b) one party must lose.

Consider the contractual renegotiation which entails mainly a reallocation of resources, for example, changes in relative product prices which call for shifts to different crops, or innovations which call for the adoptions of new seeds or new methods of cultivation. Renegotiations of this type are largely confined to share contracts, since under fixed rents the tenants are left to make their own decisions on resource use except improvements in land and maintenance of the landowner's assets. In principle, since all contracting parties expect to benefit from the revision, renegotiation can take place at any time and lease termination becomes unnecessary. However, different individual knowledge of the market may give rise to difference in opinions as to whether the revision is desirable. A relatively short lease duration is a convenient device which allows resource reallocation in the event of unsuccessful renegotiation.[44] This, together with the more complicated contractual enforcement required for share contracts, explains why durations for share leases are generally shorter than fixed rents.[45]

Consider further the contractual renegotiation which entails the revision of income distribution, when one party gains at the expense of the other. It applies to fixed and share contracts alike. Resource allocation may also be affected. For example, changes in relative asset prices of the contracted resources, a cash-rent contract with unanticipated inflation, or decision errors made in the initial contract—which call for a revision of the rental rates—are cases in point. Since some party must lose when revising the initial distributional terms, that is, the gainer either cannot or will not fully compensate the loser in making the revision, lease termination (hence, the choice

[44] With lease termination, for example, a share tenant who alone wants changes in production plan can request a fixed-rent contract, purchase the land outright, or seek tenancy with another landowner. Without lease termination, further negotiation may still take place if one party who wants the revision pays the reluctant party an amount to make the revision "convincing."

[45] Localities with higher frequencies of share leases (China, 1934) were associated with higher frequencies of short-term leases. See Nat'l Gov't, *supra* note 21, at 43, Tables 20 and 21; and at 59, Table 26.

of an appropriately short duration) is essential.[46] Again, this would not be necessary if transaction cost were zero (even if unanticipated events occur independently). In the absence of transaction cost, a contract would be designed to allow day to day changes in rental payments; within any lease duration, the distribution of income would not be held fixed throughout.

IV. Concluding Remarks

For generations economists and land tenure writers have sought to rank the relative efficiency of resource use under different leasing arrangements. But their inquiries were undertaken without explicit reference to the property right constraint involved. And in many cases, the characteristics of various lease contracts had not been carefully examined. Different contractual arrangements do not imply different efficiencies of resource allocation as long as property rights are exclusive and transferable. The characteristics of lease contracts presented above also confirm this statement.

In this article I have asked: Why are different contractual arrangements chosen under the same system of private property rights? To answer this question I have introduced transaction costs and risks. The attempt to formulate a choice-theoretic approach to explain the observed contractual behavior in agriculture has perhaps raised more questions than it has answered.

Among some related problems that I have avoided explicitly, the following are significant. First, with respect to risk aversion, a more general analysis would include all risky choices, and not contractual choice alone. The analysis would be less difficult if transaction costs were not involved. Second, with respect to transaction costs, a more general analysis would derive some specific and well-behaved cost function of transactions. This step is essential to the development of a model of general equilibrium including transaction costs.

Still other problems I have avoided implicitly. In particular, some level of law enforcement by legal authorities is taken for granted. We may well ask: What will happen to the choice of contracts if the government changes its enforcement efforts? To what extent will these efforts be consistent with the Pareto condition? What set of legal institutions is consistent with the operation of the market place? With these questions unanswered, the conditions defining efficiency with transaction costs are not all clear. Let me explain.

[46] Given an unexpired lease which fixes the rental rate, changing economic conditions may lead to a redistribution of income. However, the efficiency of resource allocation may not thereby be hindered.

In production, cost minimization requires not only the fulfillment of the familiar set of marginal equalities, but also the choice of the lowest-cost production method available. In transactions, one relevant consideration is the cost of alternative *contractual* arrangements, which we have discussed at some length. One might think that, as a cost constraint, efficiency will be attained when, other things equal, the set of arrangements with the lowest transaction cost is chosen. However, transaction costs also depend on alternative *legal* arrangements. For example, the varying effectiveness of law enforcement, or the varying corruptibility of courts, will affect the costs of transactions in the market place. Given the existing legal institutions, I have attempted to explain the observed contractual arrangements. But insofar as I have ignored the choice and development of the legal institutions, the Pareto condition with transaction costs is ambiguous.

I have also not explored the contractual behavior associated with different property right constraints. Various restrictions on the transfer of property rights, or various methods of attenuating the right of a resource owner to obtain income from his resource, will affect the leasing arrangements as well as resource allocation.

A THEORY OF CONTRACT CHOICE AND THE CALIFORNIA GOLD RUSH*

JOHN UMBECK
Purdue University

EVERY time an exchange takes place between two or more people there is a contract, either explicit or implicit. These contracts can take a variety of forms which are subject to the discretion of the contracting parties. The purpose of this paper is to examine the nature of contract choice by employing the tools of price theory. In particular (using a model developed by Cheung[1]), I will try to explain the choice of contracts observed among gold miners during the California gold rush of 1848-1850.

In his 1969 article, Cheung developed one of the first theories of contract choice. The basic proposition set forth in his paper is that individuals, in choosing between a fixed rent or a sharing contract, will select the one which minimizes risk (defined here as the variance in income), but their choice is subject to the constraint of positive transaction costs.

While I will use the same methodology as Cheung and, indeed, the same theoretical proposition, there are at least three significant differences which will require modifications of the analysis. First, Cheung's model explicitly assumes that property rights to all the factors of production are clearly delineated. However, as I will show later, this assumption cannot be used when examining contract choice in the California gold fields. Because the mineral lands were a nonexclusive resource, the theory must take into account the additional costs of privately maintaining exclusive rights. Second, Cheung's model was constructed to explain contract choice in agriculture, and so his discussion emphasized the problems in contracting in this particular industry. Yet, his theory suggests that the costs of contracting will be a function of both the production technology and the nature of the product itself. Therefore, a careful examination of the characteristics of gold and the

* To list all of those who assisted me would significantly lengthen the paper. However, I would like to give special thanks to Steven Cheung and Yoram Barzel. Without their help this work would never have begun. I am also indebted to the National Science Foundation, the Foundation for Research in Economics and Education at UCLA, and the Krannert Graduate School at Purdue University. Their financial support helped in both the research and the writing of this paper.

[1] Steven N. S. Cheung, Transaction Costs, Risk Aversion, and the Choice of Contractual Arrangements, 12 J. Law & Econ. 23 (1969).

mining techniques of the period will be required for the theory to be useful in this application. Third, Cheung's empirical work tests primarily the implications of changes in income variance across crops while holding constant the cost differences of the two types of contracts. In this study of gold mining, income variance assumes only the role of rationalizing the choice of a sharing contract. In the empirical work, the differences in income variance are assumed to be of minor importance while the focus is on differences in the contracting costs.

In Section I, Cheung's theory will be presented and modified to take into account the differences discussed above. From this theory, a set of refutable implications will be derived. In Section II, it will be shown that the actual test conditions found in the California gold fields closely conformed to the assumed theoretical constraints. Finally, in Section III, one of the implications, the effect of group size on contract choice, will be tested against the data from the gold rush period.

I. Theory

Assume that a number of wealth-maximizing individuals are placed on a limited quantity of land which contains the scarce resource gold. The gold is distributed randomly throughout and can be acquired only by adding labor effort to land—an input which is related to the final output through a linear homogeneous production function. However, there is no government or state to assign exclusive ownership rights to the gold-bearing land. If the individuals, each of whom is trying to acquire as much land as possible, are to avoid violent conflicts, they must agree, through contract, upon how the land or gold will be divided. By assumption, these agreements are limited to two alternatives: a sharing contract or a land allotment contract.

Under the sharing contract, a group of miners would agree not to fight among themselves for the rights to mine gold. Instead, they would claim, as a group, a certain amount of land from which nongroup members would be excluded.[2] Within the group, no individual has the right to exclude another member from any of the gold-bearing land. Each miner agrees to work a certain number of hours out of each production period. At the end of this period, all of the individual's gold is placed in a common pool where it is measured and then divided up among all members according to an agreed-upon formula. The contract further provides that the group will punish anyone found guilty of violating the terms of the agreement.

Under the land allotment contract, a group of miners would claim a

[2] For an explanation of the determinants of group size, see John Umbeck, A Theoretical and Empirical Investigation into the Development of Property Rights ch. 3 (unpublished doctoral dissertation, Univ. of Wash. 1975).

certain amount of land from which nongroup members would be excluded. However, unlike the sharing arrangement, each individual is alloted a particular piece of this land. This alloted land becomes private property and, as such, the individual owner can exclude all other miners, including members of the contracting group. Each miner works his own land with as much labor as he chooses to supply and keeps for himself all the gold he finds. Violators of the contractual provisions will be punished by the group.

In making a comparison between them, it will be convenient to break down the costs associated with these contracts into three separate categories: the costs of reaching agreement on the initial allocation, of measuring or metering the agreed distribution, and of enforcing the contractual provisions.

In forming either contract, the agreement on the sharing percentages or the land allowed each individual will determine the initial distribution of wealth and income among the group members. Assuming that each individual is a wealth maximizer, this initial allocation process is of crucial importance and must be negotiated and resolved before any further agreements can be made. What is of importance here is the relative costs of agreeing to a sharing contract as opposed to the land allotment contract. In one case, the agreement is in terms of gold; in the other, it is in terms of land. However, in both cases it is wealth or the present value of the initial distribution which is relevant. Thus, other things being equal, there is no reason to suppose that these costs would be significantly different.[3]

The costs of measuring and dividing the final product will depend on the characteristics of the good being produced. In this example, gold, in its pure form, requires measurement at only one margin: weight. A simple set of balances can determine the value of the final product at a trivial cost. Similarly, the division of this product can be accomplished quite easily. In general, as the product becomes increasingly complex, measurement may be required at more than one margin. As a result, measurement and division costs will be higher.[4]

[3] In the event that these negotiations fail to achieve agreement, the miners are left with one alternative, the use of personal force or violence. While a detailed analysis of this rationing process is beyond the scope of this paper, it should be noted that as long as any individual can acquire more wealth through the use of violence than he can obtain by agreement, there will be no contract. Therefore, the initial allocation of wealth between the contracting parties is constrained by the threat of personal force. Since the constraint of personal violence is the same in either contract, the costs of agreeing to the distribution of wealth should not differ significantly. Further discussion of this will be found in *id.* at chs. 2, 3, 8.

[4] For example, an automobile is a complex commodity requiring measurement at several margins such as length, width, color, engine size, fuel consumption, speed, acceleration, upholstery, etc. Compared to pure gold, the costs of measuring a car will be relatively high. Similarly, because of the complex nature of a car, the costs of dividing it up will also be relatively high. Of course, the car itself need not be physically divided. Instead the individuals

For the land allotment contract, costs will be incurred in measuring and dividing the land. If, however, the land is homogeneous with respect to its expected gold yield, the measurement of only one margin, square feet, will be required.[5] Thus, in my example, the costs of measuring and dividing land are probably insignificant. Notice, however, in comparing the two contracts that the sharing contract requires measurement and division after each production period while the land is measured and divided once at the beginning of the first production period and need not be done again.

Regardless of their choice of contract, individuals claiming exclusive rights to scarce resources will incur costs in keeping others from stealing this property. There is little reason to suppose that the costs of excluding outsiders will vary significantly with the contract choice; however, stealing among group members is a different matter.

In the land allotment contract, each person is given a measured amount of land to work for himself. If anyone violates that agreement and trespasses on another's property, it can be determined at a relatively low cost, as the trespasser is observed to be within the boundary markers of another person's land.[6] On the other hand, under the sharing agreement each individual has a right to a share of the final product produced by everyone else. The costs of enforcing these rights will depend on the characteristics of the good itself. For example, if the good is small it will be relatively easy to conceal and avoid sharing, thereby raising the costs of enforcing the contract. Similarly, the more valuable the good, the greater is the gain from the avoidance of sharing and the greater the costs of enforcement. In the mining example, even small quantities of gold would be of significant value and easily concealed, thus making the costs of sharing enforcement relatively high when compared to the alternative allotment contract.

On the basis of the above discussion alone, I would conclude that the costs

could divide the use of the car, each person acquiring the right to drive it some of the time. But, this would involve an additional contract, the costs of which would make car division more expensive than merely splitting up gold.

[5] The choice of margins to be measured is an interesting question that has for the most part been ignored by economists. For example, why do eggs sell by the dozen while apples sell by the pound? Why is lettuce sold by the head and carrots by the bunch, while strawberries sell by the quart? Wealth maximization implies that individuals will measure all economic margins. However, this will be constrained by the costs of measuring. Implicit in economic models which treat all commodities as single-dimensioned is the assumption that these measurement costs are zero.

[6] In this case, there is a close relationship between measurement costs and enforcement costs. In order to enforce exclusive rights to his property (land), an individual must first detect a trespasser. To the extent that rights are to physical things, the limit of these rights can be in part determined by measurable boundaries. The more precisely these boundaries are measured, the easier it is to determine if the rights have been violated. For example, if the boundaries between two separately-owned parcels of land are not measured, it would be impossible to determine where the rights of one individual end and the other's begin. On the other hand, if the borders are measured and marked, a trespass can be determined at a relatively low cost.

of the sharing contract would probably exceed the costs of the land allotment contract in the gold mining case. To further justify this position let me point out that the sharing contract has one additional cost which the land allotment contract does not have. Under the sharing arrangement, there will be costs of enforcing the work requirements. To the extent that individuals actually share some of their output, the cost of their leisure is lower than in the absence of sharing. For example, if I can find and keep ten dollars worth of gold per day, the cost to me of not working for one day is ten dollars. However, if I find ten dollars worth per day but share half of it with others, the cost of a day's leisure is only five dollars and the quantity of leisure demanded will increase. Therefore, under the sharing contract, some resources will have to be allocated to enforcing the work requirement.[7] Under the land allotment scheme this cost does not exist at all since each miner keeps one hundred per cent of the gold he finds.

If the costs of the share contract are greater than the costs of the land allotment contract, cost minimization dictates that the latter will always be chosen. So why use the sharing contract? In the mining example, assume that the gold is not distributed evenly throughout the land claimed by the contracting group. Two individuals working their own piece of land under the allotment contract could experience significantly different income streams. By sharing the actual gold yield, the average expected income per miner would not change but the variance would be reduced. If miners prefer a lower to a higher income variance, given the same average, and if contracting costs were the same under both arrangements, then a share contract would always be chosen.

In choosing between these two contracts, both the variance in income and the costs of contracting must be considered. To be more explicit, *in choosing between contracts, each individual will attempt to minimize the variance in his income subject to the constraint of contracting costs.* This hypothesis becomes refutable when the effect of some observable variable on either income variance or contracting costs can be determined. For example, if the gold in my previous illustration was observed to be evenly distributed, I

[7] Labor is a unique input in the production process because the physical input cannot be separated from the decision-maker. Thus, a worker can decide to reduce his labor inputs after he has agreed by contract to provide a specified amount. Because of this ability to "shirk," the enforcement of labor contracts will be relatively expensive compared to the enforcement of some nonlabor input contract. The costs of enforcing the labor inputs will depend in part on the nature of the production process. For example, if the gold miners are working a large section of land, the distance between each miner will make it more costly to observe each other in order to enforce the work requirements (assuming that the sharing can be costlessly enforced). However, when working a very small piece of land, the miners will be closer together, making it less costly to enforce the labor inputs. For a good discussion of enforcement costs and their relationship to the production process, see Armen A. Alchian & Harold Demsetz, Production, Information Costs, and Economic Organization, 62 Am. Econ. Rev. 777 (1972).

would predict that the sharing contract would not be observed. However, as the observed variance increased, the observed incidence of sharing contracts should also increase.[8] Similarly, as the population in a contracting group increases, the differences between the costs associated with the two contractual forms will increase, thereby leading to a reduction in the observed incidence of sharing contracts. A demonstration of this last proposition follows.[9]

As the population of a given group of gold miners increases, the contracting costs will rise for each individual. With more people involved in the negotiation process, the costs of agreeing will be higher. Similarly, since the land or gold must now be measured out and divided up among a larger group, these activities will be more costly. However, at least in the gold mining example, there is no a priori reason to suspect that these costs will rise at a significantly different rate with respect to the choice of contracts. In other words, considering these factors alone, the relative costs of the two contracts will probably not be noticeably affected by the change in group size.

It is in the area of enforcement that the population increase will have significantly different effects on the rate of change in the individual's contracting costs. Notice that under the land allotment contract each individual will have more potential trespassers to exclude from his property. This cost increase will be offset, at least partially, by two factors: the individual will have less land area to defend, thus reducing his total enforcement costs and, having less land, his property is a less valuable theft target to potential trespassers. Even with these offsetting factors, I expect that there will be some increase in the costs of enforcing an individual's property rights to land. However, I do not expect that it will be as great an increase as that associated with the sharing contract. In the sharing agreement, each miner has rights to a share of the gold found by everyone else. As the population increases, there are more miners to be watched, and the cost of enforcing these rights will probably rise. This cost increase will not be offset by a decline in the value of the good being stolen as in the case of the land allotment contract. To the contrary, the incentive to steal by concealing the gold discovery will increase with the population. To an individual in a group of ten miners, a one hundred dollar gold find is worth ten dollars, the other

[8] For a test of this, see Steven N. S. Cheung, *supra* note 1.

[9] From the discussion of the relative costs of contracting, it is possible to derive numerous implications in addition to those already mentioned. For example, other things remaining constant, as the physical size of the land being worked by a group of miners increases, the costs of enforcing the sharing and work requirements will rise and fewer sharing contracts should be observed. Similarly, as the final product becomes more complex and measurement must be done on more economic margins, fewer sharing contracts will be formed. And, as the final product becomes physically smaller per dollar of value, fewer sharing contracts will be chosen.

ninety going to the rest of the group. That same find is worth only one dollar to the discoverer working in a group of one hundred. In the larger group, violating the contract and hiding the gold is worth an extra nine dollars. Furthermore, to the extent that sharing is enforced, the miner in a larger group has less incentive to work. As the group gets larger and the miner gets to keep less of the product of his own efforts, the cost of leisure activity declines. Thus, more resources will have to be allocated to enforce the contractually stipulated work requirements.

While any analysis of costs ultimately is based on assertions, I believe the preceding offers a strong a priori case for assuming that population increases will raise the cost of the sharing contract more than the cost of the land allotment contract. Fortunately, when this proposition is added to the hypothesis of contract choice, a testable and potentially refutable implication can be derived. As the group size increases, the relative costs of the sharing contract will rise. If contracts are chosen to minimize the variance in income subject to the constraint of contracting costs, group size and the observed frequency of sharing contracts should be inversely related. In other words, the larger the group, the more likely it is that they will choose the land allotment contract over the sharing contract.

The preceding implication was derived under the assumption that only the relative costs of the two contract forms were changing with the increase in population. However, as the group size gets larger, the relative gains from sharing decrease. To illustrate, assume that N miners claim L units of land and they know that this land contains G amount of gold. The location of this gold is normally distributed, but until actual mining operations begin, the exact location is unknown. If the miners agree to an equal sharing contract, each will acquire G/N units of gold: there will be no variance among individuals. If they choose a land allotment contract with each miner getting a claim to L/N units of land, each will have an *expected* income of G/N. However, under this arrangement, there will be some variance in the *actual* realized returns per individual. It is the elimination of this variance that constitutes the gains from sharing. Next, assume that the population of miners doubles to $2N$ while the quantity of land and gold remains unchanged. Under the sharing contract, each person will get $G/2N$ in gold with no variance. With the land allotment contract the *expected* income will be $G/2N$ per miner but the variance will be less than before the population increase. In other words, as the size of the group increases, the variance in income under the land allotment contract decreases and, along with it, the relative gains of the sharing arrangement.[10]

[10] In the figure below, the curve furthest to the right depicts the distribution of earnings under a land allotment contract when the group size is equal to N. When the population rises to $2N$, the distribution shifts to the left as shown. It shifts in this way because where there were X

This reduction in the variance of income merely reinforces the previously discussed effect of population increases on contract costs. Not only do the costs of the sharing contract rise, but the gains decline relative to the land allotment contract. Therefore, we can still expect an inverse relationship between the size of the contracting group and the incidence of sharing contracts. This implication will be tested in Section III.

The assumptions underlying this argument define a set of conditions which must exist in order for the hypothesis to be tested. A group of individuals must be placed on a piece of land, the use of which is unconstrained by any prior contractual arrangements. The land, when combined with labor, is capable of producing gold, and except for being limited to either the sharing or the land allotment contract, the individual's choice of contracts is unconstrained in any way. Furthermore, within the time period being examined, the production technology must not change in any way that would alter the relative costs of contracting which have been discussed in this section. As I will show next, this rather restrictive set of test conditions was present during the years of the famous California gold rush.

II. Test Conditions

Legal Constraints

Prior to the year 1846, the land we now call California was governed by Mexican laws and customs. Most of the country was uninhabited and an

miners, each earning G/N before, now there are $2X$ miners earning $G/2N$. This is true for all points on the earnings axis. The dispersion of earnings is reduced as population increases. Thus, assuming the reduction in variance is not an inferior good, the increase in group size will cause a decline in the relative gains of the share contract.

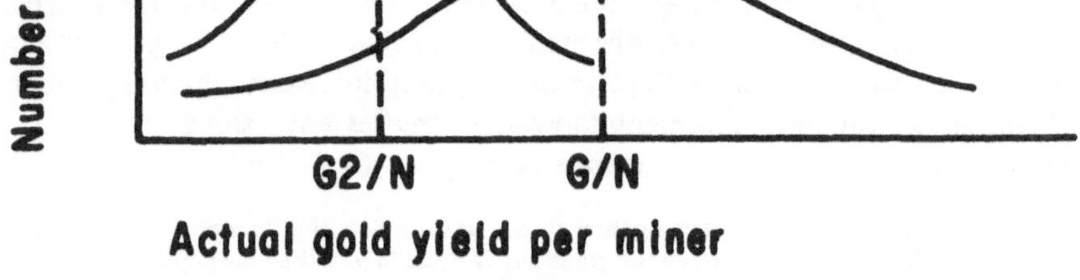

FIGURE I

individual could acquire rights to a tract of land merely by filing a request, along with a rough map showing location and boundaries, with the local government representative.[11] Mexican authority came to an end when President Polk declared war and American troops occupied California. The land was under military rule from 1846 until 1848 when the Treaty of Peace, Friendship, Limits and Settlement, between the United States and the Mexican Republic, ended the war. According to this treaty all Mexican laws not in conflict with the Constitution of the United States were to be continued in force. All nonprivately owned land, and this included all of the gold-mining areas, became the property of the United States Federal Government,[12] which at this time *had no law regulating the acquisition of privately owned mining rights in federal lands.*[13]

On January 24, 1848, just nine days before the signing of the peace treaty, gold was discovered on the American River near the present site of Sacramento. It was probably in response to this discovery and the uncertain legal position on California mineral lands that led to the following decree by the military governor, Colonel Mason: "From and after this date, the Mexican laws and customs now prevailing in California relative to the acquisition of mining rights on public lands are hereby abolished."[14] Colonel Mason offered no alternative legal system by which private property rights to mineral lands could be obtained. With Mexican laws abolished and no federal, state, or territorial law to replace it, California mineral lands remained the property of the United States Government. All individuals who claimed private mining rights were trespassers.

Had there been a legal framework to regulate private mining rights, it is doubtful that it could have been enforced. Reportedly, before the gold discovery, there were 1,059 soldiers in California.[15] Shortly after, this number was reduced to about 660,[16] primarily by desertion. The problem became so severe that on August 19, 1848, Colonel Mason wrote to the adjutant general:

> . . . what right or authority have I to exercise civil control in time of peace in a

[11] The procedure for acquiring rights to land with minerals was a bit more complicated. For details see Willoughby Rodmán, History of the Bench and Bar of Southern California 85-92 (1909).

[12] *Id.* at 87.

[13] Gregory Yale, Legal Titles to Mining Claims and Water Rights, in California, Under the Mining Law of Congress, of July 1866, at 325-54 (1867).

[14] *Id.* at 17.

[15] David Yancey Thomas, A History of Military Government in Newly Acquired Territory of the United States 239 (1904).

[16] Joseph Ellison, California and the Nation, 1850-1869, at 80 n.3 (vol. 16 Cal. Univ. Publications in Hist. 1927).

Territory of the United States? or, if sedition and rebellion should arise, where is my force to meet it? Two companies of regulars, every day diminishing by desertions, that cannot be prevented, will soon be the only military force in California. . . . In the meantime, however, should the people refuse to obey the existing authorities . . . my force is inadequate to compel obedience.[17]

While all California gold land legally belonged to the federal government, it appears that there was no economical mechanism with which to enforce their exclusive rights. Gold-bearing land was, for all practical purposes, a nonexclusive resource.

Contrary to the television westerns which claim to depict this period of American history, the reported incidence of violence in the California gold fields was remarkably low. Instead of fighting over the rights to mineral land, the miners entered into contractual arrangements which assigned mining rights in an orderly and, as I will show, predictable fashion. These contracts took one of two general forms: land allotment and sharing. The gold land which was claimed as exclusive property by the group of contracting miners was called a "mining district," and between 1848 and 1866 it is estimated that over 500 separate districts were organized, ranging in population from four individuals to 8,000.[18]

While the period from 1848 to 1866 marks the years in which there were no state or federal laws regulating the right to private contract in the gold fields, this particular study was limited to the initial rush phase, 1848-1850. This was done for three reasons: it was during these years that the most significant population increases occurred; there were no major technological changes in the mining process to alter the costs of alternative contractual arrangement; and the lands which were being claimed had little value in any nonmining alternative.

Technological Constraints

The gold that was mined between 1848 and 1850 came almost entirely from placer deposits. These superficial deposits were made by streams of water carrying particles from gold veins located higher up in the Sierra Mountains. Where the water current slowed down or was forced by the banks to change course suddenly, the gold settled to the bottom of the river bed. Because of its relatively high specific gravity, the gold flakes would sink

[17] Letter from Mason to the adjutant general on August 19, 1848. In Mary Floyd Williams, History of the San Francisco Committee of Vigilance of 1851, at 61 (vol. 12 Cal. Univ. Publications in Hist. 1921).

[18] The best single source of information concerning this period in California history will be found in 6 Hubert Howe Bancroft, History of California (1888). This is vol. 23 of Hubert Howe Bancroft, The Works of Hubert Howe Bancroft.

into the lighter surface soil until it came to rest on a harder bedrock. It was right above this bedrock that the richest "paydirt" was to be found. Using a pick and a shovel, the miners would dig down to this paying layer, remove the gold-bearing soil and place it in a pan or shallow dish usually about eighteen inches in diameter. The pan and soil were then submerged in a stream of slowly moving water and a circular motion applied. This motion would cause the lighter dirt and sand to float away leaving the much heavier gold in the bottom of the pan. As simple as this method appears, it forms the basis for all of the more advanced placer mining techniques invented after 1850.[19] Furthermore, because of the role water played in creating the gold deposits and in separating the gold from the surrounding surface soil, almost all the early mining took place along the banks of rivers and streams.

Early in 1848 a new mining device called "the cradle" was introduced in California.[20] This was a wooden box about forty inches long, twenty inches wide and four inches deep, which rested on rockers, like a child's cradle, with the head of the box elevated above the lower end. At the head was placed another box, called a riddle box, which had a bottom made of sheet iron perforated with holes about one-half inch in diameter. Paydirt was thrown into the riddle box and water added while the cradle was rocked. The smaller sized rocks, sand, dirt, and gold fell through the perforations to the floor of the cradle. The water washed the dirt over a set of cleats—which were fastened to the cradle floor—and out the lower end, leaving the heavier gold and sand trapped in the cleats. Two or three times a day the cleats were cleaned with a spoon, and the pan was used to separate the gold from the remaining dirt. Two miners together could wash an average of three hundred pans a day using the cradle, which was about three times what could be washed with the pan alone. While the cradle could be operated by one man alone, it had one disadvantage: if the rocking motion ceased, the sand would pack around the cleats thus reducing their ability to trap gold. The cleats had to be cleaned before reusing. Therefore, there appears to have been some gains from forming a contract with at least one other miner who could bring dirt and water to the cradle and avoid the necessity of interrupting the rocking motion. Together with the pan, the cradle was used in nearly all of the mining operations until the end of 1850.

Population Constraints

In May, 1848, it was estimated that the mining population within thirty miles either side of the original discovery site was eight hundred and by June

[19] John S. Hittell, The Resources of California 258-62 (1863). Contained here is an excellent, nontechnical description of all the major mining methods used throughout California.

[20] *Id.*

approached two thousand. In July, Colonel Mason visited the gold fields and estimated that there were four thousand miners. By the end of the year, various observers claimed this number to be between five and ten thousand.[21] During the same time period, the known gold fields expanded from an area immediately surrounding the site of the original discovery to nearly ten thousand square miles.

By the end of 1848, news of the gold discovery had spread around the world. During the winter, individuals in nearly every country made preparations to go to the gold fields, and in the early months of 1849, the rush was on. Between December 7, 1848 and April 17, 1849, over eight thousand people sailed out of New York for California. More than two thousand left Boston and another twelve hundred left New Orleans. It has been estimated that a total of twenty thousand left for California by boat from the east coast of the United States.[22] The Harbor Master's office at San Francisco reported that nearly forty thousand people from all over the world arrived by boat in 1849.[23] When we include those who came overland from the States, the Oregon Territory, Mexico and South America, the population in the California mines was estimated at 107 thousand by the end of the year. Two years later it was estimated at 264 thousand.[24] During the later part of 1849 and throughout 1850, the size of the gold fields did not increase significantly.

III. Evidence

Around the pan-and-cradle technology, the first contracts emerged in early 1848. With rare exception they took a form of sharing. Typically, the groups, ranging in size from two to eight, would agree to work a certain number of hours per day at one or more of the various mining operations; hauling dirt or water, rocking the cradle, and so forth. At the end of the day, the total gold yield was measured and divided evenly among the members. The contracts allowed for one exception to the sharing rule. Any nugget weighing more than one-half ounce that was found before it went into the cradle belonged to the discoverer.[25]

There were several interesting features of this contract which should be pointed out. First, the rights to all of the gold were assigned prior to the

[21] Hubert Howe Bancroft, *supra* note 18, at 70-71.

[22] New York Daily Tribune, June 7, 1849.

[23] Daily Alta California, Nov. 29, 1849 & Jan. 31, 1850.

[24] Henry G. Langley & Samuel A. Mathews, The State Register and Yearbook of Facts for 1859, at 119-22, 184-89 (1858).

[25] John S. Hittell, *supra* note 19, at 262; Edwin Bryant, What I Saw in California 457 (rev. ed. 1876) (1st ed. 1848); Hubert Howe Bancroft, *supra* note 18, at 97; J. D. Borthwick, The Gold Hunters 152-53 (1917); Henry Vizetelly [J. Tyrwhitt Brooks pseud.], Four Months Among the Gold-Finders in California 82 (Davie Bogou ed. 1849).

mining process. This implies that if enforcement costs were zero, there would have been no dissipation of income through rushing, spying, crowding, and other actions found where rights are not fully assigned.[26] Of course, to the extent that enforcement costs were greater than zero, there would have been some dissipation at other margins already discussed. Some miners would have taken more leisure than agreed upon, and others would have concealed some of their gold. The hypothesis suggests, however, that these costs may not have been significant where the group size was small. Furthermore, notice that the particular characteristics of the cradle-mining technology had the effect of reducing the costs of enforcing the contract. The dirt remaining in the cradle cleats had to removed and washed with a pan. While the cradle was being emptied, all other mining operations ceased; each individual took a pan, and the final extraction process took place in one location, the nearest stream. It would have been relatively easy for each miner to watch the others and enforce the sharing. Also, due to its high specific gravity, a nugget of gold weighing less than one-half ounce was difficult to find without the aid of the cradle. The rights to these particles, therefore, would have been relatively cheap to enforce. Larger nuggets, which were more easily found without the aid of the cradle, belonged to the discoverer, thereby eliminating any sharing problem that might arise and reducing these costs of enforcement to zero.

The observed variance in the actual gold yield of any given piece of land was significant. It is not unusual to read accounts of one group averaging over one hundred dollars a day per man, while their neighbors averaged only three or four dollars over the same time period. The costs of reducing this variance by sharing were apparently not too high within the small groups which were formed during 1848. With rare exception, sharing was the only contract form chosen.[27] I can find no evidence that the land allotment contract appeared prior to the summer of 1849.

Aside from cradle mining, the sharing arrangement was chosen by other miners to regulate slightly different activities. An examination of the enforcement problems of these contracts will provide indirect confirmation of the hypothesis.

As already mentioned, in 1848 most of the mining activities were confined to the banks of rivers and streams. But early in 1849, several miners attempted to mine the beds of rivers. This type of project involved organizing enough men to dig a ditch alongside the existing river bed. When the ditch was completed, a dam was constructed which would turn the river water out

[26] Steven N. S. Cheung, The Structure of a Contract and the Theory of a Non-Exclusive Resource 13 J. Law & Econ. 49 (1970).

[27] The only exceptions I found were some miners who hired Indians to mine gold on a wage contract.

of its natural bed and into the ditch, thus enabling the miners to work the river bottom.[28] On the north fork of the American River, where these operations originated, at least nine different groups ranging in size from eight to sixteen were formed under a sharing contract. Each group dug a ditch about three hundred yards long. Then a dam was built, at an estimated cost of eight thousand dollars, which diverted the water. After traveling the three hundred yards, the water was returned to its natural bed, whereupon another group built a dam and again diverted the water. This process was repeated at least nine times with nine separate companies each claiming that part of the river bed which they had drained.[29]

There were apparently no technological problems to prevent these nine groups from contracting together to construct only one dam and one ditch, equal in length to the sum of the separate ditches, thereby avoiding the costs of eight additional dams. However, the hypotheses offered earlier suggests that the costs of a sharing contract rise significantly with increases in group size. In this example, a doubling of the group size to eliminate the cost of an extra dam was apparently not worth the additional enforcement costs.

Further evidence to support the theory is found in the behavior of individuals who came to California as members of a mining company. These companies were formed on the East Coast or in the Midwest by individuals interested in going to the gold fields. A typical company consisted of forty to fifty members bound together by a contract which stipulated, among other things, a certain number of work hours each day and an equal share of the gold for each member. There are partial or complete records of over one hundred and twenty groups and not one of these survived more than a month after beginning mining operations.[30] It is estimated that the average daily gold yield for a member of one of these large groups was $3.16.[31] This was at a time (1849) when the average miner was earning $12 to $16 per day. When these contractual arrangements failed and the groups split up, those who chose to remain in the mines formed new contracts among themselves. The predominant rule was to organize a group of two to eight individuals and share the gold evenly.

Judging from the observed behavior of the California miners throughout 1848 and the first part of 1849, the sharing contract worked quite well. As long as gold land was relatively abundant, a small group of individuals could

[28] John S. Hittell, *supra* note 19, at 268-69.

[29] This information was found in the original record book kept by the miners on the north fork of the American River. The cost estimates for the dams are from Rodman W. Paul, California Gold: The Beginning of Mining in the Far West 126-30 (1947).

[30] Octavius Thorndike Howe, Argonauts of '49, History and Adventures of the Emigrant Companies from Massachusetts, 1849-1850 (1923).

[31] Daniel B. Woods, Sixteen Months at the Gold Diggings 175 (1851).

maintain exclusive rights to a piece of land and enforce the sharing arrangement at a nonprohibitive cost. However, when the group size exceeded about sixteen members, this contractual form ran into difficulties.

By the summer of 1849, the tremendous influx of miners was having an impact in the mining districts. Because there was little offsetting increase in the size of the gold fields, it was not unusual to read reports of hundreds or even thousands of newcomers converging on a river bank where previously there had been only four or five miners. Of course, the original miners had alternatives. They could have tried to maintain exclusive rights by keeping away all outsiders. At odds of one hundred or more to one, their chances of success approached zero. They could have left the area in search of other rich deposits, but these were becoming increasingly scarce. Or, they could admit some of the outsiders until their numbers were large enough to successfully defend their rights against future claimants. Survival in the gold fields dictated the latter choice, and group size increased.

With an increase in group size, the use of the sharing contract as a means of assigning rights to mine gold encountered difficulties. As predicted, the sharing arrangement was replaced by the land allotment contract. Each individual group member was given a particular piece of land, or "claim," along with the rights to all the gold it contained. The reports of the miners themselves reveal how the constraints were changing during this transition period.

> Wood's Creek was filled up with miners, and I here for the first time after the discovery of gold, learned what a miner's claim was. In 1848, the miners had no division of the ground into claims—they worked where it was richest, and many times four or five could be seen at work in a circle of six feet in diameter; but . . . here they were now measuring the ground off with tape measures so as to prevent disputes arising from the division.[32]
>
> All these (banks) on the Middle Fork of the American River, from Oregon Bar upwards, after the lowest estimate, employed in the summer . . . not less than 1,500 men; originally working on shares, and the assessment on the share paid out daily, so that those who had been drunk or absent did not get any part of it; but this after a while caused dissatisfaction and was the reason of breaking up the co-operative work and commencing work on claims. A claim was a spot of ground fifteen feet wide on the river front . . . .[33]
>
> In a comparatively short time we had a large community on the creek, which led to rows and altercations about boundaries, that eventuated in an arrangement, entered into by unanimous agreement, that each person should have ten feet square . . . .[34]
>
> When the mines in and around Nevada City were first opened they were solely in

[32] J. H. Carson, Early Recollections of the Mines 18 (1852).

[33] Paolo Sioli, History of El Dorado County 84 (reprint 1970) (1st ed. 1883).

[34] 2 William Kelly, Excursion to California 24 (1851).

> the ravines . . . and there was no law regulating the size of a miner's claim, and generally a party that first went into a ravine had the exclusive right there too, . . . As population increased that rule did not long maintain. The miners saw that something must be done, and therefore a meeting was called and a rule was established that each miner could hold thirty feet square as a mining claim . . . .[35]

As I mentioned earlier, over five hundred separate groups, or mining districts, were formed throughout the California gold fields. With complete records of the contracts from nearly two hundred of these districts,[36] I can find no evidence that the sharing arrangement survived after 1850. Every district chose instead the land allotment contract. While some of the contractual provisions varied from district to district, they all had a remarkably similar format illustrated by this representative contract formed in 1849 in Jackass Gulch.

First. That each person can hold "one claim by virtue of occupation," but it "must not exceed one hundred feet square."

Second. That a claim or claims if held by *purchase* "must be under a bill of sale, and certified by two disinterested persons as to genuineness of signature and of the consideration."

Third. That a "jury of five persons shall decide any question arising under the previous articles."

Fourth. That notices of claims must be posted upon the ground chosen, and must be renewed every ten days "until water to work the said claims can be had."

Fifth. That, as soon as there is a sufficiency of water for working a claim, "five days' absence" from said claim, "except in case of sickness, accident or reasonable excuse," shall forfeit the property.

Sixth. "That these rules shall extend over Jackass and Soldier gulches and their tributaries."[37]

All of the contracts defined the boundaries (provision 6) over which the rules of the group would be enforced. They allowed each miner at least one parcel of land either by preemption (provision 1) or by purchase (provision 2), provided a means of arbitration in the case of disagreement (provision 3), and specified the requirements for continued mining rights (provisions 4 and 5). There were no provisions for sharing, as each miner was allowed all of the gold contained on his property.

Before concluding this section, two additional observations are worth

[35] Charles D. Ferguson, The Experiences of a Forty-niner During a Third of a Century in the Gold Fields (M. Carson ed. 1924) (1st ed. 1888).

[36] For the location of these contracts see John Umbeck *supra* note 2, at 173-77.

[37] Charles Howard Shinn, Land Laws of Mining Districts 11 (20 ser. No. 12 Johns Hopkins Univ. Hist. & Pol. Sci. 1884).

noting. First, while every group of miners after 1849 apparently chose the land allotment form for their mining district, many of the individual miners combined their private land holdings under a private sharing arrangement. However, this was always done after the initial rights to land were assigned through land allotment. Second, the land allotment contract apparently worked so well in assigning land rights and organizing gold production that its use was continued throughout the 1850s until 1866 when the federal government adopted it within the mining statutes of that year.

IV. Conclusions

In a world where transaction costs are zero, there would be no economic reason for explicit contracts. Similarly, the logic of economics would be incapable of explaining a wide variety of other empirical phenomena, such as the existence of firms, representative governments, nonexclusive property, and people waiting in line. In order to increase the general explanatory power of economic theory, it will be necessary to increase our understanding of the nature of transaction costs. The approach used in this paper is one method by which to achieve this goal. Since all transactions are conducted through the medium of contract, an investigation of the various contract forms should yield much insight into the types of variables which affect the costs of exchange.

There are still many issues raised in this paper which have yet to be answered. For example, it was assumed that the miners only had the choice between a sharing or a land allotment contract. While this assumption conformed with the observed mining practices, in general, there are many other forms of contract. Why these were not used in California is a question that can only be answered when their costs are understood. Furthermore, the study of the constraints facing the gold miners was greatly simplified by the absence of any organized government or prior legal system. The extent to which laws and institutions affect the costs of private contract must be clearly specified in any theory of contemporary contract choice. Notice too, that laws and governmental institutions are themselves affected by the costs of transactions, and this circularity requires the specification of a well-behaved transaction cost function before a general equilibrium solution can be found.

IMPOSSIBILITY AND RELATED DOCTRINES IN CONTRACT LAW: AN ECONOMIC ANALYSIS*

*RICHARD A. POSNER*** & *ANDREW M. ROSENFIELD****

ORDINARILY the failure of one party to a contract to fulfill the performance required of him constitutes a breach of contract for which he is liable in damages to the other party. But sometimes the failure to perform is excused and the contract is said to be discharged rather than breached. This study uses economic theory to investigate three closely related doctrines in the law of contracts that operate to discharge a contract: "impossibility," "impracticability," and "frustration." These are not the only excuses for nonperformance of a contract. Among other excuses, not discussed in this study, is the closely related doctrine of mutual mistake (sometimes called "antecedent impossibility"). Also related, and only incidentally discussed herein, is the doctrine of *Hadley v. Baxendale*[1] limiting the liability of the breaching party to the foreseeable damages of the breach.

There is an extensive legal literature on the set of doctrines that, for want of a more inclusive term, we shall sometimes lump together under the name "impossibility." The main conclusions of this literature are summarized in Part IA, next, while Part IB analyzes the subject from the standpoint of economics.[2] Part II applies the economic analysis to the leading cases and

* This study was supported by a grant from the National Science Foundation to the National Bureau of Economic Research for research in law and economics. It is not, however, an official National Bureau study, because it has not undergone the full critical review accorded National Bureau publications, including approval by the Bureau's Board of Directors. The authors wish to thank Michael Boskin, Richard Epstein, Edmund Kitch, Anthony Kronman, William Landes, Peter Pashigian, George Priest, Kenneth Scott, Robert Willis, and other participants in workshops at the University of Chicago Law School, the University of California (Berkeley) Law School, and the National Bureau of Economic Research-West, for their helpful comments on a previous draft.

** Professor of Law, University of Chicago Law School; Senior Research Staff, National Bureau of Economic Research.

*** Class of 1978, University of Chicago Law School.

1 9 Ex. 341, 156 Eng. Rep. 145 (1854).

2 The subject has received relatively little attention from economic analysts. An early, but unsatisfactory, treatment is Robert L. Birmingham, A Second Look at the Suez Canal Cases: Excuse for Nonperformance of Contractual Obligations in the Light of Economic Theory, 20 Hastings L.J. 1393 (1969); see notes 15-16 *infra*, and accompanying text. Richard A. Posner, Economic Analysis of Law 49-50 (1973), discusses the economics of impossibility briefly.

recurrent situations in which the doctrine has been applied. Part III considers the remedial consequences of application of the doctrine. Our major conclusion is that the doctrine—in its typical, not its every, application—exemplifies the implicit economic logic of the common law.[3]

I. Impossibility and Related Doctrines: Basic Principles

A. *As Perceived in Conventional Legal Scholarship*

Conventional legal scholars who have dealt with the discharge cases have indicated a pervasive dissatisfaction with the prevailing doctrinal articulations.[4] Their uneasiness may reflect an inability to develop a coherent positive theory consistent with the typical outcomes in the recurring cases, and may be responsible for the tendency of courts and commentators alike to treat the field as too broad and diverse to be adequately understood within a single theoretical framework.[5] Thus, in an effort to make descriptive treat-

---

Stephen S. Ashley, The Economic Implications of the Doctrine of Impossibility, 26 Hastings L.J. 1251 (1975), is a longer treatment, but the discussion of economic principles and their applications does not go beyond Posner (see *id.* at 1272-73), the author's main emphasis being on the costs of vague contract doctrines. Paul L. Joskow, Commercial Impossibility, the Uranium Market and the Westinghouse Case, 6 J. Leg. Studies 119 (1977), which came to our attention after our own study was largely completed, is an excellent economic case study. But Joskow's discussion ot the economic principles underlying the impossibility doctrine is quite limited, while his application of those principles to the law is largely confined to section 2-615 of the Uniform Commercial Code (discussed pp. 108-10 *infra*).

On the broader subject of the economics of risk shifting (which, as we shall see, is central to an understanding of the impossibility doctrine) there is of course an extensive literature. See, *e.g.*, Jack Hirshleifer, Investment, Interest, and Capital (1970). However, its emphasis is on capital-market adjustments, formal insurance contracts, and explicit forward contracts as methods of risk shifting, and it ignores contract law as a possible such method. As a result, this literature has only limited relevance to our subject. An older institutional literature on risk shifting also seems to have ignored risk-shifting provisions in contracts other than formal insurance contracts. See Charles O. Hardy, Risk and Risk-Bearing (rev. ed. 1931). The only study of which we are aware of the noninsurance contract as a device for shifting risk (other than the impossibility studies cited earlier in this footnote) is Cheung's study of share tenancy, cited at note 105 *infra*.

[3] See Richard A. Posner, *supra* note 2, at pt. 1.

[4] See Robert L. Birmingham, *supra* note 2; John Henry Schlegel, Of Nuts, and Ships, and Sealing Wax, Suez, and Frustrating Things—The Doctrine of Impossibility of Performance, 23 Rutgers L. Rev. 419 (1969); Comment, Temporary Impossibility of Performance of Contract, 47 Va. L. Rev. 798 (1961); Malcolm P. Sharp, Promisory Liability II, 7 U. Chi. L. Rev. 250 (1940); Comment, Quasi-Contract—Impossibility of Performance—Restitution of Money Paid or Benefits Conferred Where Further Performance Has Been Excused, 46 Mich. L. Rev. 401 (1948); and J. Denson Smith, Some Practical Aspects of the Doctrine of Impossibility, 32 Ill. L. Rev. 672 (1938). See also references in note 6 *infra*.

[5] The problem has been described as one that "calls for special treatment of a type not yet fully developed by the courts. It is a field of relatively recent recognition in which the factors to be considered have not yet been fully charted." Comment, 46 Mich. L. Rev., *supra* note 4 at 403. Consider also the statement that "[t]he conclusions reached in the decided cases are not

ment of the case law more manageable, the subject has been subdivided. The principal subdivisions are "impossibility of performance," "frustration of purpose," and "extreme impracticability," and each is thought to merit separate analytical treatment.[6] "Impossibility" is the rubric used when the carrying out of a promise is no longer "physically possible,"[7] and "frustration of purpose" when performance of the promise is physically possible but the underlying purpose of the bargain is no longer attainable.[8] Impracticabil-

---

harmonious, due, perhaps in part, to the multitude of circumstances or conditions under which the question was presented. It is impossible to state a general rule which will be applicable to all classes of cases." Housing Authority v. East Tennessee Light & Power Co., 183 Va. 64, 72, 31 S.E. 2d 273, 276 (1944).

[6] "There will be found in common use such terms as physical impossibility, legal impossibility, impracticability, subjective and objective impossibility, personal inability, increased difficulty, and frustration of object. These express varying concepts; and the applicable rules of law are not uniform." 6 Arthur Linton, Contracts § 1325 (1962). See also 6 Samuel Williston, Contracts § 1935 (rev. ed. 1938). There is a tendency to treat impracticability as a subset of impossibility while continuing to treat frustration as a distinct field. Compare Restatement of Contracts §§ 288, 454 (1932). In the words of Justice Traynor: "Although the doctrine of frustration is akin to the doctrine of impossibility of performance since both have developed from the commercial necessity of excusing performance in cases of extreme hardship, frustration is not a form of impossibility even under the modern definition of that term, which includes not only cases of physical impossibility but also cases of extreme impracticability of performance." Lloyd v. Murphy, 25 Cal. 2d 48, 53, 153 P.2d 47, 50 (1944) (citations omitted). See also Arthur Anderson, Frustration of Contract—A Rejected Doctrine, 3 DePaul L. Rev. 1 (1953).

[7] See 6 Samuel Williston, *supra* note 6, at §§ 1931-1979; 6 Arthur Linton Corbin, *supra* note 6, at §§ 1320-1372; and Restatement of Contracts § 454 (1932). The leading case is Taylor v. Caldwell, 3 B. & S. 826, 122 Eng. Rep. 309 (1863), in which a contract for a musical performance in a specified auditorium was discharged on grounds of impossibility when the music hall was destroyed by fire. Similar American cases include Siegel v. Eaton & Prince Co., 165 Ill. 550, 46 N.E. 449 (1896) (discussed *infra* pp. 105-06), in which a contract calling for the manufacture of an elevator and its installation in a department store was discharged on grounds of impossibility when the store was destroyed by fire. See also, for example, Texas Co. v. Hogarth Shipping Co., 256 U.S. 619 (1921); and Emerich Co. v. Siegal, Cooper & Co., 237 Ill. 610, 86 N.E. 1104 (1908). These cases illustrate one prominent group of impossibility decisions, in which the continued existence of some material thing is considered essential; if the thing ceases to exist, performance is then said to be impossible. The other principal group of impossibility cases involves contracts discharged because of supervening illegality. The courts thus treat what is illegal as impossible, illustrating great judicial respect for the law but a disregard for normal uses of language. See, for example, Columbus Ry. Power & Light Co. v. City of Columbus, 249 U.S. 399 (1919); Stamey v. State Highway Comm'n of Kansas, 76 F. Supp. 946 (D. Kan. 1948); and Phelps v. School District, 302 Ill. 193, 134 N.E. 312 (1922) (discussed *infra* p. 101).

[8] See 6 Arthur Linton Corbin, *supra* note 6, at §§ 1353-1361; Restatement of Contracts § 288 (1932). The case law develops from the "coronation cases," for example, Krell v. Henry, [1903] 2 K.B. 740 (C.A.). See R. G. McElroy & Glanville Williams. The Coronation Cases, I, 4 Mod. L. Rev. 241 (1941). In each of these cases, an apartment was rented to view the coronation procession of Edward VII. The procession was cancelled due to Edward's illness and discharge was sought on the ground that the underlying purpose (the viewing of the procession) had been frustrated. For further discussion of these cases see text at notes 93-94, 108 *infra*. And for similar American cases see, for example, La Cumbre Golf & Country Club v. Santa Barbara

ity—a catch-all for any discharge case that does not fit snugly into either the impossibility or the frustration pigeonhole—is the term used when performance of the promise is physically possible and the underlying purpose of the bargain achievable but as a result of an unexpected event enforcement of the promise would entail a much higher cost than originally contemplated.[9]

This categorization is unhelpful. It is true that some contracts could be performed only at infinite cost, and these, though rare (Professor Corbin's use of a promise to supply a trip to the moon to illustrate impossibility showed a certain want of imagination),[10] are cases of true physical impossibility. But whether the cost is infinite, or merely prohibitive relative to the gains from performance (as in the impracticability and frustration cases), is a distinction without relevance to the purposes of contracts or contract law. There is thus no functional distinction between impossibility and frustration cases on the one hand and impracticability cases on the other.[11] In every discharge case the basic problem is the same: to decide who should bear the loss resulting from an event that has rendered performance by one party uneconomical.

The fragmentation of the discharge issue into arbitrary subtopics has had serious consequences. When a discharge case is litigated, there is much discussion of its appropriate place within the typology just described. Since the typology is empty, this amounts to an investigation of distinctions without differences and has led legal scholars to despair of generalizing fruitfully about the discharge problem. One commentator has argued that the outcomes in discharge cases are best described as being based on the equities of

---

Hotel Co., 205 Cal. 422, 271 P. 476 (1928); and Alfred Marks Realty Co. v. Hotel Hermitage Co., 170 App. Div. 484, 156 N.Y.S. 179 (1915).

[9] See 6 Arthur Linton Corbin, *supra* note 6, at § 1325; and 6 Samuel Williston, *supra* note 6, at § 1935. The early impracticability cases stressed that when performance became sufficiently difficult or costly, it could be treated as impossibile. See Restatement of Contracts § 454 (1932). Thus in Mineral Park Land Co. v. Howard, 172 Cal. 289, 156 P. 458 (1916), a contractor agreed to haul from the plaintiff's land all of the gravel necessary for the construction of a concrete bridge. The contractor took all of the immediately available gravel from plaintiff's land but purchased on the open market about half of the amount necessary to complete the project. He claimed that all of the additional gravel in plaintiff's land was below water and its extraction would have required the use of extremely expensive techniques. The Supreme Court of California held the contract discharged on the ground that, "[a]lthough there was gravel on the land, it was so situated that the defendants could not take it by ordinary means, nor except at a prohibitive cost. To all fair intents then, it was impossible for defendants to take it." 172 Cal. 293, 156 P. 459-60. However, the courts have been unable to articulate a standard as to what magnitude of cost change is necessary to justify discharge on grounds of impracticability, except to say that "mere hardship is not enough." See, for example, Wischhusen v. American Medicinal Spirits Co., 163 Md. 565, 163 A. 685 (1933); Piaggio v. Somerville, 119 Miss. 6, 80 So. 342 (1919); and Browne & Bryan Lumber Co. v. Toney, 188 Miss. 71, 194 So. 296 (1940). See also Kronprinzessin Cecilie, 244 U.S. 12 (1917); Comment, 4 Calif. L. Rev. 407 (1916).

[10] 6 Arthur Linton Corbin, *supra* note 6, at § 1325. It makes little sense to speak of an event being impossible until it is first accomplished, and possible thereafter.

[11] See J. Denson Smith, *supra* note 4; and Comment, 46 Mich. L. Rev., *supra* note 4, at 401.

the particular case,[12] another that "the decision as to whether the promise is to be enforced must rest in the end on considerations of policy and expediency,"[13] another that "fairness is arguably the foundation of all relief."[14]

Two currents of thought can be discerned in the legal literature on impossibility and related doctrines. One group of scholars argues that a broad and undefined judicial discretion, the result of such amorphous, ad hoc concepts as fairness, equity, and justice, is all that is required to handle the discharge issue adequately. Those who hold this view see their role as quantifying, or at least clarifying, the losses that result from an unexpected event so that the court can apportion them between the parties.[15] This might be termed a distributive approach to discharge.

The other group believes that the variance of the case outcomes results from the courts' lack of a consistent approach. These commentators argue for a doctrinal change of some sort, some urging greater restraint,[16] others greater liberality,[17] in allowing discharge. The proposals are complex, arbitrary, at times almost incomprehensible.[18]

In short, one group of commentators argues essentially that no general theory is possible, and hence concurs with whatever decisions the courts reach. The other group also fails to develop a systematic theory but believes that the current judicial doctrines and outcomes are inconsistent.

There is also in the literature some recognition that the problem of discharge is one of allocating risk, since the effect of granting discharge is to place the risk of the event preventing performance on the promisee, while the effect of denying discharge is to place it on the promisor.[19] But thus far

[12] See J. Denson Smith, *supra* note 4, at 675.

[13] Comment, 46 Mich. L. Rev., *supra* note 4 at 408. The considerations are not specified.

[14] Robert L. Birmingham, *supra* note 4, at 1396.

[15] "Since frustration remedies can in many cases be applied or withheld with almost equal justification, they permit the judge some freedom in allocating gain or loss between contracting parties. Their principal redistributive function should not be concealed behind bland assertions that interpretation of documents is necessarily a search for true meaning rather than an exercise of judicial discretion." Robert L. Birmingham, *supra* note 2, at 1397.

[16] See, for example, Stephen S. Ashley, *supra* note 2; Harold J. Berman, Excuse for Nonperformance in the Light of Contract Practices in International Trade, 63 Colum. L. Rev. 1413 (1963).

[17] See, for example, John Henry Schlegel, *supra* note 4; and Malcolm P. Sharp, *supra* note 4.

[18] "I would like to suggest that, where an unusual event occurs and frustration is alleged, contracts should be enforced only when the contract in question is essentially similar to the archetypical contract situation: [. . . a] contract between brokers, each essentially speculating on a narrowly fluctuating market . . . . Thus, an event shall be held frustrating when it is not one within that narrow range of events normally incidental to the average broker's or wholesaler's contract—slight delay and small market fluctuations." John Henry Schlegel, *supra* note 4, at 447.

[19] See especially 6 Arthur Linton Corbin, *supra* note 6; John Murray, Jr., Contracts §§ 197-205 (1974); and above all Edwin W. Patterson, The Apportionment of Business Risks Through Legal Devices, 24 Colum. L. Rev. 335, 348-53 (1924).

the insight has been a sterile one because of a failure to develop any criteria for assigning the risk to one party or the other. Corbin is typical in suggesting both that it is a matter of indifference who bears the risk[20] and that risk allocation is arbitrary: "Where neither custom nor agreement determines the allocation of risk, the court must exercise its equity powers and pray for the wisdom of Solomon."[21]

We shall try to give content to the concept of risk allocation as applied to the discharge question, first by sketching a theoretical framework that demonstrates why and when it is economically sensible to discharge a contract because of some unexpected event, and then by subjecting the theory to preliminary verification by comparing its implications with prevailing doctrinal positions and typical case holdings.

B. *Economic Principles*

1. *Of contract law in general.*[22] The process by which goods and services are shifted into their most valuable uses is one of voluntary exchange. The distinctive problems of contract law arise when the agreed-upon exchange does not take place instantaneously (for example, A agrees to build a house for B and construction will take several months). The fact that performance is to extend into the future introduces uncertainty, which in turn creates risks. A fundamental purpose of contracts is to allocate these risks between the parties to the exchange.

One purpose of contract *law*, but not a particularly interesting one here, is to assure compliance with the allocation of risks that the parties have agreed upon (that is, to prevent bad faith). A second purpose, central to our subject, is to reduce the costs of contract negotiation by supplying contract terms that the parties would probably have adopted explicitly had they negotiated over them. This purpose has been understood since Bentham's day:

> . . . [O]bligations may be distinguished into original and adjective. I call those original, of which express mention is made in the contract itself: I call those adjective, which the law thinks proper to add to the first. The first turn upon events which the contracting parties have foreseen; the others upon events which they could not foresee.
>
> It is thus that in every country the law has supplied [?] the shortsightedness of individuals, by doing for them what they would have done for themselves, if their imagination had anticipated the march of nature.[23]

[20] See 6 Arthur Linton Corbin, *supra* note 6, at 344.

[21] *Id.* at 371-72.

[22] See Richard A. Posner, *supra* note 2, at 41-65.

[23] Jeremy Bentham, A General View of a Complete Code of Laws, in 3 The Works of Jeremy Bentham 157, 191 (John Bowring ed. 1843).

This function of contract *law* is analogous to that performed by standard or form *contracts*. The form contract economizes on the costs of contract negotiation by providing a set of terms to govern in the absence of explicit negotiations. The parties can of course vary the terms of the form contract, but to the extent that they do not, finding the terms suitable for their needs, contracting costs are reduced. It is much the same with the law of contracts. Judicial decisions, the Uniform Commercial Code, and other sources of contract law operate to define the parties' contractual obligations in the absence of express provisions in the contract. Every contract automatically incorporates a host of (generally) appropriate terms, over which the parties do not have to negotiate explicitly unless they want to vary the standard terms supplied by the law. Incidentally, the role of contract law in supplying contract terms, like the role of the standard or form contract, is less important the larger the stakes in the contract and hence the smaller the ratio of the costs of transacting to the value of the exchange. The larger the stakes, the more it will pay the parties to negotiate contract terms finely adapted to the particular circumstances of their contract.

If the purpose of the law of contracts is to effectuate the desires of the contracting parties, then the proper criterion for evaluating the rules of contract law is surely that of economic efficiency. Since the object of most voluntary exchanges is to increase value or efficiency, contracting parties may be assumed to desire a set of contract terms that will maximize the value of the exchange. It is true that each party is interested only in the value of the contract to it. However, the more efficiently the exchange is structured, the larger is the potential profit of the contract for the parties to divide between them.

The use of economic efficiency as a criterion for legal decision-making is of course controversial. In the area of contract, however, the criterion is well-nigh inevitable once it is conceded that the parties to a contract have the right to vary the terms at will. If the rules of contract law are inefficient, the parties will (save as transaction costs may sometimes outweigh the gains from a more efficient rule) contract around them. A law of contract not based on efficiency considerations will therefore be largely futile. This is a powerful reason for expecting that the law of contract has, in fact, been informed by efficiency considerations, even if judges and lawyers may have found it difficult to articulate the underlying economic premises of the law.

Moreover, the spirit of our analysis is severely positive. We are interested not in whether a contract law based on efficiency is ultimately a good law, but in whether the assumption that contract law has been shaped by a concern with economic efficiency is a fruitful one in explaining the doctrinal positions and typical case outcomes of that law.

2. *The economics of impossibility*. The typical case in which impossibil-

ity or some related doctrine is invoked is one where, by reason of an unforeseen or at least unprovided-for event, performance by one of the parties of his obligations under the contract has become so much more costly than he foresaw at the time the contract was made as to be uneconomical (that is, the costs of performance would be greater than the benefits). The performance promised may have been delivery of a particular cargo by a specified delivery date—but the ship is trapped in the Suez Canal because of a war between Israel and Egypt. Or it may have been a piano recital by Gina Bachauer—and she dies between the signing of the contract and the date of the recital. The law could in each case treat the failure to perform as a breach of contract, thereby in effect assigning to the promisor the risk that war, or death, would prevent performance (or render it uneconomical). Alternatively, invoking impossibility or some related notion, the law could treat the failure to perform as excusable and discharge the contract, thereby in effect assigning the risk to the promisee.

From the standpoint of economics—and disregarding, but only momentarily, administrative costs—discharge should be allowed where the promisee is the superior risk bearer; if the promisor is the superior risk bearer, nonperformance should be treated as a breach of contract. "Superior risk bearer" is to be understood here as the party that is the more efficient bearer of the particular risk in question, in the particular circumstances of the transaction. Of course, if the parties have expressly assigned the risk to one of them, there is no occasion to inquire which is the superior risk bearer. The inquiry is merely an aid to interpretation.

A party can be a superior risk bearer for one of two reasons. First, he may be in a better position to prevent the risk from materializing. This resembles the economic criterion for assigning liability in tort cases.[24] It is an important criterion in many contract settings, too, but not in this one. Discharge would be inefficient in any case where the promisor could prevent the risk from materializing at a lower cost than the expected cost of the risky event. In such a case efficiency would require that the promisor bear the loss resulting from the occurrence of the event, and hence that occurrence should be treated as precipitating a breach of contract.

But the converse is not necessarily true. It does not necessarily follow from the fact that the promisor could not at any reasonable cost have prevented the risk from materializing that he should be discharged from his contractual obligations. Prevention is only one way of dealing with risk; the other is insurance. The promisor may be the superior insurer. If so, his inability to prevent the risk from materializing should not operate to discharge him from the contract, any more than an insurance company's inability to prevent a

[24] See Richard A. Posner, *supra* note 2, at 69.

fire on the premises of the insured should excuse it from its liability to make good the damage caused by the fire.

To understand how it is that one party to a contract may be the superior (more efficient) risk bearer even though he cannot prevent the risk from materializing, it is necessary to understand the fundamental concept of risk aversion. Compare a 100 percent chance of having to pay $10 with a one percent chance of having to pay $1000. The expected cost is the same in both cases, yet not everyone would be indifferent as between the two alternatives. Many people would be willing to pay a substantial sum to avoid the uncertain alternative—for example, $15 to avoid having to take a one percent chance of having to pay $1000. Such people are risk averse. The prevalence of insurance is powerful evidence that risk aversion is extremely common, for insurance is simply trading an uncertain for a certain cost. Because of the administrative expenses of insurance, the certain cost (that is, the insurance premium) is always higher, often much higher, than the uncertain cost that it avoids—the expected cost of the fire, of the automobile accident, or whatever. Only a risk-averse individual would pay more to avoid bearing risk than the expected cost of the risk.

The fact that people are willing to pay to avoid risk shows that risk is a cost. Accordingly, insurance is a method (alternative to prevention) of reducing the costs associated with the risk that performance of a contract may be more costly than anticipated. It is a particularly important method of cost avoidance in the impossibility context because the risks with which that doctrine is concerned are generally not preventable by the party charged with nonperformance. As mentioned, if they were, that would normally afford a compelling reason for treating nonperformance as a breach of contract. (Stated otherwise, a "moral hazard" problem would be created if the promisor were insured against a hazard that he could have prevented at reasonable cost.)

The factors relevant to determining which party to the contract is the cheaper insurer are (1) risk-appraisal costs and (2) transaction costs.[25] The former comprise the costs of determining (a) the probability that the risk will materialize and (b) the magnitude of the loss if it does materialize. The amount of risk is the product of the probability of loss and of the magnitude of the loss if it occurs. Both elements—probability and magnitude—must be known in order for the insurer to know how much to ask from the other party to the contract as compensation for bearing the risk in question.

The relevant transaction costs are the costs involved in eliminating or minimizing the risk through pooling it with other uncertain events, that is, diversifying away the risk. This can be done either through self-insurance or

[25] The appraisal costs are really part of the transaction costs, but to facilitate exposition we exclude them from the latter concept.

through the purchase of an insurance policy (market insurance). To illustrate, a corporation's shareholders might eliminate the risk associated with some contract the corporation had made by holding a portfolio of securities in which their shares in the corporation were combined with shares in many other corporations whose earnings would not be (adversely) affected if this particular corporation were to default on the contract. This would be an example of self-insurance. Alternatively, the corporation might purchase business-loss or some other form of insurance that would protect it (and, more important, its shareholders) from the consequences of a default on the contract; this would be an example of market insurance. Where good opportunities for diversification exist, self-insurance will often be cheaper than market insurance.[26]

The foregoing discussion indicates the factors that courts and legislatures might consider in devising efficient rules for the discharge of contracts. An easy case for discharge would be one where (1) the promisor asking to be discharged could not reasonably have prevented the event rendering his performance uneconomical, and (2) the promisee could have insured against the occurrence of the event at lower cost than the promisor because the promisee (a) was in a better position to estimate both (i) the probability of the event's occurrence and (ii) the magnitude of the loss if it did occur, and (b) could have self-insured, whereas the promisor would have had to buy more costly market insurance. As we shall see, not all cases are this easy.

3. *The analysis applied.* Two hypothetical cases will illustrate the nature of the economic analysis of a discharge case.

(1) A, a manufacturer of printing machinery, contracts with B, a commercial printer, to sell and install a printing machine on B's premises. As B is aware, the machine will be custom-designed for B's needs and once the machine has been completed its value to any other printer will be very small. After the machine is completed, but before installation, a fire destroys B's premises and puts B out of business, precluding B from accepting delivery of the machine. The machine has no salvage value and A accordingly sues for the full price. B defends on the ground that the fire, which the fire marshal has found occurred without negligence on B's part—indeed (the same point, in an economic sense), which could not have been prevented by B at any reasonable cost—should operate to discharge B from its obligations under the contract.[27]

[26] A life-insurance company, for example, self-insures by pooling the death risks of its (many) policy-holders; it holds a diversified portfolio of life expectancies. The individual could not self-insure the risk of his death.

[27] See *infra*, at notes 69-70, for a discussion of the legal treatment of the real-world counterparts to this hypothetical case.

The risk that has materialized, rendering completion of the contract uneconomical, is that a fire on B's premises would prevent B from taking delivery of the machine at a time when the machine was so far completed (to B's specifications) that it would have no value in an alternative use. The fact that the fire occurred in premises under B's control suggests that B had the superior ability to *prevent* the fire from occurring. This consideration is entitled to some weight even though the fire marshal found that B could not, in fact, have prevented the fire (economically); the fire marshal might be wrong. Certainly as between the parties B had the superior ability to prevent the fire. But in light of the fire marshal's finding, ability to prevent cannot weigh too heavily in the decision of the case.

Turning to the relative ability of the parties to *insure* against the machine's loss of value as a result of the fire, we note first that while B was in a better position to determine the probability that a fire would occur, A was in a better position to determine the magnitude of the relevant loss (the loss of the resources that went into making the machine) if the fire did occur. That loss depended not only on the salvage value of the machine if the fire occurred after its completion but also on its salvage value at various anterior stages. A knows better than B the stages of production of the machine and the salvage value at each stage.

Assuming the actuarial value of the risk has been computed, there remains the question which of the parties could have obtained insurance protection at lower cost. Depending on the volume of A's production and on A's prior experience with contingencies such as occurred in the contract with B, A may be able to eliminate the risk of such contingencies simply by charging a higher price—in effect, an insurance premium—to all of its customers; A may in short be able to self-insure. B is less likely to be able to do so: the magnitude of its potential liability to A in the event of a default may greatly exceed any amount it could hope to pass on to its customers in the form of higher prices. As for market insurance, it seems unlikely that B could obtain for a reasonable price a fire insurance policy that protected it not only against the damage to its premises (and possibly to its business) caused by a fire but also against its contractual liability to A which, as mentioned, depends on the stage in the production of the machine at which the fire occurs, a matter within the private knowledge of A.

We are inclined to view A as the superior risk bearer in these circumstances and thus to discharge B. This inclination would be strengthened if it turned out that A was a publicly held, and B a closely held, corporation, for then the owners of A could eliminate the risk of the loss of the machine's value simply by combining their shares in A with shares of other companies in a suitably diversified portfolio. It is generally more difficult for the owners of a closely held corporation to diversify away the risks associated with their holdings in the corporation, for often those holdings represent a large fraction of their net assets.[28]

(2) For our second hypothetical case,[29] let C be a large and diversified business concern engaged in both coal mining and the manufacture and sale of large coal-burning furnaces. C executes contracts for the sale of furnaces to D,E,F, etc. in which it also agrees to supply coal to them for a given period of time at a specified price. The price, however, is to vary with and in proportion to changes in the consumer price index.

A few years later the price of coal unexpectedly quadruples and C repudiates the coal-supply agreements arguing that if forced to meet its commitments to supply coal at the price specified in its contracts it will be bankrupted. Each purchaser sues C seeking as damages the difference between the price of obtaining coal over the life of C's commitment and the contract price. C argues that the rise in the price of coal was unforeseeable and ought to operate to discharge it from its obligations.

On these facts the case might be decided against C simply on the ground that the contract explicitly assigned to it all price risks (except those resulting from changes in the value of money). If, however, C were able to convince a court that the risk had not been specifically assigned in the instrument (either on the theory that C was really contracting for the sale of a furnace and the coal provisions of the contract were incidental, or that the source or magnitude of the price change that occurred was not within the parties' contemplation), it would then be necessary to determine whether C or the purchasers were the superior risk bearer(s).

With regard to the parties' relative abilities to forecast the consequences for contract performance of a steep change in the price of coal, two factors seem critical: the amount of coal that C has contracted to deliver forward at a fixed price, and the degree of C's exposure to coal price changes. C's

[28] This discussion raises the general question whether the corporate character of the contracting parties should ever be a factor in deciding who is the superior risk bearer. It has not been a factor used by courts, and they may be correct in this. While in principle the shareholders of a large publicly held corporation can, simply by holding a diversified portfolio of securities, eliminate all of the diversifiable risk associated with the corporation's activity, the practical ability of shareholders to achieve reasonably complete diversification depends on a host of economic and institutional (tax, etc.) factors, including the availability of diversified investment vehicles (for example, the new "index" or "market" mutual funds: see John H. Langbein & Richard A. Posner, Market Funds and Trust-Investment Law, pts. I and II, 1976 A.B.F. Res. J. 1; 1977 *id.* at 1). As these vehicles emerge, it may become necessary to rethink the relevance of corporate character (it is notable that most of the impossibility cases predate the rise of the modern corporation), but perhaps for now the factor should continue to be excluded from impossibility analysis.

[29] Suggested by Joskow's case study of the pending Westinghouse litigation, *supra* note 2. We mean to intimate no view on the facts or legal merits of that litigation, which at this writing is still in the trial stage.

exposure depends on the amount of coal sold forward that is not covered either by C's existing coal stocks or by its forward purchase contracts, multiplied by the spread in price between the average forward sale price and the average forward purchase price. Thus the magnitude of the potential loss from the price increase is simply C's net short position, and C is in a better position than any of its (typical) customers to estimate this magnitude since only C has precise knowledge of its own net asset position and contractual commitments.

The likelihood (as distinct from magnitude) of loss in this case *appears* to depend crucially on the probability of a large movement in the price of coal, a movement which C may have no greater ability to predict than its purchasers. But the appearance is deceptive. The critical variable is again the extent of C's exposure. If C had a perfectly neutral hedge position in coal, no movement in the price of coal could affect it. The closer C is to a neutral hedge position, the less impact a given movement in price will have on its balance sheet. Hence the ability to forecast the relevant probability here depends ultimately on knowing C's net coal position, and C knows it best.

Moreover, C can readily insure against the contingency involved in this case. Its owners can self-insure against the financial risks to C of having to make good on its coal-supply commitments at the price specified in the contract either by holding a diversified portfolio of common stocks or by purchasing shares just in the firms that are on the buying side of C's contracts. To be sure, the shareholders of C's customers may be able to insure themselves in the same fashion and at no greater cost. But an additional factor is that, as suggested above, C can self-insure by purchasing covering contracts to perfect a neutral hedge. Since there are transactional economics of scale in making forward contracts, C could execute the hedge at lower cost than each of its purchasers.

To complicate the analysis, observe that while C has better knowledge of its total exposure, it doesn't really know its potential liability to its customers since that depends on the steps they might be required by the contract doctrine of mitigation of damages to take to minimize the net cost of the unexpected increase in the price of coal. For example, at the current price of coal, oil or natural gas might become an economical substitute. If so, the measure of damages would not be the difference between the contract and current prices of coal; it would be the difference between the contract price of coal and the current price of a substitute fuel, adjusting for any differences in the quality of the substitute. Nonetheless, it seems reasonably clear to us that, everything considered, C is the superior risk bearer and its claim of discharge should fail.

4. *The costs of particularized inquiry*. In the discussion of our two hypothetical cases, we applied the standard of efficient discharge developed

earlier directly to the facts of the case. This is not necessarily the optimum approach.[30] A broad standard makes it difficult to predict the outcome of particular cases. If the purpose of contract law (so far as relevant here) is to supply standard contract terms in order to economize on negotiation, it will be poorly served by a legal standard so vague and general that contracting parties will encounter great difficulty in trying to ascertain the judicially implied terms of their contract; if the allocation of risks in the contract is unclear, neither party will know which risks he should take steps to prevent or insure against because he will be held liable if they materialize.[31]

Our second hypothetical case is a particularly good illustration of the dangers of a broad standard. The contract seemed on its face to allocate the risk of coal price changes (save those due to inflation) to C; if the allocation is instead to depend on how a court decides years later who the superior risk bearer was, the apparent definiteness of the contract terms evaporates. One way of avoiding this result in the coal hypothetical is to deem the case outside the scope of the discharge defense by noting the absence of any showing that performance under the contract was uneconomical. We assume the coal company's position is not that it could not comply with the contract at an economically reasonable price (it could buy on the open market all of the coal that it needed to fulfill its contractual obligations), but that compliance would bankrupt it. This is tantamount to arguing that a breach of contract should be excused when the breaching party for some reason lacks the resources to make good the other party's damages.

Another approach one can take in the coal case to rule out discharge is to reason that when a contract explicitly assigns the risk of price changes to one party, discharge should not be allowed simply because the price change is greater than anticipated, regardless of which party is the superior bearer of the unanticipated portion of the change. The theory here would be that since the parties must negotiate with regard to price anyway, they can, at the same time and at little additional negotiating cost, place a limit on the promisor's price exposure. If they do not do so, the court will not do it for them.

The proper use of the sort of general standard developed earlier in this section is to guide not the decision of particular cases but the formulation of rules to decide groups of similar cases. Our effort in the next part is to show that a set of such rules—rules consistent with the general standard developed

[30] On the choice between rules and standards see Isaac Ehrlich & Richard A. Posner, An Economic Analysis of Legal Rulemaking, 3 J. Leg. Studies 257 (1974).

[31] See Stephen S. Ashley, *supra* note 2, and 6 Arthur Linton Corbin, *supra* note 6, at § 1328. The other side of the coin, however, is that premature declaration of a precise rule may discourage the parties to litigation from presenting to the court evidence regarding the particular circumstances of the case that might enable a more suitable rule to be formulated. See also *infra* p. 114.

earlier—is implicit in the judicial decisions applying impossibility and related doctrines.

II. Application of the Economic Approach

Here we compare the implications of the economic analysis first with the prevailing doctrines of the discharge case law, next with the outcomes in the principal types of cases, and then with the approach of the Uniform Commercial Code. The final subpart considers what to do when the economic analysis is inconclusive. As a preliminary matter, we note that if we are correct in suggesting that any legal system characterized by positive transaction costs would be operating inefficiently if it failed to develop some version of the impossibility doctrine, the frequent assertion that the discharge concept was recognized relatively late in the development of the common law constitutes at least a minor puzzle.[32] The case most frequently cited in support of this assertion is *Paradine v. Jane,* where the court stated in dictum: "when the party by his own contract creates a duty or charge upon himself, he is bound to make it good, if he may, notwithstanding any accident by inevitable necessity, because he might have provided against it by his contract."[33] This remark, which was only tangentially related to the matter being litigated and which provides the sole basis for modern interest in the case, was not truly representative of the English case law even at the time[34] and has, of course, long since been rejected both in England[35] and in the United States.[36]

[32] See, for example, John Murray, Jr., *supra* note 19, § 197, at 389.

[33] Aleyn 26, 82 Eng. Rep. 897 (1647). A tenant had been dispossessed by a Prince Rupert, an invader. The court held that the dispossession did not excuse the tenant's independent duty to pay rent to the landlord.

[34] See William Herbert Page, The Development of the Doctrine of Impossibility of Performance, 18 Mich. L. Rev. 589 (1920). See also Brewster v. Kitchell, Salkeld 1, 91 Eng. Rep. 177 (1697) (contract discharged because of the destruction of a specific material thing); and Hyde v. The Dean and Canons of Windsor, Cro. Eliz. 552, 78 Eng. Rep. 798 (1597) (contract discharged because of the death of the promisor).

[35] See, for example, Taylor v. Caldwell, 3 B. & S. 826, 122 Eng. Rep. 309 (1863). For the complete history of the English experience with the discharge doctrine see Glanville L. Williams, The Law Reform (Frustrated Contracts) Act, 1943 (1944).

[36] See, for example, Kronprinzessin Cecilie, 244 U.S. 12, 22 (1917) (per Justice Holmes): "The seeming absolute confinement to the words of an express contract indicated by the older cases like *Paradine v. Jane,* Aleyn, 26, has been mitigated so far as to exclude from the risks of contracts for conduct (other than the transfer of fungibles like money), some, at least, which, if they had been dealt with, it cannot be believed that the contractee would have demanded or the contractor would have assumed."

The Continental legal systems have also developed a doctrine of impossibility. It appears to be similar to the Anglo-American concept (see, for example, Comment, Commercial Frustration: A Comparative Study, 3 Tex. Int'l L.F. 275 (1967)), but we have not attempted a comparison in this paper.

Professor Gilmore has used the expansion of the impossibility doctrine in recent times to argue the breakdown of an economically oriented law of contracts.[37] In his view, nineteenth-century contract law narrowly circumscribed the defense of impossibility because that defense was inconsistent with a view of contract law based on *laissez-faire* (*i.e.*, classical economic) principles. As we have seen, however, there is no inconsistency between allowing discharge in cases where the promisee is the superior risk bearer and viewing contract law as a method of maximizing efficiency viewed essentially in classical economic terms. The rise of the discharge concept vindicates rather than undermines the economic view of contract law.

A. *Prevailing Legal Doctrines*

From the standpoint of economics, contract discharge should not be allowed when the event rendering performance uneconomical was reasonably preventable by either party. This view prevails in the case law.[38] According to Corbin "it may be stated with very little qualification that if the plaintiff has himself made it impossible for the defendant to perform his promise, the nonperformance is not an actionable breach of duty."[39] Nor is "a promissor [discharged] from his contractual duty if he himself wilfully brought . . . about [the condition preventing performance], or if he could have foreseen and avoided it by the exercise of a reasonable diligence and efficiency."[40]

We said that the purpose of an economically based discharge doctrine is to supply those contract terms that the parties would have adopted if they had negotiated expressly over them. This proposition has two important corollaries: (1) the doctrine is properly limited to contingencies not specifically provided for in the contract; (2) terms expressly negotiated by the parties must be honored—they may if they wish contract to do the "impossible." The contracting parties' chosen allocation of risk must be the most efficient one possible (subject, of course, to the constraints imposed by the costs of information and other transactional frictions), since, if it were not, a reallocation of risks by the parties would be possible that would increase the utility of at least one of the parties without reducing the utility of the other.

That the explicit terms of a contract control the assignment of risk, thus

[37] Grant Gilmore, The Death of Contract 80-82, 94-96 (1974).

[38] See, for example, Gulf, Mobile & O.R.R. v. Illinois Central R.R., 128 F. Supp. 311 (D. Ala. 1954), 225 F.2d 816 (5th Cir. 1955); Martin v. Star Publishing Co., 50 Del. 181, 126 A.2d 238 (1956); Powers v. Siats, 244 Minn. 515, 70 N.W. 2d. 344 (1955); Helms v. B & L Investment Co., 19 N.C. App. 5, 198 S.E. 2d 79 (1973). See also 6 Arthur Linton Corbin, *supra* note 6, at § 1959; Restatement of Contracts §§ 281, 459 (1932); and 41 Marq. L. Rev. 314 (1957-58).

[39] 6 Arthur Linton Corbin, *supra* note 6, at § 1323.

[40] *Id.* at § 1329.

limiting the discharge doctrine to those contingencies not specifically addressed in the contract, is well accepted. In the words of Holmes:

One who makes a contract never can be absolutely certain that he will be able to perform it when the time comes, and the very essence of it is that he takes the risk within the limits of his undertaking. The modern cases may have abated somewhat the absoluteness of the older ones in determining the scope of the undertaking by the literal meaning of the words alone . . . But when the scope of the undertaking is fixed, that is merely another way of saying that the contractor takes the risk of the obstacles to that extent.[41]

Similarly, in a case in which a contract was terminated because of the promisor's death, Cardozo stated that the parties "may say by their contract what compensation shall be made in the event of that excuse [death]," and the "award will then conform to the expression of their will."[42]

The principle that parties may contract "to do the impossible" is also an accepted legal doctrine. In Williston's words:

A man may contract to do what is impossible, as well as what is difficult, and be liable for failure to perform. The important question is whether an unanticipated circumstance has made performance of the promise vitally different from what should reasonably have been within the contemplation of both parties when they entered into the contract.[43]

This statement is based on judicial language. As the Supreme Court put it:

There can be no question that a party may by an absolute contract bind himself or itself to perform things which subsequently become impossible, or to pay damages for the nonperformance. . . .[44]

Similar expressions occur throughout the discharge case law.[45]

Given that the parties may explicitly allocate risks, a problem has developed in determining when they have done so (as in our coal hypothetical). Some courts have approached the problem by asking whether the event in question could have been anticipated and so provided for in the contract.[46] If able to answer this question affirmatively they have too hastily concluded that the contract explicitly allocated the risk of that contingency:

The purpose of a contract is to place the risks of performance upon the promisor, and the relation of the parties, terms of the contract, and circumstances surrounding its

[41] Day v. United States, 245 U.S. 159, 161 (1917).

[42] Buccini v. Paterno Constr. Co., 253 N.Y. 256, 258, 170 N.E. 910, 911 (1930).

[43] 6 Samuel Williston, *supra* note 6, at § 1931.

[44] Chicago, Mil. & St. P. Ry. v. Hoyt, 149 U.S. 1, 14-15 (1893).

[45] See, for example, Annot., 84 A.L.R. 2d. 12 (1962).

[46] See, for example, Chicago, Mil. & St. P. Ry. v. Hoyt, 149 U.S. 1 (1893).

formation must be examined to determine whether it can be fairly inferred that the risk of the event that has supervened to cause the alleged frustration was not reasonably foreseeable. If it was foreseeable there should have been provision for it in the contract, and the absence of such a provision gives rise to the inference that the risk was assumed.[47]

The foreseeability test, at least in the form usually stated, is nonoperational, for it fails to indicate which contracting party is the superior bearer of the foreseeable risk. The test is disappearing, and although occasionally mentioned is seldom applied.[48] As Judge Wright correctly observed in a recent case: "Foreseeability or even recognition of a risk does not necessarily prove its allocation."[49]

B. *Typical Cases*

In this subpart we consider the major recurring issues in the discharge case law. As one would expect, there are some inconsistent holdings among the multiple jurisdictions that have considered these issues. It is not our purpose to explain or even identify every inconsistent outcome. We are content to explain the typical outcomes in the major classes of case.

1. *Contracts for personal services.* Discharge of contracts for personal services is often sought when an employee has died unexpectedly. In *Cutler v. United Shoe Mach. Corp.*,[50] a machinery company had an employment contract with an inventor. When the inventor died, the court, in a suit by the inventor's estate, held the contract discharged. This outcome—typical in employee cases—is consistent with the economic approach. The employee (1) is in at least as good a position as his employer to estimate his life expectancy, (2) has better knowledge of the value of the contract to him compared to that of any alternative employment and (3) can readily purchase life insurance.

If the employer were seeking damages as a result of the employee's death, alleging that death had caused a breach of the employee's obligations under the contract, the contract should also be discharged. Estimating life expectancy is in general no more (if no less) difficult for the employer than for the employee (if the employee knew of a condition reducing his life expectancy below the actuarial level for people of his age, sex, etc., discharge would presumably not be allowed). And the employer is better able to estimate the cost to him (in firm-specific human capital, replacement costs, etc.) if the employee dies, and can usually self-insure against such an eventuality.

[47] Lloyd v. Murphy, 25 Cal. 2d 48, 54, 153 P.2d 47, 50 (1944).

[48] See, for example, Note, 53 Colum. L. Rev. 94 (1953).

[49] Transatlantic Financing Corp. v. United States, 363 F.2d. 312, 318 (D.C. Cir. 1966).

[50] 274 Mass. 341, 174 N.E. 507 (1931).

The discharge doctrine may also be invoked in personal-services cases when an unexpected contingency prevents the completion of the promised service without physically disabling the promisor, as in *Hein v. Fox.*[51] Fox had agreed to drill a well on Hein's land. In two separate drilling attempts a boulder or layer of rock was struck, once at a depth of 250 feet and again at a depth of 350 feet, preventing completion of the well, and due to wartime regulations the special casing needed to penetrate the rock was unavailable. The court properly refused discharge. Fox, a driller, was better able than his customer to estimate the probability of encountering rock deep below the surface of the earth, the costs of alternative drilling techniques, the likelihood of failing to obtain a particular input (pipe casing), and the costs of a substitute input. And Fox could have spread the risk of these contingencies among all of his customers in his price for drilling, thereby providing effective and inexpensive self-insurance.

2. *The effects of supervening illegality on teachers' contracts and on leases.* In *Phelps v. School District,*[52] the state board of health had ordered a school closed for two months during its regular term because of a flu epidemic and the school district had laid off the teachers at that school. The district argued that its contract with the teachers was discharged because it was legally prevented from performing it. The court properly refused discharge. Although neither party could have prevented the epidemic, the school district was the superior risk bearer. It could spread the risk among all of its schools and hence among all of the teachers; it had a "diversified portfolio" of schools. If market insurance had been desired, the district could have insured all of its employees in one transaction, thereby eliminating the need for each individual to incur transaction costs.

Although the outcome in *Phelps* is the usual one in a case of this sort,[53] an Indiana decision held on similar facts that the teachers' contract was discharged by the school closing.[54] Our analysis suggests that this result is inefficient, a conclusion supported (weakly)[55] by the subsequent action of the Indiana legislature in enacting a statute assigning to the school boards the risks created by school closings.[56]

[51] 126 Mont. 514, 254 P.2d 1076 (1953).

[52] 302 Ill. 193, 134 N.E. 312 (1922).

[53] See, for example, Elsemore v. Inhabitants of Hancock, 137 Me. 248, 18 A.2d 692 (1941); and 6 Arthur Linton Corbin, *supra* note 6, at § 1357.

[54] Gregg School Township v. Hinshaw, 76 Ind. App. 503, 132 N.E. 586 (1921).

[55] There is no presumption that legislation seeks to enhance efficiency. See, for example, George J. Stigler, The Theory of Economic Regulation, 2 Bell J. Econ. & Management Sci. 3 (1971).

[56] Ind. Code Ann. § 20-6-8-2 (1971) provided: "If, during the term of a teacher's contract the school or schools are closed by order of the school corporation, or by order of the health authorities, or if, through no fault of the teacher, school cannot be held, such teacher shall

The issue of supervening illegality as a ground for discharge also arises when a leasehold is radically modified by operation of law. But here the economic analysis must remain tentative because it may not be possible to determine *a priori* which party is the superior risk bearer. In *Stratford v. Seattle Brewing & Malting Co.*, a party leased premises to be used "for saloon purposes."[57] The lease was subsequently modified to allow other related uses. When as the result of a referendum the lessee lost the liquor license necessary to continue saloon operations, the contract was held discharged. The effect was to assign the risk of the law change to the lessor. But in another group of cases, leases of automobile showrooms were held not to be discharged by federal restrictions on the sale of automobiles during World War II.[58] Here the lessees were assigned the risk.

In the liquor-license case, the referendum reduced the value of the property by disallowing its most profitable use. The loss in value was equal to the difference between the original rental value and the rental value after the referendum. And similarly in the automobile-showroom cases the loss was the difference between the original rental value and the rental value after the passage of the regulations restricting automobile production. It would seem that in both cases the lessor would be better able than the lessee to estimate the opportunity value of the premises in its next best use. But the lessee should be in a better position to estimate the other key parameter, the probability that the loss will occur. One would expect automobile dealers, for example, to be more knowledgeable with respect to the possibility of a limit on new-car production than the average commercial land owner.

When the two key parameters of the economic analysis point in opposite directions, the analysis is indeterminate on a general level and must proceed to an estimation of their relative empirical importance. The lessor in *Stratford* was a brewer,[59] and was therefore probably as competent as the lessee to estimate the likelihood of the loss of the liquor license. In the typical automobile case, the courts have found that the next best use of the leased showroom was as a showroom for the sale of second-hand automobiles or as an auto repair facility. Hence the typical lessee in the automobile cases may well have been as capable as the typical lessor of estimating the magnitude of the loss. We conclude that both the liquor-license and the automobile-showroom cases may have been correctly decided from an economic standpoint.

---

receive regular payments during such time the school or schools are closed." This statute has been superseded by a similar one. See *id.* § 20-6.1-5-8 (Supp. 1976).

[57] 94 Wash. 125, 162 P.31 (1916).

[58] See, for example, Lloyd v. Murphy, 25 Cal. 2d 48, 153 P.2d 47 (1944); Leonard v. Autocar Sales & Service Co., 392 Ill. 182, 64 N.E. 2d 477 (1945).

[59] The lease in fact required the lessee to purchase all of its beer requirements from the lessor's brewery.

But there is a question whether so microscopic an examination of the facts is an appropriate predicate for decision, in light of the administrative costs, discussed in Part I, of applying the impossibility doctrine on a highly particularistic case-by-case basis rather than on the basis of rules that decide all of the cases within a specific category in the same way—for example, a rule deciding all lease discharge cases either in the lessee's or in the lessor's favor. Unfortunately, it is unclear *a priori* which would be the more efficient rule. A relevant bit of empirical evidence is that in contracts between a large and diversified real estate owner-lessor and each of its many major, and geographically diversified, retail-chain lessees (for example, Walgreen's, Kresge's, and the A&P, National and Jewel Food Stores), the risk of loss from changes in circumstances that "prevent the lessee from doing business" is invariably and explicitly placed on the lessor.[60] Although this is only a fragment of the empirical evidence required to formulate a proper rule for applying the impossibility doctrine in lease cases, it is useful in two respects. First, it suggests that in real estate cases between *diversified* entities the lessor is the superior risk bearer.[61] Second, it indicates that there are sources available to aid in an empirical resolution of the difficult questions that are raised when the key parameters of the economic analysis of impossibility point in opposite directions. The potential role of empirical analysis both in testing and implementing economic theories of contract law is discussed further in the conclusion of this article.

3. *Transportation contracts*. Another common issue in the impossibility area is the effect of wars or other unexpected events on transportation contracts. To illustrate the relative abilities of the parties to bear risk in cases of this sort, consider the effect on shipping contracts of the closing of the Suez Canal by the Egyptian government in 1956. The closing required ships passing between Atlantic ports and ports in the Middle East to sail around Africa, a longer and more expensive voyage, and gave rise to voluminous litigation. The general result was the enforcement of the shipping contracts.[62] For example, in *Transatlantic Financing Corp. v. United States*,[63] a shipowner argued that its contract with the United States to transport

[60] This information is based upon an interview with the general counsel of one of the nation's largest real estate firms.

[61] This may be because the lessor's margin of superiority with regard to ability to estimate the magnitude of the loss to him from termination of the lease exceeds the lessee's margin of superiority with regard to estimating the probability of the loss. That margin may be small with regard to events like changes in the law that no one may be able to predict very well.

[62] See, for example, American Trading and Prod. Corp. v. Shell Int'l Marine Ltd., 453 F.2d 939 (2d Cir. 1972); Transatlantic Financing Corp. v. United States, 363 F.2d 312 (D.C. Cir. 1966); Glidden Co. v. Hellenic Lines, Ltd., 275 F.2d 253 (2nd Cir. 1960); Ocean Tramp Tankers Corp. v. V/O Sovfracht (The Eugenia), [1964] 2 Q.B. 226; and Tsakiroglou & Co. v. Noblee Thorl G.m.b.H., [1960] 2 Q.B. 348.

[63] 363 F.2d 312 (D.C. Cir. 1966).

wheat from the U.S. to Iran was discharged by the closing of the Suez Canal. The issue was framed by Judge Wright as follows:

> First, a contingency—something unexpected—must have occurred. Second, the risk of the unexpected occurrence must not have been allocated either by agreement or by custom. Finally, occurrence of the contingency must have rendered performance commercially impracticable.[64]

The court found that the closing of the canal was unexpected and that the risk of its occurrence had not been expressly allocated between the parties. It then addressed the ultimate question: was the closing grounds for discharge?

To answer the question, Judge Wright sought to determine which party—the owner of the ship or the government—was the superior risk bearer. His answer addressed itself to the precise elements of our economic framework:

> Transatlantic was no less able than the United States to purchase insurance to cover the contingency's occurrence. If anything, it is more reasonable to expect owner-operators of vessels to insure againt the hazards of war. They are in the best position to calculate the cost of performance by alternative routes (and therefore to estimate the amount of insurance required), and are undoubtedly sensitive to international troubles which uniquely affect the demand for and cost of their services.[65]

This passage makes the decision on whether to discharge the contract turn on an examination of the key economic parameters that we have identified. The shipowner is the superior risk bearer because he is better able to estimate the magnitude of the loss (a function of delay, and of the value and nature of the cargo, which are also known to the shipowner) and the probability of the unexpected event. Furthermore, shipowners who own several ships and are engaged in shipping along several different routes can spread the risks of delay on any particular route without purchasing market insurance or forcing their shareholders to diversify their common-stock portfolios. And the shipping company could, if it desired, purchase in a single transaction market insurance covering multiple voyages. Of course, the shipper in the particular case—the United States Government—was well diversified too, but decision should (and here did) turn on the characteristics of shippers as a class, if an unduly particularistic analysis is to be avoided.

It might appear that the owner of the shipment would have a better idea than the shipowner of the consequences of delayed arrival. But consequential damages of this type are not relevant to the discharge question, because the rule of *Hadley v. Baxendale*[66] places liability for such damages

[64] *Id.* at 315.

[65] *Id.* at 319.

[66] 9 Ex. 341, 156 Eng. Rep. 145 (1854).

(in the absence of express agreement to the contrary) on the shipper rather than on the carrier—and properly so from the standpoint of economics.[67] The question of discharge thus arises only with respect to that portion of the damages that the carrier can estimate without knowing the details of the shipper's business.

Parris v. Stratton Cripple Creek Mining & Dev. Co.[68] illustrates the application of the discharge doctrine in another transportation setting. A trucker contracted with a mining company to haul gold ore from the Cripple Creek mining field in Colorado to a nearby mill. The contract between the mining company and the milling company entitled the mill to suspend operations on 60 days notice. When the mill closed and was adjudged bankrupt, the mining company argued that the trucking contract should be discharged. The court agreed. The mining company was probably in a better position to estimate the probability that the mill would close, but the trucker was better able to ascertain the magnitude of the loss—being the difference between the contract price and the opportunity value of his service—and he could spread the risk by contracting to supply hauling services to customers who were engaged in other businesses and hence were unlikely to be affected by the mill closing.

4. *Contracts for the manufacture or supply of specialized equipment.* In *Siegel v. Eaton & Prince Co.*[69] a firm contracted to "furnish and erect" an elevator in the Siegel Cooper department store. The contract was held to be discharged when the store was destroyed by fire without fault on the part of Siegel Cooper. In a similar case decided a year later, *Huyett & Smith Mfg. Co. v. Chicago Edison Co.*,[70] the Edison Company, which had agreed to provide equipment to supply electric lighting and power in the First Regiment Armory Building during the Columbian Exposition (the Chicago World's Fair), subcontracted with Huyett to manufacture special fans and to install them in a ventilating system in the building. The Armory Building was destroyed by fire. The subcontract was held discharged, thereby placing the risk of loss on Huyett, the supplier of the specialized equipment.

The cases, which resemble our first hypothetical in the previous part, seem correctly decided when evaluated from the standpoint of economics. A supplier of specialized equipment is better able than a purchaser to evaluate the degree to which a given piece of equipment is specialized and to estimate the costs of converting it into something usable by other prospective purchasers; and in neither case was the purchaser better able to estimate the probability of the particular casualty. The supplier could spread the risk

[67] See Richard A. Posner, *supra* note 2, at 60-61.

[68] 116 F.2d 207 (10th Cir. 1940).

[69] 165 Ill. 550, 46 N.E. 449 (1896).

[70] 167 Ill. 223, 47 N.E. 384 (1897).

among all purchasers by discounting the expected value of these contingencies in his contract price, thus eliminating the need for each purchaser to insure; and if explicit market insurance was desired the supplier could have covered all of his sales in a single transaction.

The analysis is not limited to suppliers of equipment. In *Gouled v. Holwitz,* a supplier leased a team of horses which were to be returned by the lessee "in as good condition as they are at present."[71] One of the horses was later found to have spinal meningitis and was shot to death—against the express wishes of the lessee—by an agent of the Society for the Prevention of Cruelty to Animals. The agreement to return the horse was held to have been discharged. The result was to place the risk of death by disease on the horse's owner, and this seems correct. The owner was better able to estimate both the probability of disease and the magnitude of the loss. A horse is a wasting capital asset whose value is animal-specific, depending on particular characteristics of the horse that are likely to be better known to its owner than to a lessee. Furthermore, an owner of several horses greatly reduces the risk of animal death due to disease through the portfolio effect of his multiple ownership.

5. *Contracts for the supply of agricultural products.* The next group of cases we consider concerns contracts to supply agricultural products, and illustrates how the courts can arrive at an economically efficient result yet disguise it as an apparently meaningless semantic distinction. The cases have similar facts. A supplier contracts to deliver a particular quantity and quality of an agricultural product; an unexpected event such as a flood or an exceptionally severe drought prevents delivery; the buyer seeks damages.[72] The courts generally discharge the contract where the supplier is a grower,[73] but enforce it where the supplier is a wholesaler or large dealer.[74] The result is both consistent and efficient; it places the risk of extreme weather conditions on the superior risk bearer. The purchaser from the grower can reduce the risk of adverse weather by diversifying his purchases geographically; there is empirical evidence to suggest that in some climatic regions geographical separation of only a few miles can dramatically reduce the risk of a large loss.[75] When the seller is a wholesaler or large dealer there is no reason to

[71] 95 N.J.L. 277, 113 A. 323 (1921).

[72] See Pearce-Young-Angel Co. v. Charles R. Allen, Inc., 213 S.C. 578, 50 S.E. 2d 698 (1948); and Squillante v. California Lands, Inc., 5 Cal. App. 2d. 89, 42 P.2d 81 (1935).

[73] See, for example, Matousek v. Galligan, 104 Neb. 731, 178 N.W. 510 (1920); and Pearce-Young-Angel Co. v. Charles R. Allen, Inc., 213 S.C. 578, 50 S.E. 2d 698 (1948).

[74] See, for example, United States Co. v. Curtis Peanut Co., 302 S.W. 2d 763 (Tex. Civ. App. 1957).

[75] See Donald N. McCloskey, The Enclosure of Open Fields: Preface to a Study of Its Impact on the Efficiency of English Agriculture in the Eighteenth Century, 32 J. Econ. Hist. 15 (1972), and also his English Open Fields as Behavior Towards Risk, 1 Res. in Econ. Hist. 124 (1976).

allow discharge since he can diversify his purchases and thereby eliminate the risk of adverse weather.

Here as elsewhere the courts have not explicitly characterized the problem as one of identifying the superior risk bearer.[76] They usually state that discharge will be allowed when the contract contemplates a single crop to be grown on a specific tract of land. Similarly, a comment to the relevant section of the Uniform Commercial Code allows discharge if and only if the contract refers to crops grown on land designated explicitly in the agreement.[77] This factor is irrelevant save as a reasonable instrumental variable that distinguishes cases in which the seller is a grower from those where he is a wholesaler. However, consistently with our analysis, one observes a tendency in both the pre-Code and later cases to mitigate the mechanical operation of this rule by either expansive construction of the contract or equitable reformation of its terms.[78]

6. *Grazing contracts*. In *Berg v. Erickson*,[79] a cattle owner from Texas (Berg) contracted to pasture his cattle on Erickson's Kansas ranch. Erickson agreed to "furnish plenty of good grass, water, and salt during the grazing season of 1913."[80] There was no rain that summer and although the cattle survived they failed to reach normal weight. The court enforced the contract and thus awarded damages to Berg. This result seems correct but on a rather particularistic analysis. A cattle owner would in general be better able than a landowner to estimate the magnitude of the loss in cattle value because of inadequate water and could reduce the risk by pasturing his cattle in different ranches, but this method of self-insurance might involve con-

McCloskey, an economic historian, has studied the medieval system of open-field farming. Under the open-field system, farmers lived in the center of a large circular region approximately six miles in diameter. Each farmer owned and worked a number of small widely scattered plots. For generations historians have explained this seemingly inefficient pattern of property rights as the product of quasi-communal ownership or egalitarian sentiment. McCloskey, however, has demonstrated that the scattering was an efficient technique adopted by the farmers to diversify the risk of adverse weather conditions, notably hail. In essence, each farmer held a diversified portfolio of assets (small plots), thereby reducing his overall risk. Weather-induced (hail, frost, etc.) agricultural yield variability remains a problem in modern agriculture. See, *e.g.*, Gordon Manley, Climate and the British Scene (1952).

[76] An exception to the judicial failure to articulate the economic elements of the impossibility doctrine is Judge Wright's opinion in Transatlantic Financing Corp. v. United States, 363 F.2d 312 (D.C. Cir. 1966). See *supra* p. 104.

[77] U.C.C. § 2-615, Comment 9.

[78] An example of a pre-Code case is Snipes Mountain Co. v. Benz Bros. & Co., 162 Wash. 334, 298 P.714 (1931), in which the court allowed an equitable action to reform the contract so that specific land was mentioned, thus allowing discharge. See also Matousek v. Galligan, 104 Neb. 731, 178 N.W. 510 (1920). A case decided under the Code and holding that factors outside the writing may show that the parties contracted with reference to a particular parcel of land is Paymaster Oil Mill Co. v. Mitchell, 319 So. 2d 652 (1975).

[79] 234 F. 817 (8th Cir. 1916).

[80] *Id.* at 818.

siderable transaction costs. Moreover, *this* landowner—a rancher—was presumably knowledgeable about cattle. The other key parameter of our analysis—the ability to estimate the probability of the drought—suggests placing the risk on the rancher (depending, however, on the particular cattle owner's prior experience in the region), especially since

> It was common knowledge that droughts were not unusual in Kansas. It was common knowledge that they decreased the growth of grass. It was common knowledge that one could not tell by the examination of pastures in Kansas, of which he [Berg] had no previous knowledge, in the spring of the year before the 13th of April, whether or not they would produce sufficient grass for 1,000 cattle throughout the coming summer. Berg knew nothing of their productive capacity; Erickson knew all about it.[81]

Like the lease cases discussed earlier, *Berg* is difficult to analyze because the two key parameters seem to point in opposite directions. To reach a correct result, a thorough investigation of the facts is necessary. The court's result reached was (as in most of the cases we have examined) probably correct, in view of the superior knowledge believed by the court to be possessed by Erickson, the rancher. The question remains whether it might not be better to decide all grazing cases the same way.[82]

C. *The Approach of the U.C.C.*

Section 2-615 of the Uniform Commercial Code (U.C.C.) states a general impossibility doctrine for sales cases, limited, however, to cases where the seller of the goods is seeking discharge. The Code provides:

> Except so far as a seller may have assumed a greater obligation . . .
> (a) Delay in delivery or non-delivery in whole or part by a seller . . . is not a breach of his duty under a contract for sale if performance as agreed has been made impracticable by the occurrence of a contingency the non-occurrence of which was a basic assumption on which the contract was made. . . .[83]

This language, which is similar to that employed by the *Restatement of Contracts*,[84] uses impracticability rather than impossibility or commercial frustration as the controlling concept. The Code makes clear that the parties to the contract can control the assignment of risk by inserting appropriate terms in their agreement.[85]

[81] *Id.* at 824.

[82] Two other groups of cases, involving repair and part payment, are discussed in Part III of this article.

[83] U.C.C. § 2-615. See Paul L. Joskow, *supra* note 2, at pt. II, for a fuller economic analysis of § 2-615.

[84] See Restatement of Contracts § 454 (1932), and note 9 *supra*.

[85] U.C.C. § 1-102.

Section 2-615 appears to add little to the common law doctrines and indeed is completely silent on many important issues. As noted above, the entire section is developed exclusively from the seller's point of view. No buyer's relief is specifically contemplated in the Code.[86] This omission has been explained as a cautious reaction on the part of the Code's draftsmen to the then undecided state of the common law with regard to buyers' claims of impossibility.[87] One consequence of the omission, however, is that cases similar to our specialized-machinery hypothetical are not controlled by any provision in the Code.

The general view is that, where it does apply, section 2-615 is consistent with the non-Code case law.[88] Professor Murray has written:

> Though the Code language is not expressed in terms of risk allocation there is little question but that the courts will interpret it in keeping with the now generally recognized basic inquiry of whether the risk created by the occurrence of the contingency should be allocated to the promisor.[89]

The U.C.C. also contains several more specific sections that are relevant to the discharge of a contract on impossibility or related grounds when the event allegedly justifying discharge is the destruction of specific goods identified in the contract.[90] The Code abandons the traditional approach of making the risk of loss from destruction follow the title to the goods—an approach related, although loosely, to the ability to prevent destruction—in favor of a similarly mechanical approach but one avowedly based on risk-allocation concepts.

The Code classifies contracts for the sale of goods as either shipment or destination contracts.[91] A contract is a shipment contract if the seller is not required by the terms of the agreement to deliver the goods to a specified location, and a destination contract if delivery to a specified location is required.[92] Contracts are treated as shipment contracts in the absence of any expressed intention. Under the Code, the risk of loss from fortuitous destruction of the goods is initially on the seller, passing to the buyer when the goods are delivered to the carrier, in the case of a shipment contract, but in the case of a destination contract, only when goods are tendered at the indicated

[86] U.C.C. § 2-615, Comment 9, contains a fleeting reference to the possibility of a buyer's claim of discharge, but the issue is never pursued.

[87] 2 Grant Gilmore, Security Interests in Personal Property § 41.7, at 1105 (1965).

[88] See generally John Murray, Jr., *supra* note 21, at 412; and Paul L. Joskow, *supra* note 2, at pt. II.

[89] John Murray, Jr., *supra* note 21, at 412.

[90] See U.C.C. §§ 2-319, 2-509, 2-510, and § 2-615, Comment 9, *supra* note 80.

[91] U.C.C. § 2-319.

[92] A shipment contract will often contain the clause "F.O.B. seller's place of business," while a destination contract will often contain the clause "F.O.B. buyer's place of business." See U.C.C. § 2-504.

destination. This rule will in the usual case place the risk on the superior risk bearer. The problem dealt with by the rule is that of losses in transit and the Code in effect places the risk of that loss on the party arranging for the transportation of the goods.

In sum, the Uniform Commercial Code has not greatly affected the common law discharge doctrines.

D. *Doubtful Cases*

In many individual, and perhaps some classes of, cases economic analysis—at least of the casual sort employed by the judges and lawyers in contract cases—will fail to yield a definite answer, or even a guess, as to which party is the superior risk bearer. A good example is provided by the coronation cases.[93] Neither party was in a superior position to foresee the event (the illness of Edward VII) that prevented completion of the contract. To be sure, the building owner had a superior ability to compute the loss, which depended on his ability to rerent the rooms on short notice, and could in principle have bought a single insurance policy on Edward's health at lower cost than the renters could have insured. However, the renters may well have been superior self-insurers: enforcing the contracts would have spread the loss among a relatively large number of renters rather than concentrate it on a relatively few building owners. It is not surprising that the courts divided on whether discharge should be allowed.[94]

The choice in doubtful cases between treating nonperformance as breach or as discharge is similar to the choice in tort law between strict liability and no liability for unavoidable accidents.[95] Pending definitive empirical study, we are inclined to consider the strict-liability solution better in the contract context, though in the tort context the choice must be considered indeterminate on the basis of present knowledge.[96]

The performing party to a contract is generally the superior risk bearer. Typically, though not invariably, he is better able both to prevent the occur-

[93] See note 8 *supra*.

[94] Compare Krell v. Henry, [1903] 2 K.B. 740 (C.A.), with Chandler v. Webster, [1904] 1 K.B. 493 (L.R.), and Herne Bay S.S. Co. v. Hutton, [1903] 2 K.B. 683 (C.A.); but see note 106 *infra*. While the coronation cases on their peculiar facts could have gone either way on an economic analysis—which may explain the division in the courts—the case against discharge is much stronger in the related but more common case where, for example, a skier books a room at a ski lodge and, having paid his deposit, seeks a refund because of poor ski conditions. Skiers as a class are superior self-insurers against poor ski conditions compared to ski lodges; the skier can find adequate conditions somewhere but the lodge cannot diversify away the risk of poor conditions (save by merger with lodges in other ski areas); market insurance may also be unavailable. (Other part-payment cases are discussed at pp. 115-17 *infra*.)

[95] See Richard A. Posner, Strict Liability: A Comment, 2 J. Leg. Studies 205 (1973).

[96] *Id.*

rence of the event rendering performance uneconomical and, if it cannot be prevented at reasonable cost, to estimate the probability of its occurrence. Often, too, he is at least as able as the payor to estimate the magnitude of the loss if the event occurs. True, the payor (that is, the buyer) will have better knowledge of the consequences of nonperformance for his business, but the rule of *Hadley v. Baxendale* properly assigns the risk of consequential injury to the payor in any event. Finally, the performer can often self-insure at low cost simply by diversifying the risk across the full range of his contractual obligations.

The performer is not always the superior risk bearer; otherwise there would be no place in contract law for impossibility and related doctrines. But as long as the performer is *generally* the superior risk bearer, assigning the risk to him in cases of doubt—that is, refusing discharge in those cases—can be expected to yield correct results more often than the contrary rule. Accordingly, one is not surprised to find that the courts indeed treat discharge as an excuse, so that nonperformance is a breach of contract unless the case fits one of the exceptions to liability carved out by the impossibility or some other excuse doctrine.

This discussion raises the broader question why in general notions of strict liability seem much more important in contract than in tort law. The concept of breach of contract is one of strict liability rather than of negligence. The difference in this regard between tort and contract law appears to be related to the fact that tort cases typically involve interactive activities and contract cases typically do not. An automobile accident, for example, is produced by a collision between two automobiles or between an automobile and a pedestrian, and there is no presumption that the injurer could have avoided the accident more cheaply than the victim. But in the typical contract case the only relevant actors are performer and payor and the productive activity under the contract is controlled and conducted entirely by the former. There is a strong presumption therefore that he is better able than the payor to prevent a mishap that will render performance uneconomical. The presumption is not absolute but it is sufficient to make strict liability the appropriate general rule defining breach of contract.

III. Remedial Consequences of Discharge

Thus far we have treated the discharge issue dichotomously, as if the only choice were between on the one hand enforcing the contract and awarding full contract damages, and on the other hand discharging the contract and awarding no damages. This dichotomous treatment is not inevitable. Intermediate solutions are possible and have seemed appealing to many commentators on the impossibility doctrine.

A. *The General Case*

In a famous article Fuller and Perdue identified two components of the contract price: the reliance interest and the expectation interest.[97] The reliance interest represents the expected cost of performance, the expectation interest the expected profit from performance. If A contracts to repair the roof of B's home for $2000, A's expected cost of (say) $1500 would be his reliance interest and the difference between the contract price and his cost—$500—would be his expectation interest. If B breached the contract before A had begun to perform—for example, after A had purchased $700 worth of materials usable only on B's roof—A would claim as damages the sum of his expectation and reliance interests ($1200), A being entitled to receive a profit of $500 regardless of the time of B's breach.

The question relevant to discharge is what happens under a similar fact pattern if the event terminating the contract is deemed to have effected a discharge rather than a breach. Suppose that without negligence on anyone's part a house is destroyed by fire while under repair, and the repair contractor sues for breach. Unless there is a specific contractual provision assigning the risk to the homeowner, the courts hold that the repair contract is discharged.[98] The result appears to be sound when analyzed in an economic framework. The relevant loss is the sum of the expenses incurred (the reliance loss) and the opportunity value of the contractor's services (approximately equal to the expectation loss).[99] The magnitude of loss is presumably better known to the contractor. He has superior knowledge both of the value of the reliance loss (which depends critically on his cost schedule as a function of the stages of repair and the costs of the various inputs) and of the opportunity value of his services. Although the ability to estimate the probability of the loss will depend to some extent on the specific event giving rise to discharge, in the typical repair situation neither party has a superior ability to estimate that probability. The owner of the premises has custody, of course, but the contractor may know a good deal more about fire and other hazards that might prevent performance.

As for the remedial consequences of discharge, the contractor is entitled to no part of his lost expectation interest—this distinguishes discharge from breach. Nor can he recover his reliance losses. He would be entitled to recover in a restitution action the value of any actual benefits conferred upon

[97] L. L. Fuller & William R. Perdue, Jr., The Reliance Interest in Contract Damages, 46 Yale L.J. 52, 373 (1936-37).

[98] See, for example, Young v. City of Chicopee, 186 Mass. 518, 72 N.E. 63 (1904); and Carroll v. Bowersock, 100 Kan. 270, 164 P. 143 (1917), discussed in text at note 107 *infra*.

[99] The relationship between opportunity costs and the expectation interest varies over time; the two concepts are approximately equal when performance is nearly complete. See John H. Barton, The Economic Basis of Damages for Breach of Contract, 1 J. Leg. Studies 277 (1972).

the owner but these may be slight, depending on the completeness of the destruction.

Many legal commentators are distressed by this outcome because it places the entire loss on the contractor. Their failure to understand the efficiency basis of the discharge doctrine leads them to view the remedy issue as separable from that of liability and to argue that it is "only fair" to apportion reliance losses.[100] Typical of many proposals is the following:

> . . . [S]ince the fortuity of actual reliance expenditures provides no generally applicable guides for the placement of loss, it seems fairest to split loss according to equal innocence. . . . Apportioning these losses marks the minimal change in present law necessary to systematize somewhat the treatment of loss after discharge of burdensome contracts.[101]

The proposals to change the remedial outcome to one where reliance losses are shared result from a misplaced emphasis on ex post loss distribution rather than ex ante risk bearing.[102] Viewed from the risk-bearing perspective the refusal to apportion reliance losses is well founded; it creates an incentive for the more efficient risk bearer to adopt cost-justified risk-avoidance or risk-minimization techniques (diversification, market insurance, or whatever). The existing rule whereby discharge results in zero damages (save where restitution is appropriate) is analogous to the approach of the tort law. There too the focus is on determining which party, the plaintiff or defendant, is the lower-cost avoider of the event in question, and it is clearly not proper to approach the question by attempting to ascertain which party is in a better position ex post to bear the loss.

The ex post approach to risk assignment is in fact circular. Often the party who ex post is the superior risk bearer is the party who purchased an insurance policy covering the risk in question. But if this were the criterion of liability, it would give parties an incentive not to insure, for by not insuring they would increase the possibility that the court would assign the risk to the other party to the contract. So neither party might insure; or, fearing this possibility, both parties might insure. Neither result would be optimal.

The 50-50 loss-sharing approach favored by the commentators is at least superficially appealing in the case where it is difficult for the court to determine which of the parties is the superior risk bearer. If the parties are equally good (or bad) risk bearers, and each is risk averse, then each will prefer ex ante a solution that reduces the variance of the expected outcome of the contract. Splitting the loss does this, so long as each party estimates the same

[100] See Comment, 69 Yale L.J. 1054 (1960); Malcolm P. Sharp, *supra* note 4; Comment, 18 U. Chi. L. Rev. 153 (1950); and Comment, 46 Mich. L. Rev., *supra* note 4, at 401.

[101] Comment, 69 Yale L.J. 1054, 1060 (1960).

[102] See Stephen S. Ashley, *supra* note 2.

probability that the court will assign him the risk.[103] For in that case instead of each party facing some probability of bearing all of the costs of nonperformance each has a certainty of bearing 50 percent of those costs. Of course, if neither party is risk averse, there is no gain from such a rule. And if one party is a superior risk bearer, the *entire* loss should be placed on him in order to encourage future parties similarly situated to insure or take other measures to minimize the economic consequences of nonperformance.[104]

Whether carving out a class of indeterminate risk allocations and applying a rule of 50-50 loss sharing to them can be justified in terms of the administrative costs of seeking in each case (or class of cases) to determine the superior risk bearer may be doubted. It is easy to exaggerate those costs. The costs of deciding a question in a lawsuit ought properly to be apportioned over all future transactions that will be controlled by the rule declared in the suit. Even if it is very expensive to decide in the first case how to assign the risk of some event that renders contract performance uneconomical, once the question is decided and a rule declared, the rule will be available to guide the behavior of future contracting parties and will thus reduce the costs of future contract negotiations. To define a class of cases where the proper assignment of risk is treated as indeterminate could stifle the evolution of rules of risk allocation designed to enhance the efficiency of the contract process.

While 50-50 loss sharing seems an unappealing alternative to the law's solution of placing the loss entirely on one party or the other, in a world where the costs of using the legal system to fill in contract terms were very low a principle of *flexible* loss sharing might be superior to either approach. Loss sharing is a common characteristic of contractual arrangements: one thinks of deductibles and coinsurance in formal insurance contracts, and of joint ventures of all sorts, including sharecropping. Sometimes loss sharing is designed to deal with the moral-hazard problem in insurance; sometimes it is itself the method of insurance, as in sharecropping.[105] But it seems hardly feasible to design a legal rule that will imitate voluntary transacting in all its variety yet be administrable at reasonable cost. Here as elsewhere the law prefers the dichotomous to the continuous solution, presumably because of administrative-cost considerations, thus illustrating the second-best character of legal compared to market resource allocation.[106]

[103] If the parties do not estimate equal probabilities, then 50-50 loss-sharing can be presumed efficient only if the parties are assumed to have identical utility functions. See Alan Schwartz, Sales Law and Inflations, 50 Ind. L.J. 1, 8 n.20 (1976).

[104] The objection to loss splitting in this situation is similar to that to comparative negligence. See Richard A. Posner, *supra* note 2 at 70-71. We note parenthetically that if a rule of loss splitting were adopted there would be no reason we can think of to limit it to the reliance loss.

[105] See Steven N.S. Cheung, The Theory of Share Tenancy 68 (1969).

[106] See Richard A. Posner, *supra* note 2, at 323-34. As a detail, note that the chance of an

A further complication in the discharge remedy area has been created by a misapplication of the common law principle of restitution. In a repair case similar to our last hypothetical the court properly held the contract discharged and overturned an award entered below for full recovery of reliance damages, saying:

> The owner cannot be called on to reimburse the contractor merely because the contractor has been to expense in taking steps tending to performance. . . . It takes something more to make the owner liable for what the contractor has done toward performance. The owner must be benefitted. He should not be enriched at the expense of the contractor. That would be unjust, and to the extent that the owner has been benefitted, the law may properly consider him as resting under a duty to pay . . . . The only basis on which the law can raise an obligation on the part of the owner is the consideration he has received by way of benefit, advantage, or value to him.[107]

This statement makes good economic sense. A rule requiring a party to pay restitution for benefits actually received is consistent with the economic theory of contract law. However, the court went on to hold that materials "worked into" the house prior to the fire, although totally destroyed by it, constituted tangible benefits to the homeowner. Applying this principle, the court allowed the contractor to recover in restitution for work done in removing a floor in a house that shortly afterward was totally destroyed by fire. This result is unsound. The proper measure of benefit is the value to the homeowner during the interval before the fire deprived him of the value of the work. Any greater reward would, by conferring a windfall on the contractor, undermine the determination that he was the superior risk bearer.

B. *Partial Performance*

The remedial questions pertinent to impossibility generally arise in cases of partial performance, as in the repair cases discussed in the previous subpart. Another form of partial performance is part payment. If there has been part payment prior to delivery and delivery is prevented by some catastrophe, the question may arise whether the payee should be required to return all or part of the payment. The answer ought to depend, in an economic analysis, on whether the purpose of the prepayment was to compensate the payee for bearing the risk that something might happen to prevent him from making delivery, or whether the prepayment was unrelated. Suppose in our hypothetical repair case that the homeowner had advanced the repair contractor part of the payment before the latter com-

---

erroneous legal judgment introduces an element of risk sharing; as the probability of legal error rises, the legal solution approaches in practice the 50-50 loss-sharing rule advocated by many commentators—though it is ex ante rather than ex post loss sharing that is achieved in this way.

[107] Carroll v. Bowersock, 100 Kan. 270, 274, 164 Pac. 143, 144 (1917).

pleted the repairs. If the purpose of the advance was to compensate the repairer for bearing the risk that fire or some other event would prevent him from completing the repairs, then clearly he is entitled to keep the advance—it is his insurance premium. But the advance may be completely unrelated to such risks. It could be intended to finance the purchase of supplies by the contractor (the homeowner may be the cheapest source of the necessary capital) or to protect the contractor against the risk that the homeowner might be insolvent or otherwise difficult to collect the contract price from. It could be intended simply to avoid, for tax or other financial reasons, a large, lumpy payment at the completion of construction. Given the number of plausible reasons for prepayment that are unrelated to the provision of insurance against an event that may prevent completion of performance, there can be no presumption that prepayment is intended to compensate the performing party for the risk of such an event. Accordingly, in the absence of other evidence that the payor is the superior risk bearer, his prepayments should be returned to him. This is the generally prevailing legal rule.[108]

Where it is the performing party to the contract who has partially completed performance, rather than the paying party, there will often be a valid claim for restitution (for example, where a contract to deliver 10,000 widgets is terminated after 1,000 have been delivered), even if the performer is deemed the superior risk bearer. But where there is no basis for restitution—no value conferred on the other party to the contract by partial performance—neither is there any good economic argument for redistributing the loss between the parties. The loss should then fall entirely on the superior risk bearer.

A concept related to restitution which courts have also used in these cases is that the "divisible contract." If an event giving rise to discharge prevents the completion of a performance that has begun, payment of the completed portion of the performance will be held to be due if that portion is deemed divisible, and the recovery may include a pro rata portion of the performing party's expectation interest as well as its reliance loss. For example, in one well-known case a steamship company had contracted to supply a given number of trips at a fixed rate per trip to be paid monthly. When the

[108] See 6 Arthur Linton Corbin, *supra* note 6 at §§ 1972-1977. In many deposit situations, of course, it is understood that the payor has the right to cancel but not to recover his deposit (*e.g.*, resort bookings). Here the discharge question does not arise.

Perhaps the *Chandler* case, note 94 *supra*, can be distinguished from those coronation cases allowing discharge on the ground that the contract in *Chandler* required full payment in advance. The unusual character of the payment term arguably justified the court in concluding that the cancellation of the procession was not intended by the parties to discharge the payor's obligation. In our terms, the absence of any other apparent reason for requiring full payment in advance permitted the inference that the purpose was to insure the payee against the risk of an event that would make performance uneconomical.

steamship was destroyed by fire, the contract was held to be discharged but the steamship company was allowed to recover the agreed-upon rate for each of the trips that had already been supplied.[109] The basic rationale in such cases seems restitutionary, and appears to make good sense. But it would be cleaner to drop the fiction of divisibility and simply to view the contract as discharged, and then decide what compensation is due the performing party for having conferred benefits on the other party to the contract before the event giving rise to the discharge occurred.

Conclusion and Extensions

We have argued that economics provides a useful framework for the analysis of discharge claims. To be sure, only a subclass of potential discharge cases is within the scope of our analysis. Where the terms of a contract assign to one or the other party the risk of loss from a particular event or group of events, those terms control. But it would be a mistake to think that if only we stared hard enough at the words of the contract, all questions of risk allocation would dissolve into questions of interpretation. Interpretation depends on context, and the parties' risk-bearing capacities may be part of the context.

Also excluded from our analysis is the case where the event claimed to work a discharge was preventable by the promisor at reasonable cost; here no further inquiry is justified and the contract should be enforced. The discharge question arises only in those cases where the contract does not assign the risk in question and the event giving rise to the discharge claim was not avoidable by any cost-justified precautions. When these threshold conditions have been satisfied, economic analysis suggests that the loss should be placed on the party who is the superior (that is, lower-cost) risk bearer. To determine which party is the superior risk bearer three factors are relevant—knowledge of the magnitude of the loss, knowledge of the probability that it will occur, and (other) costs of self- or market-insurance.

This analytic framework can be used to guide empirical analysis of discharge cases, though admittedly the empirical methods used in this paper, as in the contract cases themselves, are casual and crude. Their limitations are especially serious in those situations where the relevant empirical factors point in different directions. In the lease area, for example, we were unable to discover whether lessees or lessors should bear the risk of fortuitous events that impair the value of the lease without conducting empirical research of a sort that we hope in future work to pursue in much greater depth. Studies of the provisions of actual contracts may be particularly helpful in determining

[109] Pasquotank & N.R. Steamboat Co. v. Eastern Carolina Trans. Co., 166 N.C. 582, 82 S.E. 956 (1914).

when discharge is efficient. Suppose, for example, that in some class of cases the courts of one jurisdiction allow discharge and the courts of some other jurisdiction do not. Unless there are economic differences between the jurisdictions that make the different rule in each efficient—an unlikely possibility—the rule in one jurisdiction will be the efficient rule, and the rule in the other inefficient. In the jurisdiction that has the inefficient rule, one would expect the parties to contracts to insert a provision reversing the legal rule. Therefore, by comparing contracts across states (or, in some cases perhaps, across countries) it should be possible to determine which rule is the efficient one. This could be a powerful method both of testing the empirical hunches in this paper and of determining the efficient rule in circumstances where the empirical methods used in this paper do not yield even a hunch.

Incomplete as the present paper is, it does provide an analytical framework that transforms a group of seemingly random case holdings into a generally (though not perfectly) coherent array of outcomes. Our analysis suggests, once again, that the common law has an internal economic logic stronger than many legal scholars believe. Moreover, the simple analytic framework that we have fashioned to identify the superior risk bearer in discharge cases could be used to clarify a number of other areas of contract law, and other fields as well. It has long been known that risk allocation is a fundamental purpose of contract and contract law.[110] But, as noted earlier, this insight has remained undeveloped for want of a method of determining which contracting party is the superior risk bearer and should therefore be assigned the risk. If we are correct in our analysis of whether, for example, war should be treated as a ground for discharging a certain class of transportation contracts, then the same analysis should reveal how the risk of war should be assigned in cases involving the pre-existing duty doctrine,[111] or how the risk of an unexpected pregnancy should be assigned in a case involving the purchase of a cow,[112] or how risk should be assigned in any other area of contract law. Furthermore, since issues of risk assignment become important in tort law whenever accidents are not preventable at reasonable cost,[113] our analysis has implications for that body of law as well.[114]

[110] See Edwin W. Patterson, *supra* note 19.

[111] See Listen v. Owners of Steamship Carpathian, [1915] 2 K.B. 42 (H.L.). Cf. Ling v. Schuck, 106 Md. 220, 67 A. 286 (1907) (soil conditions).

[112] See Sherwood v. Walker, 66 Mich. 568, 33 N.W. 919 (1887), discussed in Richard A. Posner, *supra* note 2 at 47-48. The mutual-mistake cases are particularly difficult to distinguish analytically from the impossibility cases. An unexpected-soil-conditions case, for example, such as *Hein v. Fox*, *supra* note 51, could equally well be regarded as a mutual-mistake case.

[113] See Richard A. Posner, *supra* note 95 at 210.

[114] Guido Calabresi, in The Costs of Accidents (1970), while pointing out that risk reduction is a goal of accident law, does not consider the problem of determining which party to the accident is the superior risk bearer, *i.e.*, can insure at lower cost. See *id.* at 46-67.

HADLEY v. BAXENDALE

Court of Exchequer, 1854.
9 Ex. 341, 156 Eng.Rep. 145.

At the trial before Crompton, J., at the last Gloucester Assizes, it appeared that the plaintiffs carried on an extensive business as millers at Gloucester; and that, on the 11th of May, their mill was stopped by a breakage of the crank shaft by which the mill was worked. The steam-engine was manufactured by Messrs. Joyce & Co., the engineers, at Greenwich, and it became necessary to send the shaft as a pattern for a new one to Greenwich. The fracture was discovered on the 12th, and on the 13th the plaintiffs sent one of their servants to the office of the defendants, who are the well-known carriers trading under the name of Pickford & Co., for the purpose of having the shaft carried to Greenwich. The plaintiffs' servant told the clerk that the mill was stopped, and that the shaft must be sent immediately; and in answer to the inquiry when the shaft would be taken, the answer was, that if it was sent up by twelve o'clock any day, it would be delivered at Greenwich on the following day. On the following day the shaft was taken by the defendants, before noon, for the purpose of being conveyed to Greenwich, and the sum of 2£. 4s. was paid for its carriage for the whole distance; at the same time the defendants' clerk was told that a special entry, if required, should be made to hasten its delivery. The delivery of the shaft at Greenwich was delayed by some neglect; and the consequence was, that the plaintiffs did not receive the new shaft for several days after they would otherwise have done, and the working of their mill was thereby delayed, and they thereby lost the profits they would otherwise have received.

On the part of the defendants, it was objected that these damages were too remote, and that the defendants were not liable with respect to them. The learned Judge left the case generally to the jury, who found a verdict with 25l. damages beyond the amount paid into Court.

Whateley, in last Michaelmas Term, obtained a rule nisi for a new trial, on the ground of misdirection.

* * *

ALDERSON, B. We think that there ought to be a new trial in this case; but, in so doing, we deem it to be expedient and necessary to state explicitly the rule which the Judge, at the next trial, ought, in our opinion, to direct the jury to be governed by when they estimate the damages.

It is, indeed, of the last importance that we should do this; for, if the jury are left without any definite rule to guide them, it will, in such cases as these, manifestly lead to the greatest injustice. The Courts have done this on several occasions; and, in Blake v. Midland Railway Company (18 Q.B. 93), the Court granted a new trial on this very ground, that the rule had not been definitely laid down to the jury by the learned Judge at Nisi Prius.

"There are certain established rules," this Court says, in Alder v. Keighley (15 M. & W. 117), "according to which the jury ought to find." And the Court, in that case, adds: "and here there is a clear rule, that the amount which would have been received if the contract had been kept, is the measure of damages if the contract is broken."

Now we think the proper rule in such a case as the present is this: Where two parties have made a contract which one of them has broken, the damages which the other party ought to receive in respect of such breach of contract should be such as may fairly and reasonably be considered either arising naturally, i. e., according to the usual course of things, from such breach of contract itself, or such as may reasonably be supposed to have been in the contemplation of both parties, at the time they made the contract, as the probable result of the breach of it. Now, if the special circumstances under which the contract was actually made were communicated by the plaintiffs to the defendants, and thus known to both parties, the damages resulting from the breach of such a contract, which they would reasonably contemplate, would be the amount of injury which would ordinarily follow from a breach of contract under these special circumstances so known and communicated. But, on the other hand, if these special circumstances were wholly unknown to the party breaking the contract, he, at the most, could only be supposed to have had in his contemplation the amount of injury which would arise generally, and in the great multitude of cases not affected by any special circumstances, from such a breach of contract. For, had the special circumstances been known, the parties might have specially provided for the breach of contract by special terms as to the damages in that case; and of this advantage it would be very unjust to deprive them. Now the above principles are those by which we think the jury ought to be guided in estimating the damages arising out of any breach of contract. It is said, that other cases such as breaches of contract in the non-payment of money, or in the not making a good title to land, are to be treated as exceptions from this, and as governed by a conventional rule. But as, in such cases, both parties must be supposed to be cognisant of that well-known rule, these cases may, we think, be more properly classed under the rule above enunciated as to cases under known special circumstances, because there both parties may reasonably be presumed to contemplate the estimation of the amount of damages according to the conventional rule.

Now, in the present case, if we are to apply the principles above laid down, we find that the only circumstances here communicated by the plaintiffs to the defendants at the time the contract was made, were, that the article to be carried was the broken shaft of a mill, and that the plaintiffs were the millers of that mill. But how do these circumstances shew reasonably that the profits of the mill must be stopped by an unreasonable delay in the delivery of the broken shaft by the carrier to the third person? Suppose the plaintiffs had another shaft in their possession put up or putting up at the time, and that they only wished to send back the broken shaft to the engineer who made it; it is clear that this would be quite consistent with the above circumstances, and yet the unreasonable delay in the delivery would have no effect upon the intermediate profits of the mill. Or, again, suppose that, at the time of the delivery to the carrier, the machinery of the mill had been in other respects defective, then, also, the same results would follow. Here it is true that the shaft was actually sent back to serve as a model for a new one, and that the want of a new one was the only cause of the stoppage of the mill, and that the loss of profits really arose from not sending down the new shaft in proper time, and that this arose from the delay in delivering the broken one to serve as a model. But it is obvious that, in the great multitude of cases of millers sending off broken shafts to third persons by a carrier under ordinary circumstances, such consequences would not, in all probability, have occurred; and these special circumstances were here never communicated by the plaintiffs to the defendants. It follows, therefore, that the loss of profits here cannot reasonably be considered such a consequence of the breach of contract as could have been fairly and reasonably contemplated by both the parties when they made this contract. For such loss would neither have flowed naturally from the breach of this contract in the great multitude of such cases occurring under ordinary circumstances, nor were the special circumstances, which, perhaps, would have made it a reasonable and natural consequence of such breach of contract, communicated to or known by the defendants. The Judge ought, therefore, to have told the jury, that, upon the facts then before them, they ought not to take the loss of profits into consideration at all in estimating the damages. There must therefore be a new trial in this case.

Rule absolute.

Sherwood v. Walker, 66 Mich. 568, 33 N.W. 919 (Mich. 1887).

MORSE, J. . . . The main controversy depends upon the construction of a contract for the sale of the cow. . . . The Walkers are importers and breeders of polled Angus cattle. The plaintiff is a banker living at Plymouth, in Wayne county. He called upon the defendants at Walkerville for the purchase of some of their stock, but found none there that suited him. Meeting one of the defendants afterwards, he was informed that they had a few head upon their Greenfield farm. He was asked to go out and look at them, with the statement that they were probably barren, and would not breed. May 5, 1886, the plaintiff went out to Greenfield and saw the cattle. A few days thereafter, he called upon one of the defendants with the view of purchasing a cow, known as "Rose 2d of Aberlone." After considerable talk it was agreed that defendants would telephone Sherwood at his home in Plymouth in reference to the price. The second morning after this talk he was called up by telephone, and the terms of the sale were finally agreed upon. He was to pay five and one-half cents per pound, live weight, fifty pounds shrinkage . . . He requested defendants to confirm the sale in writing, which they did . . .

On the twenty-first of the same month the plaintiff went to defendants' farm at Greenfield, and presented the order and [confirmation letter to an employee of the Walkers,] who informed him that the defendants had instructed him not to deliver the cow. Soon after, the plaintiff rendered to Hiram Walker, one of the defendants, $80, and demanded the cow. Walker refused to take the money or deliver the cow. The plaintiff then instituted this suit.

[At the trial, t]he defendants introduced evidence tending to show that at the time of the alleged sale it was believed by both the plaintiff and themselves that the cow was barren and would not breed; that she cost $850, and if not barren would be worth from $750 to $1,000; that after the date of the letter . . . the defendants were informed by [an employee] that in his judgment the cow was with calf, and therefore they instructed him not to deliver her to plaintiff. . . The cow had a calf in the month of October following. . .

It appears from the record that both parties supposed this cow was barren and would not breed, and she was sold by the pound for an insignificant sum as compared with her real value if a breeder. She was evidently sold and purchased on the relation of her value for beef, unless the plaintiff had learned of her true condition, and concealed such knowledge from the defendants. . . The question arises whether the [defendants] had a right to [refuse to perform the contract]. . . I am of the opinion that the [circuit] court erred in holding [that the contract should have been performed at the agreed upon price]. I know that this is a close question, and the dividing line between the adjudicated cases is not easily discerned. But it must be considered as well settled that a party who has given an apparent consent to a contract of sale may refuse to execute it, or he may avoid it after it has been completed, if the assent was founded, or the contract made, upon the mistake of a material fact,—such as the subject-matter of the sale, the price, or some collateral fact materially inducing the agreement; and this can be done when the mistake is mutual. . .

If there is a difference or misapprehension as to the substance of the thing bargained for; if the thing actually delivered or received is different in substance from the thing bargained for, and intended to be sold,—then there is no contract; but if it be only a difference in some quality or accident, even though the mistake may have been the actuating motive to the purchaser or seller, or both of them, yet the contract remains binding. . . It has been held, in accordance with the principles above stated, that where a horse is bought under the belief that he is sound, and both vendor and vendee honestly believe him to be sound, the purchaser must stand by his bargain, and pay the full price, unless there was a warranty.

It seems to me, however, in the case made by this record, that the mistake or misapprehension of the parties went to the whole substance of the agreement. If the cow was a breeder, she was worth at least $750; if barren, she was worth not over $80. The parties would not have made the contract of sale except upon the understanding and belief that she was incapable of breeding, and of no use as a cow. It is true she is now the identical animal that they thought her to be when the contract was made; there is no mistake as to the identity of the creature. Yet the mistake was not of the mere quality of the animal, but went to the very nature of the thing. A barren cow is substantially a different creature than a breeding one. There is as much difference between them for all purposes of use as there is between an ox and a cow that is capable of breeding and giving milk. If the mutual mistake had simply related to the fact whether she was with calf or not for one season, then it might have been a good sale, but the mistake affected the character of the animal for all time, and for its present and ultimate use. She was not in fact the animal, or the kind of animal, the defendants intended to sell or the plaintiff to buy. . . The court should have instructed the jury that if they found that the cow was sold, or contracted to be sold, upon the understanding of both parties that she was barren and useless for the purpose of breeding, and that in fact she was not barren, but capable of breeding, then the defendants had a right to rescind, and refuse to deliver, and the verdict should be in their favor.

The judgment of the court below must be reversed, and a new trial granted, with costs of this court to defendants.

SHERWOOD, J. (dissenting) . . . There is no question but that the defendants sold the cow representing her of the breed and quality they believed the cow to be, and that the purchaser so understood it. And the buyer purchased her believing her to be of the breed represented by the sellers, and possessing all the qualities stated, and even more. He believed she would breed. There is no pretense that the plaintiff bought the cow for beef, and there is nothing in the record indicating that he would have bought her at all only that he thought she might be made to breed. Under the foregoing facts, . . . it is held that because it turned out that the plaintiff was more correct in his judgment as to one quality of the cow than the defendants, and a quality, too, which could not by any possibility be positively known at the time by either party to exist, the contract may be annulled by the defendants at their pleasure. . . If the owner of a Hambletonian horse had speeded him, and was only able to make him go a mile in three minutes, and should sell him to another, believing that was his greatest speed, for $300, when the purchaser believed he could go much faster, and made the purchase for that sum, and a few days thereafter, under more favorable circumstances, the horse was driven a mile in 2 min. 16 sec., and was found to be worth $20,000, I hardly think it would be held, whether at law or in equity, by any one, that the seller in such case could rescind the contract. . .

In this case neither party knew the actual quality and condition of this cow at the time of the sale. . . The defendants thought [Rose could not be made to breed], but the plaintiff says that he thought she could be made to breed, but believed she was not with calf. The defendants sold the cow for what they believed her to be, and the plaintiff bought her as he believed she was, after the statements made by the defendants. No conditions whatever were attached to the terms of sale by either party. . . It is not the duty of courts to destroy contracts when called upon to enforce them, after they have been legally made. . . There was no difference between the parties, nor misapprehension, as to the substance of the thing bargained for, which was a cow supposed to be barren by one party, and believed not to be by the other. As to the quality of the animal, subsequently developed, both parties were equally ignorant, and as to this each party took his chances. . . In this case the cow sold was the one delivered. What might or might not happen to her after the sale formed no element in the contract. . .

Ora Lee WILLIAMS, Appellant,

v.

WALKER-THOMAS FURNITURE COMPANY, Appellee.

William THORNE et al., Appellants,

v.

WALKER-THOMAS FURNITURE COMPANY, Appellee.

Nos. 18604, 18605.

United States Court of Appeals
District of Columbia Circuit.

Argued April 9, 1965.

Decided Aug. 11, 1965.

Suits by furniture company to recover on contracts under which balance due on every item purchased continued until balance due on all items, whenever purchased, was liquidated. The Court of General Sessions granted judgment for furniture company and appeal was taken. The District of Columbia Court of Appeals affirmed and appeal was taken. The United States Court of Appeals for the District of Columbia Circuit, J. Skelly Wright, Circuit Judge, held that where element of unconscionability is present at time contract is made, contract should

not be enforced and that inasmuch as trial court and appellate court had not recognized that contracts could be unenforceable on that basis and record was not sufficient for Court of Appeals to decide issue as matter of law, cases must be remanded to trial court for further proceedings.

Cases remanded.

Danaher, Circuit Judge, dissented.

1. Common Law ⚿14

That Congress enacted Uniform Commercial Code specifically providing that court may refuse to enforce contract which it finds to be unconscionable at time it was made does not mean that common law of District of Columbia was otherwise at time of enactment nor preclude court from adopting similar rule in exercise of its powers to develop common law for District of Columbia. D.C.Code 1961, § 28–2–302.

2. Contracts ⚿1

Where element of unconscionability is present at time contract is made, contract should not be enforced.

3. Contracts ⚿1

"Unconscionability" includes absence of meaningful choice on part of one of parties together with contract terms which are unreasonably favorable to the other party.

See publication Words and Phrases for other judicial constructions and definitions.

4. Contracts ⚿1

Whether meaningful choice is present in particular case as to one of parties to contract claimed to be unconscionable can only be determined by consideration of all circumstances surrounding transaction and may be negated by gross inequality of bargaining power.

5. Contracts ⚿1

Manner in which contract was entered into is relevant to determining whether meaningful choice was present on part of one of parties for purposes of deciding whether contract was unconscionable.

6. Contracts ⚿1

One-sided bargain is itself evidence of inequality of bargaining parties in determining whether contract was unconscionable.

7. Contracts ⚿99(1)

Fraud can be presumed from grossly unfair nature of terms of contract.

8. Contracts ⚿93(2)

Ordinarily, one who signs agreement without full knowledge of its terms may be held to assume risk that he has entered one-sided bargain.

9. Contracts ⚿1

When party of little bargaining power, and hence little real choice, signs commercially unreasonable contract with little or no knowledge of its terms, it is not likely that his consent or even objective manifestation of his consent was ever given to all the terms and, in such case, usual rule that terms of agreement are not to be questioned should be abandoned and court should consider whether terms of contract are so unfair that enforcement should be withheld.

10. Contracts ⚿1

Usually, terms of agreement are not to be questioned.

11. Contracts ⚿1

In determining reasonableness or fairness of contract, primary concern must be with terms of the contract considered in light of the circumstances existing when contract was made, but the test is not simple and cannot be mechanically applied.

12. Contracts ⚿1

Terms of contract are to be considered in light of general commercial background and commercial needs of particular trade or case in determining whether contract was reasonable or fair.

13. Contracts ⚿1

Test to be applied in those cases where no meaningful choice was exercised upon entering into contract are whether terms are so extreme as to appear unconscionable according to mores and business practices of time and place.

14. Courts ⟹406.9(9)

Inasmuch as trial court and appellate court did not recognize that contracts whereby balance due on purchases from retail furniture store was kept on every item purchased until balance due on all items, whenever purchased, was liquidated could be unenforceable on basis of being unconscionable and record was not sufficient for Court of Appeals to decide issue as matter of law, cases must be remanded to trial court for further proceedings.

Mr. Pierre E. Dostert, Washington, D. C., counsel for appellants in No. 18,605, argued for all appellants.

Mr. R. R. Curry, Washington, D. C., for appellant in No. 18,604.

Mr. Harry Protas, Washington, D. C., for appellee.

Mr. Gerhard P. Van Arkel (appointed by this court), Washington, D. C., as *amicus curiae.*

Before BAZELON, Chief Judge, and DANAHER and WRIGHT, Circuit Judges.

J. SKELLY WRIGHT, Circuit Judge:

Appellee, Walker-Thomas Furniture Company, operates a retail furniture store in the District of Columbia. During the period from 1957 to 1962 each appellant in these cases purchased a number of household items from Walker-Thomas, for which payment was to be made in installments. The terms of each purchase were contained in a printed form contract which set forth the value of the purchased item and purported to lease the item to appellant for a stipulated monthly rent payment. The contract then provided, in substance, that title would remain in Walker-Thomas until the total of all the monthly payments made equaled the stated value of the item, at which time appellants could take title. In the event of a default in the payment of any monthly installment, Walker-Thomas could repossess the item.

The contract further provided that "the amount of each periodical installment payment to be made by [purchaser] to the Company under this present lease shall be inclusive of and not in addition to the amount of each installment payment to be made by [purchaser] under such prior leases, bills or accounts; *and all payments now and hereafter made by [purchaser] shall be credited pro rata on all outstanding leases, bills and accounts* due the Company by [purchaser] at the time each such payment is made." Emphasis added.) The effect of this rather obscure provision was to keep a balance due on every item purchased until the balance due on all items, whenever purchased, was liquidated. As a result, the debt incurred at the time of purchase of each item was secured by the right to repossess all the items previously purchased by the same purchaser, and each new item purchased automatically became subject to a security interest arising out of the previous dealings.

On May 12, 1962, appellant Thorne purchased an item described as a Daveno, three tables, and two lamps, having total stated value of $391.10. Shortly thereafter, he defaulted on his monthly payments and appellee sought to replevy all the items purchased since the first transaction in 1958. Similarly, on April 17, 1962, appellant Williams bought a stereo set of stated value of $514.95.[1] She too defaulted shortly thereafter, and appellee sought to replevy all the items purchased since December, 1957. The Court of General Sessions granted judgment for appellee. The District of Columbia Court of Appeals affirmed, and we granted appellants' motion for leave to appeal to this court.

Appellants' principal contention, rejected by both the trial and the appellate courts below, is that these contracts, or at least some of them, are unconscionable and, hence, not enforceable. In its opin-

1. At the time of this purchase her account showed a balance of $164 still owing from her prior purchases. The total of all the purchases made over the years in question came to $1,800. The total payments amounted to $1,400.

ion in Williams v. Walker-Thomas Furniture Company, 198 A.2d 914, 916 (1964), the District of Columbia Court of Appeals explained its rejection of this contention as follows:

"Appellant's second argument presents a more serious question. The record reveals that prior to the last purchase appellant had reduced the balance in her account to $164. The last purchase, a stereo set, raised the balance due to $678. Significantly, at the time of this and the preceding purchases, appellee was aware of appellant's financial position. The reverse side of the stereo contract listed the name of appellant's social worker and her $218 monthly stipend from the government. Nevertheless, with full knowledge that appellant had to feed, clothe and support both herself and seven children on this amount, appellee sold her a $514 stereo set.

"We cannot condemn too strongly appellee's conduct. It raises serious questions of sharp practice and irresponsible business dealings. A review of the legislation in the District of Columbia affecting retail sales and the pertinent decisions of the highest court in this jurisdiction disclose, however, no ground upon which this court can declare the contracts in question contrary to public policy. We note that were the Maryland Retail Installment Sales Act, Art. 83 §§ 128–153, or its equivalent, in force in the District of Columbia, we could grant appellant appropriate relief. We think Congress should consider corrective legislation to protect the public from such exploitive contracts as were utilized in the case at bar."

We do not agree that the court lacked the power to refuse enforcement to contracts found to be unconscionable. In other jurisdictions, it has been held as a matter of common law that unconscionable contracts are not enforceable.[2] While no decision of this court so holding has been found, the notion that an unconscionable bargain should not be given full enforcement is by no means novel. In Scott v. United States, 79 U.S. (12 Wall.) 443, 445, 20 L.Ed. 438 (1870), the Supreme Court stated:

"* * * If a contract be unreasonable and unconscionable, but not void for fraud, a court of law will give to the party who sues for its breach damages, not according to its letter, but only such as he is equitably entitled to. * * *"[3]

Since we have never adopted or rejected such a rule,[4] the question here presented is actually one of first impression.

[1, 2] Congress has recently enacted the Uniform Commercial Code, which specifically provides that the court may refuse to enforce a contract which it finds to be unconscionable at the time it was made. 28 D.C.Code § 2–302 (Supp. IV 1965). The enactment of this section, which occurred subsequent to the contracts here in suit, does not mean that

2. Campbell Soup Co. v. Wentz, 3 Cir., 172 F.2d 80 (1948); Indianapolis Morris Plan Corporation v. Sparks, 132 Ind.App. 145, 172 N.E.2d 899 (1961); Henningsen v. Bloomfield Motors, Inc., 32 N.J. 358, 161 A.2d 69, 84–96, 75 A.L.R.2d 1 (1960). *Cf.* 1 Corbin, Contracts § 128 (1963).

3. See Luing v. Peterson, 143 Minn. 6, 172 N.W. 692 (1919); Greer v. Tweed, N.Y. C.P., 13 Abb.Pr., N.S., 427 (1872); Schnell v. Nell, 17 Ind. 29 (1861); and see generally the discussion of the English authorities in Hume v. United States, 132 U.S. 406, 10 S.Ct. 134, 33 L.Ed. 393 (1889).

4. While some of the statements in the court's opinion in District of Columbia v. Harlan & Hollingsworth Co., 30 App.D.C. 270 (1908), may appear to reject the rule, in reaching its decision upholding the liquidated damages clause in that case the court considered the circumstances existing at the time the contract was made, see 30 App.D.C. at 279, and applied the usual rule on liquidated damages. See 5 Corbin, Contracts §§ 1054–1075 (1964); *Note,* 72 Yale L.J. 723, 746–755 (1963). Compare Jaeger v. O'Donoghue, 57 App.D.C. 191, 18 F.2d 1013 (1927).

the common law of the District of Columbia was otherwise at the time of enactment, nor does it preclude the court from adopting a similar rule in the exercise of its powers to develop the common law for the District of Columbia. In fact, in view of the absence of prior authority on the point, we consider the congressional adoption of § 2–302 persuasive authority for following the rationale of the cases from which the section is explicitly derived.[5] Accordingly, we hold that where the element of unconscionability is present at the time a contract is made, the contract should not be enforced.

[3–10] Unconscionability has generally been recognized to include an absence of meaningful choice on the part of one of the parties together with contract terms which are unreasonably favorable to the other party.[6] Whether a meaningful choice is present in a particular case can only be determined by consideration of all the circumstances surrounding the transaction. In many cases the meaningfulness of the choice is negated by a gross inequality of bargaining power.[7] The manner in which the contract was entered is also relevant to this consideration. Did each party to the contract, considering his obvious education or lack of it, have a reasonable opportunity to understand the terms of the contract, or were the important terms hidden in a maze of fine print and minimized by deceptive sales practices? Ordinarily, one who signs an agreement without full knowledge of its terms might be held to assume the risk that he has entered a one-sided bargain.[8] But when a party of little bargaining power, and hence little real choice, signs a commercially unreasonable contract with little or no knowledge of its terms, it is hardly likely that his consent, or even an objective manifestation of his consent, was ever given to all the terms. In such a case the usual rule that the terms of the

5. See Comment, § 2–302, Uniform Commercial Code (1962). Compare *Note*, 45 VA.L.REV. 583, 590 (1959), where it is predicted that the rule of § 2–302 will be followed by analogy in cases which involve contracts not specifically covered by the section. *Cf.* 1 STATE OF NEW YORK LAW REVISION COMMISSION, REPORT AND RECORD OF HEARINGS ON THE UNIFORM COMMERCIAL CODE 108–110 (1954) (remarks of Professor Llewellyn).

6. See Henningsen v. Bloomfield Motors, Inc., *supra* Note 2; Campbell Soup Co. v. Wentz, *supra* Note 2.

7. See Henningsen v. Bloomfield Motors, Inc., *supra* Note 2, 161 A.2d at 86, and authorities there cited. Inquiry into the relative bargaining power of the two parties is not an inquiry wholly divorced from the general question of unconscionability, since a one-sided bargain is itself evidence of the inequality of the bargaining parties. This fact was vaguely recognized in the common law doctrine of intrinsic fraud, that is, fraud which can be presumed from the grossly unfair nature of the terms of the contract. See the oft-quoted statement of Lord Hardwicke in Earl of Chesterfield v. Janssen, 28 Eng. Rep. 82, 100 (1751):

> "* * * [Fraud] may be apparent from the intrinsic nature and subject of the bargain itself; such as no man in his senses and not under delusion would make * * *."

And *cf.* Hume v. United States, *supra* Note 3, 132 U.S. at 413, 10 S.Ct. at 137, where the Court characterized the English cases as "cases in which one party took advantage of the other's ignorance of arithmetic to impose upon him, and the fraud was apparent from the face of the contracts." See also Greer v. Tweed, *supra* Note 3.

8. See RESTATEMENT, CONTRACTS § 70 (1932); *Note*, 63 HARV.L.REV. 494 (1950). See also Daley v. People's Building, Loan & Savings Ass'n, 178 Mass. 13, 59 N.E. 452, 453 (1901), in which Mr. Justice Holmes, while sitting on the Supreme Judicial Court of Massachusetts, made this observation:

> "* * * Courts are less and less disposed to interfere with parties making such contracts as they choose, so long as they interfere with no one's welfare but their own. * * * It will be understood that we are speaking of parties standing in an equal position where neither has any oppressive advantage or power * * *."

agreement are not to be questioned[9] should be abandoned and the court should consider whether the terms of the contract are so unfair that enforcement should be withheld.[10]

[11–13] In determining reasonableness or fairness, the primary concern must be with the terms of the contract considered in light of the circumstances existing when the contract was made. The test is not simple, nor can it be mechanically applied. The terms are to be considered "in the light of the general commercial background and the commercial needs of the particular trade or case."[11] Corbin suggests the test as being whether the terms are "so extreme as to appear unconscionable according to the mores and business practices of the time and place." 1 CORBIN, *op. cit. supra* Note 2.[12] We think this formulation correctly states the test to be applied in those cases where no meaningful choice was exercised upon entering the contract.

[14] Because the trial court and the appellate court did not feel that enforcement could be refused, no findings were made on the possible unconscionability of the contracts in these cases. Since the record is not sufficient for our deciding the issue as a matter of law, the cases must be remanded to the trial court for further proceedings.

So ordered.

DANAHER, Circuit Judge (dissenting):

The District of Columbia Court of Appeals obviously was as unhappy about the situation here presented as any of us can possibly be. Its opinion in the *Williams* case, quoted in the majority text, concludes: "We think Congress should consider corrective legislation to protect the public from such exploitive contracts as were utilized in the case at bar."

My view is thus summed up by an able court which made no finding that there had actually been sharp practice. Rather the appellant seems to have known precisely where she stood.

There are many aspects of public policy here involved. What is a luxury to some may seem an outright necessity to others. Is public oversight to be required of the expenditures of relief funds? A washing machine, e. g., in the hands of a relief client might become a fruitful source of income. Many relief clients may well need credit, and certain business establishments will take long chances on the sale of items, expecting their pricing policies will afford a degree of protection commensurate with the risk. Perhaps a remedy when necessary will be found within the provisions of the "Loan Shark" law, D.C.CODE §§ 26–601 *et seq.* (1961).

I mention such matters only to emphasize the desirability of a cautious approach to any such problem, particularly since the law for so long has allowed parties such great latitude in making their own contracts. I dare say there must annually be thousands upon thousands of installment credit transactions in this jurisdiction, and one can only speculate

9. This rule has never been without exception. In cases involving merely the transfer of unequal amounts of the same commodity, the courts have held the bargain unenforceable for the reason that "in such a case, it is clear, that the law cannot indulge in the presumption of equivalence between the consideration and the promise." 1 WILLISTON, CONTRACTS § 115 (3d ed. 1957).

10. See the general discussion of "Boiler-Plate Agreements" in LLEWELLYN, THE COMMON LAW TRADITION 362–371 (1960).

11. Comment, Uniform Commercial Code § 2–307.

12. See Henningsen v. Bloomfield Motors, Inc., *supra* Note 2; Mandel v. Liebman, 303 N.Y. 88, 100 N.E.2d 149 (1951). The traditional test as stated in Greer v. Tweed, *supra* Note 3, 13 Abb.Pr.,N.S., at 429, is "such as no man in his senses and not under delusion would make on the one hand, and as no honest or fair man would accept, on the other."

as to the effect the decision in these cases will have.[1]

I join the District of Columbia Court of Appeals in its disposition of the issues.

1. However the provision ultimately may be applied or in what circumstances, D.C. Code § 28-2-301 (Supp. IV, 1965) did not become effective until January 1, 1965.

UNCONSCIONABILITY: A CRITICAL REAPPRAISAL

RICHARD A. EPSTEIN
University of Chicago Law School

I. Introduction

THE classical conception of contract at common law had as its first premise the belief that private agreements should be enforced in accordance with their terms. That premise of course was subject to important qualifications. Promises procured by fraud, duress, or undue influence were not generally enforced by the courts; and the same was true with certain exceptions of promises made by infants and incompetents. Again, agreements that had as their object illegal ends were usually not enforced, as, for example, in cases of bribes of public officials or contracts to kill third persons. Yet even after these exceptions are taken into account, there was still one ground on which the initial premise could not be challenged: the terms of private agreements could not be set aside because the court found them to be harsh, unconscionable, or unjust. The reasonableness of the terms of a private agreement was the business of the parties to that agreement. True, there were numerous cases in which the language of the contract stood in need of judicial interpretation, but once that task was done there was no place for a court to impose upon the parties its own views about their rights and duties. "Public policy" was an "unruly horse,"[1] to be mounted only in exceptional cases and then only with care.

This general regime of freedom of contract can be defended from two points of view. One defense is utilitarian. So long as the tort law protects the interests of strangers to the agreement, its enforcement will tend to maximize the welfare of the parties to it, and therefore the good of the society as a whole.[2] The alternative defense is on libertarian grounds. One of the first functions of the law is to guarantee to individuals a sphere of influence in which they will be able to operate, without having to justify themselves to the state or to third parties: if one individual is entitled to do within the

[1] Richardson v. Mellish, 2 Bing. 229, 252; 130 Eng. Rep. 294, 303 (1824).

[2] The crucial question for the tort law concerns the scope and identification of the "interests" to be protected. On the one hand, they could be defined as to include the expectation of profit from trade, in which case all economic harm would fall within the scope of the tort law. On the other hand, they could cover the exclusive use and possession of one's person and property, in which case most forms of economic harm would fall outside the protection of the tort law. For a defense and elaboration of the second point of view, see Richard A. Epstein, Intentional Harms, 4 J. Leg. Studies 391 (1975).

confines of the tort law what he pleases with what he owns, then two individuals who operate with those same constraints should have the same right with respect to their mutual affairs against the rest of the world.

Whatever its merits, however, it is fair to say that this traditional view of the law of contract has been in general retreat in recent years. That decline is reflected in part in the cool reception given to doctrines of laissez-faire, its economic counterpart, since the late nineteenth century, or at least since the New Deal. The total "hands off" policy with respect to economic matters is regarded as incorrect in most political discussions almost as a matter of course, and the same view is taken, moreover, toward a more subtle form of laissez-faire that views all government interference in economic matters as an evil until shown to be good.[3] Instead, the opposite point of view is increasingly urged: market solutions—those which presuppose a regime of freedom of contract—are sure to be inadequate, and the only question worth debating concerns the appropriate form of public intervention. That attitude has, moreover, worked its way (as these things usually happen) into the fabric of the legal system, for today, more than ever, courts are willing to set aside the provisions of private agreements.[4]

One of the major conceptual tools used by courts in their assault upon private agreements has been the doctrine of unconscionability.[5] That doctrine has a place in contract law, but it is not the one usually assigned it by its advocates. The doctrine should not, in my view, allow courts to act as roving commissions to set aside those agreements whose substantive terms they find objectionable.[6] Instead, it should be used only to allow courts to

[3] "Laissez faire has never been more than a slogan in defense of the proposition that every extension of state activity should be examined under a presumption of error." Aaron Director, The Parity of the Economic Market Place, 7 J. Law & Econ. 1, 2 (1964).

[4] See Friedrich Kessler & Grant Gilmore, Contracts, Cases and Materials 1-14 (2d ed. 1970), for a perceptive essay that highlights and endorses the shift from laissez-faire to the regulatory state. For a typical statement of the modern position, see John E. Murray, Jr., Unconscionability: Unconscionability, 31 U. Pitt. L. Rev. 1, 2, 8 (1969).

[5] The literature on unconscionability is already quite extensive; for some of the more notable instances, see M. P. Ellinghaus, In Defense of Unconscionability, 78 Yale L. J. 757 (1969); Arthur Allen Leff, Unconscionability and the Code—The Emperor's New Clause, 115 U. Pa. L. Rev. 485 (1967) [hereinafter cited as Leff]; Robert Braucher, The Unconscionable Contract or Term, 31 U. Pitt. L. Rev. 337 (1969); Arthur Allen Leff, Unconscionability and the Crowd—Consumers and the Common Law Tradition, 31 U. Pitt. L. Rev. 349 (1969) [hereinafter cited as Leff, Unconscionability and the Crowd]; John E. Murray, Jr., *supra* note 4; John A. Spanogle, Jr., Analyzing Unconscionability Problems, 117 U. Pa. L. Rev. 931 (1969).

[6] The substantive doctrine of unconscionability appears in several forms and guises. Often, the term is used as a modern equivalent of the traditional notion of contracts against public policy. In some cases the doctrine, whatever it is called, is of common law creation. In others it is developed in connection with statutory rules which in broad outline define certain sorts of consensual arrangements as "unreasonable" or "unconscionable", or simply "unlawful". Yet even where these rules restricting the freedom of contract are of statutory origin, their language is of such looseness that a court has wide latitude in their interpretation, so judicial attitudes

police the process whereby private agreements are formed, and in that connection, only to facilitate the setting aside of agreements that are as a matter of probabilities likely to be vitiated by the classical defenses of duress, fraud, or incompetence.[7] In order to show how the doctrine of unconscionability can function usefully in this manner, we shall examine first the traditional limitations upon the freedom of contract. That done, we shall show how a doctrine of unconscionability, when properly used, enables us to further at an acceptable cost the ends served by these classical limitations.

With a place for unconscionability thus established, we shall explore the results achieved when the doctrine of unconscionability is used to oust on substantive grounds the terms of private agreements that have been formed by unexceptionable means. While this examination cannot demonstrate conclusively that the substantive doctrine necessarily will have harmful effects, it can, I think, show that use of the doctrine tends on balance to work more harm than good, and should therefore be abandoned.

II. Traditional Common Law Defenses

a. *Duress*

We begin our examination of contractual limitations with duress. In its simplest form the defense of duress allows A, a promisor, to excuse himself from performance of his part of the bargain because the promisee, B, used force or the threat thereof in order to procure his consent. The defense makes perfectly good sense even in a regime that respects the freedom of contract once it is recognized that the initial distribution of rights under the tort law protects both a person's physical integrity and his private property. Duress is an improper means of obtaining A's consent because it requires him to abandon one of these two initial rights ("your money or your life") in order to protect the other.[8] A's case is crystal clear where for example, he transfer goods, under a threat of force to his person; and it is but an easy extension to the next

remain important as well. Note, for example, the repetitive use of the term "unconscionable" in section § 2-302 of the Uniform Commercial Code, perhaps the most important statutory codification of the unconscionability principle.

§ 2-302. Unconscionable Contract of Clause. (1) If the court as a matter of law finds the contract or any clause of the contract to have been unconscionable at the time it was made the court may refuse to enforce the contract, or it may enforce the remainder of the contract without the unconscionable clause, or it may so limit the application of any unconscionable clause as to avoid any unconscionable result.

The situation is quite different where there is a complex statutory scheme, like, for example, the truth in lending laws, where the question of judicial interpretation, while important, assumes a more interstitial role. This is especially true where the statute empowers a regulatory agency to interpret the statutes by appropriate administrative regulations. In this discussion, we shall ignore the variations on the unconscionability theme, except in the few cases where they appear to be material.

[7] The concern is, in other words, with what has been aptly called "procedural unconscionability." Leff 487.

[8] "It is always for the interest of a party under duress to choose the lesser of two evils. But the

case where force is used to procure not the transfer of goods, but the promise thereof. The defense of duress allows A, as defendant in a contract action, to vindicate *both* his initial entitlements, even though he has yielded to the force of the moment. A's consent has been given, but there is good reason to set it aside.

The issue of duress is important in another class of cases, those involving the so-called problem of the "duress of goods."[9] Suppose that B has agreed to clean A's clothes for $10. After the work is done, B tells A that he will return the clothes only if A pays, or promises to pay, him $15. If A pays the $15, it is quite clear that he has an action to recover the $5 excess. B has put him to a choice between *his* clothes and *his* money. As in the case of duress by the threat of force, B has required A to abandon one of his rights to protect another, and the action to recover the $5 is designed to make certain that A will be able to protect them both. Suppose A, however, has only agreed to pay the $15 to secure the return of his goods. In B's action on the promise, A will have a defense against the $5 overcharge, similar to that available where the promise was made under the threat of force. This defense of duress of goods also vindicates the distribution rights created, not by the tort law alone, but by the tort law and private agreement in combination.[10] In neither case does the defense of duress turn upon the reasonableness of the terms of the agreement; nor does it rest upon the market position of the parties to it immediately before it was formed. The process of formation provides the court with all the information it needs to allow the promisor to escape from performance under the contract, and the court itself can and must remain unconcerned with the substantive terms of the bargain.

---

fact that a choice was made according to interest does not exclude duress. It is the characteristic of duress properly so called." Union Pacific R.R. v. Public Service Comm'n, 248 U.S. 67, 70 (1918). (per Holmes, J.).

[9] See John Dalzell, Duress by Economic Pressure I, 20 N.C. Law Rev. 237, 241-42 (1942), John P. Dawson, Economic Duress—An Essay in Perspective, 45 Mich. L. Rev. 253 (1947) [hereinafter cited as Dawson]. Principled extensions of the doctrine of duress of goods are quite straightforward. The doctrine should apply to a refusal to render services one has agreed to provide or the refusal to deliver papers on intangibles. See, on these variations of the theme, Dawson 280.

[10] The common law doctrine of consideration, that required every promise to be "purchased" by a return promise or act, can be justified in part as a way to protect promisees from threats of nonperformance by their promisors. See, for example, the classic case of Foakes v. Beer, 9 App. Cas. 605 (1884), where the House of Lords held the partial forgiveness of a debt was void for want of consideration. There was evidence in the case that the creditor released the debt because of the debtor's threat not to pay it. While the result in the case is arguably correct on its facts, it is better that the issue of duress be raised expressly by the creditor, preferably as an exception to a defense based upon the release. Ironically, consideration and unconscionability both function as indirect means of striking down promises which should be set aside because of duress. The difference between them is, in the end, that the price paid is too high under the consideration approach, but not under the unconscionability approach. See generally, on this approach to consideration, Lon L. Fuller, Consideration and Form, 41 Colum. L. Rev. 799 (1941).

The defense of duress, though capable of extension, is also subject to limitations, the most important of which concerns the question of "economic duress." Suppose that B at the outset refuses to clean A's clothes unless A pays him $15, even when B's previous price had been $10. There is no doubt that A is worse off on account of B's decision to make a "take it or leave it" offer, but it would be the gravest mistake to argue that B's conduct constitutes actionable duress because it puts A to an uncomfortable choice. Indeed the case is sharply distinguishable both from the threats or use of force and from the duress of goods. In those two cases of duress, B put A to the choice between two of his entitlements. In this situation he only puts A to the choice between entitlement and desire, between A's money, which he owns, and B's services, which he desires. It is the very kind of choice involved in all exchanges. A could not complain if B decided not to make him any offer at all; why then is he entitled to complain if B decides to make him *better off* by now giving him a choice when before he had none? If A does not like B's offer, he can reject it; but to allow him to first accept the agreement and only thereafter to force B to work at a price which B finds unacceptable is to allow him to resort (with the aid of the state) to the very form of duress that on any theory is prohibited. There is no question of "dictation" of terms where B refuses to accept the terms desired by A. There is every question of dictation where A can repudiate his agreement with B and hold B to one to which B did not consent; and that element of dictation remains even if A is but a poor individual and B is a large and powerful corporation. To allow that to take place is to indeed countenance an "inequality of bargaining power" between A and B, with A having the legal advantage as he is given formal legal rights explicitly denied B. The question of duress is not that of the equality of bargaining power in a loose sense that refers to the wealth of the parties. It is the question of what means are permissible to achieve agreement. Where, as with force, the means themselves are improper, the threat to use them is improper as well; where those means are proper, so too is the threat to use them.[11] It is a mistake to assert that the law of duress is designed to protect "freedom of the will" without specifying those things from which it should be free.[12] "Economic duress" is not a simple generalization of the common law notions of duress; it is their repudiation.[13] The integrity of the law of contract can be preserved only if that notion is flatly and fully rejected, and the

[11] But, note the opposite opinion of Holmes: "When it comes to the collateral question of obtaining a contract by threats, it does not follow that, because you cannot be made to answer for the act, you may use the threat." Silsbee v. Webber, 171 Mass. 378, 381, 50 N.E. 555, 556 (1898).

[12] But see Dawson 256, where it is argued that the concerns with the doctrines of duress were but a portion of the larger question having to do with freedom of the will.

[13] For the opposite point of view, see John Dalzell, Duress by Economic Pressure II, 20 N.C. L. Rev. 341 (1942), and Dawson. For a judicial expression of this position, see the dissenting opinion of Frankfurter, J., in United States v. Bethelem Steel Corp., 315 U.S. 289, 312 (1942).

role of duress limited to the case where one party puts the other to a choice between two of his entitlements by means, such as force or the breach of contracts that in and of themselves are valid.

b. *Fraudulent Misrepresentations*

The case against fraudulent misrepresentation is easy to make out.[14] As a moral matter, a person should not profit by his own deceit at the expense of his victim; and as a general matter, no social good can derive from the systematic production of misinformation. It is quite true that a person is in a better position to defend himself against fraud than against force, if only because he can check out the representations from his own sources or walk away from their maker without adverse legal consequences. But the carelessness of a victim does not excuse, much less justify, the perpetration of fraud. Where a promise induced by fraud is yet to be performed, the fraud is a good defense against an action for breach. Where the promise has been performed, the fraud is good reason to give the promisor the remedy of rescission,[15] or where that is inappropriate, money damages. As with duress, the agreement is not respected because of the process of its formation. The reasonableness of the terms are of no concern to the court, and the same is true of the market position of the parties. (A monopolist can be a plaintiff in a fraud action.) The conduct of the promisee alone is sufficient to allow the promisor to repudiate the agreement.

There are strong common law limitations on the reach of fraud doctrines, similar to those applied to duress. True, it has been always possible at common law to maintain actions for concealment (as with the man who papers over cracks in the walls of a house to hide evidence of termites from a prospective purchaser). Yet, by the same token, a contract cannot be set aside on account of the simple *nondisclosure* of facts, which if known might

[14] I put aside in this discussion the treatment of "innocent" misrepresentations, whether or not carelessly made. In those cases in which the representation is made in order to assist the representee, no liability should attach, absent agreement to the contrary, because the representee may be fairly said to take the risk that the information is in error. Where, however, the representation is made in order to induce the representee to act for the benefit of the representor, he should be held if the representation is false; such happens, for example, when a purchaser of real estate is allowed either rescission or damages when the seller makes a material but innocent, misrepresentation about the property sold. The "benefit test" in effect seeks to estimate the ways in which the parties would have allocated the risks if the matter had been brought to their attention. Fraud is the easy case because the allocation of risks is easy, given the deliberate nature of the defendant's conduct. For a case that recognizes the general right of action for "negligent misrepresentation," see Hedley Byrne & Co. v. Heller & Partners Ltd., [1964] A.C. 465 (1963). The defendant in that case used a disclaimer form which the House of Lords allowed, consistent with the contract analysis, to control in the particular case.

[15] The limitations on rescission are concerned, for example, with the protection of third parties, or with the restoration of benefits received by the victim of the fraud. See generally, John D. Calamari & Joseph M. Perillo, Contracts, ch. 13 (1970).

have put the other party off the agreement that was in fact reached.[16] This position has, of course, come under attack, as many have advocated the imposition of affirmative duties to disclose in a wide variety of contexts.[17] Yet that course is fraught with difficulties of its own. First, it is difficult to determine as a matter of public policy what information must be disclosed because it is "material." It is most likely much cheaper and more effective to allow the parties in question to ask for the information that *they* regard as material, after which the general rules governing fraud and misrepresentation may be applied to the responses that are given.[18] Second, disclosure requirements are always awkward because the party subject to them will have to act as a fiduciary toward someone with whom he wishes to deal at arm's length. Why must A be required to reveal to B at no cost information that he possesses no matter what its cost to him? The common law has been reluctant to impose affirmative duties to speak, just as it has been reluctant to impose affirmative duties to act. The undistinguished record of legislative disclosure laws, be it in truth-in-lending[19] or in securities regulation,[20] suggests that the traditional common law response to the prob-

[16] There is the intermediate case where there is a disclosure of some relevant information, but a nondisclosure of other information that makes its significance clearer. Given the familiar injunction to tell the "whole" truth, these have been treated as cases of fraud.

[17] See generally William L. Prosser, Handbook of the Law of Torts 695-99 (4th ed. 1971). Note, some of the exceptions to the nondisclosure rule are consistent with the traditional position. In particular, the rule that requires a fiduciary to disclose his interest in any transaction dealing with the subject matter of his trust is a fair implication from the close relationship between parties, who do not deal with each other as strangers. Again, the rule that requires the insured to make full disclosure of any information material to the question of whether the insurance company takes the risk, or the premium at which it is taken, is in almost all cases not a rule of positive law but an express provision of the insurance contract.

[18] Note, there is a "materiality" question even with actual misrepresentations, but it will in practice create many fewer problems, because there will be a strong presumption that whatever was in fact inquired of will be material, at least if it goes to the attractiveness of an investment. On the capacity for markets to provide contracting parties with the appropriate amount of information, see R. H. Coase, The Choice of the Institutional Framework: A Comment, 17 J. Law & Econ. 493 (1974); Richard A. Posner, The Federal Trade Commission, 37 U. Chi. L. Rev. 47 (1969); for a more cautious view, see Leff, Unconscionability and the Crowd. On the question of legislation to cure the defects of a market dissemination, it must be remembered that the case for regulation is not made out even if there is conclusive identification of a market defect. The costs and imperfections of the regulatory process must be considered as well, and these are apt to be great indeed, as for example, Professor Posner points out in his article on the FTC, *supra* at 60-82.

[19] See, for example, William C. Whitford, The Functions of Disclosure Regulation in Consumer Transactions, [1973] Wis. L. Rev. 400. Whitford concludes that it is likely that truth-in-lending legislation has had little, if any, impact on consumer behavior. One possible explanation is that this regulation cannot give the buyer information about personal factors—for example, desirability of location—that bulk much larger than disclosure in the purchasing decision. Although Whitford does not believe that this regulation serves its major function, he does think that non-economic justifications for it can be put forward. *Id.* at 435.

[20] See, for a general account of the disclosure requirements, 3 Louis Loss, Securities Regula-

lem was indeed a sound one, which insured that the prohibition against fraud was not by artifice allowed to swallow the basic premise in favor of freedom of contract.

c. *Defense of incompetence: infancy, insanity, and drunkenness*

Before we can turn to the question of unconscionability, we must, within the framework of the classical model, deal with questions of infancy, insanity, drunkenness, and the like, all going to the competence of the contracting parties. With the competence thereby called into question, it becomes difficult to argue that the consent, even if given, is in the best interests of the party who has given it, or that the punctual enforcement of the agreement is likely to advance the public good. The important question is, how can we minimize the cost associated with the rules governing incompetence? These costs are of two sorts: first, enforcing contracts that should not be enforced and, second, not enforcing those that should be enforced. The rules fashioned to minimize them should, I believe, take into account three considerations. First, they should attempt to identify broad classes of individuals who in general are not able to protect their own interests in negotiation. A case-by-case analysis of incompetence is for the most part too costly to administer, and it generates too much uncertainty in all transactions. Second, the rules should be designed to allow third parties to identify persons in the protected class in order that they may steer clear of contractual arrangements with them. It is one thing to prohibit exploitation of incompetents; it is quite another to say that people must deal with them, even to their own disadvantage. Third, the rules in question should not create artificial incentives for parties to lower the level of competence they bring into the marketplace. It is dangerous to allow people to plead their own incompetence in any transaction that they wish, with the benefit of hindsight, to repudiate.

These considerations suggest that the refusal to enforce contracts against infants is in general appropriate.[21] It is quite likely that most, though not all, infants will be unable to protect their own interests in negotiation, even in transactions not vitiated by fraud. Those who deal with infants will, moreover, usually be on notice of their special status and can take therefore steps to protect themselves. They can refuse to deal with the infant at all, or

tions 1445-1519 (2nd ed. 1961), 6 *id.* [supp. to vol. 3] 3556-3744 (1969) to get a sense of the complexity of the disclosure problem and the securities law. For a recent industry criticism of SEC disclosure requirements, see Concerns Say New SEC Disclosure Rules Would Sharply Boost Auditing Expenses, Wall Street Journal, March 18, 1975, at 36, col. 1.

[21] The arguments about insanity and drunkenness closely parallel those about infancy. One possible difference is that it may be more difficult for an outsider to know of the insanity (though not the drunkenness) of the person with whom he deals. If that point could be set to one side, as seems likely, then these situations could be governed by most of the same rules that apply to the contracts of infants.

they can demand that he be represented by a guardian of full age and capacity in any transaction. Finally, it is likely that most, but not all, infants will not be able to manipulate the legal rules to their conscious advantage.[22]

The recognition of the infancy defense in light of these considerations is not without its costs, as the rule in question will either block or increase the costs of certain transactions for infants who are quite capable of protecting themselves. In order to minimize the dislocations it is possible to recognize certain exceptions to the general rule consistent with its major purposes. Take for example a case of a merchant who has delivered necessaries to an infant who has consumed them. To refuse to enforce the contract will require the merchant to lose both his goods and the price for them, while leaving the infant enriched at his expense. To avoid this outcome, courts properly have allowed the merchant an action for the reasonable value of the goods consumed, a figure that may well be lower than the contract price.[23] The rejection of the contract price represents a degree of judicial intervention that prevents *both* exploitation by the merchant and the unjust enrichment by the infant, and as such is preferable to a simple refusal to give any action to the merchant. Take another instance: suppose the infant represents to the merchant that he is of full age in circumstances where that is believable. If goods have been delivered and consumed, it is again proper to protect the merchant by allowing him to recover the reasonable value of his goods, or, given the infant's fraud, even the benefit of his bargain.[24]

III. Unconscionability Applied

The merits of these exceptions to the general rule in favor of contractual enforcement is one question; their proof in particular cases is quite another. The courts could place upon the defendant a burden of proving fraud, duress or incompetence, say by the preponderance of the evidence. That approach would tend to insure that each of these defenses will be established only where the facts of the case so warrant. There is, however, a cost created

[22] In dealing with these factors, it is important to choose the right age for the infancy defense to apply. Traditionally, that age has been twenty-one. However, many teenagers leave the direct control of their parents at eighteen, either to go to college or to join the work force; and there is little reason to suppose any major increase in competence between ages eighteen and twenty-one. Eighteen has therefore in recent years been adopted in many jurisdictions as the age of majority, a sound result.

[23] Where the goods have not been consumed but only delivered, the better view is that the infant must restore them in order to escape from the consequences of the contract, it being unjust to allow him to keep both the goods and the price thereof. 2 Williston on Contracts § 238 (Jaeger ed., 3rd ed. 1959).

[24] Generally, an action is denied under these circumstances because it is impossible to restore the very goods sold and delivered. Indeed if the goods have been resold, the action for restitution is not allowed to reach the proceeds of sale. See G. C. Cheshire, C.H.S. Fifoot & M. P. Furmston, The Law of Contract (8th ed. 1972).

by putting this burden upon the defendant. Solely because he cannot meet the appropriate standard of proof, he may not be able to establish a contractual defense in a case where it in fact applies. If this last form of error results in substantial costs, then it should be appropriate to modify the rules of evidence in a manner that makes it easier for the defendant to establish fraud, duress or incompetence. It may well be that the relaxation of the standard of proof required to make out any defense will increase the number of instances where the undeserving defendant is able to defeat the plaintiff's legitimate contractual expectations. But if the costs thereby created are low, then the change in the rules of proof is justified on the grounds that it reduces the total error in enforcement, even though all error is not thereby eliminated.

The legal system has long used this rationale to justify some restrictions on the freedom of contract. The Statute of Frauds,[25] which requires that certain kinds of agreements be put in writing, has the prevention of fraud as one of its chief objects. Yet its application necessarily insures the nonenforcement of certain untainted oral transactions. The parol evidence rule, which prohibits the use of oral evidence to vary or contradict the provisions of an "integrated" written contract, is also designed to control fraud;[26] and it, too, frustrates the enforcement of legitimate consensual arrangements. One can attack either of these two rules on the ground that the control of fraud comes at too high a price (measured by the number of proper transactions nullified), given the alternative means of its control and prevention.[27] But neither rule can be attacked on the ground that it is directed toward an illegitimate end.

The doctrine of unconscionability, properly conceived and applied, serves the same general end as the Statute of Frauds and the parol evidence rule. Ideally, the unconscionability doctrine protects against fraud, duress and incompetence, without demanding specific proof of any of them.[28] Instead of looking to a writing requirement to control against these abuses, it looks both

[25] An Act for Prevention of Frauds and Perjuries, 29 Car. 2, c.3 (1677).

[26] For one version of its modern statutory expression, see U.C.C. § 2-202.

[27] Corbin has made the most powerful attacks against both these rules on precisely these grounds. "[The Statute of Frauds and the parol evidence rule] appear to have a similar purpose, at least when we regard the latter rule as in truth a rule of admissibility. That purpose is the prevention of successful fraud and perjury. Under both statute and rule, this purpose is only haltingly attained; and if attained at all, it is at the expense and to the injury of many honest contractors." Arthur L. Corbin, The Parole Evidence Rule, 53 Yale L.J. 603, 609 (1944).

[28] There is one other relevant point. The doctrine of unconscionability can be applied as well in cases in which there has been, as a matter of fact, no consent by a party to certain terms contained in standard form agreements. See, for thorough discussions, John E. Murray, Jr., *supra* note 4, at 16-18; W. David Slawson, Mass Contracts: Lawful Fraud in California, 48 So. Calif. L. Rev. 1, 11-14 (1974). Note, however, even where the terms of the written document are not an accurate expression of the agreement between the parties, it is not clear what terms should replace them, especially in more complex commercial arrangements.

to the subject matter of the agreements and to the social positions of the persons who enter into them.[29] The difficult question with unconscionability is not whether it works towards a legitimate end, but whether its application comes at too great a price.

The traditional case of undue influence, though not always so classified, falls under the general rubric of unconscionability.[30] It involves cases in which one person brings to bear psychological pressure of considerable force and duration against the will of another individual who, while of full legal capacity, may be irresolute, feeble or weak. Any agreement between the party who exerts the influence and the party who yields to it is not likely to work in the interests of both; it is much more likely to be the doing of the stronger party even if the formal expression of both. While the weakness of the party under the influence might not be easy for a stranger to detect, it is doubtless known to the party who takes advantage of it. In general the judicial position that allows agreements to be set aside if procured by undue influence seems unexceptionable, even though some cases will, no doubt, fall close to the line. Those who wish to deal with persons who might be subject to such influence are well advised to be sure that independent advice is provided them in order to forestall any possible abuse. And once that is done, whatever agreement is reached can then be enforced under the general rules of contract law.

Another similar case, no longer much litigated, involves the sale of an interest in a trust fund or in real estate.[31] The seller is a young person, but of full age, perhaps encumbered by debts. The buyer is a mature person, experienced in such transactions. The sales price is a fraction of the "real" market value of the property. The argument in favor of setting aside such transactions is not without its merit. The transaction in question could be seen as one in which the buyer takes advantage of the incompetence of the seller, perhaps even by resorting to fraud. In the alternative, we could view it, less ominously, as one where the seller took advantage of the best offer available in a thin market. The "situation sense" of most courts has been that this last construction is in general not the proper one, and on that view the case is ripe for intervention. Here the unconscionability doctrine can (at the cost of upsetting some useful transactions, or otherwise increasing their costs) act as a useful protective rule. Indeed, its greatest importance is not to set aside agreements already formed, but to insure that future transactions

[29] Rules governing incompetence, for example, can be regarded as a special case of those governing unconscionability, particularly since they are a suitable means of preventing fraud and duress. They represent an effort to minimize the errors in the administration of the law of contracts, with as much precision as the judicial process admits.

[30] See Dawson 262. The doctrine applies as well to gifts and bequests, and fits well with Dawson's theory about freedom of the will, as well as with the narrower theory developed here.

[31] See Dawson 267 for a more complete exposition.

will be conducted in a manner that avoids the question of unconscionability entirely. Once the buyer knows of the applicable rules, he can take (as in cases of undue influence) appropriate steps to limit their effect. He can insist that the seller be represented by independent counsel, or that the subject matter of sale be appraised. With these steps thus taken, the courts should then enforce the transactions in accordance with the general principles of contract law, without any resort to unconscionability doctrines, and without any independent examination of the "fairness" of the agreement's substantive terms.[32]

One of the strengths of the unconscionability doctrine is its flexibility, an attribute much needed because it is difficult to identify in advance all of the kinds of situations to which it might in principle apply. One recent case, for example, that appears to warrant the application of unconscionability rules, involves recently returned prisoners of the Vietnam war. After receipt of accumulated back pay, these men were approached by experienced salesmen who proceeded to sell them unattractive municipal bonds. These transactions should as a class be set aside at the option of the buyers. We have here a narrow class of purchasers, vulnerable by reason of their long captivity, given sudden control over substantial funds. Opposite them are salesmen who know how to exploit them. Proof of fraud is apt to be difficult in this case, even if the fraud itself is likely. Setting aside the transaction gives the shrewd buyer a chance to repudiate an arm's length deal he does not like, but it is highly unlikely that many buyers took conscious advantage of this legal benefit. It is also possible that some proper transactions will be set aside, but again those costs are apt to be small, measured against the gains derived. But the limits of the principle must be noted. The case should go the other way if, for example, these men on their own initiative went to a brokerage house to purchase these same bonds.

The limitations on the use of conscionability doctrines are as important as their application. Should, for example, the doctrine be used to protect those who are poor, unemployed, on welfare, or members of disadvantaged racial or ethnic groups? The perils of this course are great. First, it is difficult, if not impossible, to assert that the persons who fall into any or all of these classes are not in general competent to fend for themselves in most market situations. They are not infants, impressionable heirs, or gullible prisoners of

[32] There remains the question of whether courts should look to the ratio of value to price in cases when these procedural safeguards are not observed. In cases in which one deals with specialists in the purchase of such interests, the better answer is probably no, as it seems undesirable to give possible "outs" from the established procedure to those who know of its existence. When, however, the buyer is not experienced in dealings with these interests (as with a brother who buys his sister's land in order to help her out of financial difficulties; see, for example, Jackson v. Seymour, 193 Va. 735, 71 S.E. 2d 181 (1952)), the balance of convenience most likely lies in the other direction.

war. Second, the subject matter of the transactions is for the most part standard consumer goods that are sold in generally competitive markets, and not interests in trust funds or real estate difficult to value even under the best of circumstances. The costs of setting these transactions aside, moreover, are apt to be quite great, for it will be more expensive for members of the "protected" class to contract on their own behalf within a complex web of legal rules. In addition, there will no doubt be both opportunity and incentive for many to take advantage of the rights conferred upon them by law to manipulate the system to their own advantage. The absence of protective rules will have costs, measured by the tainted transactions given full legal effect, but these costs, all things considered, are apt to be lower than those incurred by demanding proof of fraud to set the transactions aside.

In consumer transactions, therefore, it will be necessary to take great care in specifying the circumstances where protective rules should be adopted in order to prevent fraud or duress. One possible case that might warrant the use of such protective rules involves door-to-door salesmen, who often rely on both high pressure tactics and outright fraud to complete a sale.[33] Yet I suspect that the unconscionability doctrine functions at best as a very blunt instrument in cases of this sort, and that it is better to adopt some legislative solution to control the problem.[34] Here for example it is possible to specify a short "cooling off" period in which the buyer is allowed as a matter of positive law to disaffirm the contract of sale at his own option without a showing of fraud or duress. In this context, moreover, it might even be desirable, given the costs of such a rule upon honest merchants, for the legislature to adopt one rule for encyclopedias and quite another for beauty products, particularly if different levels of abuse are involved in the two cases. We are not faced with an elegant question of legal theory or with a moral question of great urgency. The only issue is what combination of common law doctrine and legislative enactment will work to miminize the abuses in consumer transactions.

IV. Substantive Unconscionability

In this last section we shall deal with the doctrine of unconscionability in a way that first puts to one side all the considerations about fraud, duress, and incompetence. Instead, our attention shifts to the cases in which courts will strike down either whole contracts or, more frequently, particular clauses on

[33] See, for example, Frostifresh Corp. v. Reynoso, 52 Misc. 2d 26, 274 N.Y.S. 2d 757 (Dist. Ct. 1966), *rev'd for reassessment of damages,* 54 Misc. 2d 119, 281 N.Y.S. 2d 964 (Sup. Ct. 1967), though even there a case for fraud could be made out.

[34] There is good reason to believe that well-drafted legislation is the appropriate means to control, for example, the abuses of door-to-door selling, for there is too much fact variation between cases for a clear rule to develop by common law adjudication. See Leff, Unconscionability and the Crowd, *supra* note 5, at 353-58.

the ground that they are, as a *substantive* matter only, unfair and unconscionable. It is difficult in the abstract to insist that no contract language invites invalidation for these reasons.[35] But the crucial point is that most clauses that do *in fact* appear in agreements cannot be fairly challenged on those grounds. It is difficult to know what principles identify the "just term," and for the same reasons that make it so difficult to determine the "just price." And the problem with substantive unconscionability is further increased because the clauses so attacked are, at the time of formation, arguably in the interests of both parties to the agreement. I cannot within the compass of this paper examine most, let alone all, of the clauses that have been attacked on substantive grounds over the years. But the examination of a few typical clauses, drawn from both consumer and commercial transactions, can illustrate the pattern of argument appropriate to cases of this sort.

a. *"Add-On" Clauses*

One sort of clause that has come under both judicial and statutory scrutiny is the so-called "add-on" clause used in consumer credit sales. These clauses govern the security interest taken back by the seller, and, in one common form, provide that all previous goods purchased by the buyer from the seller will secure the debts incurred with the current purchase. The security agreement also provides that each payment made with respect to any of the items purchased would be applied against all outstanding balances, allowing the seller in effect to retain his security interest in all the goods sold until the debts with respect to all items are discharged. A single default on a single payment could trigger the plaintiff's right to repossess all the goods subject to the comprehensive security arrangement.[36]

[35] In this context I think it is dangerous to begin the analysis of unconscionability by talking about *hypothetical* clauses that have never appeared in any commercial agreement, particularly if the hypothetical case is then used as an argument in support of real control. As an instance of such clause: "The parties hereby agree that during the first year of operation of this automobile, should the automobile be operated on any Tuesday afternoon by a party wearing a red necktie, all rights in the automobile will be forfeited by the owner and ownership of the auto will revert to the seller." John E. Murray, Jr., Murray on Contracts 746 (1974). It is difficult to see how the clause so invented could ever be used; one would not expect, for example, to find it in jurisdictions that make no use of the unconscionability principle. On the dangers of arguing from imagined cases to real problems, see, R. H. Coase, *supra* note 18.

[36] One such clause, central to the important case of Williams v. Walker-Thomas Furniture Co., 350 F.2d 445 (D.C. Cir. 1965), provided that "the amount of each periodical installment payment to be made by [purchaser] to the Company under this present lease shall be inclusive of and not in addition to the amount of each installment payment to be made by [purchaser] under such prior leases, bills or accounts; and all payments now and hereafter made by [purchaser] shall be credited pro rata on all outstanding leases, bills and accounts due the Company by [purchaser] at the time each such payment is made." These add-on clauses are subject to many different forms, some of which do not extend the time for which the seller has a security interest in the earliest goods sold. See, John A. Spanogle, *supra* note 5, at 961, n.151. If, however, the

Although agreements of this kind can, and have, been attacked on unconscionability grounds, they make good sense in the cases to which they apply. One of the major risks to the seller of personal property is that the goods sold will lose value, be it through use or abuse, more rapidly than the purchase price is paid off. The buyer can, and quite often does, have a "negative" equity in the goods. The seller, therefore, who takes back a security interest only in the goods sold, runs the real risk that repossession of the single item sold will still leave him with a loss on the transaction as a whole, taking into account the costs of interest and collection. One way to handle this problem is to require the purchaser of the goods to make a larger cash down payment, but that, of course, is something which many buyers, particularly those of limited means, do not want to do. Another alternative is for the buyer to provide the seller with additional collateral; yet here the best collateral is doubtless in goods sold by the seller to the buyer. Other goods already in the possession of the buyer may be of uncertain value, and they may well be subject to prior liens. Again, they may be of a sort that the seller cannot conveniently resell in the ordinary course of his business. Even if the goods are suitable collateral for the loan, it could take a good deal of time and effort for the seller to determine that fact. The "add-on " clause allows both parties to benefit from the reduction in costs in the setting up of a security arrangement.

The case for the add-on clauses is strengthened, moreover, when we note its legal effects. As between the buyer and seller the clause allows the seller to collect on his unpaid debt without having to avail himself of the awkward procedures established for unsecured creditors. The clause assures the seller that the value he has furnished the buyer will, if need be, first be used to satisfy his own claims and not those of third parties. The only disadvantage to the buyer therefore is that he will not be able to use the goods purchased to obtain some economic benefit in a subsequent transaction. But it is difficult in a commercial context to see why a seller should not be paid before his buyer or third parties are able to use the goods he furnished for their own satisfaction.

The sense of these clauses, regardless of the particular form which they take, is demonstrated anew, moreover, once we realize that they operate

---

add-on clause used in Williams v. Walker-Thomas makes good economic sense, then these other variations will make good sense as well. In general, add-on clauses have not received a warm welcome in the academic literature. "Such [that is, add-on] clauses are forbidden in any respectable retail installment sales laws and should be held unconscionable in any contract for the purchase of consumer goods not expected to produce money income for the consumer." Robert Braucher, *supra* note 5, at 343. No reason is given why goods that are purchased for pleasure should be treated differently from those purchased for the production of income; as consumption is but a form of imputed income, it is difficult to see what justification could be offered.

within one very strong constraint, often imposed by statute,[37] which restricts the creditor in a secured transaction to the recovery of principal, interest and costs in cases of default by the buyer. Within the framework of these limitations, the add-on clause can do no harm at all, for it only makes it more certain that the seller will be able to collect that to which on any view he is entitled.

b. *"Waiver-of-Defense" Clauses*

Unconscionability arguments have been used to attack other clauses that govern the financing of consumer sales. Thus in many cases where the goods are purchased on an installment contract, the seller's rights under the contract are then sold, usually at a discount, to a finance company, which is then entitled to collect the payments as they come due from the buyer. In order to insulate itself from the disputes between the buyer and the seller of the goods, the company often insists that the original contract of sale include a term for its benefit which requires the buyer to continue to pay his installments to it even if the seller has not made good, for example, his warranty obligations.[38]

In spite of the enthusiasm for consumer protection, it is unwise to strike these clauses down as unconscionable. Suppose the seller sold goods under warranty for cash. The buyer then could only get the seller to honor the warranty by request or, that failing, by legal action; the withholding of payment is no longer a possible alternative. I take it, however, that no one would argue that this arrangement is unconscionable, even though it leaves the buyer at risk on the warranty. Why then should the position be different if he is at risk because he has waived his defenses against the finance company?

[37] See, U.C.C. § 9-501—507, for the applicable statutory provisions in the case of the sale of goods. Note, even these provisions, to the extent they cannot be varied by agreement (§ 9-501(3)), may be unwise in that they increase the administrative costs of repossession even though the goods are likely to be worth little or nothing in excess of the lien.

[38] One such clause reads as follows: "Buyer hereby acknowledges notice that this contract may be assigned and that assignees will rely upon the agreements contained in this paragraph, and agrees that the liability of the Buyer to any assignee shall be immediate and absolute and not affected by any default whatsoever of the Seller signing this contract; and in order to induce assignees to purchase this contract, the Buyer further agrees not to set up any claim against such Seller as a defense, counterclaim or offset to any action by any assignee for the unpaid balance of the purchase price or for possession of the property." Unico v. Owen, 50 N.J. 101, 106, 232 A.2d 405, 408 (1967). The court held the clause unconscionable, basing its decision on both the U.C.C. (§ 2-302; § 9-206) and the common law. These clauses are in part a response to the common law trend that makes it difficult, if not impossible, for third party transferees to be treated as "holders in due course" (U.C.C. § 3-302, *et seq.*). Holders in due course normally take free of "personal defenses," such as breach of warranty, that are effective as between the immediate parties to the contract. For an early case that rejected the plaintiff's holder in due course contention, see Commercial Credit Corp. v. Orange County Machine Works, 34 Cal.2d 766, 214 P.2d 819 (1950), where the plaintiff among other things supplied the finance forms to the seller.

The same point can be made if we consider another alternative method of financing the purchase of consumer goods. Suppose the seller says to the buyer of his goods, "If you wish to buy them on time, you must take out a bank loan for credit." Under that arrangement, the buyer remains unconditionally liable on his note to the bank even if his seller is in breach of his warranty obligation. If that arrangement is not unconscionable, why should it be unconscionable for the buyer to have no remedy against the lender because he happens to be chosen by the seller instead of the buyer?

There are also strong economic reasons that indicate that it is no one's interest, ex ante, to prohibit finance companies from disassociating themselves from the disputes between buyer and seller. The main advantage of seller financing over buyer financing is that it allows the parties to reduce the transaction costs of putting the credit arrangement together when security interests are necessary. Yet if that arrangement is incumbered by involving the finance company in disputes in which it wants no part, then there will be a shift to less desirable modes of financing. If it is argued that the finance companies should be held liable because they are better able to supervise the general activities of sellers, the quick answer is that if that is the case, then they will agree to do so as a matter of course for a fee. The fact that they do not is a strong suggestion that they have neither time nor skill to get involved in the narrow disputes which are apt to arise in consumer cases. What knowledge does the finance company have on the question of whether the buyer tampered with goods or used them in accordance with instructions? If buyers want protection against having to pay the price where there is a defect in the goods in question, then they should deal with sellers who carry their own contracts.[39] Whether that arrangement is preferable as an economic matter to one that contemplates third party financing is *not* the question that should be asked by the legal system. So long as both have their uses, as is likely the case, there is no principled justification for the judicial or legislative prohibition of either of them.

c. *Exclusion of Liability for Consequential Damage*

A close examination of still other clauses that have been incorporated into standard form contracts reveals that they too should be able to escape from the taint of unconscionability. In *Collins v. Uniroyal Inc.*,[40] a case of quite recent vintage, the defendant tire company sold a tire under a contract of sale which contained the following guarantee.

[39] Here one can even take the argument one step farther. If all parties who carry their own contracts refuse to allow breach of warranty to be a complete defense against the payment of installment obligations, there will be a good reason for them so doing: to wit, that most of the claims are manufactured as excuses for non-payment.

[40] 64 N.J. 260, 315 A.2d 16 (1974).

ROAD HAZARD—In addition, every such U.S. Royal Master tire, when used in normal passenger car service, is guaranteed during the life of the original tread against blowouts, cuts, bruises, and similar injury rendering the tire unserviceable. Tires which are punctured or abused, by being run flat, improperly aligned, balanced, or inflated, cut by chains or obstructions on vehicle, damaged by fire, collision or vandalism, or by other means, and "seconds" are not subject to the road hazard provision of this Guarantee.[41]

This Guarantee does not cover consequential damage, and the liability of the manufacturer is limited to repairing or replacing the tire in accordance with the stipulations contained in this Guarantee. No other guarantee or warranty, express or implied, is made.[42]

The purchaser of the tire was killed when the car he was driving went out of control after the tire blew out. The weight of the evidence established that no defect whatsoever in the tire caused the accident, ruling out recovery on any tort theory of products liability. The New Jersey Supreme Court held, however, that the limitation in the warranty against the recovery of consequential damages was unconscionable under the Uniform Commercial Code, and that the defendant accordingly was liable on a contract theory for the death of the decedent.[43]

The Court's argument in support of that conclusion is, I believe, erroneous.[44] Under the New Jersey law, the defendant was required by statute to sell the tire with only a warranty of merchantability, under which its liability is triggered only if the tire is defective. The defendant here gave the buyer an extra measure of protection under its supplemental warranty, without which the plaintiff concededly could have recovered nothing. What is achieved by holding the defendant liable because it gave the plaintiff protection not required by statute when the effect of the decision may well be to *reduce* the protection that sellers will give their purchasers? Is it in the general interest of consumers that Uniroyal *not* include warranties of the sort provided in this case?[45]

[41] *Id.* at 264, 315 A.2d at 19.

[42] *Id.* at 265, 315 A.2d at 19.

[43] "Consequential damages may be limited or excluded unless the limitation or exclusion is unconscionable. Limitation of consequential damages for injury to the person in the case of consumer goods is prima facie unconscionable but limitation of damages where the loss is commercial is not." U.C.C. § 2-719(3). Note that there is no explanation given of the force of the words "prima facie" or what facts might be sufficient to override them. Note too the language of § 2-719 leaves the court that applies it with ample discretion in the particular case.

[44] See, in this connection, the strong dissent of Clifford, J., 64 N.J. at 263, 315 A.2d at 18.

[45] This kind of exclusion is not only found in consumer cases. Exclusions of consequential damages in commercial cases in which there is no question of unconscionability are commonplace. See, for example, Roto-Lith, Ltd. v. F. P. Bartlett & Co., 297 F.2d 497 (1st Cir.

Thus far we have assumed that there is justification for a rule that treats all limitations against recovery for consequential damages for personal injury as prima facie unconscionable.[46] Yet even that restriction itself is not beyond criticism. In typical actions for breach of the warranty of merchantability, the plaintiff must show something beyond his own injury in the use of the goods in order to recover consequential damages. Indeed the very restrictions about proper use and maintenance incorporated into the warranty in *Collins* apply with equal force to the straightforward warranty of merchantability. It might well be wise for a seller to tell his buyers that it is too difficult for him to determine whether a particular injury is attributable to his own manufacture, to the plaintiff's conduct, or to some external cause. The best solution might be to offer the tire at a lower price, leaving the buyer, if he chooses, to purchase insurance elsewhere against this particular risk. In this manner, market mechanisms could work to bring about the best distribution of risks between the parties, superior to that ordained by statute.

d. *"Due-on-Sale" Clauses*

There still are other sorts of clauses that appear in both consumer and commercial transactions. One of these, the "due-on-sale" clause allows a lender to call in the outstanding balance on the loan when the mortgagor either sells his interest in the property or further encumbers it with a second mortgage.[47]

The "due-on-sale" clause has been enforced in order to protect the lender against the deterioration of the underlying property or against the "moral risk" of foreclosure. Its use, however, is quite controversial where there is no threat to the lender's security interest. Suppose, for example, the borrower has a seven per cent mortgage with twenty years left to run. He now wishes to sell his equity, at a time when the interest rate for new loans is ten per

1962) (warranty that excluded the buyer's right to consequential damages if seller's emulsions did not work as described; replacement of emulsion at seller's expense was, however, required); Construction Aggregates Corp. v. Hewitt-Robins, Inc., 404 F2d 505 (7th Cir. 1968) (seller provided buyer with a conveyor system to be used in large engineering works; warranty excluded responsibility for consequential damages).

[46] Note the case could not be decided on process-unconscionability grounds. The exclusion clause was in italics, and the circumstances of sale presumably above suspicion. The Court sought to make something of the defendant's advertisements. "If it only saves your life once, it's a bargain." [64 N.J. 263, 315 A.2d 18] Here, there was, moreover, no proof that the plaintiff purchased on the faith of that advertisement. Even, however, if he did, it could be read to say that the risk of blowouts is quite small, *not* that the defendant took that risk, given the express and conspicuous limitation in the document.

[47] On due-on-sale clauses, see generally, Note, Judicial Treatment of the Due-on-Sale Clause: The Case for Adopting Reasonableness and Unconscionability, 27 Stan. L. Rev. 1109 (1975); and the literature cited, *id.* at 1110, n.4.

cent. In this context, the due-on-sale clause has been challenged as a unreasonable restraint on alienation.[48] The concern is, however, quite misplaced, for it fails to distinguish between restraints on alienation that can be ousted by private agreement and those that cannot. In the latter case, the restraint may well have adverse social effects, by preventing the movement of real estate to its highest and best use. A restriction that may be undone, however, serves a quite different function. It only determines the distribution of the purchase price between the bank (as mortgagee) and the seller (as mortgagor). The clause shifts to the bank the advantage from the increase in interest rates which would otherwise belong to the seller. The truth of this proposition is borne out by an examination of a recent California case, *Tucker v. Lassen Savings & Loan Association*.[49] There the property in question was subject to a mortgage which contained the standard due-on-sale clause. The seller, who had arranged to resell his interest in the property on an installment sale contract, challenged the clause as an unreasonable restraint on alienation, at least where resale was by installment contract. The court unanimously, but mistakenly, upheld his contention. It noted that the due-on-sale clause is acceptable in the normal case because the seller gets from his buyer sufficient funds to pay off the mortgage. With an installment resale, however, it argued that the clause works an unreasonable restraint on alienation because the seller does not receive from the sale the funds to discharge the bank's mortgage. As the bank could not show that the sale impaired its security, its justification for the restraint was weak, and it followed that the restraint as applied was unreasonable.

The first point in the court's argument is that the clause functioned as a restraint on alienation. That view of the situation, however, was belied by the very facts of the case. Before the case had been decided, the three parties involved had provisionally renegotiated the terms of the sale. The buyer received the property as before, although he paid a higher rate of interest to the bank and a smaller sum to the seller. The clause had no effect upon the alienation of the property as such; and indeed the suit was brought by the seller in order to recapture that portion of the price that the clause deflected from him to the bank.

The clause, therefore, was designed to protect the bank against rising interest rates in the event of resale. That protection could have been achieved in other ways, without ever raising the question of unreasonable restraints on alienation. Suppose that the original loan was for two years; no

[48] The applicable section of the California Civil Code, § 711, provides: "Conditions restraining alienation when repugnant to the interest created are void." The "reasonableness" language is of judicial creation. The crucial case is Coast Bank v. Minderhout, 61 Cal.2d 311, 38 Cal. Rptr. 505, 392 P.2d 265 (1964).

[49] 12 Cal.3d 629, 116 Cal. Rptr. 633, 526 P.2d 1169 (1974).

doubt it could be renewed at a higher rate of interest. Or suppose the original loan was for twenty years at a variable rate of interest, but one which did not fall below a certain minimum. No matter: the borrower will be able to exact some benefit for insulating the lender from the downside risk, perhaps in the form of a lower basic interest figure, for the lender will not get something for nothing. If loans of this sort are proper, then due-on-sale clauses, which are but a different means to achieve that same end, must be proper as well.

The opinion of the Court is difficult to accept on a second point. For the restraint on alienation to be reasonable, it demands that the bank show that it has a "legitimate interest" in invoking the clause, where its own financial gain cannot count as that interest.[50] But why must there ever be justification to enforce a contract in accordance with its terms? Why is it inappropriate for a bank to improve its returns from its loans? Is that any more improper than borrowing at the most favorable rates of interest? The Court suggests that the lender's action amounts to an improper exaction of some collateral benefit from its borrower. That argument appeals implicitly to a tort model, as it treats the bank as though it used force to exact benefits from a stranger. But here the bank demands only the imposition provided for in the agreement, while borrower's imposition, for such it is, stands in defiance of the agreement. The burden should be on the borrower to show why the clause should not be enforced, not on the bank to show otherwise. As there is no impact on the alienability of property, one must look elsewhere for that justification, but none is forthcoming.

Its internal logic aside, the effects of the decision are apt to be unfortunate. First, as the case restricts the use of due-on-sale clauses, it is likely that banks will try to offset that loss in part by increasing the rates of interest that they will charge. It is difficult, however, to regard the mandated shift in contractual terms as a benefit to the parties; for if it were, then in a competitive market that solution would be adopted voluntarily. Second, the decision in *Tucker* should create an artificial (though not necessarily compelling) incentive to cast real estate sales in the installment mold, as that mold alone allows buyer and seller to divert to themselves cash that otherwise would go to the bank. A final effect of the *Tucker* rule is that it is likely to subject banks, particularly savings and loan associations, to great financial stress when interest rates rise. These institutions rely on short-term deposits to

[50] Note if the lender's legitimate interests are restricted to the protection of the security and the like, it will follow that clauses that demand repayment when the buyer makes a further *incumbrance* upon the property in general will be treated as improper restraints on alienation, as the original debtor still remains in possession of the property and liable on the note. Indeed, that was the position reached by the California court in La Sala v. American Sav. & Loan Ass'n, 5 Cal. 3d 864, 97 Cal. Rptr. 849, 489 P.2d 1113 (1971). The major exception to this is apt to be in the rare case where the second mortgage is part of a scheme for a disguised sale of the equity, where it is planned at the outset that the "mortgagee" will take possession by virtue of "foreclosure".

fund their long term commitments, particularly for home mortgages. The increase in rates can lead to a withdrawal of short-term deposits, requiring banks to go borrow at high short-term rates, as their long-term mortgages can not be called in. The due-on-sale clauses allow the banks to use the natural turnover in real estate to make themselves relatively short-term lenders, able to participate in the upturn in interest rates. In the long term, banks may be able to use variable interest loans or other devices to reduce the risks arising from sharp changes in the interest rates; but there is no guarantee that this sort of arrangement will meet with consumer acceptance.

e. *"Termination-at-will" Clauses*

Unconscionability arguments are not restricted to consumer contexts. To take but one instance of its application in commercial cases, consider a provision common to many franchise agreements that allows the franchisor to terminate the franchise at will, without, in other words, having to give any justification for his actions. The attack against such clauses is based upon the belief that they allow the franchisor to act as a tyrant, who can cut off his franchisee at whim, even before he has recouped his start-up costs in the venture.[51]

While these clauses are indeed open to this kind of abuse, there are reasons that make their adoption work in general in the interests of both parties to the agreement. The franchisor is concerned with, first, the profitability of the particular outlet and, second, with the impact that its operation will have upon his entire enterprise. If the franchise could be terminated only "with cause," his settlement costs on termination are apt to be high no matter what the circumstances, for the franchisee always could litigate the matter. If those costs deter the franchisor from termination, he loses the benefits of a substitute franchisee, while being forced to suffer from the continued erosion of his good will. All these costs are reduced, if not eliminated, if termination can be at will.

From the point of view of the franchisee, the clause need not work harm, and may do good. If the franchisee makes a good profit, it will not, in general, be in the economic interest of the franchisor to invoke the clause, as termination of the franchise will make him worse off. Indeed, the good

[51] See, for example, M. P. Ellinghaus, *supra* note 5, at 809, for a statement of the position. The argument against the clause based upon "public policy" was rejected, though uneasily, in Bushwick-Decatur Motors, Inc. v. Ford Motor Co., 116 F.2d 675 (2d Cir. 1940). The argument in favor of the franchisee received, at least in part, legislative sanction in the Automobile Dealer's Day in Court Act of 1956, 70 Stat. 1125, 15 U.S.C. § 1221-25 (1956), which provides, inter alia, that the termination of an automobile franchise must be made in "good faith." The "good faith" requirement is defined negatively, as the "duty of each party to any franchise . . . to act in a fair or equitable manner toward each other so as to guarantee . . . freedom from coercion, intimidation, or threats" thereof, § 1221(e). The position implicit in the negative portion of this good faith requirement echoes the arguments advanced in the body of the paper on the proper grounds for disregarding contractual arrangements. The affirmative requirement of "good faith" is in itself of uncertain effect.

franchisee may well want a termination-at-will clause to be included in *all* franchise agreements, because he may rightly perceive that the franchisor acts in his interest when he terminates a weak franchisee whose conduct erodes the goodwill of the entire enterprise, including his own. The real conflict, in other words, is not between franchisor and franchisee, but between franchisee and franchisee, as the franchisor acts in effect as the *de facto* agent of the superior franchisees. Where termination appears warranted, moreover, a franchisor has incentives to act in a manner which, no matter how informal, appears to be fair if he wishes to retain his other franchisees and attract new franchisees. When we look, therefore, at both the economic pressures and the contract terms, the termination-at-will clause may well be the best solution for both parties. The issue is not whether the clause will be required, but only whether it should be allowed. On that question, there is no need for judicial or legislative intervention so long as there are common circumstances in which the use of this clause is appropriate. Those who might wish to ban the use of the clause labor under a much greater burden than those who only want to permit its use, and that burden is not met by the invocation of unconscionability arguments.

CONCLUSION

In this paper I have sought to defend against modern attacks the principle of freedom of contract which was central to the classical common law. Properly understood, that position does not require a court to enforce every contract brought before it. It does, however, demand that the reasons invoked for not enforcing the contract be of one of two sorts. Either there must be proof of some defect in the process of contract formation (be it duress, fraud or undue influence); or there must be, but only within narrow limits, some incompetence of the party against whom the agreement is to be enforced. The doctrine of unconscionability is important in both these respects because it can, if wisely applied, allow the courts to police these two types of problems, and thereby improve the general administration of the contract law. Yet when the doctrine of unconscionability is used in its substantive dimension, be it in a commercial or consumer context, it serves only to undercut the private right of contract in a manner that is apt to do more social harm than good. The result of the analysis is the same even if we view the question of unconscionability from the lofty perspective of public policy. "[I]f there is one thing which more than another public policy requires, it is that men of full age and competent understanding shall have the utmost liberty of contracting, and that their contracts when entered into freely and voluntarily shall be held sacred and shall be enforced by Courts of justice."[52]

[52] Printing and Numerical Registering Co. v. Sampson, L.R. 19 Eq. 462, 465 (1875).

Rings and Promises

MARGARET F. BRINIG
George Mason University

1. INTRODUCTION

My mother had an engagement ring, but neither of my grandmothers did, although both my grandfathers were wealthy enough to afford them. Before 1930, diamond rings were certainly available. The South African diamond mines were discovered in 1880, and they soon replaced the rapidly disappearing supply of diamonds from India and Brazil (McCarthy). In fact, the first reported diamond engagement ring was given by the Emperor Maximilian to Mary of Burgundy in 1377 (Kunz: 234–35). Diamonds were associated in this country with engagement beginning in the 1840s, although they were at first given to men as well as women (Rothman: 161).

However, before the Depression, diamond rings were not considered a requisite for betrothal by most Americans. (Kunz: 230; Rothman: 161). What then made women rather suddenly demand diamonds on the occasion of their engagement, so that by 1945 the "typical" bride wore "a brilliant diamond engagement ring and a wedding ring to match in design?" (McCarthy: frontispiece).

I wish to acknowledge the thoughtful contributions of many colleagues, especially including Barry Adler, William Bishop, Steven Crafton, and Steven Eagle of the law faculty, and Michael Alexeev, Robert Tollison, and Jenny Wahl of the economics departments of George Mason University and St. Olaf's College. David Levy of George Mason gave invaluable help with the econometrics. Thanks is also owed to my research assistant, Laurie LaCorte, and three anonymous referees.

Journal of Law, Economics, and Organization vol. 6, no. 1 Spring 1990
 ISSN 8756-6222

The diamond ring rapidly changed from a relatively obscure token of affection to what amounted to an American tradition. It is customary to explain such a shift in demand in terms of an increase in income, a change in relative prices, or a change in tastes. This assumes a stable legal setting—that contracts are enforceable. But if the enforceability of a contract is problematic, what formerly was a relatively costly (hence unused) form of private ordering may become more viable (Kronman: 5).[1] This paper looks at the change in America's demand for diamonds during the period 1930–1985, not as a Madison Avenue success story, but rather as a natural outgrowth of economic processes. The event beginning the movement toward diamond engagement rings was the abolition, with great fanfare, of a now relatively obscure cause of action called the "breach of promise to marry."

2. THE BREACH OF PROMISE ACTION

The breach of promise action entitled a woman whose fiancé had broken off their engagement to sue him in assumpsit for damages, including the actual expenses she had incurred in reliance on the marriage. She might also recover for her embarrassment, humiliation, and loss of other marriage opportunities.[2]

Until fairly recently, a woman's marriage was necessary to secure her social position. An "old maid" would not only be scorned because she was not attractive enough to snag a husband, but also would be disadvantaged because in later life she would not be secure financially (*Wightman v. Coates*, 15 Mass. 2, 2–4 (1918); Glendon: 31–32; Craik: 166–67; Grossberg: 36). Marriage was, as one writer noted, the "one career open to her," and once she had made her choice of husbands, the woman's "options were suddenly, irrevocably gone" (Rothman: 163; Brinig and Carbone: 872–74).

But there was more to the doctrine than this. Many, if not most, women

1. Other forms of property have been exchanged at engagement or marriage since antiquity. The dower gift of land or livestock by the bride's father would be returned by the man if the marriage was not consummated, but it did not belong to the woman in any event. Since the man could presumably marry his second choice, obtaining a like dower price, he would not be substantially damaged. She, however, might be precluded from marrying as well, and she might be precluded from marrying at all if she had lost her virginity (Jenks: 313). The transformation of agrarian forms of wealth to less tangible assets may be one reason why rings, as opposed to other gifts, became useful (Glenn, 1981). The breaking of a formal engagement, with return of property, was the type of "divorce" originally contemplated by Joseph in the Bible story when he was confronted by Mary's pregnancy (Matthew 1:19–20).

2. The early action for breach of promise to marry was within the jurisdiction of the English ecclesiastical courts, and in many cases the filing of the action resulted in specific performance of the marriage contract rather than an award of damages since the man was financially coerced into marriage to prevent the suit (Jenks: 303; Grossberg: 34). One of the reasons given in favor of abolishing the action was that these forced marriages ought not to be encouraged (*Fearon v. Treanor*, 272 N.Y. 268, 5 N.E.2d 815, 817 (1936); *Virginia Law Review:* 314; *Marquette Law Review:* 341).

who brought such actions had not only lost a husband, but also their virginity. Particularly during the period between the two world wars, a woman was expected to remain chaste until the time of her engagement (Kinsey, 1948a: 336, 1948b: 364; Gebhard and Johnson: 288). Once she was betrothed, however, sexual intimacy with her fiancé reportedly occurred nearly half the time (Kinsey, 1948a: 336; 1948b: 364). All this was well and good, but if the marriage never came about, she was irretrievably barred from offering an unblemished self to a new suitor[3] and suffered a loss in "market value" (Feinsinger, 1935a: 983). While a man could pretend inexperience, a woman's virginity or lack of it was a verifiable physical fact.[4] Because of the importance of premarital chastity, damages in breach of promise actions where seduction (intercourse) had occurred were far more substantial than in cases where no sexual intimacy was alleged (*Paul v. Frazier*, 3 Mass. 71, 73 (1807); Grossberg: 46–47). The trials themselves frequently became public spectacles because of testimony regarding the woman's previous chastity (or lack of the same).[5] By the beginning of the Depression, the breach of promise suit came to be regarded as legally sanctioned blackmail, a threat to marriage and the family (Grossberg: 62–63).[6]

In 1935, a legislator from Indiana sponsored a bill abolishing the heart-balm actions in that state (Byrnes: 94; *Marquette University*). Almost immediately thereafter, similar statutes were passed in most of the other major urban jurisdictions,[7] so that by 1945, sixteen states had eliminated breach of marriage promise.[8] Today, there are only scattered reported breach of marriage promise decisions from those few jurisdictions where the action remains viable.

3. *Bennett v. Beam*, 42 Mich. 346, 351 (1880); *Scharringhaus v. Hazen*, 269 Ky. 425, 107 S.W.2d 329 (1937); *Berry v. Da Costa* [1966] L.R., 1 C.P. 331); Cousens: 372.

4. One author notes that "our courts seem to demand only that the plaintiff be *virgo intacta*. All is a question of the condition of the flesh. The mind may be poisoned with filth, and the character hardened by ugly habits; in short, the spiritual hymen may have suffered many a breach, but if the physical one is not intact, the defendant will have no better alternative than to marry her or pay damages" (Brockelbank: 8).

5. *Van Houten v. Morse*, 162 Mass. 414, 38 N.E. 705 (1894); *Barrett v. Vander-Meulen*, 264 Ky. 441, 94 S.W.2d 983 (1936); *Baylor Law Review.*

6. There are relatively few appellate breach of promise cases that have been reported at any time. This might be because the action has never had a great deal of use. It is more probable, however, that in most cases there was no interesting legal question involved that was worth the various costs of an appeal to the defendant, that the case was "settled" by marriage of the parties either before a trial or after a verdict for damages, or that the very fact that the action existed deterred men from breaking engagements. For a discussion of the deterrent effect of laws regarding morality, see Devlin.

7. In 1935, in addition to Indiana, breach of promise actions were abolished in Alabama, Illinois, New York, New Jersey, Michigan, and Pennsylvania.

8. These states, with the year of legislation, are North Dakota (1877), Illinois (1935), Indiana (1935), New Jersey (1935), Pennsylvania (1935), Alabama (1935), New York (1935), Michigan (1935), Colorado (1937), Massachusetts (1938), California (1939), Maine (1941), Wyoming (1941), New Hampshire (1941), Nevada (1943), and Florida (1945).

3. DEMAND FOR DIAMONDS

At the same time the cause of action for breach of promise was being reconsidered, the diamond industry had faced a period of lessened demand and increased supply. For a few years following 1932, diamonds were stockpiled in Europe to prevent a glut on the market (Epstein, 1982a: 85–87). By the mid-1930s, DeBeers, the diamond-importing institution, was holding stocks valued at four times its annual sales (Koskoff: 272). New sources of diamonds had been discovered, particularly in the Soviet Union, and the price of diamonds had been in decline for some years (Koskoff: 272).[9]

There was not only a greater supply but also a reduced demand, for sales during the twenty-year period prior to 1939 declined by nearly 100 percent (Epstein, 1982b: 122–23). National advertising was thought of as "vulgar" before the Great Depression (Koskoff: 272), but in 1939, four years after the first states abolished the breach of promise action, DeBeers formed an alliance with a prominent New York advertising agency, Ayers, and prepared to release a significant advertising campaign focused on the slogan that "a diamond is forever" (Koskoff).

The advertising agency from the start aimed at a national market. One of its more successful techniques was exploitation of the burgeoning film industry: Hollywood stars were given large and conspicuous diamonds to wear off stage, and special scenes involving the presentation of engagement rings were introduced into popular movies after intervention by Ayers (Epstein, 1982b: 123–32), a notable example of which is the Mae West–Cary Grant classic *She Done Him Wrong.*[10]

The industry enjoyed a phenomenal success during the period following 1935, and by 1965, 80 percent of all brides chose diamond engagement rings (Ward et al.: 144). DeBeers attributed the changing market to the Ayers advertising campaign (Epstein, 1982b: 125–63), but, in fact, the market for diamonds began its growth four years before national advertising when the breach of promise action was first abolished in a significant number of important states. (North Dakota had abrogated breach of marriage promise actions

9. The diamond industry, which is represented by one importer, DeBeers (Epstein, 1982a: 23), has completely controlled the quantity of diamonds brought into the United States since its organization in South Africa in 1888 (Epstein, 1982a: 23; 1982b: 81). DeBeers therefore could meter the supply of diamonds, setting price according to the downward-sloping demand curve characteristic of a monopoly.

10. The sentiments of the heroine in that movie are echoed in the trial court's observations in *Goldstein v. Rosenthal*, 56 N.Y. Misc. 2d 311, 288 N.Y.S.2d 503 (1968): "When the burning blue white flames of romance died out, all that was left was the blue white diamond. The defendant does not wish to keep plaintiff's hand, but she does wish to keep his ring on her finger. In the words of the popular song: 'She took it off her finger, now it doesn't mean a thing.'"

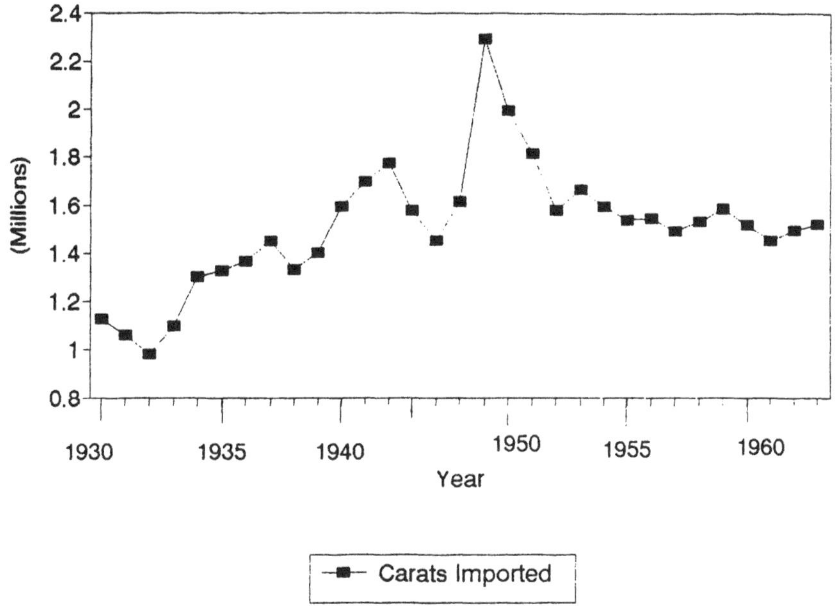

Figure 1. Diamond imports by year.

in the nineteenth century, but they were at least theoretically available in the other 47 states.[11])

The selection of states that abolished the action in the ten years following 1935 itself presents an interesting study. A glance at a map shows that they appear to have little in common: both urban and farm states, with an average per capita income approximating the norm for the period. What is interesting, however, is that the marriage rate in these states before abolition of the action greatly exceeded the contemporary national rate (67 percent of the United States marriages in 1935, with only 47.7 percent of the population). This suggests that the action for damages made people marry who otherwise would not. The scanty legislative history for the statutes abolishing breach of promise indicates that one motivation, and perhaps the primary one, may have been removal of a vestige of women's historic legal inferiority to men

11. In most of the discussion in the text, I have ignored the fact that North Dakota apparently has had a statute abolishing breach of promise since 1877. This may have been because it was one of the original "divorce mill" states, enjoying popularity for dissolution of marriage during the period 1871–99 (Jones: 25 (map), 33 (text)). As with Nevada, there may have been a corresponding rise in the marriage rate during that time. Unfortunately, the best statistical study (U.S. Bureau of the Census, 1968: Table 7, p. 28) does not contain any information about the Dakotas prior to 1890.

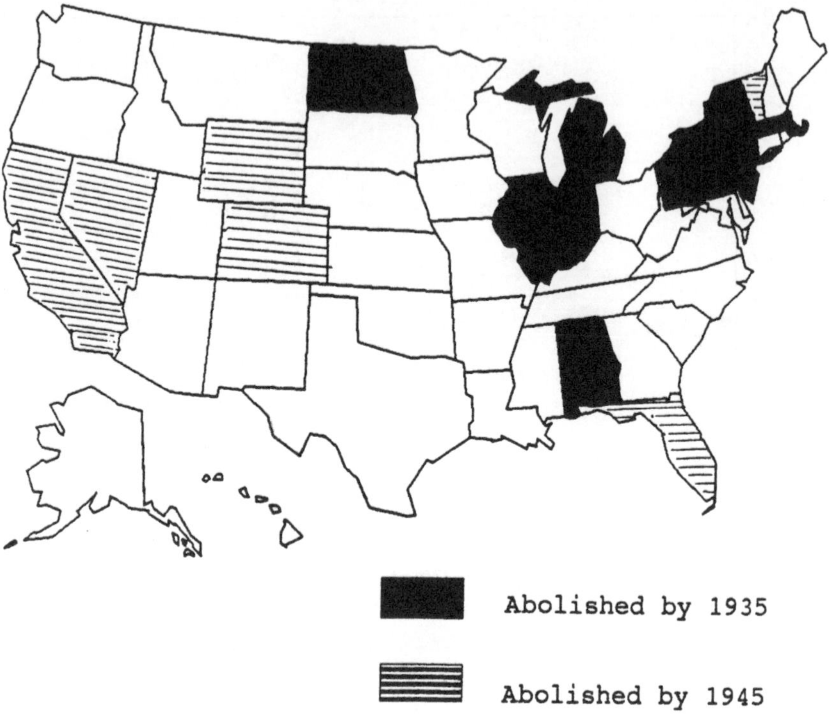

Figure 2. States abolishing breach of promise.

(Feinsinger, 1935a). States especially concerned with gender equality would therefore be expected to be the leaders in this reform, and some were involved at an early stage in the abolition movement. Other states abolishing breach of promise before 1945, including Nevada, Alabama, Florida, and Indiana, had always been important sources for migratory divorces.

4. EXPLAINING THE CHANGE IN DEMAND

The change in demand for diamonds can be studied empirically by analyzing the various factors that might have led to an increased desire for diamonds and observing what turns out to be the most significant. The dramatic increase in demand could be the result of a dramatic decrease in price. Or DeBeers' national advertising campaign could have caused the surge in popularity of diamonds.[12] This has certainly been the position taken by the industry (Epstein, 1982b). The hypothesis of interest here, the bond or

12. This does not explain the changes before 1939, the year when the Ayers agency assumed the DeBeers account.

pledge hypothesis,[13] is that the statutory changes abolishing the breach of promise action explain the increase in the demand for diamonds.

An alternative explanation is that Americans during and after the Depression began to prefer holding their portfolio in tangible assets that would be more secure than paper currency or bank deposits. In particular, it is possible that diamonds served an investment function during the uncertain financial climate of World War II. The thesis that investment patterns changed does not fit the more modern data, however, because the decline of interest in diamond engagement rings began before the relaxation in regulation of financial institutions that has led to Americans holding wealth in more liquid forms. In addition, advertising by the diamond industry should have tempered any trend toward the substantial use of diamonds for investment. One important component of the massive advertising campaign was designed to convince the public that diamonds could not be resold, and the DeBeers cartel has enforced this by threatening to cut off supply to dealers who bought diamonds back from purchasers (Epstein, 1982a: 25).

It is difficult, if not impossible, to get information about engagement ring sales fifty or more years ago, since even the large and well-known New York jewelers did not keep sales records by such categories at that time. A proxy for diamond sales in general, of which engagement rings were by all accounts the largest portion (Koskoff; Epstein, 1982b), can be found by examining the quantity of diamonds imported into the United States. However, even these figures become complicated by the emigration of most diamond cutters from Europe to the United States during the period 1938–40 (Historical Abstracts). Before this time, most diamonds used in engagement rings were cut in Europe and imported as cut diamonds. After this time, the cutting took place in New York, so that uncut diamonds of gem quality made up the majority of imports (Epstein, 1982b). My analysis therefore uses as a dependent variable a composite of figures reflecting cut gem quality diamonds before 1939 and uncut diamonds thereafter.[14] Independent variables to test

13. The utility of a diamond ring as collateral depends upon whether it belongs to the nonbreaching party. Even in Roman law, this was true in the case of engagement rings (*Tulane University*: 501). "The ring is a pledge to bind the contract to marry and it is given on the understanding that the party who breaks the contract must return it" (*Jacobs v. Davis*, [1917] K.B. 532). This conditional gift rule has survived the abolition of the breach of contract to marry in most states. See, e.g., *Bohn v. Lowe*, 146 Mich. App. 325, 379 N.W.2d 485 (1985); *Friedman v. Geller*, 82 Misc. 2d 291, 368 N.Y.S.2d 980 (1975); *Urbanus v. Burns*, 300 Ill. App. 207, 20 N.E.2d 869 (1939); *Gikas v. Nicholis*, 71 A.2d 785 (N.H. 1950); *Pavlicic v. Vogtsberger*, 390 Pa. 502, 136 A.2d 127 (1957); *Ruehling v. Hornung*, 98 Pa. Super. 535 (1939). Great Britain reaches a similar result by statute. Law Reform (Miscellaneous Provisions) Act 1970 (c.33) section 3(2).

Of course the reciprocal is true: a breach by the donor (man) would enable the donee (woman) to retain the ring. (*Sloine v. Levine*, 11 N.J. Misc. 899, 168 A. 849 (1933); *Notre Dame Lawyer*: 687).

14. The industry, which has kept detailed records of sales only for the last eight years and has been organized (through the Ayers agency) only since 1938, has no records by state, by

the hypotheses of interest are price (PRICE), advertising (ADSDUMMY),[15] the percentage of population living in states abolishing the action (PERCENT), and investment during World War II (WARDUMMY).[16] I also include as an explanatory variable the population of marriageable age (POP), as that surely will affect demand independent of the various hypotheses. Given the number of endogenous right-hand side variables in this demand equation, a system of equations—with dependent variables demand, price, and percentage of states with statutes abolishing breach of promise actions—was estimated by Three Stage Least Squares (3SLS).

The explanatory variables for the price chosen by DeBeers (PRICE) are the presence of the advertising campaign conducted by DeBeers (ADSDUMMY), per capita income (PCINC), and the stock of "used" diamonds (USEC).[17] The explanatory variables for the third equation, explaining which states abolished the breach of promise action, are the marriage rate (MARRIAGE), per capita income (PCINC), and a time series function (YEAR).

A Box-Cox study (Judge et al.: 555) of these equations revealed that they were not linear. Logarithmic transformations were therefore done on the non-dummy variables, and a 3SLS regression was performed on the transformed equations. The regression results are summarized in Table 1.

The data show that four factors explain much of the increase in the number of diamonds demanded in the period 1935–1960. The most important explanatory variable is the abolition of the breach of promise action. The standardized β coefficient of the bonding hypothesis variable is the largest at 0.52, and it is statistically significant. The population of marriageable age was also significant, with the second largest β coefficient of 0.36. The World War

---

merchant, or even by type of jewelry for these earlier years. The most reliable data come from *Navigation and Trade*, a journal available in the U.S. Department of Commerce library, and the original source for the Statistical Abstracts. These figures at least separate diamonds suitable for jewelry from those useful only in industry. Not even these figures are available for 1939, 1943, 1945, and 1947.

15. A dummy variable was included to represent the presence or absence of advertising because expenditures for the DeBeer's campaign are not available.

16. Because World War II might have made importation difficult or increased the desire to hold diamonds for investment purposes, a dummy variable for war/no war was put into the regression equation. Ruling out a more general investment hypothesis involves substantial data collection problems. One problem, again, is that the jewelry industry has no figures on jewelry sales during this period, and in any event, does not keep data for diamonds as opposed to other jewelry sold. Both gold and silver might have been used for secure investment as well as diamonds, but both are produced to some extent in the United States, so that import data do not account for the whole supply. Further, both precious metals are used industrially as well as for investment purposes. Government import figures separate gem-quality from industrial-type diamonds.

17. Since diamonds are a durable good, the stock of diamonds already sold should have an effect on price (Bulow). Although DeBeers' campaign was in part designed to convince the public that "diamonds were forever" and not to be resold, the stock of diamonds in the United States was also included as a variable.

Table 1. Regression Analysis (3SLS)

Variable	Coefficient	St. Error	*T*-Ratio	β
PRICE[a]				
ADSDUMMY	0.35772	0.11383	3.1425	0.53298
LOGPCINC	0.59504	0.12517	4.7538	1.2019
LOGUSEC	−0.19363	0.63622E-01	−3.0434	−0.85784
LOGCOMPOSIT[b]				
WARDUMMY	−0.87820	0.24987	−3.5146	−0.32495
ADSDUMMY	−0.19739	0.60364	−0.32699	−0.095013
LOGPERCENT	0.33977	0.11866	2.8635	0.51525
LOGPOP	2.4111	0.87293	2.7621	0.36042
LOGPRICE	0.86328	0.71901	1.2007	0.27891
LPERCENT[c]				
LOGMARR	4.3610	1.0878	4.0089	0.45748
LOGPCINC	0.076996	0.90321	−0.085247	−0.033133
LOG YEAR	218.43	103.23	2.1160	0.83156

Note: System $R^2 = 0.9797$; χ^2 −116.91 with 11 D.F.
[a]*f*(ADSDUMMY, LOGPCINC, LOGUSEC)
[b]*f*(WARDUMMY, ADSDUMMY, LOGPERCENT, LOGPOP, LOGPRICE)
[c]*f*(LOGMARR, LOGPCINC, LOGYEAR)

II dummy was almost as important as marriageable population (β = 0.33) and was also significant, although it is negatively related to diamond demand. This suggests that the hardships and absences of the war had a greater effect on demand than the desire to purchase diamonds as investment instruments. Although there is a fourth variable with a sizable β coefficient, price (β = 0.28), it is not statistically significant.[18] These results support the hypothesis that abolition of the breach of promise action created a need for a bonding device, a need fulfilled by the diamond engagement ring.

5. MODERN DEMAND FOR DIAMOND ENGAGEMENT RINGS

Another way of testing the hypothesis that diamond engagement rings serve as pledges is to see what happened to the demand for rings when social mores changed so that sexual intimacy was no longer confined to marriage and engagement.[19] Although from 1965 to 1980 real per capita income con-

18. The insignificance of the estimated coefficient shows that nothing can be assumed from the addition of price to the equation. To the extent that the positive sign means anything, it is suggestive of a series of positive supply points or the outward movement of the demand curve. As Table 1 indicates, the price of diamonds set by DeBeers was largely a function of its advertising campaign (raising the price), per capita income, showing that prices could be raised as people had more to spend on "luxury" goods, and the increasing stock of diamonds (negatively related).

The final endogenous variable, the abolition of the breach of promise action, was positively related to a state's high marriage rate and to the time trend variable.

19. This is not to say that there is no current relationship between permission for sexual

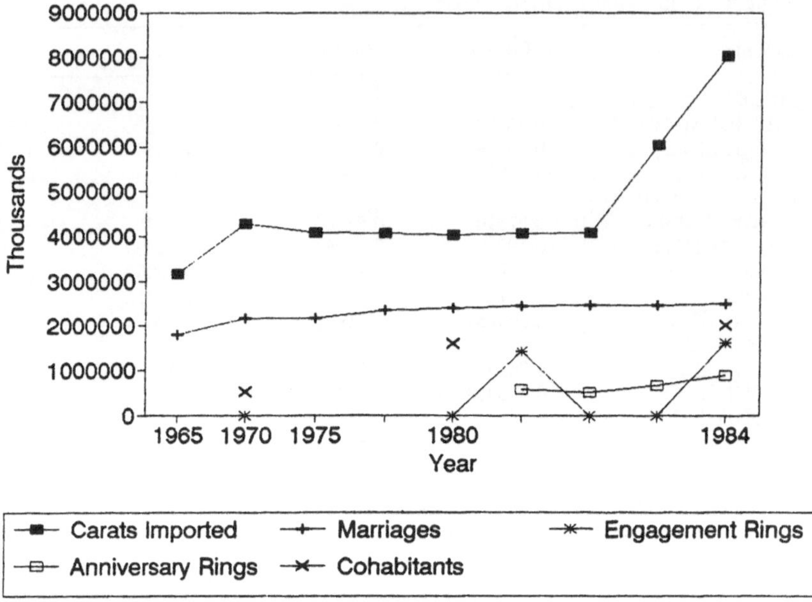

Figure 3. Modern trends.

tinued to increase, the demand for engagement rings leveled off and actually decreased for this more recent period, when cohabitation of nonmarried couples was no longer a curiosity (Koskoff: 273–74, 277).

There has been a recent decline in the number of marriages as more women enter the job market and more couples postpone marriage until education is complete and careers established (England and Farkas). However, since sexual activity by women is not so completely confined to marriage, the current need for a bonding device before consent to intercourse is greatly diminished. DeBeers has had to reach a new market: diamond ads of the late 1980s no longer show engagement rings, but rather diamond-studded wedding bands, anniversary rings, and other diamond jewelry. Ayers' statistics show that since 1980, and unlike the earlier period, engagement rings have never exceeded 20 percent of diamond jewelry sales (Ayers Research: 6–7).[20] Although diamond sales in general increased, the demand for

intercourse and the wearing of the engagement ring. Interestingly, Ayers, the public relations firm for the DeBeers organization, notes that the element of "surprise, even if it is feigned, plays the same role of accommodating dissonance in accepting a diamond gift as it does in prim sexual seductions: it permits the woman to pretend that she has not actively participated in the decision" (Epstein, 1982b: 138). A recent *Life* magazine ad for DeBeers is suggestively captioned "Want to Turn on the Heat?" (February, 1989).

20. Unfortunately, because no statistics were kept in the earlier period, one must rely on

engagement rings has changed, for the wearing of a diamond symbolic of engagement is no longer a prerequisite to premarital intimacy and because the cost to a woman of a broken engagement is no longer as significant.

6. CONCLUSION

Students of economics are told that demand curves shift outward because of changes in demographics or, less frequently, tastes. Becker and Stigler argued that, in fact, tastes are relatively constant: that any widespread human behavior can be explained by utility maximization (76). They illustrated their theory by discussing such "tastes" as those for addiction, custom and tradition, and advertising. Although they presented a sophisticated mathematical model, they did not attempt to test their hypotheses empirically. This is an empirical study that proves them as well as Kronman right: looking at one such change in tastes with a less than obvious economic explanation, I have found some evidence that engagement rings were part of an extralegal contract guarantee, so that the "ring is a pledge to bind the contract to marry and it is given on the understanding that the party who breaks the contract must return it" (*Jacobs v. Davis*, [1917] 2 K.B. 532).

The change in demand for diamond engagement rings may therefore be explained by an increase in need for such a bond because of the abolition of a cause of action for breach of marriage promise. My guess, having apparently found a reason for the change in demand for diamond engagement rings, is that many other mysterious demand changes could be accounted for as well, given some thought as to what the commodity might mean to consumers and some exploration of the legal or other changes of the time during which the demand change occurred.

REFERENCES

Ayers Research. 1987. *The Market for Diamond Jewelry—United States—1986*. New York: N. W. Ayers.

Baylor Law Review. 1965. "Comment: Breach of Promise to Marry," *Baylor Law Review* 51.

Becker, Gary, and George Stigler. 1977. "De Gustibus Non Est Disputandum," 69 *American Economic Review* 76.

Brinig, Margaret, and June Carbone. 1988. "The Reliance Interest in Marriage and Divorce," 62 *Tulane Law Review* 855.

Brockelbank, W. J. 1946. "The Nature of the Promise to Marry—A Study in Comparative Law," 41 *Illinois Law Review* 1.

---

qualitative evidence that engagement rings constituted the bulk of the diamond trade. Certainly the secondary sources believe that this is so (Epstein, 1982b; Koskoff, 1981). Further, the massive advertising directed at the market for diamond engagement rings suggests their importance to the industry.

Bulow, Jeremy. 1982. "Durable-Goods Monopolists," 90 *Journal of Political Economy* 314.

Byrnes, Jane. 1943. "The Illinois Anti-Heart Balm Law," 38 *Illinois Law Review* 94.

Cousens, Theodore. 1932. "The Law of Damages as Applied to Breach of Promise of Marriage," 17 *Cornell Law Quarterly* 367.

Craik, Elizabeth. 1984. *Marriage and Property.* Aberdeen: Aberdeen University Press.

Devlin, Sir Patrick. 1961. *Law and Morals.* Birmingham: Holdsworth Club of the University of Birmingham.

Ellman, Ira. 1989. "The Theory of Alimony," 77 *California Law Review* 1.

England, Paula, and Gary Farkas. 1986. *Households, Employment and Gender.* New York: Aldine Publications.

Epstein, Edward, 1982a. "Have You Ever Tried to Sell a Diamond?" *Atlantic Monthly* 23.

———. 1982b. *The Rise and Fall of Diamonds.* New York: Simon and Schuster.

Feinsinger, N. P., 1935a. "Legislative Attack on 'Heart Balm,'" 33 *Michigan Law Review* 979.

———. 1935b. "Current Legislation Affecting Breach of Promise to Marry, Alienation of Affections, and Related Actions," 10 *Wisconsin Law Review* 417.

Gebhard, Paul, and Alan Johnson. 1979. *The Kinsey Data: Marginal Tabulations of the 1938–63 Interviews Conducted by the Institute for Sex Research.* Philadelphia: Saunders.

Glendon, Mary Ann. 1981. *The New Family and the New Property.* Boston: Butterworths.

Grossberg, Michael. 1985. *Governing the Hearth.* Chapel Hill: University of North Carolina Press.

Jenks, Edward. 1913. *A Short History of English Law.* Boston: Little, Brown.

Jones, Mary. 1987. *An Historical Geography of Changing Divorce Law in the United States.* New York: Garland.

Judge, George, Carter Hill, William Griffiths, Helmut Luthepohl, and Lee Tsoung-Chao. 1988. *Introduction to the Theory and Practice of Econometrics.* New York: John Wiley.

Kane, Frederick. 1936. "Heart Balm and Public Policy," 5 *Fordham Law Review* 66.

Kinsey, Alfred, Wardell Pomeroy, and Clyde Martin. 1948a. *Sexual Behavior in the Human Female.* Philadelphia: Saunders.

———. 1948b. *Sexual Behavior in the Human Male.* Philadelphia: Saunders.

Koskoff, David. 1981. *The Diamond World.* New York: Harper & Row.

Kronman, Anthony. 1985. "Contracts in a State of Nature," 1 *Journal of Law, Economics, and Organization* 5.

Kunz, George. 1917. *Rings for the Finger.* Philadelphia: J. B. Lippincott.

Marquette Law Review. 1959. "Comment, Abolition of Breach of Promise in Wisconsin—Scope and Constitutionality," 43 *Marquette Law Review* 341.

McCarthy, James. 1945. *Rings Through the Ages.* New York: Harper and Brothers.

Notre Dame Lawyer. 1956. "Comment: Recovery of Antenuptial Gifts," 25 *Notre Dame Lawyer* 684.

Rothman, Ellen. 1987. *Hands and Hearts: A History of Courtship in America.* Cambridge, MA: Harvard University Press.

Tulane Law Review. 1950. "Note, Obligations—Breach of Promise to Marry, Art. 1934, La. Civil Code of 1870," 24 *Tulane Law Review* 501.

United States Bureau of the Census. 1987. *The Historical Abstracts.*

United States Department of Commerce, various years. *Navigation and Trade.*

United States Department of Health, Education and Welfare, 1968. *100 Years of Marriage and Divorce Statistics, United States, 1867–1967.*

Virginia Law Review. 1947. "Comment, Twelve Years with the 'Heart Balm Acts,'" 33 *Virginia Law Review* 314.

Ward, Ann, John Cherry, Charlotte Gere, and Barbara Cartlidge. 1981. *Rings Through the Ages.* New York: Rizzoli.

Wisconsin Law Review. 1935. "Comment, Current Legislation Affecting Breach of Promise to Marry, Alienation of Affections, and Related Actions," 10 *Wisconsin Law Review* 417.

THE ECONOMICS OF THE BABY SHORTAGE*

*ELISABETH M. LANDES*** and *RICHARD A. POSNER****

INTRODUCTION

Although economists have studied extensively the efforts of government to regulate the economy, public regulation of social and personal life has largely escaped economic attention. With the rapid development of the economic analysis of nonmarket behavior, the conceptual tools necessary for the economic study of social (as distinct from narrowly economic) regulation are now at hand.[1] Nor is there any basis for a presumption that government does a good job of regulating nonmarket behavior; if anything, the negative presumption created by numerous studies of economic regulation[2] should carry over to the nonmarket sphere. An example of nonmarket regulation that may be no less perverse than the widely criticized governmental efforts to regulate imports, transportation, new drugs, bank entry, and other market activities is the regulation of child adoptions—the subject of this paper.

Sometimes natural parents do not want to raise their child; the typical case is where the birth is illegitimate. And in some cases where the natural parents do raise the child initially, their custody is later terminated for one reason or another—death or other incapacity, abuse, or extreme indigence. In either case—the unwanted infant or the abused, neglected, or abandoned child—there are potential gains from trade from transferring the custody of the child to a new set of parents. Where the new parents assume full parental rights and obligations over the child, one speaks of adoption; where they obtain simply a temporary custody (usually being partially compensated for their custodial services by the state), one speaks of foster care. An alternative to foster care in a home is foster care in an institution.

* Research for this study was supported by the Center for the Study of the Economy and the State at the University of Chicago. The authors wish to express their gratitude for comments received at workshops at the University of Chicago and the University of Lund.

** Charles R. Walgreen Postdoctoral Fellow, Graduate School of Business, University of Chicago.

*** Professor of Law, University of Chicago Law School.

[1] Particularly relevant here is the recent economic work on marriage and the family. See, *e.g.*, Economics of the Family (Theodore W. Schultz ed. 1974) (Nat'l Bureau Econ. Res.).

[2] See, *e.g.*, William A. Jordan, Producer Protection, Prior Market Structure and the Effects of Government Regulation, 15 J. Law & Econ. 151 (1972).

Ordinarily, potential gains from trade are realized by a process of voluntary transacting—by a sale, in other words. Adoptions could in principle be handled through the market and in practice, as we shall see, there is a considerable amount of baby selling. But because public policy is opposed to the sale of babies, such sales as do occur constitute a "black market." Recent hearings before the Senate Subcommittee on Children and Youth,[3] as well as a well-publicized indictment of baby sellers,[4] have brought into renewed focus the existence of the black market in babies. The hearings in particular constitute a rich if unsystematic source of data and opinions on the adoption problem, facilitating appraisal of a major and, we shall argue, probably misguided example of public regulation of nonmarket behavior.

Part I of this paper develops a model of the supply and demand for babies for adoption under the existing pattern of regulation and shows (1) how that regulation has created a baby shortage (and, as a result, a black market) by preventing a free market from equilibrating the demand for and supply of babies for adoption, and (2) how it has contributed to a glut of unadopted children maintained in foster homes at public expense. Part II explores the objections to allowing the price system to equilibrate the adoption market and argues that the objections do not justify the existing regulations though they might justify a more limited regulation of the baby market. In Part III we consider, in the spirit of the new economic analysis of the political process,[5] some of the reasons why the government has curtailed the operation of the market in this area. Part IV proposes a method of practical experimentation with introducing a market in adoptions. Parts III and IV are highly tentative. In the course of the analysis we attempt to sketch how the world would look if a free market in babies were permitted to come into existence. We also discuss, though much more briefly, the problem of foster care.

I. Disequilibrium in the Adoption Market

A. *The Baby Shortage and the Baby Glut*

Students of adoption agree on two things. The first is that there is a shortage of white babies for adoption; the second is that there is a glut of

[3] Adoption and Foster Care, 1975: Hearings before the Subcomm. on Children & Youth of the Senate Comm. on Labor & Public Welfare, 94th Cong., 1st Sess. (1975) [hereinafter cited without cross-reference as Adoption and Foster Care]. A further round of hearings on baby selling began on March 22, 1977 before the Criminal Justice Subcommittee of the House Judiciary Committee, in connection with a bill to make the sale of babies in interstate commerce a federal crime. See Chicago Sun-Times, March 3, 1977, at 55, col. 3. At this writing, those hearings are still going on, and none of the testimony given at them has yet been published.

[4] See New York Times, September 8, 1976, at 1, col. 4.

[5] See, *e.g.*, George J. Stigler, The Theory of Economic Regulation, 2 Bell J. Econ. & Management Sci. 3 (1971); Sam Peltzman, Toward a More General Theory of Regulation, 19 J. Law & Econ. 211 (1976).

black babies, and of children who are no longer babies (particularly if they are physically or mentally handicapped), for adoption. The dimensions of the problem are suggested in Table 1. The very high ratio of illegitimate black births to black adoptions suggests why there is no shortage of black babies for adoption.

Contrary to popular impression, Table 1 indicates that the increased availability of contraception and abortion has not perceptibly diminished the number of illegitimate births. A partial explanation may be that the availability of contraception and abortion, by reducing the risk of producing an unwanted child (but not to zero), has reduced the expected cost and hence increased the incidence of sexual intercourse outside of marriage. However, while the illegitimate birth rate remains high the availability of babies for adoption has declined, apparently because a larger proportion of parents of illegitimate children are keeping them.[6] This trend may be due to inexplicable (on economic grounds) changes in moral standards; or it may be due to the fact that the increased opportunities for women in the job market have made them less dependent on the presence of a male in raising a child. An additional feature is that, given the increased availability of contraception and abortion, an illegitimate baby is more likely than formerly to be a desired baby.

Students of adoption cite factors such as the declining proportion of illegitimate children being put up for adoption as the "causes" of the baby shortage. But such factors do not create a shortage, any more than the scarcity of truffles creates a shortage; they merely affect the number of children available for adoption at any price. At a higher price for babies, the incidence of abortion, the reluctance to part with an illegitimate child, and even the incentive to use contraceptives would diminish because the costs of unwanted pregnancy would be lower while the (opportunity) costs to the natural mother of retaining her illegitimate child would rise.

[6] Some indication of this is the recent decline in the ratio of illegitimate babies put up for adoption to illegitimate births, as shown in the following table (thousands).

	Babies Born[a] Out of Wedlock	Adoption of Babies[b] Born Out of Wedlock	Ratio
1957	183	48	.26
1960	225	60	.27
1965	292	88	.30
1970	399	110	.28
1971	402	101	.25
1972	404	N.A.	—
1973	407	77[c]	.19

[a] *Source:* Time of Transition, tab. 1-L, at 198. (Heather L. Ross & Isabel Sawhill eds. 1975).

[b] *Source:* U.S. Dep't of Health, Education, & Welfare, Nat'l Center for Social Statistics, Adoptions in 1971 (1973).

[c] This number is projected by a method similar to that used in Table 1, notes e and f. Thirty-eight states reported a total of 46,763 adoptions of out-of-wedlock children in 1973. These 38 states contributed 61% of out-of-wedlock adoptions reported in 1971.

TABLE 1
BIRTHS OUT OF WEDLOCK, ADOPTIONS, AND NONRELATIVE ADOPTIONS BY RACE, 1957-1974 (thousands)

Year	Births out of Wedlock[a] White	Births out of Wedlock[a] Nonwhite	Adoptions[b] White	Adoptions[b] Nonwhite	Nonrelative Adoptions[b] White	Nonrelative Adoptions[b] Nonwhite
1957	64[c]	119[c]	82.8	8.2	44.3	3.9
1960	83	142	96.3	10.7	52.6	5.2
1965	124	168	126.4	15.6	69.8	6.9
1970	175	224	154.0	21.0	78.5	10.7
1971	164	238	147.0	22.0	70.8	12.0
1972[d]	161	243				
1973[e]	163	244	125.1	22.8	48.87	11.6
1974[f]			110.6	24.5	37.9	11.5

[a] *Source:* Time of Transition, tab 1-L, at 198 (Heather L. Ross & Isabel Sawhill eds. 1975).

[b] *Source:* U.S. Dep't of Health, Education, & Welfare, Nat'l Center for Social Statistics, Adoptions in 1971 (1973). 1973 and 1974 data are reported in *id.*, Adoptions in 1973 and *id.*, Adoptions in 1974. The data for these two years are incomplete with only 38 and 41 states reporting, respectively. Note that these figures are not limited to adoption of babies born out of wedlock as in note 6 *supra*.

[c] Data are for 1955.

[d] Adoption data for 1972 were not sufficiently complete to permit calculation.

[e] Adoptions in 1973 are projected from available information. The 38 states reporting in 1973 were responsible for 76% of total adoptions reported in 1971 and for 73% of nonrelative adoptions reported in 1971. We project adoptions by race in 1973 by multiplying total adoptions reported in 1973 by 1/.76, and nonrelative adoption reported in 1973 by 1/.73.

[f] Adoptions in 1974 are projected from available data as described in note e to this table. The 41 states reporting adoptions in 1974 were responsible for 81% of total adoptions reported in 1971 and 76% of nonrelative adoptions reported in 1971.

The principal suppliers of babies for adoption are adoption agencies. Restrictive regulations governing nonagency adoption have given agencies a monopoly (though not a complete one) of the supply of children for adoption. However, while agencies charge fees for adoption, usually based on the income of the adoptive parents, they do not charge a market-clearing (let alone a monopoly-profit-maximizing) price. This is shown by the fact that prospective adoptive parents applying to an agency face waiting periods of three to seven years.[7] And the (visible) queue understates the shortage, since by tightening their criteria of eligibility to adopt a child the agencies can shorten the apparent queue without increasing the supply of babies. Thus some demanders in this market must wait for years to obtain a baby, others never obtain one, and still others are discouraged by knowledge of the queue from even trying. Obtaining a second or third baby is increasingly difficult.

The picture is complicated, however, by the availability of independent adoptions. An independent adoption is one that does not go through an agency. Most independent adoptions are by a relative, for example a stepfather, but some involve placement with strangers and here, it would seem, is an opportunity for a true baby market to develop. However, the operation

[7] Adoption and Foster Care 6.

TABLE 2
CHILDREN RECEIVING FOSTER CARE FROM PUBLIC AND VOLUNTARY CHILD WELFARE AGENCIES, 1961-1972
(thousands)

		Number of Children Receiving Foster Care Services		
Year	Total	Public Agencies	Served by Public and Voluntary Agencies[a]	Voluntary Agencies
1961	244.5	133.3		111.2
1965	283.3	173.9		109.4
1970	326.0	226.0	57.0	42.2
1971	330.4	231.4	59.8	39.2
1972	319.8	223.4	61.4	35.0

Source: Numbers for 1961 and 1965 are derived from U.S. Dep't of Health, Education, & Welfare, Children's Bureau, Child Welfare Statistics, 1961 and 1965.
Numbers for 1970, 1971, and 1972 are derived from U.S. Dep't of Health, Education, & Welfare, Children Served by Public Welfare Agencies and Voluntary Child Welfare Agencies and Institutions, for 1970, 1971, and 1972.
[a] For the great majority of these children, the public agency was purchasing foster care from the voluntary agency.

of this market is severely curtailed by a network of restrictions, varying from state to state (a few states forbid independent adoption by a nonrelative) but never so loose as to permit outright sale of a baby for adoption.[8]

Just as a buyer's queue is a symptom of a shortage, a seller's queue is a symptom of a glut. The thousands of children in foster care revealed by Table 2 are comparable to an unsold inventory stored in a warehouse. Child welfare specialists attribute this "oversupply" to such factors as the growing incidence of child abuse, which forces the state to remove children from the custody of their natural parents, and the relatively small number of prospective adoptive parents willing to adopt children of another race, children who are no longer infants, or children who have a physical or mental handicap. No doubt these factors are important. However, some children are placed in foster care as infants and remain there until they are no longer appealing to prospective adoptive parents. We believe that the large number of children in foster care is, in part, a manifestation of a regulatory pattern that (1) combines restrictions on the sale of babies with the effective monopolization of the adoption market by adoptive agencies, and (2) fails to provide effectively for the termination of the natural parents' rights.

B. *A Model of the Adoption Market*

Here we present a simple analytical model of the adoption market as it exists today in the United States. Queues for some children (mainly white

[8] The relevant state laws are described in Note: Black-Market Adoptions, 22 Catholic Lawyer 48 (1976), and in Daniel R. Grove, Independent Adoption: The Case for the Gray Market, 13 Vill. L. Rev. 116 (1967).

infants) in the legal market, overstocks of others (older, nonwhite, or physically or mentally handicapped children), and black-market activity in infants are all shown to be the result of the peculiar market structure in adoption that has been brought about by public regulation.

Whereas in 1957 only 53 percent of all nonrelative adoptions went through adoption agencies, in 1971 the proportion was almost 80 percent.[9] This would be a matter of limited significance from the economic standpoint if adoption agencies were both numerous and free from significant restrictions on their ability to operate as efficient profit-maximizing firms. The first condition is more or less satisfied but not the second. While agencies are generally not limited in the fees they may charge prospective adoptive parents, they are constrained to other inefficient restrictions. For example, they are constrained to operate as "nonprofit" organizations which presumably retards, perhaps severely, their ability to attract capital, and may have other inefficient effects as well.[10] The most significant restriction is the regulation of the price at which the agencies may transact with the natural parents. Adoption agencies that are also general child-welfare agencies must accept all children offered to them at a regulated price (but may place them in foster care rather than for adoption); and they may offer no additional compensation to suppliers (the natural parents) in order to increase the supply of babies. The regulated price is generally limited to the direct medical costs of pregnant women plus (some) maintenance expenses during the latter part of the pregnancy. To be sure, agencies have some flexibility in the kinds of services they may offer the natural parents, such as job counseling, but they cannot thereby transfer to the natural parents anything approaching the free-market value of the child.

There are rough counterparts to such regulation in many explicit markets. Banks as a group have a monopoly of banking services, though most banking markets contain several competing banks; the prices of banking services are unregulated (save for usury laws which are applicable to some bank loans); but banks are forbidden to pay a market-clearing price for an essential input, demand deposits (corresponding to babies in the adoption market). Similar regulatory patterns are found in industries as otherwise diverse as taxi service and television broadcasting. Nevertheless the regulation of adoption has several peculiar characteristics reflected in our model: collusion among agencies, including market division (often along religious lines), is permitted; there exists a very close substitute for the good supplied by the

[9] See U.S. Dep't of Health, Education, & Welfare, Nat'l Center for Social Statistics, Adoptions in 1971 (1973).

[10] In particular, it may lead the agencies to dissipate their profits in expenditures that reduce welfare—*e.g.*, unnecessarily intrusive inspections of the home of the adoptive parents.

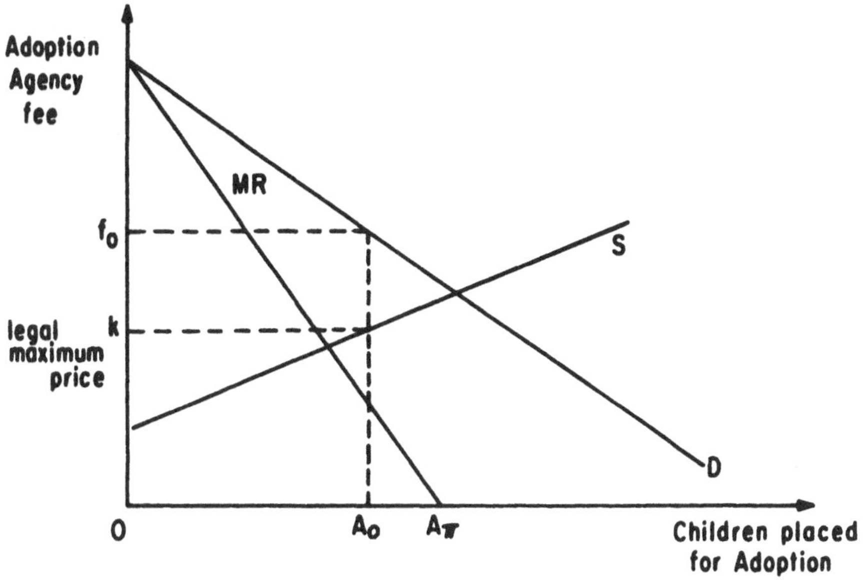

FIGURE 1

agencies—independent adoption; and the agency has, as mentioned, no power to refuse to take the children tendered to it.[11]

We begin by analyzing a monopoly model of the adoption market that would exist if agencies acted jointly as a monopolist (*i.e.*, if there were no competition among agencies or substitution in the independent-adoption markets and the agencies' only objective were to maximize economic profits). Agencies face a demand curve for children for adoption described by D in Figure 1. One can conceive of all families as being in the adoption market, with their location along the demand curve determined by the value they place on adopting a child. The supply curve of babies for adoption is described by S in Figure 1. It is assumed to be upward sloping. The supply curve reflects the transfer in wealth that natural parents would demand in exchange for giving up a child for adoption, and is determined by such things as the natural mother's direct and opportunity costs in carrying the child to term and any psychic costs she incurs by giving birth to a child she will not keep, over the direct, opportunity, and psychic costs of either having the child and keeping it or aborting it. For some women the supply price will

[11] This applies only to those agencies—the majority, however—that are general child-welfare organizations rather than solely adoption agencies.

be low, perhaps because of a strong aversion to abortion relative to giving up the child; for others the price will be high, perhaps because of high opportunity costs of bearing the child. At the legally prescribed maximum price that agencies may offer natural parents, A_0 children will be placed with the agencies for adoption.

Abstracting from the administrative costs of placing children for adoption, it is clear that there is no marginal cost of children to the agencies in this model. In each period agencies have only a fixed cost of k times the number of children they must accept under the regulation, where k is the regulated price at which they must take any child tendered to them.[12]

Under these extreme assumptions the agency-monopoly would be willing to place up to A_π children, since marginal revenue from placing children is positive up to that number. However, the actual number of children the agency has to place may exceed or fall short of A_π. When the number of children it has, denoted by A_0 in Figure 1, falls short of A_π, all the children will be placed for adoption. When A_0 exceeds A_π, as in Figure 2, some of the children will be placed in foster care. The number placed in foster care will depend upon the cost to the agency of maintaining them there. The lower that cost is, the more children the agencies will place in foster care and the fewer they will offer for adoption. Clearly, if the cost to the agency of foster care is zero, because, for example, the state reimburses it for the full cost of maintaining children in foster care,[13] all of the children in excess of A_π will be placed in foster care and the number placed for adoption will never exceed A_π.

To be sure, if adoption agencies could price discriminate perfectly, children in excess of A_π would be placed in foster care only when the number supplied to the agencies at the regulated price exceeded the demand for children at that price. There is evidence that adoption agencies do price discriminate (though not perfectly): adoption fees are usually determined by, among other things, the income of the prospective adoptive parents.

What fee will the agency charge for the children placed for adoption? In Figure 1, which depicts the case where $A_0 < A_\pi$, the profit-maximizing fee is f_0. In Figure 2, which depicts the case where $A_0 > A_\pi$, the price will be somewhere between f_π and f_1, depending on the cost to the agency of maintaining the children in excess of A_π in foster care.

[12] Actually, there is some variation in this price, depending on the particular medical or maintenance costs incurred by the natural mother. This variation is immaterial to our analysis and will be ignored.

[13] In 1965, 41.6% of state and local foster care payments were for children living in foster family homes and institutions supervised or administered by voluntary agencies. This amounted to $95 million. We do not know what fraction of expenditures on total foster care provided by voluntary agencies was offset by this $95 million. See U.S. Dep't of Health, Education, & Welfare, Children's Bureau, Child Welfare Statistics (1965).

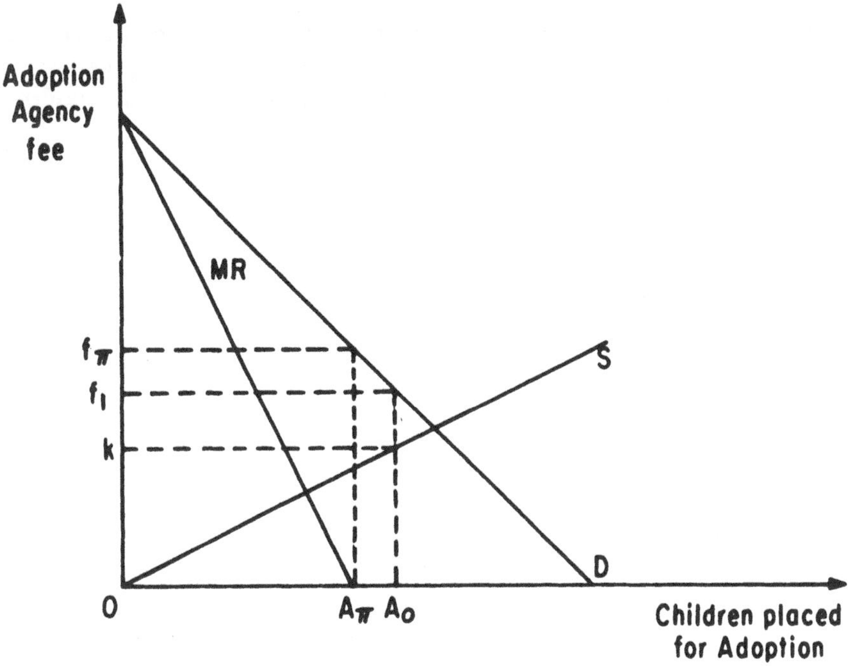

FIGURE 2

But such prices are not being charged by adoption agencies, the most telling evidence of this being the long queues that prospective adoptive parents must undergo to obtain a child through an agency even when they are willing to pay the agency fee. What constrains the agencies from charging f_0 in Figure 1? Probably not the fact that they are nominally nonprofit agencies: profits obtained in adoption activities could readily be used to support other activities in which these agencies engage. We suggest that the presence of competition from the independent adoption market may be one constraining force. This suggestion is consistent with the vigorous efforts by adoption agencies to restrict independent adoptions.

To understand how the presence of the independent market constrains the agencies, we must model the interaction between the agency and independent markets. To do this we make two assumptions: (1) Price in the independent market is determined competitively, and (2) babies available for adoption at any price are allocated in fixed proportions between the agency and the independent market depending on the costs of information in the independent market and the potential criminal and professional penalties from handling independent adoptions. Clearly, the assumption of fixed proportions is unrealistic; the proportion of babies in the agency market is presumably responsive to the price that could be obtained in the independent market relative to the supply price in the agency market. However, the assumption facilitates a graphic exposition of the model at only a small sacrifice of explanatory power.

Assuming for simplicity linear demand and supply curves, the market supply of children to the adoption market is described, as in Figures 1 and 2, by

$$S_M = e + gp.$$

The supply of children to be placed through agencies is a fixed fraction, γ, of market supply at the regulated price, k, which agencies may offer for children.

$$S_A = \gamma(e + gk) = A_0.$$

The supply of children to the independent market is also a fixed fraction, $1 - \gamma$, of market supply:

$$S_I = (1 - \gamma)(e + g(p_I - C_{IS})),$$

where p_I is the transaction price for children in the independent market, and C_{IS} represents the information and expected penalty costs that are incurred by suppliers to this market. Hence C_{IS} must be netted out of the gross supply price.

Market demand for adopted children is described, as in Figures 1 and 2, by

$$D_M = a - bp.$$

Demand in the independent market is assumed to be some fraction, δ, of market demand that is not satisfied through agency adoptions:

$$D_I = \delta(a - b(p_I + C_{ID}) - A_0),$$

where C_{ID} represents the information costs that must be incurred in order to obtain a child in the independent market. Hence C_{ID} must be included in the full price of independent adoption.

To complete the model, we assume that because of political considerations the agency may not charge a fee for adoption in excess of the full price paid for children in the independent market. We assume further (for simplicity of graphical exposition) that if the agency faces excess demand for children at that price, it will allocate its available children among its prospective parents so as to maximize consumer satisfaction (*i.e.*, among the highest-value bidders).

In equilibrium,

$$D_I = S_I,$$

and

$$p_I = \frac{\delta(a - bC_{ID}) - (1 - \gamma)(e - gC_{IS}) - \delta\gamma(e + gk)}{\delta b + (1 - \gamma)g}. \quad (1)$$

Assuming that the agency adoption fee is equal to the full price of independent adoption, the agency fee is

$$p_A = p_I + C_{ID} = \frac{\delta a - (1 - \gamma)(e - g(C_{ID} + C_{IS})) - \delta\gamma(e + gk)}{\delta b + (1 - \gamma)g}. \quad (2)$$

The queue facing the agency at this adoption fee can be determined from the difference between the total number of children demanded in the market at a full price of p_A and the total number supplied:

$$Q = D_M - S_M = \frac{(1 - \gamma)(1 - \delta)[be - \gamma g(e + gk) + g\delta(a - b(C_{IS} + C_{ID}))]}{\delta b + (1 - \gamma)g}.$$

This equilibrium is depicted in Figure 3. From our assumption that the agency allocates its available children among the highest-value bidders, demand in the independent market is represented by a linear demand curve D_I (in panel (b)) that is equal to a fraction δ of market demand in excess of agency supply. (The fraction of demanders who do not receive children in the agency market but appear as demanders in the independent markets will be a function of, among other things, the information and expected penalty costs of buying in the independent market.) This demand curve is gross of information costs. Assuming that the costs of information are the same for all demanders and are proportional to the number of children demanded, we can subtract the costs of search from D_I to get the net demand curve D'_I. The number of children adopted independently is determined by the intersection of D'_I and S_I.

From equation (2) it is clear that an increase in either the expected penalty or information costs of suppliers in the independent market or the information costs of demanders in that market would increase the equilibrium fee that agencies may charge. If an expected penalty equal to $f_0 - C_{IS} - C_{ID}$ were imposed on suppliers in the independent market, that market would vanish. It would reemerge, however, whenever the supply conditions of children shifted so that the (unconstrained) profit-maximizing agency fee exceeded f_0. Hence we predict that in times of relatively short supply of babies for adoption the private market will become more active and the agencies will agitate to have the restrictions on private placement tightened.

The above analysis is consistent with observed characteristics of the adoption market. It explains why agencies charge less than market-clearing fees in the face of baby shortages and why they agitate for stringent regulation of

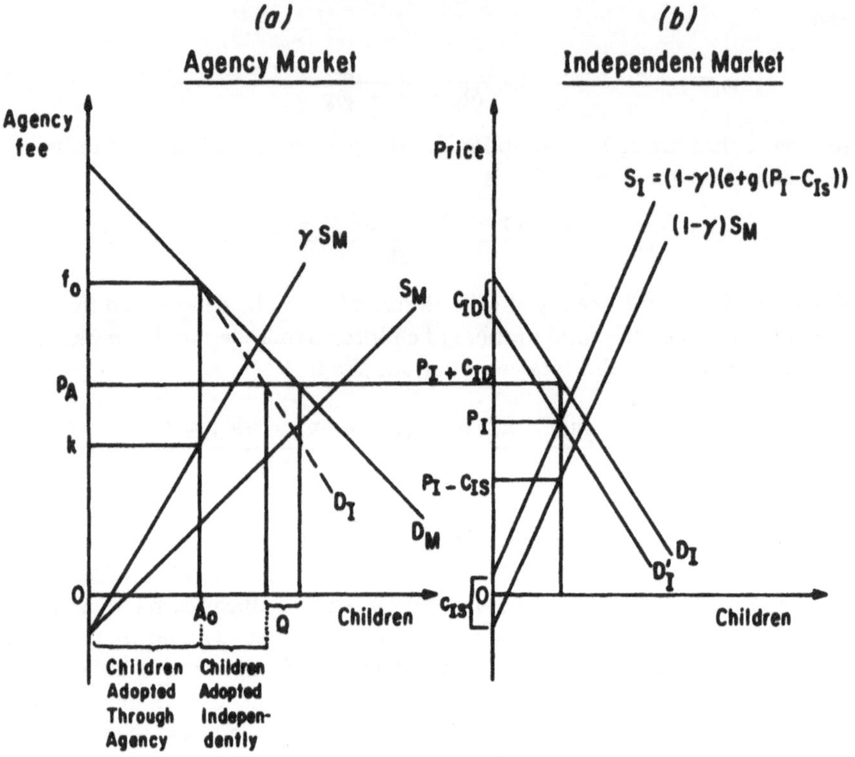

FIGURE 3

the independent market. The substantial costs of information in the independent market for both demanders and suppliers explain why there are queues at adoption agencies rather than simply a diversion of all unsatisfied demanders in the agency market to the independent market.

C. *The Effects of the Baby Shortage*

The baby shortage generates social costs in excess of the traditional welfare loss of monopoly. The counterpart to that loss would be the lost consumer surplus from sales not made at all because of the artificial unavailability of the product and is measured by triangle DBC in Figure 4. But assuming the nonprice rationing methods used by agencies to allocate children are random with respect to willingness to pay (rather than based on willingness to pay, as we assumed in Figure 3),[14] the loss in consumer surplus is the area

[14] This is a plausible assumption because length of time in the queue is presumably uncorrelated with income (it would be negatively correlated if the queue were "literal"—*i.e.*, involved real opportunity costs of time—but it does not).

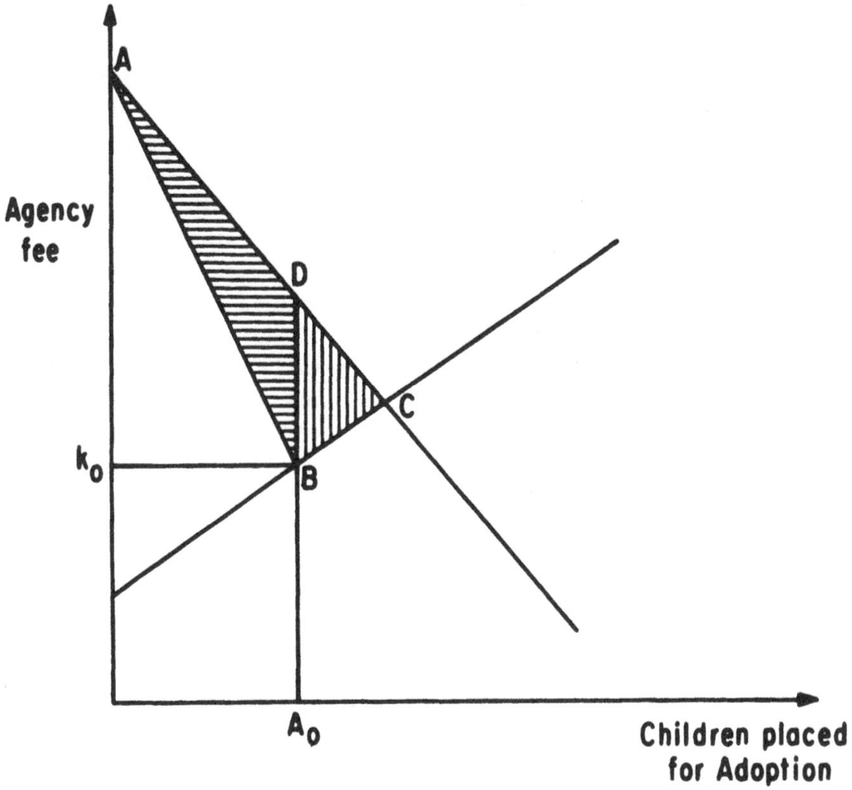

FIGURE 4

of the larger triangle ABC in Figure 4. To be sure, some of this loss is offset by the availability of children in the independent market, but the search costs in the independent market also represent a substantial social cost.

No effort will be made in this paper to quantify the social cost of the baby shortage (and hence of the governmental regulations that have generated it) or to measure its impact on the number of children adopted. However, the potential magnitude of the problem will be explored briefly.

A crude estimate of the potential size of the baby market can be obtained from a comparison of the fraction of married women who are childless throughout their married lives with the (much smaller) fraction of women who report, early in their marriage, that they do not intend to have any children. In 1975, 10.8 percent of white American women aged 50 or over who had ever been married were childless.[15] Many of these were childless by

[15] See U.S. Bureau of the Census, Statistical Abstract of the United States, 1976, tab. 75, at 56 [hereinafter cited without cross-reference as Statistical Abstract]. We limit our attention to

choice, but another statistic suggests that many were not: in 1975 only 4.4 percent of white American wives aged 18-24 *expected* to have no children.[16] The difference between these figures is some clue to the potential demand for babies that cannot be satisfied by natural means. Still another clue is the high cost (nominal, time, and risk) that childless couples incur in order to increase the probability of giving birth.

Of course, adopted children may not be a perfect substitute for natural children. The genetic characteristics of natural children are highly correlated with their parents' genetic characteristics, and this correlation could conceivably increase harmony within the family compared to what it would be with an adopted child.[17] Nevertheless, there is considerable substitutability between natural and adopted children and it might be much greater if better genetic matching of adopted children with their adoptive parents were feasible—as might occur, as we shall see, under free market conditions.

Given that the number of white marriages has averaged close to two million a year over the past decade,[18] about 130,000 married couples might be potential "buyers" in the baby market every year.[19] And this is probably an underestimate. Couples who have adopted children are not counted among the 10.8 percent of couples who are childless. More important, most natural parents want more than one child, and presumably the same is true of adoptive parents. This alone might double the 130,000 figure for potential demand. Offsetting this to some extent is the fact that some childless couples may not consider an adopted child a substitute for a natural child. But on balance it seems clear that the 37,000 white nonrelative adoptions a year (estimated in Table 1) fall far short of satisfying the potential demand.

In light of these statistics it may seem surprising that only about 17,000 nonrelative adoptions in 1971 (the last year for which adequate data are available)—a mere 21 percent—were independent rather than agency adoptions. Why do not a larger fraction of the potential demanders utilize the independent method, free from the restrictions that hamper the agency adoption process? The probable answer, already suggested, is that governmental restrictions on the fees that may be paid in an independent adoption artificially depress the net price of providing babies through this process. The result is to reduce the number of babies supplied below the free-

whites because, as mentioned earlier, there appears to be no shortage of black babies for adoption.

[16] Statistical Abstract, tab. 78, at 57.

[17] Cf. Gary S. Becker, A Theory of Marriage, in Economics of the Family, *supra* note 1, at 299.

[18] Statistical Abstract, tab. 97, at 68.

[19] This obviously crude estimate was obtained by multiplying the difference between the childless rate for older married women and the expected childless rate of younger married women by the number of marriages per year (whites only).

market level while simultaneously restricting the use of price to ration the existing, and inadequate, supply.

In independent adoption, normally the only payments that may be made are (1) compensation to the natural mother for her medical, and some maintenance, costs plus (2) compensation to the obstetrician and the lawyer for their professional (*i.e.*, medical and legal) services, excluding any search costs they may have incurred in arranging for the adoption. The included items represent only a part of the costs of producing and selling a baby. The major omitted items are (1) the opportunity costs of the natural mother's time during the period of pregnancy or hospitalization when she is precluded from working, over and above her maintenance costs, (2) any pain or other disutility of the pregnancy and delivery to her, (3) any value which she attaches to keeping the child rather than putting it up for adoption, and (4) the costs of search of the middleman—usually an obstetrician or lawyer—in locating and bringing together the supplier and demander.

In practice the constraints on full compensation to producer and middleman are less rigid than suggested. The difficulties of monitoring the fees and activities of the attorney, obstetrician, and natural mother enable these individuals to charge somewhat more than the technically permitted amounts without running any appreciable risk of punishment. This is why independent placement of babies for adoption (other than to relatives) is often referred to as the "gray market." However, the constraints placed on independent adoption are sufficiently stringent to prevent it from approximating a free market. Women have little or no incentive to put a child up for adoption rather than retain or abort it (since abortions are relatively inexpensive, and public assistance is ordinarily available to cover their medical expenses and maintenance costs regardless of whether they keep or give up the child). At the same time, the constraints on payment discourage the emergence of an effective middleman function to match up the prospective sellers and buyers—the middleman activity *per se* cannot be compensated. This is particularly serious in a market of this sort where the sellers and buyers tend to be geographically and socially remote, are not professional businessmen, do not participate in this market on a regular basis, and are dealing in a highly individualized commodity.

In these circumstances, the economist expects a black market to emerge. Some fraction—we do not know what—of the 17,000 independent adoptions are indeed black-market adoptions in the sense that the compensation paid either the natural parents or the middlemen, or both, exceeds the lawful limits.[20] However, the potential criminal and professional sanctions for the

[20] Regardless of how obtained—whether lawfully or in the black market—most babies are formally adopted and hence most black-market activities show up in the statistics of independent adoption. In some cases, however, where an adoption is arranged prior to the birth of the

individuals involved in baby selling not only drive up the costs and hence the price of babies (and so reduce demand) but necessarily imply a clandestine mode of operation. This imposes significant information costs on both buyers and sellers in the market, which further raise the (real) price of black-market babies to buyers and reduce the net price to sellers, as demonstrated in panel (b) of Figure 3.

The legally permissible compensation to the natural parents is unlikely to exceed \$3,000.[21] However, prices for babies in the black market are alleged to range between \$9,000 and \$40,000.[22] To some extent these prices reflect search costs and other middleman expenses that would be found in a free market, but they may to a greater extent reflect the expected penalties suppliers face and the additional costs of search entailed by operating in a clandestine market.

A further consideration is that there will be more fraud in a black market for babies than in a lawful market, so fear of being defrauded will further deter potential demanders. In lawful markets the incidence of fraud is limited not only by the existence of legal remedies against the seller but also by his desire to build a reputation for fair dealing. Both the clandestine mode of operation of current baby sellers and the lack of a continuing business relationship between seller and buyer reduce the seller's market incentives to behave reputably. To summarize, we cannot, simply by observing the black market, estimate the market-clearing prices and quantities of babies in a lawful baby market.

The constraints on the baby market may also be responsible in part for the glut of children in foster care—and this quite apart from the possible incentives of adoption agencies to place children in foster care rather than for adoption. Since the natural parents have no financial incentive to place a child for adoption, often they will decide to place it in foster care instead. This is proper so long as they seriously intend to reacquire custody of the child at some later date. But when they do not the consequence of their decision to place the child in foster care may be to render the child unadoptable, for by the time the parents relinquish their parental rights the child may be too old to be placed for adoption. This would happen less often if parents had a financial incentive to relinquish their rights at a time when the child was still young enough to be adoptable.

The *total* effect of the baby-market constraints on the number of foster children is, to be sure, a complicated question. In particular, the limited

---

adopted child, the adoptive parents' name may simply be entered directly on the birth certificate, thus obviating any formal adoptive procedure.

[21] See Adoption and Foster Care 132, 139.

[22] See Adoption and Foster Care 160, 165-166, 175, 182; Chicago Tribune, March 22, 1977, sec. 1, at 3.

supply of desirable babies for adoption may lead some prospective adoptive parents to substitute children who would otherwise be placed in foster care. We suspect that this substitution effect is small, but in any event it is partly controlled by the agencies; they can manipulate the relative "prices" of infants and children residing in foster care by modifying the criteria for eligibility that must be satisfied by prospective adoptive parents.

II. Objections to a Free Baby Market

The foregoing analysis suggests that the baby shortage and black market are the result of legal restrictions that prevent the market from operating freely in the sale of babies as of other goods. This suggests as a possible reform simply eliminating these restrictions. However, many people believe that a free market in babies would be undesirable. Representative of this point of view is the conclusion of a recent law-review note on baby selling:

> The black market in adoptions is a thriving business. Destructive of the best interests of parents, children, and society, such dealings in human flesh should be thwarted by strong, strictly enforced state laws and equally stringent barriers to interstate trade. . . . If state and federal governments show a determination to discover and punish black-market activities, this taint on civilized society can be removed.[23]

The objections to baby selling must be considered carefully before any conclusion with regard to the desirability of changing the law can be reached.

A. *Criticisms Properly Limited to the Black Market*

We begin with a set of criticisms that in reality are applicable not to the market as such, but only, we believe, to the *black* market. The first such criticism is of the high price of babies and the bad effects that are alleged to flow from a high price, such as favoring the wealthy.[24] This criticism of the use of the price system is based on the current prices in the black market. There is no reason to believe that prices would be so high were the sale of babies legalized. On the contrary, prices for children of *equivalent quality* would be much lower.[25]

The current black-market price is swollen by expected punishment costs which would not be a feature of a legalized baby market. In a legal and competitive baby market, price would be equated to the marginal costs of producing and selling for adoption babies of a given quality. These marginal

[23] Note, Black-Market Adoptions, *supra* note 8, at 69.

[24] See, *e.g.*, Adoption and Foster Care 11, 27.

[25] The importance of this qualification is emphasized at p. 341 *infra*.

costs include certain well-known items, such as the natural mother's medical expenses and maintenance during pregnancy and the attorney's fee for handling the legal details of the adoption proceeding, that are unlikely to exceed \$3,000 in the aggregate. The question marks are the additional fees that would be necessary (1) to compensate a woman either for becoming pregnant or, if she was pregnant already, for inducing her to put the baby up for adoption rather than abort or retain it, and (2) to cover the search costs necessary to match baby and adoptive parents.

With regard to the first item (the natural mother's opportunity costs of adoption), the most important point to be noted is that these costs may be no greater than the cost savings to the adoptive mother of not undergoing pregnancy and childbirth herself. Adoption is a process by which the adoptive mother in effect contracts out one of the steps in the process of child production and rearing, namely the actual pregnancy and childbirth. The anxieties and inconveniences of pregnancy are a cost to the biological mother but a cost saving to the adoptive mother. Equally, all or most of the out-of-pocket expenses of the natural mother, including the obstetrician's fee, represent a cost saving to the adoptive mother. Therefore, at least as a first approximation, the only *net* cost of purchasing a baby in a free and competitive market should be the cost of the search, which would presumably be low.

Also, because the adoption agencies give substantial emphasis to the employment and financial situation of adoptive parents, a baby market might actually provide more opportunities for the poor to adopt than nonprice rationing does. If we are correct that the (acquisition) costs of babies in a lawful and competitive market would often be small, perhaps no more than the cost of an automobile, low-income families who would normally be considered financially ineligible by adoption agencies would be able in a free market to obtain a child.

Another prevalent criticism of the market, and again one that pertains primarily to the operations of the black market, is that fraud and related forms of dishonesty and overreaching pervade the market method of providing children for adoption. It is contended, for example, that the health of the child or of the child's mother is regularly misrepresented and that frequently after the sale is completed the seller will attempt to blackmail the adoptive parents.[26] Such abuses are probably largely the result of the fact that the market is an illegal one. Sellers cannot give legally enforceable guarantees of genealogy, health, or anything else to the prospective parents, and even the seller's adherence to the negotiated price is uncertain given the buyer's ina-

[26] Adoption and Foster Care 20-21.

bility to enforce the contract of sale by the usual legal procedures. Any market involving a complex and durable good (*i.e.*, one that yields services over a substantial period of time) would probably operate suboptimally in the absence of legally enforceable contracts or, at a minimum, regular, repetitive business relations between (the same) sellers and (the same) buyers. Both conditions are absent from the illegal baby market and this is the likeliest explanation for the number of complaints about the honesty of the sellers in that market.

To be sure, there are probably inherent limitations on the use of legal remedies to protect purchasers even in a legal baby market. For example, consideration of the welfare of the child might lead courts to refuse to grant rescission to a buyer as a remedy for breach of warranty (*i.e.*, allow him to return the child). And courts might be reluctant to order specific performance of a contract to put up a child for adoption. However, similar limitations are a traditional feature of remedies for personal-service contracts, yet do not appear to prevent effective enforcement of those contracts. Why should they do so in the case of baby sale contracts?

The foregoing analysis also enables us to place in perspective allegations that the sellers in the baby black market include a number of ex-convicts and other unsavory types and that the market reveals commercial "trafficking" at its ugliest.[27] An illegal market will naturally attract people who are less sensitive to the threat of criminal punishment than is normal and this group may include a large proportion of ex-convicts. But these characteristics of the market are an artifact of its illegality.

This analysis suggests a qualification to our earlier conclusion that legalizing the baby market would result in a reduction in the price of babies below the current black market level: the conclusion refers to a *quality-adjusted* price. The current illegality of baby selling reduces the benefits of transacting to the buyer by depriving him of the contractual protections that buyers in legal markets normally receive. Prospective adoptive parents would presumably be willing to pay more for a child whose health and genealogy were warranted in a legally enforceable instrument than they are willing to pay under the present system where the entire risk of any deviation from expected quality falls on them. Thus the effect of legalizing the baby market would be not only to shift the marginal cost of baby production and sale downward but to move the demand curve for adoptive children upward. Conceivably these movements could cancel each other out, resulting in no change from the current black-market prices, but even if they did consumer satisfaction would be increased. The same price would buy a higher-quality package of rights.

[27] Adoption and Foster Care 11, 159, 173.

B. *Criticisms of a Legal Market*

We now consider criticisms of baby selling that are applicable to a legal market rather than just to the present illegal market. The first is that the rationing of the supply of babies to would-be adoptive parents by price is not calculated to promote the best interests of the children, the objective of the adoption process.[28] This criticism cannot be dismissed as foolish. The ordinary presumption of free-enterprise economics is no stronger than that free exchange will maximize the satisfaction of the people trading, who in this case are the natural and adoptive parents. There is no presumption that the satisfactions of the thing traded, in most instances a meaningless concept, are also maximized. If we treat the child as a member of the community whose aggregate welfare we are interested in maximizing, there is no justification for ignoring how the child's satisfactions may be affected by alternative methods of adoption.

Very simply, the question is whether the price system would do as good a job as, or a better job than, adoption agencies in finding homes for children that would maximize their satisfactions in life. While there is no direct evidence on this point, some weak indirect evidence is provided in a followup study of independent adoptions which suggest that children adopted privately do as well as natural children. Witmer and her coauthors find that the distribution of I.Q. and a measure of school achievement, both at age 11, between children adopted privately and natural children of comparable socioeconomic backgrounds are virtually identical, although they also find that the adopted children did not perform as well on certain psychological tests as did the natural children.[29] It is true that some, perhaps most, independent adoptions do not involve price rationing, but the most important thing is that independent adoption involves a minimum of the sort of screening of prospective parents that the adoption agencies do. If children adopted without the screening seem nevertheless to do about as well as natural children, then one is entitled to be skeptical of the need for or value of the screening.

This conclusion is reinforced by the way in which adoption agencies screen. Agencies attempt to allocate children only to "fit" or caring parents. But after determining the pool of fit, or eligible-to-adopt, couples, they allocate available children among them on a first-come, first-served basis. The "fittest" parents are not placed at the head of the queue.

Further, and perhaps most important, agencies have no real information on the needs of a particular child they place for adoption beyond its need for

[28] Adoption and Foster Care 7.

[29] Helen L. Witmer, Elizabeth Herzog, Eugene A. Weinstein, & Mary E. Sullivan, Independent Adoptions: A Followup Study (1963).

love, warmth, food, and shelter. One cannot read from the face of a newborn whether he or she will be of above or below normal intelligence, or be naturally athletic, musical, or artistic. Hence agencies cannot be presumed to match these very real, if inaccessible, qualities of infants with the qualities of the adoptive parents any more effectively than a market would.

One valuable function agencies may perform is screening out people whose interest in having children is improper in an uncontroversial sense—people who wish to have children in order to abuse or make slaves of them. The criminal statutes punishing child abuse and neglect would remain applicable to babies adopted in a free market, but the extreme difficulty of detecting such crimes makes it unlikely, at least given current levels of punishment, that the criminal statutes alone are adequate. This may make some prescreening a more effective method of prevention than after-the-fact punishment. But the logical approach, then, is to require every prospective baby buyer to undergo some minimal background investigation. This approach would be analogous to licensing automobile drivers and seems as superior to the agency monopoly as licensing is to allocating automobiles on a nonprice basis.

Moreover, concern with child abuse should not be allowed to obscure the fact that abuse is not the normal motive for adopting a child. And once we put abuse aside, willingness to pay money for a baby would seem on the whole a reassuring factor from the standpoint of child welfare. Few people buy a car or a television set in order to smash it. In general, the more costly a purchase, the more care the purchaser will lavish on it. Recent studies suggest that the more costly it is for parents to obtain a child, the greater will be their investment in the child's quality attributes, such as health and education.[30]

A further point is that today some fetuses are probably aborted because the cost to the mother of carrying them to term and placing them for adoption exceeds the permissible return. In a free adoption market, some of the 900,000 fetuses aborted in 1974[31] would have been born and placed for adoption. If the welfare of these (potential) children is included in the calculation of the welfare of adopted children, both actual and potential, the heavy costs imposed on the market by adoption regulation may actually decrease child welfare.

Another objection to the market for babies is the alleged vulnerability of both natural and adoptive parents to overreaching by middlemen. Par-

[30] Gary S. Becker & H. Gregg Lewis, Interaction between Quality and Quantity of Children, in Economics of the Family, *supra* note 1, at 81; Gary S. Becker & Nigel Tomes, Child Endowments and the Quantity and Quality of Children, 84 J. Pol. Econ. S143-S162 (August 1976). Even critics of baby selling seem generally satisfied with the quality of the families who obtain children in the black market. See Adoption and Foster Care 13.

[31] Statistical Abstract, tab. 83, at 59.

enthood is thought to be so emotional a phenomenon that people cannot reason about it in the same way they reason about the goods and services normally traded in the market.[32] But many of those goods and services, such as medical care, also involve a strong emotional component, yet it has rarely been thought appropriate to exclude such goods from market exchange. And studies of marriage and procreation have shown that people in fact calculate in family matters, whether implicitly or explicitly, in the same way they do when purchasing ordinary goods and services.[33]

Other objections to legalizing the market in babies are more symbolic than pragmatic. For example, to accord a property right in the newborn child to the natural parents seems to some observers to smack of slavery.[34] But allowing a market in adoptions does not entail giving property rights to natural parents for all purposes. Laws forbidding child abuse and neglect would continue to be fully applicable to adoptive parents even if baby sales were permitted. Further, we are speaking only of sales of newborn infants, and do not suggest that parents should have a right to sell older children. The creation of such a right would require identification of the point at which the child is sufficiently mature to be entitled to a voice in his placement. However, the question is largely academic given the lack of any significant market for adopting older children.

Moreover, it is incorrect to equate the possession of property rights with the abuse of the property, even if the property is a human being. For example, a serious problem with foster care is the foster parents' lack of any property rights in the foster child. The better the job the foster parents do in raising the child, the more likely are the natural parents to reclaim the child and thereby prevent the foster parents from reaping the full fruits of their (emotional as well as financial) investment. This possibility in turn reduces the incentive of foster parents to invest in foster children, to the detriment of those children's welfare.

The antipathy to an explicit market in babies may be part of a broader wish to disguise facts that might be acutely uncomfortable if widely known. Were baby prices quoted as prices of soybean futures are quoted, a racial ranking of these prices would be evident, with white baby prices higher than nonwhite baby prices. One is reminded of Professor Tribe's objection to instructing the jury on the numerical probability implicit in the concept of proof beyond a reasonable doubt.[35] He argues that while the system of criminal justice would be unworkable if subjective certainty of guilt were re-

[32] See Adoption and Foster Care 12, 44.

[33] See studies in Economics of the Family, *supra* note 1.

[34] See Adoption and Foster Care 2-3.

[35] Laurence H. Tribe, Trial by Mathematics: Precision and Ritual in the Legal Process, 84 Harv. L. Rev. 1329 (1971).

quired, to acknowledge explicitly that people are convicted on less than such certainty might tear the social fabric. Similarly, anyone who thinks about the question will realize that prices for babies are racially stratified as a result of different supply and demand conditions in the different racial groups,[36] but perhaps bringing this fact out into the open would exacerbate racial tensions in our society.

Some people are also upset by the implications for the eugenic alteration of the human race that are presented by baby selling. Baby selling may seem logically and inevitably to lead to baby breeding,[37] for any market will generate incentives to improve the product as well as to optimize the price and quantity of the current quality level of the product. In a regime of free baby production and sale there might be efforts to breed children having desirable characteristics and, more broadly, to breed children with a *known* set of characteristics that could be matched up with those desired by prospective adoptive parents. Indeed, one can imagine, though with some difficulty, a growing separation between the production and rearing of children. No longer would a woman who wanted a child but who had a genetic trait that might jeopardize the child's health have to take her chances on a natural birth. She could find a very close genetic match-up to her and her husband's (healthy) genetic endowment in the baby market. However, so long as the market for eugenically bred babies did not extend beyond infertile couples and those with serious genetic disorders, the impact of a free baby market on the genetic composition and distribution of the human race at large would be small.

The emphasis placed by critics on the social costs of a free market in babies blurs what would probably be the greatest long-run effect of legalizing the baby market: inducing women who have unintentionally become pregnant to put up the child for adoption rather than raise it themselves or have an abortion. Some of the moral outrage directed against the idea of "trafficking" in babies bespeaks a failure to consider the implications of contemporary moral standards. At a time when illegitimacy was heavily stigmatized and abortion was illegal, to permit the sale of babies would have opened a breach in an otherwise solid wall of social disapproval of procreative activity outside of marriage. At the same time, the stigma of illegitimacy, coupled with the illegality of abortion, assured a reasonable flow of babies to the adoption market. Now that the stigma has diminished[38] and abortion has become a constitutional right, not only has the flow of babies to the (lawful) adoption market contracted but the practical alternatives to selling an unwanted baby have increasingly become either to retain it and raise

[36] See Table 1 *supra*.

[37] See Adoption and Foster Care 22-23.

[38] An economic reason for the diminution is suggested at p. 325 *supra*.

it as an illegitimate child, ordinarily with no father present, or to have an abortion. What social purposes are served by encouraging these alternatives to baby sale?[39]

The symbolic objections to baby sale must also be compared with the substantial costs that the present system imposes on childless couples, aborted fetuses (if they can be said to incur costs), and children who end up in foster care. In particular, many childless couples undergo extensive, costly, and often futile methods of fertility treatment in order to increase their chances of bearing a child. Some people produce unhealthy offspring (due to various genetic disorders) because of their strong desire to have children. And no doubt many people settle for childlessness because of the difficulties of obtaining an adopted child.

III. The Sources of Opposition to Baby Selling

Even though the benefits of free baby selling might well outweigh the costs, still it will come as no surprise to students of government regulation to find that there are well-organized interests opposed to an improvement in social welfare. The most vocal and organized opponents of the baby market are the adoption agencies. This is logical: we showed in Part I that both the supply of babies to agencies and agency revenues from adoption would be greater if the private market were regulated out of existence. Assuming that agencies would have no cost or efficiency advantage over private firms in an unregulated market, they would be reduced to operating at the competitive margin if such a market were permitted. They might even be competed out of the market.

To be sure, adoption agencies are generally not specialized in adoptions but engage in a variety of child welfare services—the primary one being foster care. Children placed in foster care are maintained at agency expense, although some fraction of the maintenance expenditures may be offset by government reimbursement. Today some 350,000 children are in foster care at an annual expense to the U.S. government alone of some $700 million.[40] Clearly, healthy infants and older, perhaps less healthy, children are substitutes in adoption, albeit imperfect substitutes. By obtaining exclusive control over the supply of both "first-quality" adoptive children and "second-quality" children residing in foster care but available for adoption, agencies are able to internalize the substitution possibilities between them. Agencies

[39] Cf. Raymond M. Herbenich, Remarks on Abortion, Abandonment, and Adoption Opportunities, 5 Philo. & Pub. Affairs 98, 103 (1975), proposing a tax credit for the natural parents to encourage carrying a fetus to term and placing the baby for adoption rather than aborting it.

[40] Opportunities for Adoption Act of 1977, S. Rep. No. 95-167, 95th Cong., 1st Sess. 17 (1977).

can charge a higher price for the children they place for adoption, thus increasing not only their revenues from adoption but also the demand for children who would otherwise be placed or remain in foster care at the agency's expense. Conversely, if agency revenues derive primarily from foster care, the agencies can manipulate the relative price of adopting "first-quality" children over "second-quality" children to reduce the net flow of children out of foster care.

The group that has the largest stake in the adoption agencies' net revenues is their professional personnel. If the principal effect of eliminating the agency monopoly in adoptions was to force agencies to operate at the competitive margin, it would surely reduce any rents now being received by agency personnel. Nor can it be argued that if baby selling were legalized the agency personnel would simply become the middlemen of the legal market; if the Securities and Exchange Commission were abolished, few of its personnel would become stockbrokers. One is not surprised that professional social workers' organizations have been strong proponents of governmental restrictions on nonagency adoptions.

Potentially allied to the agencies and the social welfare professionals who staff them in opposition to baby selling are those prospective adoptive parents who by virtue of their contacts and general sophistication are able to jump to the head of the queue or procure a baby easily in the (lawful) independent market, either way paying less than they would have to pay in a free market. The analogy is to the effect of usury laws in reducing the interest rate paid by the most credit-worthy borrowers.

The potential supporters of baby selling are difficult to organize in an effective political coalition. They consist of unborn babies, children in foster care, taxpayers (each only trivially burdened by the costs of foster care), and people who have only a low probability of ever wanting to adopt a baby, as well as couples currently wanting to adopt one. The members of this last group have the most concentrated interest in a free baby market, but they are relatively few and widely scattered at any given time.

IV. Interim Steps Toward a Full-Fledged Baby Market

We close by speculating briefly on the possibility of taking some tentative and reversible steps toward a free baby market in order to determine experimentally the social costs and benefits of using the market in this area. Important characteristics of a market could be simulated if one or more adoption agencies, which typically already vary their fees for adoption according to the income of the prospective parents, would simply use the surplus income generated by the higher fees to make side payments to pregnant women contemplating abortion to induce them instead to have the child and put it up for adoption.

This experiment would yield evidence with respect to both the demand and supply conditions in the adoption market and would provide information both on the value that prospective adoptive parents attach to being able to obtain a baby and on the price necessary to induce pregnant women to substitute birth for abortion. Follow-up studies of the adopted children, comparing them with children that had been adopted by parents paying lower fees, would help answer the question whether the payment of a stiff fee has adverse consequences on the welfare of the child.

Some states appear not to limit the fees that adoption agencies pay to natural parents. The experiment we propose could be implemented in such states without new legislation.

The Market for Children: Evidence from Early Modern Japan

J. Mark Ramseyer
University of Chicago

Using a data set of about 1,000 Japanese contracts, I study the relationships among urban labor markets, peasant employment contracts, and parental control over work-age children. From 1600 to the mid-18th century, the use of contracts for the sale, pledge, or long-term employment of children fell drastically. The reason apparently lies in the development of a large nonagricultural labor market. Because this market (with its informal, at-will contractual terms) made it profitable for so many children to abscond, it threatened any property right that parents may once have had in their children's work. And absent that property right, most employers no longer offered long-term contracts on attractive terms. By making it profitable for dissatisfied children to abscond, this new labor market also reduced the control that parents had over their children. Indirectly to be sure, it shaped relations within the family and constrained domestic exploitation as well.

1. Introduction

As Thomas Hardy told it in 1886, Michael Henchard sold her in a tavern at a wayside fair. He was poor, drunk, unhappy, and unhappily married. He owned her. "I don't see why men who have got wives and don't want 'em, shouldn't get rid of 'em as these gipsy fellows do their old horses," he explained (Hardy, 1920: vol. 1, 8). If a passing sailor wanted her, well, for five guineas he could have her.[1]

I received helpful suggestions from Gary Becker, Frank Bennett, Philip Brown, Stanley Engerman, Harry First, Mark Fischer, David D. Friedman, Lawrence Friedman, David Galenson, Clayton Gillette, Farley Grubb, Richard Helmholtz, David Howell, Daniel Klerman, John Langbein, Gary Leupp, Fred McChesney, Curtis Milhaupt, Geoffrey Miller, Hiroyoshi Noto, Eric Rasmusen, Frances Rosenbluth, Arthur Rosett, Richard Ross, Alan Schwartz, David Skeel, Robert Smith, Hiroo Sono, Kathryn Spier, Anne Walthall, James W. White, John Wiley, Oliver Williamson, Ken Yamada, Stephen Yeazell, two anonymous referees, and participants in workshops at UCLA, the University of Chicago, Princeton University, and the University of Virginia. I received generous financial help from the Lynde and Harry Bradley Foundation and The Sarah Scaife Foundation.

1. Note that according to modern scholars (e.g., E. P. Thompson, 1991; F. M. L. Thompson, 1988: 91), the women "sold" in Britain probably often left their husbands because they hated them. They agreed to the deal as their best alternative in a world without ready divorce, and often arranged to be "bought" by their lovers.

From time to time, scholars have told similar tales of Tokugawa (1600–1868) Japan. The late Takeyoshi Kawashima, probably the best-known legal sociologist in Japan, claimed Tokugawa men routinely sold their wives and children or rented them long-term. It was endemic to the brutality of Asiatic patriarchal feudalism, he explained (Kawashima, 1950). During the early Tokugawa period, echoes historian Mikiso Hane, "peasants frequently sold their family members into temporary servitude," but, he notes, "In reality, this resulted in permanent enslavement, because the contract could not be dissolved until the debt was repaid, and this the impoverished peasants could seldom do. . . . [I]ndentured servants [had] terms of service [that] might run from ten years to a lifetime" (1972: 170–71).

One might have thought the sold children would resist. According to many scholars, though, out of ideological conformity or cultural docility, the children eventually complied. Living as they did within a hierarchical or familistic world, they thought working in a place like a brothel for the sake of the family "a supreme example of filial self-sacrifice" (Hendry, 1986: 21). Within the household, such scholars continue, the male members dominated the female. The elder members dominated the younger. And because of the ideology "in the air," the female and younger members usually did as they were told. For the good of the house, for greed, or perhaps from sheer folly, fathers worked the other members on the farm, rented them under long-term contracts, and sold them into slavery.

Unfortunately, these discussions miss the way markets shape family relations. The issue touches both on Oliver Williamson's (1985) work on the relation between external markets and internal hierarchies, and on Gary Becker's (1991: 14) analysis of how "bargaining within marriages takes place in the shadow of competition in marriage markets." In the article that follows, I explore these theoretical issues with empirics from Tokugawa Japan.

I first reconstruct the contractual arrangements themselves (Section 2). Second, I show that by the mid-18th century, sales contracts, pledge contracts, and long-term indenture contracts had largely disappeared (Section 3). I argue that the reason for the disappearance lies in the growing market for nonagricultural labor. By making it possible and profitable for workers to abscond, this market apparently destroyed the ability of workers and their parents to transfer long-term "property rights" in a worker's labor.

Third, I explore the apparent absence of any contracts for infants (Section 4). Peasants did not use contracts to sell them, I suggest, because infants in early modern Japan (like infants elsewhere for much of history) fetched a market price close to zero. I conclude by exploring the way the nonagricultural labor market increasingly prevented parents from controlling their work-age children (Section 5).

2. The Contracts

I base this study on 1,016 contracts found in 63 sources. These contracts represent all contracts or records of contracts (i) that I could find in published sources, (ii) that were written between 1601 and 1860, (iii) that dealt with the sale or rental of humans, and (iv) that concerned periods of at least six months.[2] Several basic qualifications are in order. First, for reasons that will become clear, I would have preferred to measure the accessibility of urban centers from the place of contracting. Unfortunately, that much specificity proved unworkable. Note, though, (a) that the places of contracting remained predominantly rural throughout the period, and (b) that, for better or for worse, they included a wide variety of domains across the country. Second, I would have preferred to know the age of the worker involved. Unfortunately again, most sources do not include that information.

Last, these 1,016 contracts, enumerated in Table 1, obviously represent a small sample of all employment contracts actually written. That sampling, however, was not done by me. It was done by the vagaries of floods, fires, worms, and the historians and archivists upon whose efforts I have relied. To be sure, these processes introduce potential biases. When they do, I address them in the course of the analysis.[3]

2.1 Indentures

The contracts in this data set took one of four forms: indentures, pledges, sales, and adoptions. In most of these contracts, the principal parties were the employer E and the head H of worker W's household (generally W's father). The reason is straightforward: Tokugawa law (based as it was on neo-Confucian patriarchal premises) and custom dictated that arrangement, and local authorities often required parties to clear the contract with them at the outset.[4]

Under a typical indenture contract, W promised to work for a given term, H guaranteed W's performance, and employer E paid the promised cash wages at the outset.[5] This timing presents a puzzle, for the parties had strong incentives to have E pay the cash wages at the end. Between the workers and the employers, the workers were the more mobile and numerous. Necessarily, they were the less constrained by reputational sanctions; necessarily, they were more likely

2. In some cases only partial records of the contracts were available. Where critical aspects of the contracts are missing, I exclude them from the set. A list of the sources used is available from the author. For translations of several of the contracts, see Ramseyer (1994).

3. One of the clearest cases of bias caused by academic fashions derives from the recent fascination with prostitution. Because of this interest, several studies have uncovered relatively large numbers of prostitution contracts (e.g., Usami, 1986, 1993). Since very peculiar considerations drive the terms of these contracts (discussed at length in Ramseyer, 1991), I have in places explicitly distinguished prostitution from nonprostitution contracts.

4. See Miyamoto (1948: 112). Under the federal legal system in effect, the law of the Tokugawa shogunate applied only to the Tokugawa domains—land producing about one quarter of the country's total crops. Yet Tokugawa law generally served as the model elsewhere. See also Ishii (1948: 395; 1964: 161–62); Maki (1977: 175); Murao (1977: 48–50, 185, 220); Yoshida (1977: 53–55).

5. For straightforward incentive reasons, some employers added discretionary bonuses later (Hidemura, 1950: 120; Ishii, 1961: 189; 1967: 136; Shitanaka, 1959/60: 226–27). H generally guaranteed W's performance and added extra guarantors as well. Because few peasants would have made good guarantors, E probably did not realistically expect to be made whole. Instead, E demanded guarantors because W's *in*ability to provide them signaled (however imperfectly) that he or she may have absconded in the past, and was in any event a bad risk.

Table 1. Pledge, Indenture and Sales Contracts in Tokugawa Japan

Date	Pledge	Indenture	Sale
	Number of observations n (%)		
1601–1620	8 (47)	0 (0)	9 (53)
1621–1640	6 (50)	3 (25)	3 (25)
1641–1660	32 (67)	6 (13)	10 (20)
1661–1680	24 (52)	14 (30)	8 (18)
1681–1700	9 (43)	8 (38)	4 (19)
1701–1720	14 (27)	38 (73)	0 (0)
1721–1740	4 (10)	35 (83)	3 (7)
1741–1760	1 (1)	95 (99)	0 (0)
1761–1780	4 (9)	43 (91)	0 (0)
1781–1800	0 (0)	165 (100)	0 (0)
1801–1820	2 (1)	135 (96)	3 (3)
1821–1840	1 (1)	95 (97)	2 (2)
1841–1860	5 (2)	217 (94)	10 (4)

Notes: *Pledge contracts* are contracts that could function as disguised sales: contracts where the borrower pledged to transfer a human should the borrower default on the loan, but where the pledged human did not work for the lender in the interim; and contracts where the borrower pledged a human to work for the lender during the term of the loan, but where that labor did not reduce the principal amount of the loan.

Indenture contracts are employment contracts for specified lengths of time; and contracts denominated as pledges where the labor of the pledged human reduced the principal amount of the loan.

Sales contracts are contracts denominated as sales, and adoptions in which the transferor received compensation.

Only contracts for terms of six months or longer are included.

Sources: List available from the author.

to abscond than the employers were to refuse the promised wages. All else equal, therefore, most parties should have negotiated contracts in which the workers worked first and the employer paid last. And indeed, in the West most indentured workers (other than those indentured for transatlantic carriage) did perform first (Grubb, 1992b).

In the longer-term (six- to eight-year) contracts that the peasants negotiated at the start of the Tokugawa period, the reason for the odd timing seems straightforward: cash-constrained peasant parents apparently coupled loans with their children's labor contracts.[6] Nonetheless, with the far more common short-term contracts (the one- or two-year arrangements), the puzzle remains: in these, too, E almost always paid the cash wages in advance. Granted, perhaps all peasants wanted loans, even if only of one or two years. Yet Western peasants were presumably cash-constrained too. Notwithstanding, unlike Japanese peasants, they almost always received their cash wages at the end of the year. Some reason for the difference thus seems appropriate.

6. In some cases, the long terms may have reflected investments specific to the employment relationship, as discussed in note 23, *infra*. Those investments, however, would explain only the length of the contract—not the payment of all cash wages at the start of the term.

The explanation for the apparently perverse timing in Japan probably lies in the way the Tokugawa government limited access to courts. In order to make litigation practice consistent with its official neo-Confucian hierarchical premises, the government generally let employers sue their workers but banned workers from suing their employers.[7] If W absconded, E thus could sue and—depending on the quality of the guarantees—recover. If W worked for a promised period and E refused to pay, W had no legal recourse. Faced with these legal asymmetries ex post, the parties negotiated compensating asymmetries ex ante: effectively, they required E to post a large bond with H (or W).

2.2 Pledges

The second most common contracts were pledges. Some pledges were disguised sales. For example, H might borrow money from E and pledge family member W as security. If H defaulted, E obtained W as a hereditary servant. Alternatively, H might send W to work for E during the term of the loan, and apply W's services against the interest. In these cases, if W's work did not reduce the outstanding principal, W ended the loan term no freer than when he started.

Peasants probably negotiated sales as pledges to circumvent Tokugawa law. Several times during the 17th and 18th centuries, the government banned the sale of humans.[8] Apparently, however, it continued to enforce security interests in human labor. Hence, if H wanted to sell W to E, H borrowed from E an amount equal to the sale price, gave E a security interest in W, and defaulted.

Other pledges were disguised indentures. Under these arrangements, H sent W to work for E during the term of the loan, but W generated a net return for E that exceeded market interest on E's loan to H. As a result, W reduced (often to zero) the amount due at the end of the term. If H did not have the funds to repay any residual principal, H could then do one of two things: (a) H could renew the contract with E and have W work longer to reduce further the amount outstanding, or (b) H could borrow the amount still payable to E from third party T, and pledge W to T.

As with sales, peasants probably also negotiated indentures in pledge form to avoid Tokugawa regulatory restrictions. During the 17th century, the Tokugawa government limited the indenture contracts that workers and employers could use. Several times, for example, it banned them from contracting for periods of more than 10 years—before permanently repealing that ban in 1698.[9] Workers who wanted longer terms could thus disguise their contracts as se-

7. For a discussion of these legal provisions, see Henderson (1974: 70–75): Ishii (1961: 189); Kaneda (1927: 1325); Maki (1970: 462; 1977: 57).

8. The edicts are detailed in Maki (1970: chap. 1 sec. 3). The government also banned the sale of rice paddies, and peasants circumvented the ban with mortgage arrangements similar to the schemes described here.

9. Initially, the ban was on contracts of more than three years (Maki, 1970: chap. 1, sec. 3). Within Edo (Tokyo), the government during the early part of the Tokugawa period also banned indentures of less than one year, but Maki argues that the ban applied primarily to samurai (1970: 69–70; 1977: 82–88). See generally Yoshida (1977: 57–66).

cured loans. Moreover, in several domains the local government capped the wages that private-sector employers could pay (Nakabe, 1974: 106–7; Yoshida, 1977: 188–93). In the labor market, these governments (and the samurai they employed) competed against private employers for hired servants. Gradually, that competition raised market wages. In response to the competition, some domainal governments capped wages. In response to those caps, some private employers probably disguised the wages they paid as loans.

2.3 Sales and Adoptions

Of two other contractual arrangements, the records disclose a smaller number. Both sales and adoptions were transfers in perpetuity. Under one scheme, H straightforwardly sold W to E. Under the other, E "adopted" W from H, but paid H for the privilege. The probable reason for the adoption is again regulatory: Tokugawa law allowed adoptions but (from time to time) banned sales. Accordingly, those who wished to sell a worker could denominate the transaction as an adoption. Table 1 lists both straightforward sales and adoptions for cash as sales.

3. Contractual Terms

Tables 1 and 2 identify two central puzzles.[10] First, over the course of 260 years, indenture contracts eventually replaced sales and pledges. Second, over the same period, the mean length of the contractual terms steadily declined. I consider the first puzzle in Section 3.1, the second in Section 3.2.

3.1 Sales and Pledges

After 1740, contracts where W faced a significant risk of sale largely disappeared. Workers, families, and employers substituted rental agreements for sales and pledge contracts. For both men and women (the data show no real difference by sex), they abandoned slavery for indentured servitude.[11]

3.1.1 Urban Growth. The explanation for the decline in the use of sales contracts is simple: sales contracts declined because of an increase in a basic form of postcontractual opportunism (Klein, Crawford, and Alchian, 1978; Williamson, 1979)—namely, running away; the incidence of that opportunism increased because of the growth in the nonagricultural labor market. During the 17th century, the Japanese population grew from 12 million to 28 million

10. Other puzzles concern the relation of these changes to household production decisions such as family size. Although such issues are beyond the scope of this essay, readers should note the extensive literature on Tokugawa demography, including T. C. Smith (1977); Hanley and Yamamura (1977); and the many studies by Hayami (1968, 1971, 1992) and Saito (1978, 1987, 1992).

11. Nor does this seem an artifact of sample bias. One would expect families to retain a document that gave them title to their hereditary servants—and this may explain why larger numbers of sales survive from the 17th century than indentures. It could also explain why so many pledge contracts survive—for the borrowers may have defaulted on these contracts and transferred workers who became the family's hereditary servants. The point does *not* explain, however, why the number of sales and pledges dramatically declined by the mid-1700s.

Table 2. Contractual Substance by Sex

	Part A Mean Contract Length in Years $(n)^b$		Part B Number of Sales and Pledges[a]			
			Sales		Pledges	
Date	Male (M)	Female (F)	M	F	M	F
1601–1620	*	*	4	5	2	6
1621–1640	*	8.4 (5)	1	2	2	4
1641–1660	6.7 (23)	*	2	8	23	9
1661–1680	7.7 (25)	8.2 (9)	4	4	14	10
1681–1700	*	6.2 (10)	3	1	2	7
1701–1720	5.1 (21)	4.5 (30)	0	0	6	8
1721–1740	3.9 (24)	4.0 (14)	0	3	3	1
1741–1760	1.9 (66)	1.5 (28)	0	0	0	1
1761–1780	2.9 (42)	3.8 (6)	0	0	2	2
1781–1800	2.1 (122)	2.6 (29)	0	0	0	0
1801–1820	1.6 (99)	1.0 (24)	2	1	2	1
1821–1840	2.0 (68)	1.8 (14)	0	2	0	1
1841–1860	3.1 (56)	3.4 (77)	1	9	5	0

a. Sales and pledges are as defined in Table 1.
b. The mean length is for all contracts in Table 1 that specify a term: contractual terms were rounded to nearest year before being aggregated. Female contracts exclude contracts for prostitution.

*. Four or fewer observations.

Sources: See Table 1.

(Hayami and Miyamoto, 1988: 44), and the urban centers captured much of that growth. Many peasants flocked to the largest of the cities, and by the mid-18th century Edo (Tokyo) boasted a population of over one million and Osaka and Kyoto over 400,000 each (Hauser, 1983: 149). Many others, however, flocked to the regional centers scattered over the entire country—to the 200-odd castle towns and the "hundreds of local and regional port cities, post towns, and small commercial and craft centers" (Rozman, 1986: 318–21). Urbanization was rapid, and it was pervasive. Over two Tokugawa centuries, the urban population grew nearly 400 percent (Rozman, 1973: 285). By the end of the Tokugawa period, 12 to 13 percent of the 30 to 32 million Japanese lived in cities of at least 10,000, and 16 to 17 percent in towns of at least 3,000 (Rozman, 1986: 323).

With this increase in the cities and towns, the demand for nonagricultural workers grew apace. As shortages developed, brokers who placed workers by the day appeared. Indeed, over 400 brokers appeared in Edo alone (Steenstrup, 1991: 144; Saito, 1987: 70, 113). As workers arbitraged their services, wage differentials among markets declined (Saito, 1978). And as lucrative by-employment opportunities appeared, even many families in the farm villages came to earn the bulk of their income from nonagricultural work (T. C. Smith, 1969).

To the new towns and cities, adolescent boys and girls could now run and find work. With their "highly variegated life, very large populations, and the drama and excitement of the bustling amusement and business centers," writes anthropologist Robert Smith, the cities "provided a large measure of anonymity" (1963: 417). "Although people in the castle towns register on the city records," complained political theorist Ogyu Sorai in 1722, "they can freely leave their establishment or switch to another. Because they came to the city from elsewhere, they have no relatives around and no one knows their history" (15). Indeed, by the mid-19th century, a quarter to a third of all Edo residents had been born elsewhere (Hayami, 1992: 255).

For both men and women, mobility was a fact of life. In one province in the 18th century, reports historian Mark Fruin, towns and villages "recorded migration-related population changes of as much as 20 percent in one year" (1973: 3). Demographer Akira Hayami (1992: 101) notes a similar phenomenon: during the latter half of the Tokugawa period, half of the men and 62 percent of the women left the village he studied for a job at least once during their life. Of those who left, only 44 percent of the men and 55 percent of the women ever returned.[12]

3.1.2 Agricultural Labor Contracts. For the Japanese men and women bound for life or at least for many years, the urban labor markets promised new gains to absconding.[13] Because of the economics of agricultural labor contracting, at the outset of the Tokugawa period these workers would have found it hard to find work if they absconded. The landlords on large farms needed nonfamily workers only during peak seasons. To obtain that peak-season help, the landlords faced a choice. They could either (i) hire help on the spot market at high wages during times of peak demand, or (ii) hire workers on contracts that extended beyond those peak months and pay them their total product over the contractual term.

To avoid holdups, most Japanese landlords chose contracts at least a year long. Given the limited transportation facilities, they hired their help in small (and necessarily "lumpy") labor markets. Like landlords in many other agricultural societies, if they sought help only when their crops stood ripe and the frost was but a few days away, they ran tremendous risks.[14] Because everyone needed to harvest their crops at the same time, they could easily fail to find help. If they failed, they lost their crops. Even if they found someone, the worker (depending on the availability of other help) could potentially extract wages that captured much of the employer's revenue for the year. To avoid these bargaining problems, they hired help during slack seasons on contracts of at

12. Although legislation often purported to ban migration, most such decrees were highly porous. See Fruin (1973: 14; 1980); Hayami (1971: 67, note 2); Hayami and Uchida (1971); Murao (1977: 124–25).

13. On the use of the risk of absconding to explain the decline of bound labor in other societies, see Barzel (1989: 83–84); see also Bloch (1975: chap. 2), discussing risk in the Middle Ages.

14. See Galenson (1989). On the use of annual agricultural contracts elsewhere, see Bardhan (1984: chap. 5) on India (also citing evidence from Denmark, Sweden, Germany, Egypt, and Chile); Karsten (1990) on Britain and the U.S.; Kussmaul (1981) on England: Roback (1984: 1171–73) on the postbellum American South.

least a year. Perhaps to split the risks of year-to-year crop fluctuations with their workers, they (like farm workers in the West; see Grubb, 1992b) generally negotiated the contracts in the spring before either party knew whether that year's harvest would be fat or lean.

Because employees could not sue a defaulting employer (see Section 2.1), landlords who negotiated annual contracts had to pay their employees their cash wages at the outset. This, coupled with the necessarily uncertain character of contractual guarantees from poor peasants, meant they would generally hire only those workers whom they could effectively force to work. Absent that coercive power, workers had an incentive to collect room and board and wages during the slack seasons and then quit.

Now consider a simple example. Suppose peasant father F sold his 17-year-old son S to wealthy landlord E. Suppose too that all jobs in the areas to which S could realistically escape were agricultural. In such a world, if S tried to escape, he would have had a very hard time locating anyone willing to hire him.[15] No new employer would advance him a year's wages without guarantors. Yet because he had already left his father and guarantor liable on his labor contract once, no one would likely guarantee his work. Being a demonstrably bad risk, he would have found work only if he could locate a rare farmer who needed extra help by the day.[16]

Suppose, by contrast, that S worked in an area with a large nonagricultural labor force. S would then have had a greater incentive to abscond. As industrial and commercial work is seldom seasonal, employers can dispense with advance wage payments, guarantees, and formal long-term contracts. Instead, they can hire workers on at-will contracts.[17] S might still suffer a handicap on the market. After all, by absconding (or by refusing to divulge his past) he necessarily signals some unreliability. Depending on how easily his potential employer can monitor his work, however, that employer might yet find it profitable to hire him.

Because F had guaranteed his performance to E, S would still impose a large loss on F by absconding. To date, most scholars have assumed that ideology or religion prevented children like S from absconding—that ideology and religion induced them to sacrifice their personal welfare for the sake of the family. Yet perhaps more skepticism is in order. F did, after all, sell S into slavery. By all logic, S ought to care less about F than most sons care about most fathers.

---

15. Because few spot-market jobs were available, earlier runaways would have had trouble finding work. As a result, it was less important in early Tokugawa Japan than in some other societies that potential employers maintain a cartel against hiring runaways (see Engerman, 1994; Bloch, 1975: 52).

16. By the end of the Tokugawa period, transportation improvements would have reduced the earlier hold-up problems by letting both workers and employers compete in a larger labor market. As a result, even spot-market agricultural contracts would have become more feasible.

17. Or, if for official reasons they chose to sign the standard indenture contract, the employer and employee could agree to name fake guarantors, parties, etc.—a phenomenon noted by Ogyu Sorai at the time (1722: 15). On the use of short-term contracts in the cities, see Saito (1987: chap. 2), who notes differences between Osaka and Edo.

Indeed, notwithstanding any ideology or religion, many peasant children faced with the new nonagricultural jobs in the cities and towns did escape and leave their parents liable on their contracts. By the middle of the Tokugawa period, workers fleeing their contracts crowded the cities (Murao, 1977: 124–25). Court documents detail their exploits, village registries record their absence, and absconding prostitutes became the theater's stock in trade.[18] Contemporary philosopher Ogyu Sorai spoke for many aristocrats when he complained that "indentured servants now often steal and abscond. Loyal ones have grown rare" (1722: 14). Those who absconded were not just peasants: in a single year in 18th century Edo, samurai employers filed 600 complaints against their absconded valets, and from 1837 to 1867, 44 (13 percent) of the employees of one prominent Edo dry goods store absconded (Leupp, 1992: 86–88).

Runaways pose a problem for bound labor contracts in any society, of course, but the ethnic homogeneity in Japan compounded the problem. Compare it to the antebellum United States. American slaves could not easily abscond, for they were a different race from most freemen (e.g., Engerman, 1973: 61; Hicks, 1969: 133; Barzel, 1989: 83). The indentured servants from Europe were the same race, but often could not speak English. Moreover, they worked under short enough contracts that many were probably free before they did learn the language: four-year contracts during the 17th and 18th centuries, and two-year contracts by 1821. Because they often received large "freedom dues" at the end of their contract, even in the 18th century workers effectively repaid a past debt only during the first two years of their service (Grubb, 1992a: 171, 180–81; 1994a: 4, 10; 1994b).

Given the Japanese homogeneity, by the mid-18th century the increasing risk that a worker might abscond radically changed agricultural contracting practices. Suppose employer E bought 17-year-old daughter D from her father F. To the extent that D could credibly threaten to escape, E would have needed regularly to pay D herself a large portion of the wage she could earn elsewhere if she left. E would have needed to pay her this wage whether or not he already had paid F for D. That purchase price was sunk, and largely irrelevant to whether D would stay.

Necessarily, however, when E must pay D directly a large portion of the wage she could earn elsewhere, he will pay F less for D ex ante. More precisely, when E buys D, he will pay F D's present-valued lifetime productivity, *less* the present-value of all payments he expects to pay D directly. If he must pay D her potential wage elsewhere, he will pay F only D's lifetime earnings less that wage elsewhere. Effectively, the nonagricultural labor market will drive the price of children down, potentially to levels approaching zero.

Suppose now that parents vary in their willingness to sell children (e.g., that they vary in their affection or in the value they obtain from using their children at home). If so, then some parents necessarily will have a higher reservation

18. Hayami (1971: 581, note 2); Maki (1970: 241, note 6); Nakabe (1974: 106); Yoshida (1977: 205). Hayami (1992: 276) finds that about 12 percent of the workers in his village study may have absconded on their contracts.

price for their children than others. As the market price for children falls, more and more parents will withhold them from the market. Effectively, therefore, the sale of children may have disappeared in Tokugawa Japan because (i) the urban labor market prevented parents from transferring an enforceable property right in their offspring, and (ii) that inability to transfer an enforceable right reduced the price of children to levels at which almost no parents were willing to part with them.

3.1.3 Hereditary Servants. This logic may explain a further curiosity in Tokugawa history: during that period, hereditary servants disappeared (Fruin, 1973: 34; Maki, 1970: 98–100; Nakabe, 1974: 104). Where such hereditary servants had been common in 1600, by the 18th century they had all but vanished from most communities. "The number of temporary servants has recently jumped," Ogyu Sorai observed in 1722 (30). "Hereditary servants have vanished from the samurai houses. Even in the rural farm houses, few remain." Unless owners encouraged their hereditary servants not to reproduce—a thesis no one has argued[19]—such a decline necessarily implies that owners freed them on a wide scale. That they would do so presents a puzzle: people rarely discard valuable assets, and slaves in most societies are significant capital assets.

Perhaps, however, by the middle of the 18th century Japanese hereditary servants were no longer very valuable. If they could credibly threaten to abscond, they could successfully demand a large portion of their wage elsewhere. If they did, their value as capital assets would have fallen substantially. Paying slaves is not uncommon. To motivate them, owners in many societies have paid them substantial wages (Fogel and Engerman, 1974: 239; Barzel, 1989: 79–81). The more readily a slave can run away, however, the higher the wage an owner will need to pay to induce the slave to stay and work. In Tokugawa Japan, that dynamic would simultaneously have caused two phenomena: it would have lowered the value of hereditary servants as capital assets, and raised the wealth of those servants themselves. Inevitably, it would have increased the frequency with which owners and hereditary servants found manumission mutually beneficial.[20]

2 Contractual Length

The mean terms of indenture and pledge contracts, shown in Table 2, start at six to eight years but decline steadily to one or two years by the end of the 18th century. The phenomenon applies to both sexes: by the 19th century, only prostitution and apprenticeships—both relatively unusual arrangements—

19. Although if slaves *were* less valuable one would expect owners to work less hard to encourage them to reproduce—a point consistent with the argument here.

20. Note that manumission need not explicitly take the form of a cash-for-freedom deal: "if you pay me X, you can go free." Instead, it can (and in Japan apparently often did) take the form of an implicit understanding that accomplished the same result: "if you work faithfully for me for Y years, I will help you set up a modest household of your own."

Table 3. Mean Age of Male Workers, by Length of Contract

Contractual Term	Mean Age in Years (*n*)		
	1601–1680	1681–1760	1761–1840
$x \leq 2$ yrs	*	29.7 (6)	29.4 (43)
$3 \leq x \leq 5$ yrs	28.5 (11)	*	20.8 (16)
$x \geq 6$ yrs	19.1 (16)	12.0 (6)	12.7 (6)

Notes: Ages are as noted in the contracts (contracts not giving the worker's age are excluded). By custom, a newborn baby was considered one year old, and gained a year each New Year's Day. Prostitution contracts are excluded. Female contracts are excluded because of small numbers. Term lengths are as defined for Table 2.

*. Four or fewer observations.

Sources: See Table 1

involved long-term contracts.[21] Men and women did not now work outside the home for *total* periods that were progressively shorter. Instead, where earlier they had worked under a series of fewer but longer contracts, increasingly they worked under a greater number of successive shorter-term contracts.

Apparently, the mean contractual term declined for the same reason that sales disappeared: once a market in nonagricultural labor developed, workers became a bad credit risk. The more profitably workers could escape, the more reluctant landlords were to advance to them or their parents several years' wages except in highly discounted form. At those discount rates, most parents and workers preferred to eliminate much of the runaway risk by negotiating one-year contracts instead. Accordingly, employers hired workers for the shortest term possible, given the technological constraints of agriculture.

Evidence consistent with this hypothesis appears in the age of the workers hired for long-term contracts: over the course of the period, not only did the mean length of all contracts fall to one or two years, but the mean age of the workers hired for the longest-term contracts fell to ages 12 or 13 (see Table 3). All else equal, if workers generally became bad risks for long terms, employers would hire them for such terms only (i) when the efficiency reasons for the terms (e.g., the need to pay for any training received) were greatest, (ii) when the adverse-selection problems were least, and (iii) when the employees found it hardest to escape. All factors tend to point toward children at the start of their careers: ages 12 or 13.

First, these younger workers had less training, and took longer to pay for any training they received.[22] Employers who hired such workers often needed to

21. On the reason for the use of long-term contracts in prostitution, see Ramseyer (1991). On the use of such contracts in apprenticeships, see Saito (1987: chap. 2).

22. These children hired under long-term contracts were at the beginning of their careers. In general, peasant children left home for work in their early teens, returned in their mid- to late 20s, and then married (Hayami and Uchida, 1971: 232–33, 238–39). For other data showing that the

train them extensively before they became productive. If they invested substantial time in that training, however, they were less likely to recoup the room and board they provided unless they kept the children for several years. Without long-term contracts, 12-year-olds thus were likely to obtain training only if their parents subsidized their employment. By contrast, older children could pay for any training they received more quickly, and were more likely to already have the requisite training anyway.[23]

Second, the youngest children presented the smallest adverse-selection problems. Parents (and the child himself or herself) had relatively imperfect information about how productive an 11-year-old might be; about an 18-year-old who had worked at home for several years, they had far better information. Potential employers, however, often had coarse information about both children. As a result, parents (and the child) had an incentive either to keep high-quality older children at home or to rent them under a succession of single-year contracts. If they offered an 18-year-old child under a 10-year contract, employers necessarily had reason to suspect that the child was relatively less productive.

Third, the youngest workers were less able to abscond successfully, for they were less likely to have the "street smarts" necessary to succeed on their own.[24] Even an employer who could not stop a 20-year-old from escaping might yet be able to keep a 12-year-old. For all these reasons, therefore, peasants stopped negotiating long-term contracts for the older workers. Instead, they primarily used them only for the younger children—only those who needed several years to pay for the training they received, who presented smaller adverse-selection problems, and who could not easily escape.[25]

---

length of the indenture correlated inversely with age over the relevant range, see Yamazaki (1961: 201).

23. Note that the education could (though did not necessarily) involve relationship-specific investments—a factor that contributes to the use of long-term contracts (see Crocker and Masten, 1988; Joskow, 1985, 1987; Williamson, 1979).

24. Intuitively, one also might have thought that female children would find it harder to survive on the street than would males. In fact, however, other historical records indicate that female workers did regularly abscond, and Table 2 shows no real differences in sex in the willingness of the parties involved to negotiate longer-term contracts.

25. One could ask whether the decline in contractual length might not reflect different survival rates for long- and short-term contracts over time, rather than any difference in the contracts actually negotiated. After all, families might have preserved long-term contracts more carefully than short-term contracts. A longer contract did represent a larger cash investment.

Suppose, however, that the decline in mean contractual length did merely reflect differential survival rates. If there were no difference in the mean of the contracts actually negotiated, then one would still expect to see significantly more long-term contracts from the last decades of the Tokugawa period than from the first—if only (i) because the population more than doubled (and thus more contracts of all kinds were negotiated) and (ii) because a higher percentage of contracts of all kinds were likely to survive from 1860 than from 1601. Notwithstanding, my data set contains no evidence of that phenomenon: 37 long-term (six or more years) nonprostitution contracts survive from 1601–1680, 28 from 1681–1760, and 32 from 1761–1860.

3.3 Alternatives

3.3.1 Ideological Change. Consider now three alternative hypotheses about the disappearance of sales contracts and the decline in the mean length of indentures and pledges.[26] First, some observers (e.g., Ishio, 1975: 437–61) invoke Henry Maine's (1906: 173–74) famous transition from status to contract. In the 17th century, the rich preferred hired help for whom that function was their fixed status. As time passed, they learned to think contractually and began renting their help instead. Even the perceptive historian Thomas C. Smith (1959: 116) advances ideological change to explain the shortening of contractual terms in Japan: "This drastic shortening of the employment period," he writes, "reflects the fact that labor was being slowly lifted out of the context of the social group and recognized as having an economic value independent of social relations." Unfortunately, describing a shift does not explain it, and "explaining" an economic shift by positing an ideological shift is usually less an explanation than a description.

3.3.2 Rising Incomes. Alternatively, perhaps peasants abandoned sales and long-term contracts because their incomes increased. During the Tokugawa period, average peasant incomes did rise (Hanley and Yamamura, 1977). If peasants in 1600 sold their children out of desperation, then an increase in income should have caused a decrease in sales. Promising as the hypothesis may seem, two factors militate against it.

First, higher incomes do not explain why existing hereditary servants disappeared. The full puzzle, recall, is not just why peasants stopped negotiating sales contracts. It is also why existing hereditary servants disappeared, and the rising-incomes hypothesis does not answer that question. By contrast, the hypothesis above suggests that the urban labor market facilitated manumission by simultaneously raising servant wealth and lowering servant value.

Second, because peasant incomes continued to vary over a broad range during the period, some peasants remained desperately poor. Necessarily, therefore, even if an increase in peasant incomes might have reduced sales contracts, it should not have eliminated them. According to Table 1, though, sales all but disappeared by the mid-18th century. Even from the desperate years of the Temmei famine (1782–1787) when 130,000 to 200,000 people died, no sales or pledges survive.[27] By contrast, the hypothesis above predicts that sales and pledges would largely disappear. If peasants everywhere were by the mid-18th century within a few days' walk of a modest urban center, then anyone who

26. Alternatively, one could try to explain the contractual shifts by positing the development of financial innovations that enabled landless peasants to obtain credit without using human mortgages. The explanation does not work: although the sophistication of rural financial markets did increase during this time, even by the late 19th century landless peasants still had access to little credit.

27. On famine mortality, see Kokushi (1988). For the five years preceding the famine years the mean length of the contracts with stated terms (22 contracts) was 3.6 years; for the famine years and the five succeeding years, the mean length (89 contracts) was 2.9 years. During and immediately after the famine, in other words, the length of the contracts negotiated *fell*. Note, of course, that during famines the *demand* for agricultural laborers would probably decline.

bought a 16-year-old or rented one long-term risked losing the child to the city. Unable to distinguish the likeliest runaways in advance except by age, employers were apt to demand an extremely high discount rate before agreeing to long-term arrangements for any but the youngest adolescents.

3.3.3 Technological Change. Alternatively, perhaps peasants abandoned sales and multiyear contracts because changes in agricultural technology reduced the variance to agricultural yields. Suppose, for instance, that they had earlier negotiated the longer-term contracts (whether sales or multiyear indentures) to mitigate the risks associated with year-to-year variations in the harvest. If new agricultural technology decreased these fluctuations, then the later peasants should have negotiated long-term contracts less frequently than the earlier. Unfortunately, this hypothesis too leaves two gaps.

First, like the rising-incomes hypothesis, technological change does not explain why existing slaves disappeared. Although it explains why peasants negotiated fewer longer-term contracts, it does not explain why the existing hereditary servants vanished. Second, the hypothesis does not explain the contracts the peasants actually negotiated. In negotiating contracts where the employer paid several years' wages in advance, early Tokugawa peasants created enormous moral hazard (runaway) problems. Had they wanted primarily to reduce the risk from harvest fluctuations, these problems were entirely unnecessary. To avoid the harvest fluctuation risk, the peasants could simply have negotiated multiyear employment contracts but transferred each year's cash wages separately at the start of each year. That they did not negotiate such contracts suggests, therefore, that they were addressing something else entirely.

4. Infants

In 1978, Elisabeth Landes and Richard Posner proposed a radical experiment in American adoption practice: allow adoption agencies to pass a portion of the adoption fee onto the birth mother, even when the amount exceeds her maintenance and medical expenses. Doing so would reduce, they argued, many of the more egregiously inefficient aspects of modern adoption. Curiously, however, apparently none of the contracts in Table 1 involves a newborn—virtually no evidence of Landes–Posner contracts survives.[28] To be sure, many of the Table 1 contracts do not give the age of the child transferred. When they do, though, the child is never a newborn. Again, two explanations suggest themselves.

First, the phenomenon could reflect data bias rather than the underlying market. Perhaps peasants did transfer newborns for cash but left no contractual evidence of their deals.[29] Although the data set itself does not disprove this hypothesis, two considerations militate against it. First, I know of no allusions

28. Ishii (1978: 556) does include an 1812 contract for the sale (denominated an adoption) of a two-year-old boy.

29. T. C. Smith (1977: 68) notes that adoptions recorded in village registries were almost exclusively of males over age 12; in his study, Fruin (1973: 155) finds no adoptees under age 15.

to such transactions either in contemporary literary accounts or in the Marxist histories that try so hard to show the destitution to which Tokugawa peasants fell. Extant accounts instead detail the ways peasants abandoned their babies while others rescued them—transfers at a price of zero. Second, Table 1 suggests that peasants eagerly documented the ways they sold or rented older children. If they transferred infants for cash too, all else equal one might expect some of the contracts to survive. Apparently, none do.

Instead, perhaps peasants negotiated no baby-sale contracts because the market price of babies approached zero. Even in the antebellum South in the U.S., newborn slaves had a market value of only four percent of their peak adult price (Fogel and Engerman, 1992: 472, note 9). Given the apparent low sales price of Japanese adults by the mid-18th century (see Section 3.2), perhaps infants just fetched an extremely low price. Recall, in this regard, that Tokugawa peasants had neither effective birth control nor safe abortion technology. Birth control involved little more than abstinence, and most abortions involved either toxic drugs or dangerous mechanical ploys (Sakurai, 1993; Shitanaka, 1959/60: 210). Faced with these choices, many peasants—according to demographic studies—killed their babies instead (T. C. Smith, 1977: 83–85; Mosk, 1978, 1979).

That peasants routinely killed "surplus" babies (both girls *and* boys) itself implies that infants commanded a market price near zero. All else equal, one might ask, why kill your baby if you can sell it for cash? Or why pay much for your neighbor's baby (except to insure adequate prenatal care) if you can find an abandoned one for free? Perhaps, therefore, peasants seldom sold babies because babies had little market value; they seldom negotiated elaborate contracts for babies because the low economic value of the asset transferred did not justify the transactions costs of contractual draftsmanship.[30]

If infants in Japan did have a zero market price, the recent proposals to allow adoptive parents to pay birth mothers may be largely artifacts of modern birth control, abortion technology, and information about prenatal care. Babics may indeed warrant nontrivial positive payments where professional couples defer childbirth until their mid-30s, where parents who do not want children use the pill, where inadvertently pregnant mothers safely and cheaply abort in the first trimester, and where adoptive parents realize the importance of prenatal care. Landes and Posner advanced their proposal in such a world—but for most of history the world has been very different. In Tokugawa Japan, couples married in their 20s and practiced little effective birth control. Rather than abort, they often brought their children to term, and killed or abandoned those born at inconvenient times or those of inconvenient sex.

30. Because the adoptive father could register the baby as his own, even without a sales contract he could still protect his "title" to the newborn.

5. Labor Markets and Family Norms

Indirectly, to be sure, the analysis above (in Section 3) also suggests that most scholars of Tokugawa Japan have exaggerated the power parents had over their work-age children. To date, most have assumed that the real parties to these contracts were the employers and the heads of the workers' households—generally the fathers. The fathers decided which children would work where for how long. They negotiated the contracts and they kept the money.

Fundamentally, though, who signed these contracts tells us nothing about who negotiated them and who kept the money. Tokugawa law and custom required the parties to draft labor contracts as though the household head negotiated the terms and pocketed the money (Ishii, 1961: 181; Miyamoto, 1948: 112). The parties largely complied, and included appropriate contractual recitals.

5.1 Parental Control

Granted, in some cases the parents did control the transaction. In the sale contracts, for example, they probably negotiated the deal and took the money. So too in the indentures for six-year-old children. But contracts involving very young children were always rare, and by the middle of the Tokugawa period sales contracts had virtually disappeared. Most contracts instead concerned indentured arrangements for teenagers and workers in their 20s. The important questions concern these.

Indirectly, but necessarily, the analysis above implies that by the mid-18th century many of the workers in these run-of-the-mill contracts exercised significant control over their own lives. Recall first that sales and long-term contracts seem to have disappeared because the growing market in nonagricultural labor destroyed employer E's ability to enforce his property right in worker S's labor. Because E no longer could readily prevent S from absconding, he refused to advance S's father F several years' cash wages except at an unacceptably (to F or S) high discount rate. Accordingly, E, F, and S negotiated contracts for the minimum technologically feasible unit. With agricultural contracts, that unit was one year.

Consider how Tables 1 and 2 would look if father F in 1750 could still have prevented his son S from absconding. If F had had that power—either by force or by normative authority—he would have been able to continue to persuade E to accept sales and long-term indenture arrangements. Presumably, if some parents wanted to trade their children's long-term service for cash advances in 1650, some still wanted to do so in 1750. Yet if F in 1750 could still control S, then E would not have much feared that S would abscond. Similarly, if S in 1750 were not so heartless as to abscond and leave F liable for several years' cash wages, then E would not have feared that S would abscond. Instead, in either case E could have relied on S to stay. Accordingly, if some parents wanted to sell their children long-term, E could safely have bought the children. Notwithstanding, by 1750, all parties—E, F, and S—abandoned such contracts.

Hence the necessary conclusion, indirect as it may be: by the middle of the 18th century, parents could no longer reliably control their sons and daughters.

Perhaps precisely because a father's real control had grown so attenuated, the parties themselves often came to ignore his role. Noted Ogyu Sorai in 1722 (15): "the household heads they recite in the contracts often have no address. In fact, they often are merely fictitious names."

5.2 Parental Expropriation

The proposition that many children by 1750 kept much of the cash they earned (or gave it to their parents with the implicit understanding that they received it back with interest when they established their own household) again follows—indirectly but necessarily—from this logic. If by the mid-18th century son S *could* profitably abscond, father F generally had to let S keep much of the money. Otherwise, S often *would* abscond. Recall that the fathers were liable on their sons' contracts. Even when absconding left their families liable for several years' cash wages, many children willingly ran to the city. Tables 1 and 2 thus imply that S often did as F said only if F made it worth his while. Unless S found it worthwhile not to leave home, and even if leaving home left F liable on the contract, S left. If E had to pay S the wage S could earn elsewhere to keep him, so did F.

In effect, a father who expropriated the money his children earned substantially raised the risk that they would abscond, even when they worked under a succession of one-year contracts. Necessarily, in deciding whether to abscond, S weighed the extra wages he could earn at a new job against the risk of punishment he incurred by absconding and the social dislocation he suffered. To explore the implications of this calculus for whether F could keep the cash S earned, assume S earned market cash wages of 4 *ryo* a year. Suppose first that S kept any cash he earned. If he absconded from a one-year contract, he could expect to gain at most 4 *ryo*: he could pocket the 4 *ryo* he received in advance from his rural employer E_1, and earn an extra 4 *ryo* from urban employer E_2 under an at-will contract. If he instead absconded from a 10-year contract he could expect (at a 10 percent discount rate) gains of up to 27 *ryo*: he could pocket the 27 *ryo* E_1 paid him up front, and over time earn extra cash wages under an at-will contract from E_2 with a present value of 27 *ryo*. Effectively, through absconding he increased his net cash income by up to 27 *ryo*. Unless the expected costs to absconding were much higher under 10-year contracts than 1-year contracts,[31] he would have had a substantially greater incentive to abscond under a 10-year contract.

Suppose now that S worked for E_1 under a succession of one-year contracts, but that F kept all cash wages S earned and that S expected this to continue for the next 10 years. If S stayed with E_1, he earned cash wages of zero, for F levied an annual income tax of 100 percent. If he absconded, he earned cash wages from E_2 with a present value of 27 *ryo*. Effectively, and precisely because of F's expropriative conduct, S had the same incentive to abscond as he would have

31. Presumably they were somewhat higher, since E would invest more resources in searching for workers who absconded with 27 *ryo* than for workers who absconded with 4 *ryo*.

had if he were working under a 10-year contract: by absconding, he increased his net cash income by up to 27 *ryo*.

5.3 Ideology

But early modern peasants were not like this, readers will protest. Such an a-historical and a-ideological approach misses the way Tokugawa peasants saw the world. Integrated into family networks, they would not have found it profitable to abscond. Trapped by cultural notions of filial piety, most would not even have tried. The poor, as F. Scott Fitzgerald once almost put it, are different from you and me.

Apparently not so. That norms and ideology tightly bound peasants to their family is a claim that Tables 1 and 2 (and the large anecdotal evidence of absconded servants) potentially contradict. Once a market for nonagricultural labor developed, E no longer advanced several years' wages. Notwithstanding any familistic ideology, E apparently could no longer trust his workers to stay. Notwithstanding any norms of filial piety, many sons and daughters apparently ignored their parents and pursued their selfish interests instead. Yes, the poor are different from you and me, as Ernest Hemingway once almost replied to Fitzgerald. They have less money.

At least as important as the fact that many of the peasants did abscond is the fact that many of the rest could credibly threaten to abscond. For if peasants could credibly threaten to leave, then in equilibrium relatively few would. In equilibrium, most sons and daughters would stay in their jobs. They would stay because their parents (a) knew they could profitably leave, (b) knew that they might indeed leave if the parents did not let them keep most of the money they earned, and (c) therefore let them keep that money. Indirectly, to be sure, Tables 1 and 2 testify to the probable establishment by the middle of the Tokugawa period of precisely that equilibrium.

6. Conclusions

From the 17th century to the 19th, Japanese parents, children, and employers radically changed the labor contracts they negotiated. In the early 17th century, some parents still sold their children into hereditary servitude. Within a century, they had stopped, and employers who had owned such hereditary servants had freed them. In the early 17th century, some parents still rented their children under multiyear indenture contracts. Within a century, they had stopped this too.

Japanese parents, children, and employers changed the contracts they negotiated, I argue, because of changes in the labor market they faced. By the mid-18th century, workers could readily negotiate at-will contracts in towns and cities. Because they could now dispense with contracts, advance payments, and guarantors, they could profitably abscond. Because they could abscond—because their threat of postcontractual opportunism was credible—employers and parents no longer bought and sold them outright or rented them under long-term contracts. And for exactly the same reason, by the mid-18th century many work-age children probably chose the jobs they took, kept much of the cash they earned, and generally ran their own lives.

In the end, the labor market itself shaped the internal organization of the family. By the mid-18th century, many peasant children who found themselves in circumstances not to their liking absconded. Many more did not abscond, but even they may have used the threat of absconding to their private advantage. The point follows from the contracts themselves: by the mid-18th century, employers, parents, and children negotiated contracts that seemed to reflect an awareness that an exploited child could readily leave. In effect, the external labor market shaped the internal dynamics of the family. Scholars have detailed how competitive markets mitigate exploitation within firms. According to the data from Japan, they mitigate it within the family as well.

References

Bardhan, Pranab K. 1984. *Land, Labor, and Rural Poverty: Essays on Development Economics*. New York: Columbia University Press.

Barzel, Yoram. 1989. *Economic Analysis of Property Rights*. Cambridge, England: Cambridge University Press.

Becker, Gary S. 1991. *A Treatise on the Family, Enlarged Edition*. Cambridge, Mass.: Harvard University Press.

Bloch, Marc. 1975. *Slavery and Serfdom in the Middle Ages*. Berkeley: University of California Press.

Crocker, Keith J., and Scott E. Masten. 1988. "Mitigating Contractual Hazards: Unilateral Options and Contract Length," 19 *RAND Journal of Economics* 327–43.

Engerman, Stanley L. 1973. "Some Considerations Relating to Property Rights in Man," 33 *Journal of Economic History* 43–65.

———. 1994. "Slavery, Serfdom, and Other Forms of Coerced Labor: Similarities and Differences," unpublished manuscript, University of Rochester.

Fogel, Robert William, and Stanley L. Engerman. 1974. *Time on the Cross: The Economics of American Negro Slavery*. Boston: Little, Brown.

———, and ———. 1992. "The Slave Breeding Thesis," in R. W. Fogel and S. L. Engerman, eds., *Without Consent or Contract: The Rise and Fall of American Slavery—Conditions of Slave Life and the Transition to Freedom: Technical Papers II*. New York: W. W. Norton.

Fruin, William Mark. 1973. "Labor Migration in Nineteenth Century Japan: A Study Based on Echizen Han." Unpublished Ph.D. dissertation, Stanford University.

———. 1980. "Peasant Migrants in the Economic Development of Nineteenth-Century Japan," 54 *Agricultural History* 261–77.

Galenson, David W. 1989. "Labor Market Behavior in Colonial America: Servitude, Slavery, and Free Labor," in D. W. Galenson, ed., *Markets in History: Economic Studies of the Past*. Cambridge, England: Cambridge University Press.

Grubb, Farley W. 1992a. "The Long-Run Trend in the Value of European Immigrant Servants, 1654–1831: New Measurements and Interpretations," 14 *Research in Economic History* 167–240.

———. 1992b. "Does Bound Labor Have to Be Coerced Labor: The Case of Immigrant Servitude in English Colonial America," University of Delaware Working Paper No. 92-08.

———. 1994a. "The Disappearance of Organized Markets for European Immigrant Servants in the United States," 18 *Social Science History* 1–30.

———. 1994b. "The End of European Immigrant Servitude in the United States: An Economic Analysis of Market Collapse, 1772–1835," 54 *Journal of Economic History* 794–824.

Hane, Mikiso. 1972. *Japan: A Historical Survey*. New York: Charles Scribner's Sons.

Hanley, Susan B., and Kozo Yamamura. 1977. *Economic and Demographic Change in Preindustrial Japan*. Princeton, N.J.: Princeton University Press.

Hardy, Thomas. 1920. *The Life and Death of the Mayor of Casterbridge: A Story of a Man of*

Character (Two Volumes). London: Macmillan.

Hauser, William B. 1983. "Economic History: Premodern Economy," in *Kodansha Encyclopedia of Japan*. Tokyo: Kodansha.

Hayami, Akira. 1968. *Nihon keizai shi e no shikaku [Perspectives on Japanese Economic History]*. Tokyo: Toyo keizai shimpo sha.

______. 1971. "Tokugawa koki jinko hendo no chiiki teki tokusei [Regional Characteristics of Population Movement in the Late Tokugawa Period]," 64 *Mita gakkai zasshi* 67–80.

______. 1992. *Kinsei Nobi chiho no jinko, keizai, shakai [Population, Economy, and Society in the Early Modern Nobi Region]*. Tokyo: Sobunsha.

______, and Matsuo Miyamoto. 1988. "Gaisetsu [Overview]," in Akira Hayami and Matsuo Miyamoto, eds., *Keizai shakai no seiritsu [The Establishment of an Economic Society]*. Tokyo: Iwanami shoten.

______, and Nobuko Uchida. 1971. "Kinsei nomin no kodo tsuiseki chosa [An Investigation into the Movement of Early Modern Peasants]," 1971 *Tokugawa rinsei shi kenkyu jo kenkyu kiyo* 217–56.

Henderson, Dan Fenno. 1974. "'Contracts' in Tokugawa Villages," 1 *Journal of Japanese Studies* 51–90.

Hendry, Joy. 1986. *Marriage in Changing Japan*. Rutland, Vt.: Charles E. Tuttle.

Hicks, John. 1969. *A Theory of Economic History*. Oxford: Oxford University Press.

Hidemura, Senzo. 1950. "Tokugawa ki hokubu Kyushu ni okeru noson hokonin no shoso [Aspects of Agricultural Village Laborers in Northern Kyushu in the Tokugawa Period]," 16 *Keizaigaku kenkyu* 97–133.

Ishii, Ryosuke. 1948. *Nihon hoseishi gaisetsu [An Outline of Japanese Legal History]*. Tokyo: Kobundo.

______. 1961. *Zoku Edo jidai manpitsu [More Random Notes on the Edo Period]*. Tokyo: Inoue shobo.

______. 1964. *Hosei shi [Legal History]*. Tokyo: Yamakawa shuppan sha.

______. 1967. *Yoshiwara [Yoshiwara]*. Tokyo: Chuo koron sha.

______. 1978. *Nihon dantai ho shi [A History of Japanese Group Law]*. Tokyo: Sobun sha.

Ishio, Yoshihisa. 1975. *Nihon keisei ho no kenkyu [Studies in Early Modern Japanese Law]*. Tokyo: Bokutakusha.

Joskow, Paul L. 1985. "Vertical Integration and Long-term Contracts: The Case of Coal-burning Electric Generating Plants," 1 *Journal of Law, Economics, & Organization* 33–80.

______. 1987. "Contract Duration and Relationship-Specific Investments: Empirical Evidence from Coal Markets," 77 *American Economic Review* 168–85.

Kaneda, Heiichiro. 1927. "Tokugawa jidai ni okeru koyo ho no kenkyu [A Study of Employment Law in the Tokugawa Period], 41 *Kokka gakkai zasshi* 1103–39, 1299–1341, 1441–1473, 1651–74.

Karsten, Peter. 1990. "'Bottomed on Justice': A Reappraisal of Critical Legal Studies Scholarship Concerning Breaches of Labor Contracts by Quitting or Firing in Britain and the U.S., 1630–1880," 34 *American Journal of Legal History* 213–61.

Kawashima, Takeyoshi. 1950. *Nihon shakai no kazokuteki kosei [The Family Structure of Japanese Society]*. Tokyo: Nihon hyoron sha.

Klein, Benjamin, Robert G. Crawford, and Armen A. Alchian. 1978. "Vertical Integration, Appropriable Rents, and the Competitive Contracting Process," 21 *Journal of Law & Economics* 297–326.

Kokushi daijiten henshu iinkai (eds.). 1988. *Kokushi daijiten [The Great Encyclopedia of National History]*. Tokyo: Yoshikawa kobunkan.

Kussmaul, Ann. 1981. *Servants in Husbandry in Early Modern England*. Cambridge, England: Cambridge University Press.

Landes, Elisabeth M. and Richard A. Posner. 1978. "The Economics of the Baby Shortage," 7 *Journal of Legal Studies* 323–48.

Leupp, Gary P. 1992. *Servants, Shophands, and Laborers in the Cities of Tokugawa Japan*. Princeton, N.J.: Princeton University Press.

Maine, Henry Sumner. 1906. *Ancient Law*. London: John Murray. Reprint, Buffalo, N.Y.: William

S. Hein and Co., 1983.
Maki, Hidemasa. 1970. *Kinsei Nihon no jinshin baibai no keifu [The Geneology of the Sale of Humans in Early Modern Japan]*. Tokyo: Sobunsha.
______. 1977. *Koyo no rekishi [A History of Employment]*. Tokyo: Kobundo.
Miyamoto, Mataji. 1948. *Kinsei shogyo keiei no kenkyu [A Study of Commercial Management in the Early Modern Period]*. Kyoto: Daiyashima shuppan K. K.
Mosk, Carl. 1978. "Fecundity, Infanticide, and Food Consumption in Japan," 15 *Explorations in Economic History* 269–89.
______. 1979. "The Decline in Marital Fertility in Japan," 33 *Population Studies* 19–38.
Murao, Yasuhei. 1977. *Awaguni jinshin baibai shi ko [Thoughts on the Sale of Humans in the Awa Domain]*. Tokushima: Kyoiku shuppan sentaa.
Nakabe, Yoshiko. 1974. *Kinsei toshi shakai keizai shi kenkyu [Studies in the Social Economic History of Early Modern Cities]*. Kyoto: Koyoshobo.
Ogyu, Sorai. 1722. *Seidan [Political Discourses]*. Reprint, *Ogyu Sorai zenshu [The Complete Works of Ogyu Sorai]*. Vol. 6. Tokyo: Kawade shobo shinsha, 1973.
Ramseyer, J. Mark. 1991. "Indentured Prostitution in Imperial Japan: Credible Commitments in the Commercial Sex Industry," 7 *Journal of Law, Economics, & Organization* 89–116.
______. 1994. "The Market for Children: Evidence from Early Modern Japan." University of Chicago Law and Economics Working Paper (2d series) no. 24.
Roback, Jennifer. 1984. "Southern Labor Law in the Jim Crow Era: Exploitative or Competitive," 51 *University of Chicago Law Review* 1161–92.
Rozman, Gilbert. 1973. *Urban Networks in Ch'ing China and Tokugawa Japan*. Princeton, N.J.: Princeton University Press.
______. 1986. "Castle Towns in Transition," in M. Jansen and G. Rozman, eds., *Japan in Transition*. Princeton, N.J.: Princeton University Press.
Saito, Osamu. 1978. "The Labor Market in Tokugawa Japan: Wage Differentials and the Real Wage Level, 1727–1830," 15 *Explorations in Economic History* 84–100.
______. 1987. *Shoka no sekai, Uradana no sekai [The World of the Merchant Houses, the World Behind the Houses]*. Tokyo: Riburopoto.
______. 1992. "Infanticide, Fertility and 'Population Stagnation': The State of Tokugawa Historical Demography," 4 *Japan Forum* 369–81.
Sakurai, Yuki. 1993. "Mabiki to datai [Infanticide and Abortion]," in R. Hayashi, ed., *Nihon no kinsei, 15 [Early Modern Japan, Vol. 15]*. Tokyo: Chuo koro sha. Shitanaka, Kunihiko. 1959/1960. *Nihon zankoku monogatari [Accounts of Cruelty in Japan]*. Vols. 1, 3. Tokyo: Heibonsha.
Smith, Robert J. 1963. "Aspects of Mobility in Pre-Industrial Japanese Cities," 4 *Comparative Studies in Society and History* 416–23.
Smith, Thomas C. 1959. *The Agrarian Origins of Modern Japan*. Stanford, Calif.: Stanford University Press.
______. 1969. "Farm Family By-Employments in Preindustrial Japan," 29 *Journal of Economic History* 687–715.
______. 1977. *Nakahara: Family Farming and Population in a Japanese Village, 1717–1830*. Stanford, Calif.: Stanford University Press.
Steenstrup, Carl. 1991. *A History of Law in Japan Until 1868*. Leiden: E. J. Brill.
Thompson, E. P. 1991. *Customs in Common*. New York: The New Press.
Thompson, F. M. L. 1988. *The Rise of Respectable Society: A Social History of Victorian Britain, 1830–1900*. Cambridge, Mass.: Harvard University Press.
Usami, Misako. 1986. "Tokaido yado eki ni okeru meshimori onna no sonzai keitai [The Situation of Prostitutes at Inns Along the Tokaido]," in R. Hayashi, ed., *Ronshu: Kinsei josei shi [Essays on Early Modern Women's History]*. Tokyo: Yoshikawa kobundo.
______. 1993. "Meshimori onna [Prostitutes]," in R. Hayashi, ed., *Nihon no kinsei, 15 [Early Modern Japan, Vol. 15]*. Tokyo: Chuo koro sha.
Williamson, Oliver E. 1979. "Transaction Cost Economics: The Governance of Contractual Relations," 22 *Journal of Law and Economics* 233–61.
______. 1985. *The Economic Institutions of Capitalism*. New York: The Free Press.

Yamazaki. Ryuzo. 1961. "Settsu ni okeru nogyo koyo rodo keitai no hatten [The Development of Agricultural Labor in Settsu]," in T. Ichikawa, N. Watanabe and T. Furushima, eds., *Hoken shakai kaitai ki no koyo rodo [Employed Labor During the Period of Dissolution of Feudal Society].* Tokyo: Aoki shoten.

Yoshida. Masashi. 1977. "Kinsei koyo ho no kozo to sono shiteki tenkai katei josetsu [An Introduction to the Historical Developmental Process and to the Structure of Early Modern Employment Law]." 41 *[Tohoku Daigaku] Hogaku* 53–102, 165–208.

Paris v. Stepney Borough Council
1951 A.C. 367 (H.L.)

[A workman employed as a garage hand had, as defendants, his employers, knew, only one good eye. In working on the back axle of a vehicle to remove a U-bolt, which had rusted in, he struck it with a hammer, and a metal chip flew off, seriously injuring his good eye. He was not wearing goggles. He claimed damages against his employers on the ground that they were negligent in failing to provide and require the use of goggles as part of the system of work. The trial court gave judgment for the plaintiff, but this was reversed by the Court of Appeal, and plaintiff appealed to the House of Lords.]

LORD SIMONDS. . . .

My Lords, a study of the evidence leaves me in no doubt that an employer could not be held guilty of negligence if he did not generally provide goggles for the use of his employees engaged in this kind of work. The respondents' public cleansing officer, Mr. Boden, to whom I have already referred, a witness of wide experience, being asked, "Have you seen in work of this kind workmen wearing goggles to do such work?" replied, "Not in my experience. I have never seen any mechanic working in any of the repair shops that I have visited during that thirty-seven years wearing goggles doing that repair work." . . . The appellant himself gave evidence, which, so far as it bears on the obviousness of the risk and corresponding duty, cannot be disregarded. I make nothing of the fact that he did not complain that goggles were not provided, for he might well hesitate to do so. But being asked, "Have you considered as to whether it was dangerous to do this sort of job without eye protection?" he answered, "Well, we were always working through years just doing the same thing. It became natural to get in there without protection." Then he was asked, "You did not think about it?" and answered, "We had been doing it for years and never thought of it." It is true that he added that if goggles had been provided and he had been told to use them, he would have done so. But this does not appear to carry the matter any further. For the appellant, a Captain Paterson said, in answer to the judge, that in the whole of his experience he had about a dozen times seen a man wearing goggles when he was using a hammer to knock a rusted bolt in dismantling a car, adding that that would be when working under a vehicle. It is not clear whether on these occasions the man was wearing goggles for fear of a splinter of metal piercing his eye or of grit or dirt falling into it. . . .

The evidence in regard to practice appears to me overwhelming. But however unlikely such an event may be in such an organized community as ours is today, it is possible that the practice, however widespread, is carried on in disregard of risks that are obvious. Let me then examine this aspect of the evidence. There was undisputed evidence that, when a piece of steel, and particularly of steel corroded with rust, is struck with a steel hammer, chips or splinters of steel may fly off. It could hardly be otherwise. But the question is what is the risk. Captain Paterson, whom I have already mentioned, deposed to having had personal knowledge of about half-a-dozen eye injuries in the course of thirty-two years' experience, the first of them having taken place some six or seven years before. . . .

On this evidence, my Lords, no other conclusion can be reached than that the respondents were not under a duty to provide goggles for their workmen engaged on this work, at least if they were two-eyed men, and the reason why they were under no such duty was because the risk was not one against which a reasonable employer was bound to take precautions. It was from this premise that the inquiry should proceed, whether, nevertheless, in the case of a one-eyed man they were bound to do so. This clearly must depend on whether it should be manifest to the reasonable employer that in the case of a one-eyed workman the possible damage in the event of accident was so much graver than in the case of a two-eyed workman that in the former case he ought to take precautions though in the latter case he need not. I see no justification for such a conclusion. A two-eyed man might, if a splinter struck him in the eye, suffer an injury which in any scale would be considered very grave. He might even suffer injury in both eyes either by immediate damage to both or by the infection of one from the other. The eye which was left to him might have perfect vision or might be defective in a degree varying from the slightest imperfection to almost total blindness. But, however grave, even calamitous, the damage that he suffered by the loss of one eye, the two-eyed man would have no remedy. The question therefore is not of a contrast between damage in the case of one man trivial and in the case of another very grave, but rather of an accident so serious in its consequence to any man, whether one-eyed or two-eyed, that, if the risk of it was appreciable, it would be the clear duty of the employer to provide and enforce the use of proper precautions against it. Yet the risk was not guarded against, for it was regarded, and rightly regarded, as a risk which could reasonably be run. . . . For these reasons I would dismiss this appeal. But as the majority of your lordships are in favour of allowing the appeal, the judgment of Lynskey, J., upon liability must be restored and it will remain for the Court of Appeal to deal with the appellant's appeal upon the quantum of damages.

LORD NORMAND. . . .

The Court of Appeal reversed the judgment for reasons which are very clearly stated by Asquith, L.J.: "The plaintiff's disability could only be relevant to the stringency of the duty owed to him if it increased the risk to which he was exposed. A one-eyed man is no more likely to get a splinter or a chip in his eye than is a two-eyed man. The risk is no greater although the damage may be to a man with only one good eye than to a man with two good eyes. But the quantum of damage is one thing and the scope of duty is another. A greater risk of injury is not the same thing as a risk of greater injury; the first alone is relevant to liability." . . .

. . . The test is what precautions would the ordinary reasonable prudent man take. The relevant considerations include all those facts which could affect the conduct of a reasonable and prudent man and his decision on the precautions to be taken. Would a reasonable and prudent man be influenced, not only by the greater or less probability of an accident occurring, but also by the gravity of the consequences if an accident does occur? In Mackintosh v. Mackintosh Lord Neaves, considering a case of alleged negligence in muir [moor]-burning, said: "It must be observed that in all cases the amount of care which a prudent man will take must vary infinitely according to circumstances. No prudent man in carrying a lighted candle through a powder magazine would fail to take more care than if he was going through a damp cellar. The amount of care will be proportionate to the degree of risk run and to the magnitude of the mischief that may be occasioned." In Northwestern Utilities Ld. v. London Guarantee and Accident Co. Ld. Lord Wright, dealing with the risk of grave damage which may be caused by gas escaping from a main, said: "The degree of care which that duty involves must be proportioned to the degree of risk involved if the duty should not be fulfilled." The learned editor of Salmond on Torts similarly says: "There are two factors in determining the magnitude of a risk – the seriousness of the injury risked, and the likelihood of the injury being in fact caused." These are, in my opinion, accurate statements both of the law and of the ordinary man's conduct in taking precautions for his own safety. "No reasonable man handles a stick of dynamite and a walking-stick in the same way." . . .

The facts on which the judge founded his conclusion, the known risk of metal flying when this sort of work was being done, the position of the workman with his eyes close to the bolt he was hammering and on the same level with it or below it, and the disastrous consequences if a particle of metal flew into his one good eye, taken in isolation, seem to me to justify his conclusion. But even for a two-eyed man the risk of losing one eye is a very grievous risk, not to speak of the foreseeable possibility that both eyes might be simultaneously destroyed, or that the loss of one eye might have as a sequel the destruction of vision in the other. It may be said that, if it is obvious that goggles should have been supplied to a one-eyed workman, it is scarcely less obvious that they should have been supplied to all the workmen, and therefore that the judgment rests on an unreal or insufficient distinction between the gravity of the risk run by a one-eyed man and the gravity of the risk run by a two-eyed man. I recognize that the argument has some force but I do not assent to it. Blindness is so great a calamity that even the loss of one of two good eyes is not comparable; and the risk of blindness from sparks of metal is greater for a one-eyed man than for a two-eyed man, for it is less likely that both eyes should be damaged than that one eye should, and the loss of one eye is not necessarily or even usually followed by blindness in the other. . . .

"Square Deal" or Raw Deal? Market Compensation for Workplace Disamenities, 1884–1903

PRICE V. FISHBACK AND SHAWN EVERETT KANTOR

Early twentieth-century social reformers claimed that public insurance was necessary because employers ignored the financial needs of their unemployed, injured, or ill workers. Reformers dismissed the idea that competition in the labor market would boost the wages of workers who faced greater chances of job-related financial distress. This article reports a test of the compensating-wage-difference hypothesis on wage samples of men, women, and children from 1884 to 1903. We found mixed support for the reformers' claims: unemployment risk tended to be fully compensated; accident risk was only partially compensated; and occupational illness went unremunerated.

At the end of the nineteenth century, American workplaces were substantially more dangerous than they are today: layoffs were more common, and unsanitary conditions contributed to the transmittal of diseases. Progressive Era reformers publicized the adverse working conditions in a number of industries and sought new government regulations that would provide workers with safe and more healthful work environments. In addition, social reformers pointed to the financial hardship that workers and their families faced if the primary wage-earner became ill or unemployed or was injured or killed as the result of an industrial accident. Reformers called on government, as the "protector of the weak," to institute social insurance schemes that would compensate the injured, ill, or unemployed.[1] Although advocates of reform acknowledged that there were some private attempts to provide for unemployed workers, they maintained that formal payments from firms to their unemployed workers were generally nonexistent. Similarly, employers' payments to injured workers were meager at best. Under the negligence liability system, many workers received nothing after being injured, some settled out of court, and a lucky few received

The Journal of Economic History, Vol. 52, No. 4 (Dec. 1992). ISSN 0022-0507.

Price V. Fishback is Associate Professor of Economics at the University of Arizona, Tucson, AZ 85721. Shawn Everett Kantor is Assistant Professor of Economics at the University of Arizona and Faculty Research Fellow at the National Bureau of Economic Research, Cambridge, MA 02138.

The authors wish to thank Susan Carter, Roger Ransom, and Richard Sutch for sharing the data used in this study and for providing comments. Jeremy Atack, Robert Margo, Joshua Rosenbloom, Kenneth Sokoloff, participants at the Kansas Conference on Historical Labor Statistics, and two anonymous referees provided helpful suggestions, for which we are thankful. We assume responsibility for any remaining shortcomings.

[1] "Protection of the Dumb Animal," p. 226.

large awards after wending their way through the courts for several years.

In pushing for formal mechanisms of public compensation for work-related illnesses, injuries, and unemployment, the reformers focused exclusively on the absence of monetary payments to workers after the "bad event" had occurred. Economists since Adam Smith, however, have discussed implicit forms of compensation for the negative attributes of jobs. Competition among employers may force them to pay higher wages to workers up-front for accepting greater risks of layoffs, accidents, and illness. Reformers clearly understood the theoretical notion of compensating wage differentials, but argued that the theory was inconsistent with the "facts of the actual world."[2] One of the early leaders in the reform movement, economist Richard T. Ely, dismissed what he believed to be a defunct theory of wage determination:

> The eighteenth century economic philosophy was . . . based on a now discredited and discarded belief in the beneficent code of nature, ruling the economic life as all other social life spheres, and which, if not interfered with, would bring to all classes and especially the workers, the maximum amount of economic well-being. . . . But experience has shown conclusively that . . . unregulated contract does not always conduce to freedom and fair opportunity—"the square deal"—but frequently means bondage and degradation.[3]

If wages and working conditions were to be negotiated in a free market environment, the reformers claimed, then the benefits from trade would accrue to "the man who is most unscrupulous in driving a hard bargain." This outcome implied that "the worker shall become virtually the bondsman of the employer" and that uncompensated illnesses, accidents, and layoffs would simply become the by-products of the ill-negotiated labor contract.[4]

Was the social reformers' focus on ex post compensation for occupational disamenities a complete picture of how workers were remunerated for the various threats to their standards of living? Workers, as theory suggests, might have received wage premiums as compensation for the chance that bad events would occur. A more accurate description of the way in which workers were compensated for workplace disamenities, therefore, requires that we carefully examine the extent to which wages rose in response to those various contingencies.

Studies showing the presence of compensating wage differences for workplace disamenities in the modern era are legion. Modern workers not only receive wage premiums up-front to accept various types of job-related risks, but they also receive workers' compensation, disability payments, and unemployment benefits once the insured event has

[2] Ely, "Economic Theory," p. 13.
[3] Ibid., pp. 13–14.
[4] Farnam, "Labor Legislation," p. 39.

occurred. The few empirical tests of compensating differences that have used historical data suggest that workers around the turn of the century in fact received higher wages for negative job attributes. Timothy Hatton and Jeffrey Williamson, for example, found that unskilled workers in Michigan in the 1890s received compensation for higher unemployment risk.[5] Williamson and John Brown estimated that urban wages in nineteenth-century Britain were higher than rural wages, in part, to compensate for urban disamenities.[6] Moreover, Clark Nardinelli concluded that British children in the 1800s received higher wages in factories in which they were subject to corporal punishment.[7] American coal miners in the 1920s received higher wages than most manufacturing workers as compensation for more dangerous working conditions and limits on days worked.[8] Seung-Wook Kim and Price Fishback found that railroad workers received compensating differences for both fatal and nonfatal accident risks during the two decades prior to 1910.[9] Although the coal and railroad studies found evidence of compensating differences, their principal shortcoming is that they relied on aggregate data and, therefore, could not control for individual-level differences in productivity or working conditions.

The disadvantages of aggregated historical data are overcome in this study. Beginning in 1874 and continuing until World War I, state bureaus of labor sought to provide a detailed, quantitative, and impartial investigation of labor conditions in their respective states; therefore, they published full survey responses from working men, women, and children in raw form. The Historical Labor Statistics Project (HLSP) at the University of California (Berkeley and Riverside) has coded many of the state labor reports and has made them available in machine-readable form.[10] To test whether workers received higher wages for workplace disamenities, we made use of five quite diverse samples from the more than one hundred that the HLSP has identified: Kansas workers from 1884 through 1887, Maine workers in 1890, California wage earners in 1892, female workers in Indianapolis in 1992, and child laborers in New Jersey in 1903. By comparing the labor market experiences of workers of different ages and sexes, we can examine the robustness of our conclusions.[11]

[5] Hatton and Williamson, "Unemployment, Employment Contracts."

[6] Williamson, "Was the Industrial Revolution Worth It?"; and Brown, "The Condition of England."

[7] Nardinelli, "Corporal Punishment"; and Nardinelli, "The Productivity of Corporal Punishment."

[8] Fishback, *Soft Coal*, chap. 6.

[9] Kim and Fishback, "Wages and Accident Risk."

[10] See Carter, Ransom, and Sutch, "The Historical Labor Statistics Project."

[11] The samples focus almost exclusively on workers in manufacturing and mechanical pursuits and in trade and transport; they underrepresent people working in agriculture or domestic and personal service. Moreover, the samples tend to focus more heavily on skilled workers and union members. Because social reformers directed most of their attention to manufacturing workers and

BASIC MODEL AND RESULTS

For each sample we estimated hedonic wage regressions in semi-log form using ordinary least squares.[12] The functional relationship that we estimated can be written as

$$w_{ij} = f(X_i, U_i, \bar{U}_j, S_i, \bar{S}_j, \bar{A}_j, e_i) \tag{1}$$

where w_{ij} represents the logarithm of individual i's hourly earnings in industry j, X_i corresponds to individual i's productivity attributes—like age, work experience, and schooling—and U_i and S_i measure the individual's propensity for unemployment and sickness.[13] A model of compensating differences also predicts that workers received wage premiums for unemployment, sickness, and accident risk associated specifically with employment in industry j—$\bar{U}_j$, $\bar{S}_j$, and $\bar{A}_j$, respectively, in equation 1. Finally, e_i is random error.

Because our focus is on the compensating differences discussed in the next few sections, the full set of regression results are not reported here.[14] Similar to the findings of other hedonic wage studies, ours suggest that individual attributes affected workers' wages as theory might predict. Greater levels of human capital—measured by age, tenure within the firm, and experience in the current occupation—increased wages, but at a decreasing rate. Skilled workers earned relatively more than unskilled workers and laborers, whereas professionals and proprietors tended to earn more than the skilled. Women earned less than men, which is consistent with Claudia Goldin's

to women and children, the relative nonrandomness of the samples actually provides us with an appropriate data set to test reformers' claims that workers were left unremunerated for workplace disamenities.

[12] Hedonic regressions are typically used to determine the market values of various attributes of jobs and workers. The semi-log hedonic wage regression is standard for the type of analysis we provide in this article. See, for example, Thaler and Rosen, "The Value of Saving a Life"; and Viscusi, "Labor Market Valuations." Although hedonic wage equations are typically used to test models based on neoclassical assumptions, researchers have used hedonic equations in situations in which they believe that the strict assumptions underlying neoclassical models are not satisfied. See, for instance, Krueger and Summers, "Efficiency Wages."

[13] The California sample included workers paid by the day, by the week, and by the month. Before computing the hourly earnings, we converted the weekly and monthly wages into daily earnings by dividing by 6 and 26, respectively. In all samples we also ran the regressions with the daily (or weekly) wage as the dependent variable and hours per day (per week) as an independent variable. The results were essentially the same as those reported here. For the samples that reported annual earnings, we performed consistency checks using the annual earnings and days worked (308 minus days lost for various reasons) to calculate a daily wage. In all cases the daily wage calculated using annual earnings had means similar to the daily wage reported by the workers; the correlations between the two were 0.88 in Maine, 0.935 in California, 0.932 in Kansas, and 0.97 in Indiana.

[14] These results are presented in an earlier working paper version of this article, which is available from the authors.

findings.[15] Immigrants in general earned less than native workers, whereas union members earned relatively higher hourly wages.[16]

Compensation for Layoff Risk

The risk of layoffs and unemployment was potentially a serious problem for workers at the turn of the century. Some industries were more susceptible to seasonal layoffs; others were more susceptible to plant closings related to troughs in the business cycle. Days lost to no-work averaged 25.0 days in California, 5.3 weeks in Indianapolis, 37.1 days in Maine, and 45.6 days in Kansas. In the absence of private or public unemployment insurance schemes, the payment of wage premiums for accepting a higher risk of layoff became the primary mechanism through which workers were compensated for unemployment.[17] In the data that we consider here, every state but New Jersey published information on the number of days that the worker was unemployed because no work was available and because of other, unspecified, reasons. We would expect that employers would have been forced to pay a compensating differential to workers who expected to be laid off because of the nature of the work (seasonal or cyclical, for example) or inadequate planning by the employer.

We used the reported number of days lost due to no-work as a direct measure of unemployment risk. As a worker might have been unemployed because of his or her own productivity characteristics or because of industry-specific reasons, we attempted to disentangle those effects by using the reported days of unemployment to construct two variables: the mean number of days lost because no work was available in each worker's industry (denoted $\bar{U}_j$ in equation 1) and the individual's deviation from his industry's mean ($\bar{U}_i$). The industry mean seeks to capture layoffs that were common to all workers within a particular industry. Compensating differences for industry-related lost days of work would lead to a positive coefficient on the industry mean variables.[18] If less productive workers were likely to be unemployed longer than

[15] Goldin, *Understanding the Gender Gap*, chap. 4. The coefficient of the sex dummy variable in the analysis of New Jersey children is statistically insignificant from zero, which is consistent with the argument in Goldin and Sokoloff, "Women, Children, and Industrialization," that women, male children, and female children were close substitutes.

[16] Immigrants did not fare poorly in all states, however. In Maine, immigrants did not earn less than Maine natives. Contrary to the findings from the other states, Kansas immigrants were paid a premium, holding other factors constant. According to the U.S. Bureau of the Census *Report on the Population*, nearly 80 percent of Kansas immigrants were from the United Kingdom, Britain, Germany, or Scandinavia, and those immigrants were less likely to be the victims of discrimination. See McGouldrick and Tannen, "Did American Manufacturers Discriminate?"

[17] Topel, "Equilibrium Earnings," notes that with unemployment insurance available, wage regressions that do not control for unemployment insurance fail to find compensating differences for unemployment risk. Once the unemployment insurance variable is included in the equations, the wage premium for layoff risk is found.

[18] We also experimented with calculating industry means after controlling for individual

the industry average, we would anticipate a negative coefficient on the deviations of days lost from the industry means.[19]

Workers indeed received higher wages for longer layoffs at the industry level. All of the coefficients reported in Table 1 for the industry means of days lost to "no-work" are positive and statistically significant. As in Hatton and Williamson's findings for unskilled laborers in Michigan, there was a wide disparity in the amount that workers in our samples were compensated for unemployment. Consider that one day lost is 0.33 percent of a 300-day work year. Workers received a wage boost of 0.18 percent per day lost to no-work in Kansas, 0.23 percent in Maine, and 0.61 percent in California. The Indianapolis coefficient of 1.9 percent per week lost implies a 0.32 percent increase in hourly wages per day lost (assuming a six-day week). Therefore, it appears that workers in Kansas and Maine were only partially compensated for each day of layoff, whereas Indianapolis women and California workers received full compensation.

Some of the industry layoffs might have been included under the category of days lost because of unspecified other reasons. In most of the samples, the coefficients imply an even larger compensating difference for industry differences in mean days lost because of other reasons than for differences in days lost to no work. In Kansas and Maine, the coefficient is positive and statistically significant, suggesting a wage increase of roughly 1 percent for a one-day increase in days lost because

characteristics that would influence days lost due to unemployment (also days lost due to illness and other, unspecified reasons discussed in the text). We ran regressions for all workers with days of no-work as a function of age, work experience, a number of other variables, and dummy variables for each industry. We then used the coefficients of the industry dummies to develop an index for the industry layoff experience. The wage regression results using that index were basically the same as those reported in this article.

[19] There might be a potential problem with the days-lost variables, to the extent that wages and layoffs might have been simultaneously determined in the labor market. If the data were rich enough, we would be able to estimate a simultaneous equations model that took into account both the workers' labor supply responses to higher wages and the labor market's wage adjustments to compensate for higher unemployment risk. Hatton and Williamson, "Unemployment, Employment Contracts," used a two-stage least squares procedure because they worried about the simultaneous relationship between wages and layoffs. They first estimated an equation of days of lost working time on various personal characteristics. They then estimated a wage equation with the predictons of lost working time replacing the reported lost working time. To ensure that they could perform the two-stage procedure, they left some variables out of the wage equation and placed them in the days-lost equation. However, one could easily argue that the variables—whether workers were paid by the month or by the week—also belong in the wage equation. Because there seem to be no clear a priori reasons to assert that some variables in the unemployment equation do not belong in the wage equation, the effectiveness of the two-stage procedure is questionable. For California, where we had pay period information similar to that used by Hatton and Williamson, we followed their methods: (1) we estimated a probit equation for having lost time because no work was available and then used the predicted probabilities in the wage equation; and (2) we estimated a tobit equation for days lost for any reason and then used the tobit predictions in the wage equation. For different specifications of the wage equation, using the actual reported amount of lost time or the predicted values from the two-stage process yielded similar results.

TABLE 1
HEDONIC WAGE REGRESSION COEFFICIENTS[a]

Variables	California	Maine	Kansas	New Jersey Children	Indianapolis Women
Intercept	1.823*	1.96*	−2.89*	−3.45*	−3.91*
	(15.8)	(23.6)	(18.7)	(18.1)	(19.4)
Industry means of time lost due to[b]					
Illness	−0.0063*	−0.0038*	−0.002	0.036*	−0.014
	(3.01)	(1.91)	(0.62)	(2.31)	(0.53)
No-work	0.0061*	0.0023*	0.0018*	—	0.019*
	(8.53)	(7.89)	(4.91)	—	(3.55)
Paid vacation	—	—	—	—	−0.39*
	—	—	—	—	(3.12)
Unpaid vacation	—	—	—	—	0.228*
	—	—	—	—	(6.81)
Other	−0.0028*	0.009*	0.012*	—	—
	(1.97)	(6.50)	(4.86)	—	—
Individual time lost minus industry average time lost due to[b]					
Illness	0.00008	0.00049	−0.0001	0.00005	−0.007
	(.18)	(1.16)	(0.33)	(1.08)	(1.47)
No-work	−0.00025	0.00006	0.0002	—	−0.01*
	(0.89)	(0.28)	(0.99)	—	(4.50)
Paid vacation	—	—	—	—	0.01
	—	—	—	—	(0.25)
Unpaid vacation	—	—	—	—	0.15*
	—	—	—	—	(2.06)
Other	−0.00022	0.00125*	0.0005	—	—
	(0.39)	(4.07)	(0.43)	—	—
Pay period					
Weekly pay	−0.137*	—	—	—	—
	(5.65)	—	—	—	—
Monthly pay	−0.294*	—	—	—	—
	(4.98)	—	—	—	—
Health variables					
Health worse since began working	−0.047	—	—	—	—
	(1.452)	—	—	—	—
Job injurious to health	—	—	—	—	−0.0019
	—	—	—	—	(0.004)
Amount paid in doctor bills	—	—	—	—	0.001
	—	—	—	—	(1.22)
Accident risk measures					
Benefit society member	0.084*	0.069*	0.079*	—	—
	(3.41)	(4.63)	(3.48)	—	—
Has accident insurance	—	—	0.128*	—	—
	—	—	(3.04)	—	—
Ohio WC premium, 1923	0.088*	—	0.003	−0.031	−0.095
	(4.58)	—	(0.21)	(1.28)	(1.28)
Adjusted Ohio WC premium, 1923[c]	—	0.012	—	—	—
	—	(1.07)	—	—	—
Selected personal characteristics					
Age	0.039*	0.016*	0.03*	0.068*	0.063*
	(5.845)	(4.18)	(4.31)	(5.54)	(6.02)
Age squared	−0.00055*	−0.00017*	−0.0004*	—	−0.0008*
	(6.40)	(3.78)	(4.26)	—	(5.50)
Male	0.466*	0.466*	—	0.022	—
	(11.11)	(11.34)	—	(1.16)	—

TABLE 1—continued

Variables	California	Maine	Kansas	New Jersey Children	Indianapolis Women
Union member	0.097*	0.066*	0.051*	—	—
	(3.39)	(4.47)	(2.51)	—	—
N	845	1042	836	666	500
R^2	0.67	0.60	0.49	0.57	0.48

* Significant at the 10 percent level.

[a] Dependent variable is natural log of hourly earnings.

[b] All of the days-lost information was reported in terms of days, except for that in Indianapolis, which was reported in weeks. For comparisons of Indianapolis coefficients with the coefficients of the other states, divide the Indianapolis coefficients by 6.

[c] The Ohio measure of job risk is set at 1.917 for sawmill workers, instead of 5.40. See note 40 for a discussion.

Notes: The absolute values of *t*-statistics are shown in parentheses.

The California mean (unlogged) wage for the sample is 25.1 cents per hour. In addition to the variables reported above, the California regression includes variables on whether the worker was married; the number of dependents; interactions between the male dummy variable and the aforementioned two variables; years in the occupation and years squared; years with employer and years squared; nativity dummy variables; and skill-level dummy variables. In California there was some confusion about how to treat blanks in the information on days lost. The procedure we followed was to treat the data as missing when the observation contained blanks for every type of lost day. We included zeros for observations where there was a value listed for at least one of the other types of lost day. We also estimated the equations including zeros for every blank and obtained similar results.

The mean (unlogged) wage for the Maine sample is 18.0 cents per hour. In addition to the variables reported above, the Maine regression includes variables on whether the worker had a family; his family size; interactions between the male dummy variable and the aforementioned two variables; the percentage of the family's earnings from other members; nativity dummy variables; and skill-level dummy variables.

The mean (unlogged) wage for the Kansas sample is 20.5 cents per hour. In addition to the variables reported above, the Kansas regression includes variables on the earnings of other family members; nativity dummy variables; skill-level dummy variables; type of industry dummy variables; year dummy variables; and whether hospital fees were withheld from the worker's pay.

The mean (unlogged) wage for the New Jersey sample is 8 cents an hour. In addition to the variables reported above, the New Jersey regression includes variables on whether the child worked at night; hours of overtime; whether profane language was used in the child's presence; whether the child's work required lifting heavy loads; percentage of earnings going to parents; whether the parents were still living; whether the child currently attended school and night school; whether the child could do math and write; experience in the labor force and experience squared; years of education; parents' nativity dummy variables; whether the child was an apprentice; and the father's skill level.

The mean (unlogged) wage for the Indianapolis sample is 10.2 cents an hour. In addition to the variables reported above, the Indianapolis regression includes variables on whether the woman was widowed; number of dependents; whether she currently lived at home, helps with the housework, sews, or supports others; whether she was reared in an urban area; years in her occupation and years squared; experience in the workforce; nativity dummy variable; parent's nativity dummy variables; skill level dummy variables; and father's skill level.

Sources: All data except the Ohio Accident risk measure are from the University of California Historical Labor Statistics Project. The data for California, New Jersey, and Indianapolis are described in Carter, Ransom, and Sutch, "Codebooks." Data for Maine and Kansas are Ransom and Sutch, "Codebooks." The accident risk measure matches the workers' occupations with the workers' compensation premium paid per $100 on the payroll by Ohio employers in 1923. The premiums are reported in Ohio Industrial Commission, *The Ohio State Insurance Manual.*

of unspecified reasons. The only exception is California, where the coefficient is negative and statistically significant.

In most cases, the coefficients of the individual deviations of days lost from the industry means do not imply that workers lost hourly earnings when they displayed propensities to be laid off greater than the industry average. Nearly all the coëfficients were very small and statistically insignificant. Only the coefficient in the Indianapolis sample was consistent with expectations. Indianapolis women who lost an extra week to no-work beyond the industry mean received about 1 percent lower hourly earnings.

The sample of Indianapolis women offered some additional detail on lost working time, including information on weeks lost for paid and unpaid vacations. Roughly 6.2 percent of the women reported vacations with pay, and another 31.8 percent reported vacations without pay. For both paid and unpaid vacations, we calculated industry means and individual deviations from the means. The coefficients of the industry mean variables are consistent with compensating differences. There was a negative coefficient on the industry mean for weeks of paid vacation, which was an unusual positive job attribute at this time. On the other hand, weeks of unpaid vacation may have just been predictable, unpaid layoffs. The workers received higher compensation for such "vacations," with a positive coefficient implying a 22.8 percent wage increase for each additional week that the industry, on average, gave an unpaid vacation.

The nature of wage payments—whether paid by the day, week, or month—may imply something about unemployment risk. Hatton and Williamson and Robert Margo and Georgia Villaflor have speculated that workers paid by the month and by the week were much less susceptible to layoff risk in the nineteenth century than were workers paid by the day.[20] The California results are consistent with this hypothesis. Relative to workers paid by the day, workers paid by the week and by the month received 13.7 and 29.4 percent lower hourly earnings, respectively.

The results generally tend to support the compensating-wage-difference hypothesis. At least for unemployment, workers received wage premiums that would have covered from about half to all of the income lost because of more days of unemployment. Although the Progressive Era reformers' position is undermined by our results, we cannot categorically reject a weaker version of their hypothesis. It might have been the case that unemployment risk was only partially, not fully, compensated.

[20] Hatton and Williamson, "Unemployment, Employment Contracts"; and Margo and Villaflor, "The Growth of Wages."

Compensating Differences for Unhealthful Workplaces

"The need for labor legislation for the protection of workers in unhealthful trades is so apparent to anyone at all familiar with the facts that argument upon the subject is unnecessary," wrote reformer John B. Andrews.[21] Dusts, fumes, gases, vapors, acids, compressed atmospheres, improper lighting, extreme temperatures and humidity, and excessive strain were some of the hazards from which reformers sought to protect workers. In fact, by 1912 the American Association for Labor Legislation (AALL), one of the most vocal proponents of workplace reform, had compiled a bibliography of over 500 American references on occupational diseases and industrial hygiene and had collected another list of non-American titles almost as long.[22] It was not until 1911, for example, that Illinois legislated laws that to modern observers seem commonsensical: factories in which acid, lead, brass, zinc, and paint were manufactured or processed were required to provide lavatories where workers could wash before changing into street clothes, as well as separate rooms for lunch. Although a handful of states did have laws that regulated the health conditions in factories, reformers dismissed them as ineffective. According to John B. Andrews, Secretary of the AALL in 1912, health reform in the workplace was simply a matter of dollars and cents: "One reason that many safe methods are not in operation at the present time is simply that many employers, busy with the making of profits, have had no sufficient incentive to turn their attention to factory sanitation. . . ."[23]

All five state bureaus apparently recognized the potential for work-related health problems and collected evidence on the number of days each individual lost because of illness. Empirically, the individual's number of sick days may have conflicting effects on the wage. If more days of illness purely reflected the worker's propensity for illness, then more days lost because of sickness might have been associated with lower productivity and, consequently, lower wages. If the job tended to cause the illness instead, then the employer may have had to pay a positive wage premium in order to attract workers. We used the procedure discussed earlier for layoffs to try to separate the job-related aspects of illness from aspects unique to a particular individual. For each sample we calculated the mean number of days lost due to illness for the industry in which the worker was employed ($\bar{S}_j$ in equation 1), and then we calculated the individual's deviation from the industry mean (S_i). Increases in industry-related illnesses would lead to higher wages, if there were compensating differences. The deviations from the industry means measure the extent to which the individual's propensity

[21] Andrews, "Legal Protection," p. 356.

[22] American Association for Labor Legislation, "Bibliography," pp. 369–97.

[23] Andrews, "Legal Protection, " p. 360.

for illness differs from the experience of the average worker in his industry. Someone with a greater likelihood of sickness presumably was less productive, and we might expect a negative coefficient in the wage regressions.

The results in Table 1 show that child workers received higher hourly earnings in industries associated with more days lost to illness, but adult workers generally did not. In the typical industry New Jersey children lost an average of 6.1 days because of sickness. A one-day rise in the industry mean for days ill raised the children's hourly earnings by about 0.36 percent.[24] In contrast, in every sample of adult workers, the coefficients of the industry mean days of sickness were negative, inconsistent with the hypothesis of compensating differences for industry-related illness. Put another way, our results lend credence to social reformers' claims that the private market inadequately compensated workers and failed to provide a financial incentive for employers to make the workplace more healthful.

Other variables describing how the workplace environment affected an adult worker's health also show no sign of a compensating difference. In California, the 11.4 percent of the workers who said that their health was worse since they began working received lower hourly earnings, but the coefficient was not statistically significant. Similarly, in the Indianapolis regression, the coefficient on whether the job was injurious to the woman's health was negative, small, and not statistically significant.[25] Moreover, Indianapolis women who had relatively higher doctor bills did not receive any wage premiums.

The regression results do not support the hypothesis that individuals with higher propensities for illness received lower hourly earnings. The coefficients on the variables that measured deviations from the mean were generally very small and statistically insignificant, and they were positive in three of the samples. For adult workers, the incidence of illness, whether related to the workplace or to individual attributes, had very little impact on wages in the late nineteenth century.

Compensation for Accident Risk

Until workers' compensation was implemented at the state level, beginning in 1911, workers were not guaranteed compensation for workplace injuries. In the states under study, negligence liability was the basis for determining compensation.[26] To receive compensation for

[24] Given that one day is 0.33 percent of a 300-day year, the result suggests a full-wage offset. New Jersey also reported information on the character of illnesses. We ran regressions with dummy variables for specific types of illnesses, but few of the coefficients of the dummies were statistically significant, and the coefficient on the number of sick days stayed the same.

[25] There was little sign of multicollinearity between sick days and the statement that the job was injurious to health in Indianapolis or in California. The correlation between sick days and the health question was very low in both cases.

[26] Prior to 1909 some states passed employer liability laws that either clarified the common law

a job-related accident, a worker was required to prove in a court of law that the employer's negligence had caused the worker's mishap. In the legal battle the employer could escape liability using any of three common-law defenses: that the worker had assumed the normal risks of the job when employed; that a fellow worker had caused the accident; or that the worker's own negligence had contributed to the accident's cause.[27] Relatively few cases resulted in court-awarded compensation for injuries, as most claims were settled out of court. The Minnesota Bureau of Labor, Industries and Commerce found that 77 percent of the victims (or their families) of serious and fatal accidents received some compensation for injuries under the negligence liability system, even though suits were filed in only 11 percent of the cases.[28] Fishback found that over 50 percent of the families of fatal and nonfatal accident victims in coal mining received some compensation at a group of nonunion Virginia mines in the late 1910s (before workers' compensation was enacted in Virginia).[29] In general, the compensation did not come close to fully covering the lost wages caused by the injury and was much smaller than the payments under workers' compensation laws.[30] As such payments did not fully compensate workers for the lost wages and medical expenses caused by an accident, we might expect that firms would be forced to pay wage premiums to workers in more dangerous jobs. Reformers dismissed this idea.

According to Mary K. Conyngton of the U.S. Bureau of Labor Statistics, the negligence liability system, compared with workers' compensation, "presented a nightmare of suffering and destitution."[31] Crystal Eastman, in her seminal study on workplace accidents in Allegheny County, Pennsylvania, concluded that "the whole economic

---

or eliminated some of the employers' common-law defenses. New Jersey and Maine passed no employer liability laws prior to 1907. California's 1885 Code of Statutes includes a restatement of the common law before it was amended in 1907; Kansas (1901) and Indiana (1893) passed laws focusing on railroads. Thus, none of the employers' liability laws affected the common-law standards of negligence for the states and time periods under consideration. See Clark, "The Legal Liability of Employers."

[27] See ibid.; Weiss, "Employers' Liability"; and Epstein, "The Historical Origins," for lucid discussions of the employers' liability system.

[28] The Minnesota Bureau of Labor, Industries and Commerce, *Twelfth Annual Report*, pp. 166–86, examined the compensation paid by companies for a sample of accidents. Croyle, "Industrial Accident Liability," claims that the sample is representative and that the workers benefited from filing suit because they received more compensation. Of 54 families of fatal accident victims, 41 received some compensation, ranging from $32.50 to $6,352; only 6 filed lawsuits. Of six permanent total disability cases, four received compensation, with only one lawsuit. Of 50 permanent partial disability cases, 38 received compensation; only 11 involved lawsuits. In 51 cases of serious temporary disabilities, 41 received compensation, with only one suit. In 132 not-serious temporary disability cases, 82 received compensation, with only one suit. In most cases, the compensation was less than the wage loss and other expenses incurred by the accident victim.

[29] Fishback, "Liability Rules," p. 311.

[30] See Fishback and Kantor, "Did Workers Gain."

[31] Conyngton, "Effect of Workers' Compensation," p. 109.

burden of work-accidents [is] borne by the injured workman and his dependents, with consequent hardship and privation."[32] Summarizing the views of many reformers who sought workers' compensation laws, Daniel L. Cease of the AALL argued as follows:

> American industry has been protected in every way possible by law and court decisions, but the employes [sic], the foundation of American industry, have been thrown aside as scrap, and their bruised and broken bodies added to the long roll of human wreckage to attest to the unrecompensed sacrifices made on its behalf.[33]

The editor of the labor periodical *Steam Shovel and Dredge* perhaps best captured the essence of the reform movement's goals. "It is cheaper to kill human beings than to apply safety devices. . . . If they [employers] will not take the necessary precautions to safeguard the lives of the toilers for humane reasons, they must be made to do so by law."[34]

In this section we provide an empirical test of the competing hypotheses. The state labor bureaus offered no direct measures of accident rates for the workers or industries, so we included in the regressions reported in Table 1 two types of proxies for the extent of accident risk: first, the individual's choice to purchase accident insurance or to join a benefit society; and second, premiums paid by employers for accident insurance to the Ohio state workers' compensation insurance fund in 1923. In other regressions, summarized in Table 2, we used insurance premiums for employers' liability in 1901 and 1910 as alternative measures of accident risk.

If workers joined a benefit society or purchased accident insurance, it might be a sign that they considered their jobs to be dangerous.[35] Neither accident insurance nor benefit societies fully compensated workers for the full extent of lost wages. Therefore, a positive coefficient for the benefit society and accident insurance variables is consistent with the hypothesis that companies paid a risk premium to workers who faced more dangerous working conditions. There is one caveat, though. A positive coefficient also is consistent with the hypothesis that accident insurance or benefit society membership was a normal good.[36]

[32] Eastman, *Work-Accidents*, p. 220.

[33] Cease, "Compulsory Compensation," p. 47.

[34] "Human Life Cheaper than Coal," pp. 12–13.

[35] Higher injury risk shifted the workers' demand for accident insurance outward, while shifting back the insurance companies' willingness to supply insurance. Both shifts would raise the insurance premium for higher-risk jobs, but would have conflicting effects on the amount of insurance purchased. The workers' demand shift is likely to be larger than the insurance companies' supply shift, because the insurance companies were better able to diversify against risk. Most workers' wealth was in the form of their own human capital; thus, an accident could be devastating to their wealth position. Relatively few workers had enough other assets to develop a diversified portfolio of risks. Insurance companies, on the other hand, specialized in insuring a diverse portfolio of risks that were independent from each other.

[36] See Whaples and Buffum, "Fraternalism, Paternalism."

TABLE 2
REGRESSION COEFFICIENTS OF VARIOUS ACCIDENT RISK MEASURES

Variables	California	Maine	Kansas	New Jersey Children	Indianapolis Women
Equations with Industry Average Days Lost and Individual Deviations					
Ohio WC premium, 1923	0.088* (4.58)	— —	0.003 (0.21)	−0.031 (1.28)	−0.095 (1.28)
Adjusted Ohio WC premium, 1923	— —	0.012 (1.07)	— —	— —	— —
Employers' liability premium, 1910	0.093* (4.16)	0.069* (4.38)	−0.008 (1.14)	0.028 (0.86)	0.22 (0.86)
Employers' liability premium, 1901	0.070* (7.40)	0.0008 (0.14)	−0.019* (2.38)	0.012 (0.75)	0.044 (0.387)
Equations with Individual Days Lost					
Ohio WC premium, 1923	0.091* (4.49)	— —	0.025* (1.69)	−0.039 (1.60)	−0.11 (1.60)
Adjusted Ohio WC premium, 1923	— —	0.015* (1.66)	— —	— —	— —
Employers' liability premium, 1910	0.153* (7.46)	0.027* (2.76)	0.012 (1.47)	0.016 (0.48)	0.033 (1.16)
Employers' liability premium, 1901	0.047* (5.72)	0.003 (0.64)	0.004 (0.55)	0.008 (0.50)	0.12 (1.19)

* Significant at the 10 percent level.

Note: The absolute values of *t*-statistics are shown in parentheses.

Sources: The first two rows of coefficients under the first heading are the coefficients from the regressions for each state in Table 1. The coefficients of the third row under the same heading are from equations with the same variables for each state underlying Table 1, but replace the Ohio accident measure with the Employers' liability premium in 1910, and similarly for 1901. In essence, the three rows for each state represent coefficients from three different regressions. Each regression uses the risk measure listed and the same set of other control variables described in Table 1. The 1901 and 1910 employers' liability premiums were obtained from Spectator Company, *The Insurance Yearbook*, pp. 383–93, and from Dawson, "Cost of Employers' Liability," pp. 825–28, respectively.

The coefficients under the second heading are from regressions in which the control variables for days lost to illness, no-work, and other reasons are not the industry means and deviation from means in Table 1, but instead are the values reported by the individual. Each cell represents the coefficient of the accident measure from a separate regression, with the accident measure listed on the left, the individual days lost to illness and so on, and the remaining control variables underlying Table 1. The full set of regression results can be obtained from the authors.

In California, 42 percent of the workers had joined benefit societies, compared with 33 percent in Maine and 25 percent in Kansas. In addition, 7 percent of the Kansas workers purchased accident insurance. In all of the samples, joining the benefit society or purchasing accident insurance was associated with higher wages, lending credence to our hypothesis that employers paid a wage premium for accident risk.[37]

[37] The Kansas and Maine samples also included information on life insurance purchases. When the variable was included in the Kansas sample, its coefficient was positive and significant, which is consistent with the idea that fire and life insurance was a normal good, and the coefficients on the

We developed an alternative measure of risk using information from the *Ohio State Insurance Manual.* The industries and jobs in the historical samples were matched with the premiums that employers paid per $100 on the payroll to the Ohio state workers' compensation fund in 1923. We chose Ohio over other states because Ohio had a wider range of industries than most. The measure should be correlated with fatal and nonfatal accident risk, because the Ohio Industrial Commission sought to price the insurance so that industries paid for the accident costs that they generated. The information from 1923 may be more accurate than that from the 1910s, as the Commission gained experience in assessing accident risk. We should point out, however, that contemporary observers suggested that Ohio's assignment of premiums was still crude and arbitrary.[38] Our proxy for accident risk may be biased, as it is based on accident risks 20 to 40 years after the period we are studying. Measurement error is present to the extent that safety improved in some industries but not in others during the intervening years.

Although we focus the discussion on the Ohio Workers' Compensation measure, we also matched the individual's information with industry-level employers' liability premiums from the *Manual of Liability Insurance* of 1910 and from the table of liability rates in the *Insurance Yearbook for 1901.*[39] These premiums have the advantage of being closer to the time period under consideration, but may mismeasure risk differences across industries because of the way in which workers were compensated under the negligence liability system. Under this system, insurance companies had to compensate workers for accidents only when the employer was shown to have been negligent and was unable to invoke one of the three defenses. Thus, differences in employers' liability premiums across industries may reflect less the differences in accident risk experienced by workers than the workers' relative ability to show that the employer was negligent or the employers' inability to show that they were not negligent or to invoke their common-law defenses. Alternatively, under workers' compensation virtually all accidents that caused death or disablement were compensated. Therefore, the premiums under workers' compensation would seem to be a better proxy for the workers' accident risk across industries.

Each cell in Table 2 contains the coefficient from a separate regression using different accident measures and different methods of controlling for days lost to illness, no-work, vacations, and other reasons. The first two rows of the table repeat the rows in Table 1 where the Ohio workers' compensation premium is used as the accident measure. The

---

benefit society and accident insurance variables were smaller. In Maine, inclusion of the life insurance variable did not affect the coefficient of the benefit society variable.

[38] Downey, *Workmen's Compensation*, p. 104.

[39] The 1901 data were obtained from Spectator Company, *The Insurance Yearbook*, pp. 383–93; data from 1910 are from Dawson, "Cost of Employers' Liability," pp. 825–28.

third and fourth rows replace the Ohio workers' compensation premium with the employers' liability premiums, while continuing to use the same empirical specification that controls for differences in days lost using industry means and deviations from means. In the bottom half of Table 2, we report the accident risk coefficients from a regression that uses the individual's reported days lost, rather than industry means and deviations from the means. We report both sets of estimates because the results are sensitive to how we control for days lost. When we include the industry means for days lost (to illness, no-work, etc.) in the regressions, the accident risk coefficients are affected, most likely because now there are a total of four variables anchored to the industry in which the worker was employed. Our objective in creating the industry means of days lost was to more explicitly test for compensating differences of various types of unemployment and illness risk. However, if the only goal is to estimate the coefficient of accident risk, it is not clear which specification of days lost is more appropriate.

The specifications most favorable to the hypothesis of compensating differences for accident risk are reported in rows 5 and 6 of Table 2 and combine the 1923 workers' compensation risk measure with the individual's reported information on days lost. In the samples largely composed of male workers, the results suggest that workers were paid higher wages in industries that had higher incidences of workplace accidents. An increase of $1 in the Ohio workers' compensation premium raised wages by 2.5 percent in Kansas, and by 9.1 percent in California. In Maine, an increase of $1 in an adjusted Ohio premium led to an increase in wages of 1.5 percent.[40]

Using the Ohio workers' compensation premium, there is no evidence of a compensating differential for accident risk in the Indianapolis women and New Jersey childrens samples.[41] The coefficients are

[40] When we used the Ohio premium in the Maine wage regression, the coefficient on the accident risk variable was negative. This result was caused by the observations for sawmill workers, who account for roughly 10 percent of the sample. Sawmill workers, we found, were paid less than most other workers, but faced the highest value for the Ohio accident risk measure. However, it appears that the Ohio employers' premium for sawmill workers exaggerates the relative accident risk at $5.40 per $100 on the payroll, which is twice the level for coal mines. Note that the premium for sawmills in West Virginia was $1.25 per $100 on the payroll, which is only 71 percent of the premium for coal mining (see West Virginia State Compensation Commissioner, *Annual Report*, p. 22). Further, comparisons of fatal accidents from the 1920s show that sawmills had only one-fourth the level of fatal accidents as coal mines (Fishback, *Soft Coal*, p. 87). Therefore, we estimated the Maine wage equation with the sawmill employers' premium adjusted to $1.917, which is 71 percent of the Ohio coal-mining premium: the same percentage as in West Virginia. The reestimated accident coefficient, which is statistically significant, implies an increase of 1.5 percent in the hourly wage for every $1 increase in Ohio employers' accident premium.

[41] The New Jersey regression included some extra disamenity variables. We had information in the New Jersey sample that might be correlated with accident risk: whether or not the children worked at night and whether or not the work required lifting heavy loads. Children who worked the night shift were paid 19 percent more than day workers, and children who were required to lift

negative and statistically insignificant. The lack of a risk premium might stem from two differences between the situations for adult males and for women and children. First, women and children were generally employed in industries with much lower accident risk and smaller variances in risk. The means of the Ohio accident risk measure are lower in the New Jersey children (0.65) and Indianapolis women (0.34) samples than they are in the California (0.73), Maine (1.71), or Kansas (1.45) samples, which include mostly men. Moreover, the relative standard deviations of the risk measure in New Jersey (0.54) and Indianapolis (0.74) tend to be less than those found in the other samples—Kansas (0.59), Maine (0.88), and California (0.84). Given the presence of transaction and information costs in the labor market, labor markets probably did not adjust as effectively to small differences in risk at lower levels. Second, the risk measure may suffer from more measurement error for women and children than for males, because it only measures differences at the industry level. Studies of modern data show that within the same occupations women have substantially lower injury rates than males.[42] At the turn of the century, social concern often focused on the protection of women and children, implying that more hazardous jobs within industries were probably assigned to adult males.

Was the risk premium enough to cover the workers' losses from accidents in Kansas, California, and Maine? Given that the goal of the Ohio workers' compensation fund was to force the industries to pay their own accident costs, a $1 rise in the industry premium seems to imply that the industry would have produced an additional dollar in workers' compensation costs to the state for every $100 it paid in wages. How does this translate into the accident losses for workers? Roughly one-third of the money in workers' compensation funds went to medical expenses; two-thirds went to compensate workers for lost earnings.[43] Carl Hookstadt found that statutory maximums on weekly payments meant that Ohio workers would have received only about 25 to 40 percent of their average daily wage in compensation for accidents.[44] Assume that workers' compensation payments covered only 25 percent of the workers' wage and medical losses, because Ohio limited the

heavy loads were paid 12.4 percent more. Both of these results tend to be supportive of the compensating difference hypothesis.

[42] Dillingham, "Sex Differences," p. 120.

[43] Hobbs, *Workmen's Compensation Insurance*, pp. 245–46.

[44] Hookstadt, "Enforcement of Workmen's Compensation Laws," pp. 67–69. A Pennsylvania study in 1920 found that only about 22.7 percent of the workers' wage losses were covered by workers' compensation. However, exclusive state funds, as in Ohio, were more liberal with payments than were competitive state funds, as in Pennsylvania (Hookstadt, pp. 14, 67). The 25 percent figure seems to fit the payments for fatal accidents. Compensation for fatal accidents was roughly two or three times the average workers' annual income, whereas the present value of the lifetime stream of earnings at a 10 percent discount rate approached ten times the average annual income. See Fishback, "Liability Rules," p. 313.

payment of medical expenses and some workers' lost working time extended beyond the time period that the compensation fund covered. Thus, a $1 rise in the Ohio employers' premium implies that for every $100 the workers received in wages, the workers' expected losses in earnings and medical expenses had risen by $4, or 4 percent.[45] In Kansas and Maine, wages rose only 2.5 and 1.5 percent, respectively, for each $1 increase in the Ohio employers' premium—not fully covering the estimated 4 percent rise in the workers' expected accident losses. In California, wages rose 9.1 percent, more than covering the rise in expected wage losses. Note that losses from accidents are understated, because we did not estimate losses due to pain and suffering, nor losses due to delays in the receipt of compensation. Our estimate of the workers' expected losses may also be understated, to the extent that the mean and variance of accident risk were higher in the late nineteenth century during the 1920s. On the other hand, our estimates of a risk premium in the wage may be understated, because we must rely on industry averages for accident risk proxies. Michael Moore and W. Kip Viscusi noted that using industry aggregate-risk measures often leads to a downward bias in the coefficients, as well as to an upward bias in the standard errors.[46]

Modern studies have found a number of settings in which union members receive larger compensating differences for accident risk than nonunion workers.[47] Table 3 shows the regression coefficients of an interaction term between union membership and the Ohio workers' compensation premium. Union workers in California clearly received higher compensation for accepting risk. In Kansas and Maine, however, the negative and statistically insignificant coefficients of the interaction terms suggest that union workers received no more compensation than their nonunion counterparts.

Except for California, the results described above are not fully robust to differences in specification and risk measures. When the employers' liability premiums from 1901 and 1910 are used as the risk measure and

[45] Our estimate of the workers' losses from a $1 increase in the Ohio premium may be overstated, because workers' compensation often covered a much higher percentage of injured workers' medical expenses than of their wage losses. Michelbacher and Nial, *Workmen's Compensation Insurance*, pp. 149–51, found that "the insurance companies . . . usually offer unlimited treatment in all states, irrespective of the provisions of the state laws." The Ohio state fund, however, did impose limits of $200 on the medical expenses that it would pay (Reede, *Adequacy of Workmen's Compensation*, p. 160). If Ohio had fully covered medical expenses, a $1 increase in the Ohio employers' premium would have led to a $0.33 increase in the workers' expected medical costs and a $2.67 increase in the workers' expected wage losses—a rise of $0.667 in compensation costs to the employer divided by Hookstadt's ("Enforcement of Workmen's Compensation Laws") 25 percent estimate of how much of the workers' wage losses were paid by workers' compensation. Thus, a $1 increase in the Ohio employers' premium meant a $3 rise in the workers' expected accident losses per $100 on the payroll.

[46] Moore and Viscusi, *Compensation Mechanisms*, p. 16.

[47] See, for example, Fairris, "Compensating Payments"; Fairris, "Compensating Wage Differentials"; and Moore and Viscusi, *Compensation Mechanisms*, pp. 27–28.

TABLE 3
COEFFICIENTS OF UNION AND RISK PREMIUM INTERACTIONS

Variables	Kansas	Maine	California
Equations with Industry Averages and Individual Deviations of Days Lost			
Union	0.071*	0.076*	0.035
	(1.76)	(3.076)	(0.807)
Ohio WC premium measure	0.014	0.016	0.067*
	(0.64)	(1.162)	(3.030)
Union × WC premium	−0.003	−0.0079	0.083*
	(0.12)	(0.497)	(1.960)
Equations with Individual Days Lost			
Union	0.066	0.099*	0.042
	(1.63)	(3.904)	(0.926)
Ohio WC premium measure	0.033	0.024*	0.047*
	(1.56)	(1.974)	(2.008)
Union × WC premium	−0.012	−0.018	0.163*
	(0.49)	(1.108)	(3.796)

* Significant at the 10 percent level.
Notes and Sources: The absolute values of *t*-statistics are shown in parentheses. The coefficients in the first panel are from a single regression for each state. The regression for each state includes the same variables underlying Table 1, with the addition of the interaction term between Union and the Ohio accident measure.

The coefficients in the second panel are from a single regression for each state with the same variables as the regressions discussed in rows for the Ohio accident measure in Table 2 and the addition of the interaction term between Union and the Ohio accident measure. The full set of regression results can be obtained from the authors.

the specification uses individual days lost, the coefficients in all five samples are positive; however, only the California coefficients and the Maine coefficient for the 1910 employers' liability premium are statistically significant. When we switch the specification by replacing individual days lost with the industry means, we see two major sets of changes. Using the Ohio accident risk measure, we cannot reject the hypothesis that differences in accident rates had no effect on wages in Maine and Kansas. Further, the Kansas coefficients of the employers' liability premiums for 1910 and 1901 switch signs, with the 1901 coefficient being statistically significant.

CONCLUSIONS

Social reformers around the turn of the century saw the very small payments to injured or unemployed workers and presumed that the system was "unjust."[48] Reformers dismissed as unrealistic Adam Smith's theoretical suggestion that employers had to entice workers with higher wages to attract enough workers to fill hazardous or uncertain jobs. The results reported here show that compensating

[48] Eastman, *Work-Accidents*, p. 220.

differences were paid for a variety of workplace disamenities in the late nineteenth century, but generally did not fully compensate workers for their expected losses in income.

Adult workers received higher wages as compensation for longer layoffs. The compensation for days lost due to no-work ranged from covering about half the loss in earnings in Kansas in the 1880s to more than fully covering the loss in California in the 1890s. The compensating differences, however, did not extend to days lost because of illness among adults. It might have been that the health risks from factory work were more long-term in nature and not readily measured by contemporary evidence on days lost to illness. Alternatively, workers may have been aware that factory work could be damaging to their health, but were unable to determine the differences in health risks across industries.

There are several indications that workers also received wage premiums for accepting more dangerous jobs. Workers who joined benefit societies or purchased accident insurance, signs that they considered their jobs dangerous, were paid higher wages. When we used measures of accident risk based on the workers' compensation premiums paid by employers in Ohio in 1923, we found that workers (primarily males) in Kansas, California, and Maine were paid higher wages for accepting more accident risk, but that only California workers were compensated on a par with what they would have received later under workers' compensation. Wages did not adjust as effectively to the smaller and less varied accident risk faced by women and children in the labor market. The estimates of compensating differences for adult workers, moreover, are sensitive to equation specifications and alternative measures of job risk by industry. Only the presence of compensating differences in California seem to be robust to these alternative approaches.

Did workers in fact get "the square deal"? Or, as social reformers maintained, were workers who faced higher incidences of work-related illnesses, accidents, and unemployment getting a raw deal? Our evidence provides mixed support for both hypotheses. Whereas workers may have received wage premiums for unemployment and accident risk to at least partially offset the income loss from the bad event, occupational diseases went unremunerated. Although our empirical results offer some evidence to support the reformers' claims of market failure and their call for government intervention, the presence of compensating differences at the turn of the century raises new questions about how much workers actually benefited from labor market reforms. Consider the introduction of workers' compensation. Contemporaries concluded that workers benefited from the passage of workers' compensation laws, because under the new laws workers on average received much higher payments after they were injured.[49] A complete description of accident compensation would have to include an analysis of how the compensating differences in wages changed in response to the laws. It might be the case that labor market adjustments caused accident premiums to fall after the workers' compensation system was enacted and postaccident payments were guaranteed. The social reformers' eventual victory in providing the average worker with "the square deal"—at least in regard to unemployment insurance and workers' compensation—may have, after all of the economic consequences are accounted for, been illusory. Ironically, given their repudiation of the competitive market for labor, for which we find some evidence here, the reformers might not have realized that their well-intentioned programs could have been undermined by a "beneficent code of nature."

[49] See, for instance, Hookstadt, "Comparison of Experience"; and Fisher, "American Experience."

REFERENCES

American Association for Labor Legislation, "Bibliography on Industrial Hygiene," *American Labor Legislation Review*, 2 (June 1912), pp. 369–97.

Andrews, John B., "Legal Protection for Workers in Unhealthful Trades," *American Labor Legislation Review*, 2 (June 1912), pp. 356–66.

Brown, John C., "The Condition of England and the Standard of Living: Cotton Textiles in the Northwest, 1806–1850, this JOURNAL, 50 (Sept. 1990), pp. 591–614.

Carter, Susan B., Roger L. Ransom, and Richard Sutch, "Codebook and User's Manual: Survey of 3,493 Wage Earners in California in 1892. Reported in the *Fifth Biennial Report of the California Bureau of Labor Statistics for 1893*" (Berkeley, 1990).

Carter, Susan B., Roger L. Ransom, and Richard Sutch, "Codebook and User's Manual: Survey of 500 Women Wage Earners in Indianapolis in 1893. Reported in the *Fifth Biennial Report of the Indiana Department of Statistics for 1893–94*" (Berkeley, 1990).

Carter, Susan B., Roger L. Ransom, and Richard Sutch, "Codebook and User's Manual: Survey of 943 Child Laborers in New Jersey, 1903. Reported in the *26th Annual Report of the Bureau of Statistics of Labor and Industries of New Jersey, for the Year Ending October 31st, 1903*" (Berkeley, 1990).

Carter, Susan B., Roger L. Ransom, and Richard Sutch, "The Historical Labor Statistics Project at the University of California," *Historical Methods* 24 (Spring 1991), pp. 52–65.

Cease, Daniel L., "Compulsory Compensation for Injured Workmen," *Association for Labor Legislation Review*, 1 (Jan. 1911), pp. 41–48.

Clark, Lindley D., "The Legal Liability of Employers for Injuries to Their Employees, in the United States," U.S. Bureau of Labor Bulletin No. 74 (Washington, DC, 1908), pp. 1–120.

Conyngton, Mary K., "Effect of Workmen's Compensation Laws in Diminishing the

Necessity of Industrial Employment of Women and Children," U.S. Bureau of Labor Statistics Bulletin No. 217 (Washington, DC, 1918).

Croyle, James L., "Industrial Accident Liability Policy of the Early Twentieth Century," *Journal of Legal Studies*, 7 (June 1978), pp. 279–97.

Dawson, Miles M., "Cost of Employers' Liability and Workmen's Compensation Insurance," *Bulletin of the Bureau of Labor* No. 90 (Washington, DC, 1910).

Dillingham, Alan, "Sex Differences in Labor Market Injury Risk," *Industrial Relations*, 20 (Winter 1981), pp. 117–22.

Downey, E. H., *Workmen's Compensation* (New York, 1924).

Eastman, Crystal, *Work-Accidents and the Law* (New York, 1910).

Ely, Richard T., "Economic Theory and Labor Legislation," *Proceedings of the First Annual Meeting of the American Association for Labor Legislation* (Madison, WI, 1908), pp. 10–39.

Epstein, Richard A., "The Historical Origins and Economic Structure of Workers' Compensation Law," *Georgia Law Review*, 16 (Summer 1982), pp. 775–819.

Fairris, David, "Compensating Wage Differentials in the Union and Nonunion Sectors," *Industrial Relations*, 28 (Fall 1989), pp. 356–72.

Fairris, David, "Compensating Payments and Hazardous Work in Union and Nonunion Settings," *Journal of Labor Research*, 13 (Spring 1992), pp. 205–21.

Farnam, Henry W., "Labor Legislation and Economic Progress," *Proceedings of the Third Annual Meeting of the American Association for Labor Legislation* (New York, 1910).

Fishback, Price V., "Liability Rules and Accident Prevention in the Workplace: Empirical Evidence from the Early Twentieth Century," *Journal of Legal Studies*, 16 (June 1987), pp. 305–28.

Fishback, Price, *Soft Coal, Hard Choices: The Economic Welfare of Bituminous Coal Miners, 1890–1930* (New York, 1992).

Fishback, Price V., and Shawn Everett Kantor, "Did Workers Gain from the Passage of Workers' Compensation Laws?" Paper presented at the 1992 Cliometrics Conference, May 1992.

Fisher, Willard C., "American Experience with Workmen's Compensation," *American Economic Review*, 10 (Mar. 1920), pp. 18–47.

Goldin, Claudia, *Understanding the Gender Gap: An Economic History of American Women* (New York, 1990).

Goldin, Claudia, and Kenneth Sokoloff, "Women, Children, and Industrialization in the Early Republic: Evidence from the Manufacturing Censuses," this JOURNAL, 42 (Dec. 1982), pp. 741–74.

Hatton, Timothy J., and Jeffrey G. Williamson, "Unemployment, Employment Contracts, and Compensating Wage Differentials: Michigan in the 1890s," this JOURNAL, 51 (Sept. 1991), pp. 605–32.

Hobbs, Clarence W., *Workmen's Compensation Insurance* (New York, 1939).

Hookstadt, Carl, "Comparison of Experience Under Workmen's Compensation and Employers' Liability Systems," *Monthly Labor Review*, 8 (Mar. 1919), pp. 230–48.

Hookstadt, Carl, "Enforcement of Workmen's Compensation Laws, April 1922," in U.S. Bureau of Labor Statistics Bulletin No. 301 (Washington, DC, 1922).

"Human Life Cheaper than Coal," *Steam Shovel and Dredge*, 12 (Jan. 1908), pp. 12–13.

Kim, Seung-Wook and Price V. Fishback, "Wages and Accident Risk Under Different Labor Market Institutions: Railroads, 1892–1945" (Unpublished working paper, 1991).

Krueger, Alan B., and Lawrence H. Summers, "Efficiency Wages and the Inter-Industry Wage Structure," *Econometrica*, 56 (Mar. 1988), pp. 259–93.

Margo, Robert A., and Georgia C. Villaflor, "The Growth of Wages in Antebellum America: New Evidence," this JOURNAL, 47 (Dec. 1987), pp. 873–95.

McGouldrick, Paul, and Michael Tannen, "Did American Manufacturers Discriminate Against Immigrants Before 1914?" this JOURNAL, 37 (Sept. 1977), pp. 723–46.

Michelbacher, G. F., and Thomas M. Nial, *Workmen's Compensation Insurance* (New York, 1925).

Minnesota Bureau of Labor, Industries and Commerce, *Twelfth Annual Report, 1909–1910.*

Moore, Michael, and W. Kip Viscusi, *Compensation Mechanisms for Job Risks: Wages, Workers' Compensation and Product Liability* (Princeton, 1990).

Nardinelli, Clark, "Corporal Punishment and Children's Wages in Nineteenth Century Britain," *Explorations in Economic History*, 19 (July 1982), pp. 283–95.

Nardinelli, Clark, "The Productivity of Corporal Punishment: A Reply to MacKinnon and Johnson," *Explorations in Economic History*, 21 (Apr. 1984), pp. 224–28.

Ohio Industrial Commission, *The Ohio State Insurance Manual, Rules and Rates Effective July 1, 1923* (Columbus, OH, 1923).

"Protection of the Dumb Animal," *Journal of the Switchmen's Union of North America*, 12 (Feb. 1910), pp. 226–27.

Ransom, Roger L., and Richard Sutch, "Codebook and User's Manual: A Survey of 1,165 Workers in Kansas, 1884–1887. Reported in the *First, Second, and Third Annual Reports of the Kansas Bureau of Labor and Industrial Statistics*" (Berkeley, 1989).

Ransom, Roger L., and Richard Sutch, "Codebook and User's Manual: A Survey of 1,085 Workers in Maine, 1890. Reported in the *Fifth Annual Report of the Maine Bureau of Industrial and Labor Statistics*" (Berkeley, 1990).

Reede, Arthur H., *Adequacy of Workmen's Compensation* (Cambridge, MA, 1947).

Spectator Company, *The Insurance Yearbook, 1901–1902* (New York, 1901) pp. 383–91.

Thaler, Richard, and Sherwin Rosen, "The Value of Saving a Life: Evidence from the Labor Market," in N. Terleckyj, ed., *Household Production and Consumption* (New York, 1976).

Topel, Robert, "Equilibrium Earnings, Turnover, and Unemployment: New Evidence," *Journal of Labor Economics*, 2 (Oct. 1984), pp. 500–22.

U.S. Bureau of the Census, *Report on the Population of the United States at the Eleventh Census: 1890, Parts I and II* (Washington, DC, 1897).

Viscusi, W. Kip, "Labor Market Valuations of Life and Limb: Empirical Evidence and Policy Implications," *Public Policy*, 26 (Summer 1978), pp. 359–86.

West Virginia State Compensation Commissioner, *Annual Report, July 1, 1923–June 30, 1924.*

Weiss, Harry, "Employers' Liability and Workmen's Compensation," in John R. Commons, ed., *History of Labor in the United States, 1896–1932* (New York, 1935), pp. 564–610.

Whaples, Robert, and David Buffum, "Fraternalism, Paternalism, the Family, and the Market: Insurance a Century Ago," *Social Science History*, 41 (Apr. 1991), pp. 97–122.

Williamson, Jeffrey G., "Was the Industrial Revolution Worth It? Disamenities and Death in 19th Century British Towns," *Explorations in Economic History*, 19 (July 1982), pp. 221–45.

PROPERTY RIGHTS, RISK SHARING, AND PLAYER DISABILITY IN MAJOR LEAGUE BASEBALL*

KENNETH LEHN
Washington University School of Business

In *The Economic Organization* Frank Knight describes five tasks performed in all economic systems. In logical order the first of these tasks is determination of what is to be produced. Knight describes the second function: "The second step, logically speaking, after the ranking and grading of the uses to which productive power may be put, is that of actually putting them to use in accordance with the scale of values thus established. From a social point of view, this process may be viewed under two aspects, (a) the assignment or *allocation* of the available productive forces and materials among the various lines of industry, and (b) the effective *coordination* of the various means of production in each industry into such groupings as will produce the greatest result."[1] Economists frequently have assumed that the "effective coordination" of inputs is primarily an engineering problem and have directed their attention to questions dealing with allocative efficiency. For example, Knight goes on to state that the effective coordination of inputs "properly belongs to technological rather than to economic science, and is treated in economics only with reference to the interrelations between the organization of society as a whole and the internal organization of the industries."[2]

Recent literature in the area of property rights and agency relationships has assumed that the effective coordination of inputs depends on the available contracting technology as well as on the available engineering

* Generous financial support for this research was provided by the Center for the Study of American Business and the H. B. Earhart Foundation. I would like to thank Lee Benham, Alexandra Benham, Edward Greenberg, William Landes, William Marshall, David Schap, and Barry Weingast for helpful comments.

[1] Frank H. Knight, The Economic Organization (1951) at 10.

[2] *Id.*

[*Journal of Law & Economics*, vol. XXV (October 1982)]

technology.[3] In this literature, organizations are viewed as networks of contracts involving the voluntary interaction of individuals in pursuit of their self-interest. Embodied in these contracts is an incentive structure which is determined in part by legal arrangements defining property rights and in part by transaction costs, including the costs of monitoring performance. As alternative specifications of property rights result in different incentive structures within the organization, production functions are viewed as more than simply technological relationships. Jensen and Meckling have stated that, "Since such sets of contracts specify the disposition of rewards and costs arising out of the organization's activities, they are important in determining the behavior of the participants and thereby the behavior of the organization as a whole. In particular, in the case of the firm, the nature of the rights and the contracts affects output. This in turn means that the production function of the firm depends on the specification of rights and the laws or rules of the game governing contracting."[4]

The property rights–agency literature provides a theoretical perspective from which to examine some effects that recent changes in the assignment of the right to player services have had on contractual incentives in major league baseball. Traditionally, club owners had possessed a well-defined and transferable property right to players' services by virtue of the reserve clause. A labor arbitrator's ruling in 1975 led to a collective bargaining agreement (hereafter referred to as the Basic Agreement) that partially transferred the rights to players' services from the club owners to the players themselves. In addition to affecting the distribution of rents, this transfer has also resulted in a reallocation of risk bearing from players to club owners via a proliferation of guaranteed multiyear player contracts. To the extent that alternative risk-sharing arrangements alter incentives, the behavior of players and club owners will be affected by the allocation of risk bearing and, thus, by the specification of the property right to player services.

In this paper we empirically investigate some effects of the Basic Agreement on the allocation of risk bearing in the market for players' services. In Section I, we briefly describe how the property rights to

[3] See, for example, Armen A. Alchian & Harold Demsetz, Production, Information Costs and Economic Organization, 62 Am. Econ. Rev. 777 (1972); Michael C. Jensen & William Meckling, The Theory of the Firm: Managerial Behavior, Agency Costs and Ownership Structure, 3 J. Fin. Econ. 305 (1976); Rights and Production Functions: An Application to Labor Managed Firms and Codetermination, 52 J. Bus. 469 (1979); and Steven Cheung, Transaction Costs, Risk Aversion and the Choice of Contractual Arrangements, 12 J. Law & Econ. 23 (1969).

[4] Jensen & Meckling (1979), *supra* note 3, at 470.

players' services were redefined in the Basic Agreement. Section II examines the effect that the Basic Agreement had on the allocation of risk bearing between players and club owners. In Section III empirical results are presented on the effects that the reallocation of risk bearing has had on the disability rate among players. Finally, in Section IV, the results of this study are summarized.

I. The Property Rights of Baseball's Labor Market

The first professional baseball league, the National Association of Professional Baseball Players, was formed in 1871. From 1871 through 1901, professional baseball experienced the entry and exit of several leagues. In an attempt to control both the movement of players across clubs and the level of players' salaries, in 1884 the two existing leagues (the National League and the American Association) signed the National Agreement, which contained a provision commonly known as the "reserve clause." The reserve clause provided club owners with an exclusive option to renew the contracts of eleven players (later changed to all players) on their rosters, thereby precluding negotiation between these players and other clubs for the players' services.

In *Federal Baseball Club of Baltimore v. National League of Professional Baseball Clubs*,[5] the Supreme Court unanimously upheld both the legality of the reserve clause and professional baseball's exemption from federal antitrust laws, on the grounds that baseball was not interstate commerce, and thus was not subject to federal antitrust laws. For more than fifty years after the Supreme Court ruling in *Federal Baseball Club*, organized baseball's antitrust exemption and the absence of competition from other professional baseball leagues combined to give major league club owners a well-defined and transferable right to the services of major league players.

The contractual changes which provide the impetus for this paper arose from legal developments which occurred in the 1970s. In 1975, pitchers Andy Messersmith and Dave McNally challenged the reserve clause and, in December 1975, labor arbitrator Peter Seitz ruled that both players were eligible to sell their services to any major league club. Upheld in a U.S. district court, this decision resulted in a collective bargaining agreement in July 1976 (retroactive to January 1976) between the players' association and baseball management that substantially altered the structure of contracting rights in the market for players' services. Under the Basic Agreement, players with at least six years of major league experience,

[5] Federal Baseball Club of Baltimore v. National League of Professional Baseball Clubs, 259 U.S. 200 (1922).

who had not signed a contract with their current club for the following baseball season, were eligible to participate in a "reentry draft." The reentry draft, held in November each year, established the clubs' negotiating rights to eligible players. This draft was described in the Basic Agreement:

At the Selection Meeting, Clubs shall select in inverse order of their standing in the championship season just concluded. . . . Each of the 24 (26 beginning in 1977) participating Major League Clubs may make one selection in each round. As the proceedings advance, round by round, each Player may be selected by a maximum of 12 Clubs (13 beginning in 1977), not counting the Player's former club which need not select such a Player. The selections will continue until each eligible Player has been selected by 12 Clubs (13 beginning in 1977) or until each Club has indicated that it desires to make no further selections. At the conclusion of the selections, the former Club of each Player will be asked to indicate whether it wishes to have negotiation rights with respect to that Player, and if it does desire to have such rights, it will then be added to the list of Clubs eligible to negotiate and contract with that Player.[6]

Under the Basic Agreement, a club which lost a player through the reentry draft was compensated by the club which signed the player. The signing club provided the player's former club with one of its selection rights in the Amateur Player Draft the following June. While this compensation system partially attenuated a player's right to contract with clubs which selected him in the reentry draft, it is generally acknowledged that the relatively low value of amateur draft choices in professional baseball had not affected the mobility of most players who participated in the reentry draft.[7]

II. Property Rights, the Distribution of Rents, and Risk Sharing in the Market for Player Services

Since an ostensible purpose of the reserve clause had been to promote an equitable distribution of playing talent across clubs, most eco-

[6] Basic Agreement between the American League of Professional Baseball Clubs and the National League of Professional Baseball Clubs and Major League Baseball Players Association, effective January 1, 1976 (retroactively), art. XVII, C(1b) and (1c), at 35–36.

[7] Three reasons account for the relatively low value of amateur draft choices in professional baseball vis-à-vis the value of amatur draft choices in other professional sports. First, most players selected in the amateur player draft are not ready to perform at the major league level when selected and require, on average, three to five years of seasoning in the minor leagues. In football and basketball, draft picks are usually expected to play at the major league level immediately. Second, unlike college football and college basketball, college and high school baseball does not have a wide national following. Thus, there is little name recognition value in baseball draft picks. Third, there likely is greater variance attached to forecasting player talent in baseball than other major sports. The higher degree of specialization in pro football and the dominance of size and quickness in pro basketball make it relatively easier to rank prospects in these sports than it is in pro baseball.

nomic analyses of the market for player services have studied the reserve clause for its effect upon two phenomena: the distribution of rents between the players and club owners and the allocation of players across clubs.[8] Because the reserve clause did not preclude clubs from transacting player contracts among themselves, there are theoretical grounds to believe that the allocation of players across clubs is independent of the assignment of the property right to player services. In a classic paper on the market for player services, Rottenberg stated: "It seems, indeed, to be true that a market in which freedom is limited by a reserve rule such as that which now governs the baseball labor market distributes players among teams about as a free market would. . . . The difference is only that in a market subject to the reserve rule part of the price for the player's services is paid to the team that sells his contract and part of his value is kept by the team that holds his contract; in the free market the player gets his full value."[9]

With the existence of binding roster constraints, the reserve clause had no effect on the total stock of major league players. Consequently, the

[8] See, for example, Simon Rottenberg, The Baseball Players' Labor Market, 64 J. Pol. Econ. 242 (1956); Mohamed El Hodiri & James Quirk, An Economic Model of a Professional Sports League, 79 J. Pol. Econ. 1302 (1971); Joseph W. Hunt, Jr. & Kenneth A. Lewis, Dominance, Recontracting, and the Reserve Clause: Major League Baseball, 66 Am. Econ. Rev. 936 (1976); William L. Holahan, The Long-Run Effects of Abolishing the Baseball Player Reserve System, 7 J. Legal Stud. 129 (1978); Matthew Spitzer & Elizabeth Hoffman, A Reply to Consumption Theory, Production Theory and Ideology in the Coase Theorem, 53 S. Cal. Law Rev. 1187 (1980); and George Daly & William J. Moore, Externalities, Property Rights and the Allocation of Resources in Major League Baseball, 19 Econ. Inq. 77 (1981).

[9] Rottenberg, *supra* note 7, at 255. Rottenberg's article preceded publication of the "Coase theorem" (see Ronald H. Coase, The Problem of Social Cost, 3 J. Law & Econ 1 [1960]). His argument, however, is consistent with Coase's proposition, which states that in a world of zero transaction costs and neutral wealth effects, the allocation of resources is both efficient and invariant with respect to the initial assignment of ownership rights. The efficiency result is tautologically true with the assumption of zero transaction costs, and the assumption of neutral wealth effects assures the invariance result. Since there are differences in the revenue potential of the markets in which major league clubs perform, a player's marginal revenue product may be dependent on the club for which he plays. The Rottenberg-Coase insight is that, independent of whether clubs or players possess the property right to player services, equilibrating market forces result in an allocation of players across clubs such that each player performs in the market in which his marginal revenue product is highest. Spitzer & Hoffman, *supra* note 7, have empirically examined the first-year effect of the Basic Agreement on the allocation of players across clubs. They could not reject the null hypothesis that the same percentage of players changed clubs during the first year of the Basic Agreement as had changed clubs in the nine previous years. Introduction of positive transaction costs and/or nonneutral wealth effects may result, however, in a relationship between the assignment of the right to players' services and the allocation of players across clubs. Generally, cash sales of front-line players in baseball, from one club to another club, are prohibited. This prohibition can be viewed as increasing the costs associated with the transaction of players' contracts, since clubs must engage in barter exchange (that is, trades of players' contracts are the way in which clubs transact players). Daly and Moore, *supra* note 7, argue that this transaction cost results in a systematic effect between the assignment of the right to players' services and the allocation of players across clubs.

TABLE 1
AVERAGE NOMINAL PLAYER SALARY, AVERAGE REAL PLAYER SALARY (in 1975 Dollars), AND PERCENTAGE OF CHANGE IN AVERAGE REAL PLAYER SALARY, 1971–80

Year	Average Nominal Salary	Average Real Salary	Change in Average Real Salary (%)
1971	31,543	41,918	. . .
1972	34,092	43,860	4.63
1973	36,566	44,285	0.97
1974	40,839	44,570	0.64
1975	44,676	44,676	0.24
1976	51,501	48,692	8.99
1977	76,066	67,560	38.75
1978	99,876	82,392	21.95
1979	113,558*	84,204	2.20
1980	130,592†	85,299	1.18

SOURCE.—Average nominal salary data are from Sports Illustrated 36 (January 5, 1981).
* This was the first year that the Players Association discounted deferred payments. They used a 9 percent rate to discount deferred payments without interest.
† This figure is based on the Players Association's estimate that salaries increased by about 15 percent in 1980. The Player Relations Committee's estimate of the average 1980 salary is $146,500.

conventional efficiency loss resulting from underutilization of the seller's resource in a monopsonistic market cannot be associated with the reserve clause. As a result, the reserve clause primarily has been viewed as affecting the distribution of rents between club owners and players.[10]

Available empirical evidence supports the hypothesis that the relaxation of the reserve clause has involved a redistribution of rents from club owners to players. Table 1 lists the average nominal salary for major league players on an annual basis for the years 1971–80. We have deflated these figures by the Consumer Price Index and also list the average real salary in 1975 dollars for each year. These figures show a dramatic increase in average real salary from 1976 to 1977. As the Basic Agreement

[10] Holahan, *supra* note 7, examines an argument which states that teams which were marginally profitable with the reserve clause would become insolvent with the abolition of the reserve clause. One implication of this argument is that if some teams dissolve, then clearly the Coase theorem is violated. Holahan argues, however, that with sufficient interteam transfers of revenue, no team's existence is dependent on the retention of the reserve clause. Furthermore, Holahan states that these transfers would be consistent with joint maximization of teams' profits since league balance presumably is directly related to league profits. Holahan also examines whether or not the reserve clause is necessary for the continued existence of the minor leagues, where young players are trained. Applying Becker's theory of human capital (see Gary S. Becker, Human Capital [1964]), Holahan argues that the assignment of rights to player services affects the way in which training costs are shared between players and club owners, but it should have little effect on the overall level of investment in player development.

was signed in mid-1976, the 1977 season was the first full season played under the Basic Agreement. Thus, in the first full year of the Basic Agreement, the average real salary of major league players increased by more than 38 percent. After a 21.95 percent increase in 1978, the average real salary of major league players has leveled off during the past two years.[11]

In addition to the average salary data, there are also frequent media reports of the wealth effect associated with the Basic Agreement. A popular magazine reported two cases in which players received dramatic increases in their compensation: "The bonanza is all so new, so overwhelming, that recent free-agent prospectors like Larry Hisle and Lyman Bostock, former Minnesota Twins, give the impression that they have struck fool's gold. Hisle, whose salary leaped from $47,200 to $525,833 when he joined the Milwaukee Brewers this season, will not talk about his good fortune. . . . Bostock talks about his big raise—from $20,000 to $450,000, compliments of the California Angels. . . ."[12] This anecdotal evidence provides additional support for the view that the Basic Agreement has involved a large redistribution of rents.

Effect of the Basic Agreement on the Allocation of Risk Bearing between Players and Club Owners

In addition to redistributing rents from club owners to players, the Basic Agreement has had a substantial effect on the way in which players and club owners share the risk associated with the value of the players' performance. Data are not available on individual player contracts prior to 1976, but several baseball executives have indicated in private conversation that prior to the Basic Agreement virtually all of the 600 major

[11] While these numbers are strongly suggestive, there are several problems associated with using these data to estimate the wealth transfer induced by the Basic Agreement. First, only in 1979 did the source for these data begin discounting deferred compensation in calculating the players' average salary. Because the number of contracts with deferred compensation began to increase in 1977, an upward bias is introduced in the 1977 and 1978 average salaries that are reported in Table 1. Second, these figures do not control for possible changes in the demand for baseball that would have affected the value of the players' marginal product during this period. Third, the average salary figures in Table 1 are calculated for all players in the major leagues. In 1980, more than 60 percent of players had less than six years of major league service. Thus, they were unable to sell the right to their services in a competitive market. Assuming that more than 60 percent of players in all included years had less than six years of experience, the average salary figures underestimate the wealth effect involved when individual players receive the property right to their services.

[12] Ray Kennedy & Nancy Williamson, Money in Sports: Part 2, Sports Illustrated 36 (July 24, 1978).

TABLE 2
NUMBER OF PLAYERS BY THE NUMBER OF GUARANTEED YEARS ON THEIR CONTRACT FOR 650 PLAYERS IN 1980

Guaranteed Years on Contract (*N*)	Players (*N*)
0	352 (54.15)
1	26 (4.00)
2	45 (6.92)
3	57 (8.77)
4	41 (6.31)
5	92 (14.15)
6	29 (4.46)
7	4 (.62)
8	0 (.00)
9	0 (.00)
10	4 (.62)

NOTE.—Figures shown in parentheses are percentages.

league players had a one-year contract.[13] Furthermore, these contracts typically were not guaranteed by the club. Depending on his seniority, if a player was released by his club or sent to the minor leagues during a baseball season, he received a prorated share of his salary for the time that he spent in the major leagues. During the Basic Agreement there was a sizable increase in the number of guaranteed multiyear player contracts. Table 2 lists the number of players by the number of guaranteed years on their contract for 650 players who were on the active opening-day roster of a major league club in 1980.[14] Thirty-five percent of the players in 1980 had at least three guaranteed years on their contract.

This contractual change under the Basic Agreement can be viewed as a reallocation of risk bearing from players to club owners. The risk associated with the value of a player's performance involves the risk of disability and the risk that expectations of the player's performance will not be met. In part, player contracts stipulate the way in which this risk is to be shared between the player and the club owner. The post-1976 increase in the number of guaranteed multiyear player contracts indicates that players are bearing less employment risk under the Basic Agreement than

[13] C. Raymond Grebey, director of the Major League Baseball Player Relations Committee; John Claiborne, former senior executive vice-president and chief operating officer of the St. Louis Cardinals; Robert Fontaine, director of player personnel for the San Francisco Giants; Joseph McDonald, general manager of the St. Louis Cardinals; and Martin Appel, former associate director of information for the commissioner's office, have all stated this in private conversation.

[14] Contract data were obtained from the Major League Baseball Player Relations Committee on all players who performed in the major leagues in 1980.

they were under the reserve clause. This observation leads to the following question: Why is the allocation of risk bearing between players and club owners dependent on the rules governing contracting rights in the market for player services?

To address this question it is useful to view the reserve clause as an implicit long-term contract between players and club owners that provided the owners with an option to renew the contract annually. Since the standard explicit contract was for one year, the risk associated with the discounted value of a player's performance was shared by both the player and the owner under the reserve clause. To illustrate this, for simplicity assume a two-state world in which i is a discrete index that defines the state of a player's disability. Let $i = 0$ if the player is not disabled, 1 if the player is disabled. Further assume that the value of the rent associated with a player's skills is dependent on whether the player is disabled: $R_t(i)$ = rent associated with the player's skills in year t, and $R_t(0) > R_t(1)$, all t. Assume that players perform for T years. The discounted value of rents that are lost due to the occurrence of the risky event, that is, the total size of the wager, is

$$W = \sum_{t=1}^{T} \frac{R_t(0) - R_t(1)}{(1 + r)^t}.$$

Let α = players' share of the rents under the reserve clause, $0 < \alpha < 1$; and $1 - \alpha$ = club's share of the rents under the reserve clause. The total wager can be written as: $W = W_p + W_c$, where

$$W_p = \alpha \sum_{t=1}^{T} \frac{R_t(0) - R_t(1)}{(1 + r)^t} = \text{player's wager}$$

and

$$W_c = (1 - \alpha) \sum_{t=1}^{T} \frac{R_t(0) - R_t(1)}{(1 + r)^t} = \text{club's wager.}$$

Thus, under the reserve clause, players and club owners bore risk in proportion to their respective shares of the rent associated with the players' performance.

For a given assignment of property rights, the terms of a contract (including, of course, the way in which risk is shared) are negotiated to the mutual advantage of the contracting parties. If both players and club owners preferred alternative contractual arrangements to the explicit one-year contract observed under the reserve clause, presumably these preferred arrangements would have evolved. Note that the pre-1976 contracts did not preclude players from purchasing the clubs' option to renew their contracts annually. Assuming that both players and club owners are risk averse, a player could have signed a guaranteed multiyear contract with his club, by accepting a guaranteed wage that was less than his expected future wage. That the standard explicit contract under the reserve clause was a one-year contract implies that the club owners valued the option to renew the players' contract annually more than the players valued the security of guaranteed multiyear contracts.

Now consider the effect that a transfer of the right to player services (from club owners to players) has on the choice of contractual arrangements. As a benchmark against which the observed contractual changes can be contrasted, consider the case in which the transferred right affects only the distribution of rents. If all other contractual stipulations are independent of the assignment of the right to player services, then clubs would retain the option to renew the players' contracts annually, that is, the standard contract would continue to be an annual contract. Since the player owns the right to his services, he receives the full value of the rent associated with his skills (that is, $\alpha = 1$ in the example above). Accordingly, under this contractual arrangement the player bears the entire risk associated with the value of his performance.

We have indicated, however, that there has been an increase in the number of guaranteed multiyear player contracts under the Basic Agreement. At first glance, this contractual change may appear to be an attempt by clubs to replicate the reserve clause by signing players to multiyear contracts, thereby precluding the players from joining other clubs. But a multiyear contract is consistent with any risk-sharing arrangement. Clubs could replicate the reserve clause with an explicit long-term contract that takes the form of a series of one-year contracts, renewable each year at the club's option. Under this contractual arrangement, in each year that a club renews his contract, the player receives a predetermined wage which is an unbiased estimate of his marginal revenue product, plus a premium that reflects the shadow value of the club's option.[15] Thus, while the increased number of long-term contracts under the Basic Agreement can be explained, at least in part, by a desire of clubs to replicate the reserve clause, this explanation cannot account for the fact that, in practice, clubs typically guaranteed every year of a player's multiyear contract.

Coase's proposition, referred to earlier,[16] provides an analytical framework within which to examine the observed increase in the number

[15] Joe Sullivan, former general manager of the St. Louis Football Cardinals, has indicated in private conversation that a series of one-year contracts is the typical form that long-term contracts take in professional football.

[16] Coase, *supra* note 9.

of guaranteed multiyear contracts under the Basic Agreement. Coase stated that with zero transaction costs and neutral wealth effects, the allocation of resources is independent of the initial assignment of property rights. In the case of baseball contracts, we have observed that the allocation of risk bearing is dependent on the initial assignment of the right to players' services. Since the transaction costs associated with the allocation of risk bearing between players and club owners are presumably low, this observed relationship suggests the following: the value which players place on insuring their stream of income, relative to the value which clubs place on the option to renew the players' contracts annually, is dependent on the assignment of the right to the players' services.

One explanation for the relationship between the allocation of risk bearing and the assignment of the rights to players' services is that the wealth transfer associated with the Basic Agreement has increased both the willingness and the ability of players to insure their stream of income. An increase in the players' willingness to sign guaranteed multiyear contracts is consistent with the postulate of nondecreasing relative risk aversion, a postulate that is conventionally assumed to characterize behavior toward risk when an individual's wealth and wager increase in the same proportion.[17] From the example above, if α goes from a value of less than one during the reserve clause to a value of one during the Basic Agreement, both the players' wealth and their wager increase by a factor of $(1/\alpha)$. The hypothesis of constant or increasing relative risk aversion predicts that players are willing to pay a higher premium to insure their stream of income under the Basic Agreement than they were willing to pay to insure their stream of income under the reserve clause. Given the size of the wealth transfer associated with the Basic Agreement, this wealth-induced effect is likely to be nontrivial. In addition to affecting the players' willingness to sign guaranteed multiyear contracts, the increase in their wealth position has increased their capacity to "purchase" these contracts. With a positive wealth elasticity of demand for security, then, players will choose to consume part of their additional wealth in the form of increased security.

One implication resulting from the reallocation of risk bearing in the market for players' services concerns the incentive effects of alternative risk-sharing arrangements.[18] If the probability of a risky event is in part

[17] Pratt and Arrow independently developed the concepts of absolute risk aversion and relative risk aversion. See John Pratt, Risk Aversion in the Small and in the Large, 32 Econometrica 122 (1964); and Kenneth J. Arrow, Aspects of the Theory of Risk-bearing (1965).

[18] A large body of literature exists on these incentive effects. Among the most important articles are Kenneth J. Arrow, Uncertainty and the Welfare Economics of Medical Care, 53

endogenous to the behavior of at least one party to a contract, then the way in which the parties share the risk may affect the probability that the event occurs. The cost borne by an individual from the occurrence of a risky event is inversely related to the extent to which the individual has insured against the event, resulting in an inverse relationship between the extent to which an individual has insured against an event and the incentive that the individual has to prevent the event from occurring.

Since the probability of both player disability and deviations in player performance is, in part, endogenous to the behavior of players and clubs, the use of guaranteed multiyear player contracts has implications for the likelihood that these events occur. As the risk associated with these events is shifted from players to club owners, there is a reduced incentive for players to prevent the risky events. This effect unambiguously predicts that the probability of player disability and unmet expectations in player performance is directly related to the extent to which players have insured their future income through guaranteed multiyear contracts.

In addition to the behavior of players, the behavior of clubs is also likely to affect the probability of player disability and/or unmet expectations in player performance. As the risk associated with these events is shifted from players to club owners, the owners have an increased incentive to prevent the occurrence of these events. For two reasons, however, we do not expect guaranteed multiyear contracts to affect the owners' behavior significantly with respect to prevention of these events. First, since clubs received most of the rents associated with the players' employment under the reserve clause, the incremental increase in the clubs' wager is likely to be small. Guaranteed player contracts in part simply transform the club's wager from one that had consisted of potentially foregone losses under the reserve clause into one that consists of potentially explicit losses. If the value of the club's wager had not changed during the Basic Agreement, then this distinction would not alter the club's behavior with respect to its prevention of the risky events. The only part of a guaranteed contract that will elicit a behavioral response from the club owners is the proportion of the risk, which the players bore under the reserve clause, that is now borne by the owners. Even in the limiting case where the club guarantees the entire stream of the player's future income, its wager increases only by $\alpha/1 - \alpha$ percent, and not by the entire value of the guaranteed contract.

Am. Econ. Rev. 941 (1963); Mark V. Pauly, The Economics of Moral Hazard: A Comment, 58 Am. Econ. Rev. 531 (1968); Richard J. Zeckhauser, Medical Insurance: A Case Study of the Tradeoff between Risk-spreading and Appropriate Incentives, 2 J. Econ. Theory 10 (1970); and John M. Marshall, Moral Hazard, 66 Am. Econ. Rev. 880 (1976).

A second reason for suspecting that guaranteed multiyear contracts have induced a relatively small behavioral response from club owners is that, in part, the owners can diversify this risk across players. With frictionless markets, players would also be able to diversify this risk through buying and selling shares in their uncertain future income. Since there are limited diversification opportunities for players, however, clubs have a comparative advantage in bearing the risk associated with future player performance. As a result, an incremental change in risk bearing is likely to elicit a greater behavioral response from players than from club owners.

III. Empirical Evidence: The Effect of Guaranteed Multiyear Contracts on Player Disability

In the previous section, we attempted to show that the Basic Agreement resulted in both a transfer of wealth from club owners to players and a reallocation of risk bearing from players to club owners. In this section the effect that guaranteed multiyear player contracts have had on player disability is examined.[19]

Concomitant with the Basic Agreement has been a significant increase in the disability rate among players in major league baseball. To document this increase, data have been collected for each year from 1974 to 1980 on all players who spent time on a major league club's disabled list.[20] Conveniently, the rules concerning placement of players on a club's disabled list have not changed over this period. These rules are described in *The Baseball Blue Book:*

Upon written application to its League President and the Commissioner, a club may request that a player, unable to render service because of a specific injury or ailment, be placed on the disabled list. The Commissioner may approve such

[19] We are also in the process of examining the effect of guaranteed multiyear contracts on players' performance. Since one player's performance depends in part on the performance of both his teammates and his opponents, this is a more formidable task than examining the effect of guaranteed multiyear contracts on player disability. It is difficult to detect the effect that the Basic Agreement has had on the absolute level of pitching and batting, since a pitcher's performance statistics depend in part on the quality of batters, and vice versa. Thus, if the absolute quality of both pitching and batting has declined during the Basic Agreement, unless the relative quality of the two has changed, there will be no change in overall batting and pitching statistics.

[20] There are two difficulties involved with using time spent on the disabled list as a proxy for player disability. First, not all disabled players are placed on a club's disabled list. Since players must spend a minimum of fifteen days on the disabled list and clubs are limited in the number of players that they are allowed to have on the supplemental and regular disabled lists simultaneously, players with minor injuries frequently will not be placed on a disabled list. The second difficulty with this proxy is that, on occasion, clubs allegedly place healthy players on the disabled list in order to free a spot on their active roster for another player. Thus, it is unlikely that all players on the disabled list are actually disabled.

requests when certified by the League President, but only after the Commissioner has received written evidence from a doctor detailing the extent of the disability. . . . Players on the Regular Disabled List shall count on the overall roster but not on the active list. . . . Clubs must designate at the time they request permission to place [a] player on a disabled list whether he is to be placed on the Emergency Disabled List for not less than sixty (60) days, on the Regular Disabled List for not less than twenty-one (21) days or on the Supplemental Disabled List for not less than fifteen (15) days.[21]

Clubs are not permitted to have more than three players on the regular disabled list at the same time nor more than one player (excluding pitchers) on the supplemental disabled list at the same time. Clubs are permitted, however, to have an unlimited number of players on the emergency disabled list simultaneously.

The total number of players who spent time on a major league club's disabled list is shown in the second column of Table 3 for each of the seven years for which we have compiled these data.[22] The average number of players who spent time on the disabled list has increased from 89 players per season in the 1974–76 period to 131 players per season in the 1977–80 period. Part of the 47 percent increase in the average number of disabled players is the result of an expansion of the major leagues in 1977. This expansion increased the stock of active major league players by 8.33 percent from 600 players in each of the 1974–76 seasons to 650 players in each of the subsequent seasons. To adjust the disability data for the 1977 expansion we have divided the flow of disabled players in each season by the stock of active players in each of these seasons. These figures are reported in the third column of Table 3. As a percentage of the total stock of active players, the per season flow of disabled players in the major leagues has increased from approximately 15 percent in the 1974–76 period to 20 percent in the 1977–80 period. This represents a 33 percent increase in the percentage of active players who spent time on a disabled list in the 1977–80 period over the same percentage during the 1974–76 period.

The total number of days spent by all players on a major league club's disabled list is shown in the fourth column of Table 3 for each of the seven seasons. To calculate the average number of days spent on a disabled list by all players, this total has been divided by the total stock of active players in each season. These averages are reported in the fifth column of

[21] The Baseball Blue Book (1981), § MR2 (e), at 511.

[22] The disability data for the years 1974–79 were obtained from The Baseball Yearbook for each corresponding year. Disability data for 1980 were obtained from the Player Relations Committee.

TABLE 3
DISABILITY STATISTICS FOR ALL PLAYERS IN MAJOR LEAGUES DURING EACH SEASON, 1974–80

Year	Total Number of Players Who Spent Time on Disabled List	Players Who Spent Time on Disabled List (%)	Total Number of Days Spent by All Players on Disabled List	Average Number of Days Spent by All Players on Disabled List	Average Number of Days Spent by Disabled Players on Disabled List
1974	83	13.8	4,177	6.962	50.325
1975	103	17.2	5,210	8.683	50.583
1976	81	13.5	4,700	7.833	58.025
1977	128	19.7	6,155	9.469	48.086
1978	114	17.5	5,393	8.297	47.307
1979	141	21.7	7,738	11.905	54.879
1980	142	21.9	7,311	11.248	51.486
1974–76	267	14.8	14,087	7.826	52.760
1977–80	525	20.2	26,597	10.230	50.661

Table 3. The average number of days spent on a disabled list by all players increased by approximately 31 percent during the 1977–80 period over the same average during the 1974–76 period.[23]

Several explanations for baseball's increased disability rate have been offered by baseball executives, team physicians, sportswriters, and baseball fans. Some conventional explanations which have been offered are:[24]

1. *Artificial turf.* Allegedly, artificial turf results in more injuries.

2. *Advent of the "designated hitter" rule in the American League.* This rule apparently allows pitchers to pitch more innings per game than they would in the absence of the rule. It has been hypothesized that this places greater strain on pitchers' arms and thereby increases the likelihood of injuries among American League pitchers.

3. *Growing sophistication of sports medicine.* It has been hypothesized that injuries which previously went undetected are now diagnosed.

[23] The post-1977 increase in this average has resulted from an increase in the frequency of player disability rather than from an increase in the average number of days spent by disabled players on a disabled list. The latter average has been calculated for each year from 1974 through 1980 and it is listed in the sixth column of Table 3. This average has actually declined in the 1977–80 period by approximately 4 percent when compared to the same average over the 1974–76 period.

[24] For a discussion of these explanations, see Tom Singer, Why Is the Major League Injury Rate Rising? 39 Baseball Dig. 33 (1980).

4. *The 1977 expansion of the American League*. This expansion supposedly has increased the proportion of younger players in the league. Proponents of this theory contend that young players, particularly young pitchers, are more susceptible to injuries than are older players.

While there has been much speculation concerning the increase in player disability, there is little empirical support for the offered explanations. This is illustrated in the following excerpt from an article dealing with baseball's disability rate:

> The difficulty of deriving an intelligent trend from the increased number of injuries is underlined by the two distinct ways baseball's two leagues differ. The N. L. has the majority of baseball's artificial turf fields. So one could expect a greater injury rate. Yet, at one point in the 1980 season, 22 nonpitchers were disabled in the N. L., compared to 39 in the A. L. (whose two extra franchises can't account for the difference). And the A. L. with its DH would seem more threatening to the welfare of pitchers. But 15 of its hurlers went on the disabled list, compared to 18 Nationals during the early part of the season.[25]

The explanation which is offered here for the increase in baseball's disability rate is that the proliferation of guaranteed multiyear player contracts under the Basic Agreement has reduced the price of disability to players, thereby inducing an increase in the players' "consumption" of disability. This hypothesis assumes, of course, that the probability of a player becoming disabled is in part endogenous to the player's behavior. While undoubtedly there is a large random element associated with disability, it is also clear that players' behavior can affect the probability that they become disabled. First, it is likely that proper physical conditioning reduces the probability of a disabling injury. Two club physicians, discussing the increased disability rate, have explicitly commented on the relationship between conditioning and disability: ". . . it behooves us, as doctors, to try to work out a bonafide off-season program for players. It requires sacrifice on their part. They must dedicate themselves."[26] "A guy who works out has less chance of injury. Players don't use muscles the way they should. If you don't loosen up regularly, you stretch those muscles in the spring and they get pulled."[27] Assuming that conditioning is not costless for players, that monitoring the players' condition is not costless for clubs, and that guaranteed multiyear contracts reduce the cost borne by players from "improper" conditioning, it follows that a guaran-

[25] *Id*. at 35.

[26] *Id*.

[27] *Id*.

teed multiyear contract reduces a player's incentive to prevent disability through physical conditioning.

For a given level of conditioning, the behavior of players can affect the probability that they spend time on the disabled list in another way. The cost of both revealing an injury and recovering from an injury is lower for players with guaranteed multiyear contracts than it is for players who have short-term contracts that reward the players for their playing performance. Since it is costly for clubs to diagnose player disability and to monitor the players' recovery, alternative contractual arrangements are likely to affect the willingness of players to perform when they are injured. Even if clubs could costlessly detect player disability, however, the increased wealth position of players is likely to affect the players' marginal rate of substitution between playing when they are injured and leisure. Thus, both the price and wealth effects of guaranteed multiyear contracts reduce the probability that players will perform when they are injured.

We wish to test the hypothesis that the increase in baseball's disability rate has resulted, in part, from changes in contractual incentives. Specifically, the following two hypotheses are tested:

H1: At a point in time, players with guaranteed long-term contracts are more likely to be disabled than are players with short-term contracts.

H2: Players experience more disability after signing guaranteed long-term contracts than they do prior to signing such contracts.

Empirical Evidence

To test the first hypothesis, disability data are analyzed for all players in the sample who played the entire 1980 season at the major league level. In this analysis, we do not include players who at any time during the 1980 season (*a*) were sent by their club to the minor leagues,[28] (*b*) were released

[28] The sample for this section consists of all 576 players who were on the opening day roster of a major league club in 1980 and who had at least one full season of major league experience prior to 1980. The following players are excluded from the sample because they were sent to the minor leagues during 1980: Joe Kerrigan, Stan Papi, Miguel Dilone, Don Werner, Mike Paxton, Andres Mora, Julio Gonzales, Jerry Terrell, Willie Norwood, Kevin Kobel, Dave Hamilton, Glenn Burke, Donnie Moore, Roy Thomas, Mike Parrott, Gary Wheelock, Dave Rajisch, Nelson Norman, and Willie Upshaw. In 1980 a rule was instituted whereby clubs could send disabled players to one of the club's minor league teams for a period of rehabilitation not to exceed twenty days. Officially, these players remain on the major league club's disabled list and this time is counted as major league service for the players. Thus, players who were sent to the minor leagues under this clause are included in the sample.

by their club,[29] (*c*) were suspended by their club (or by their league),[30] or (*d*) voluntarily retired.[31]

Summary statistics on player disability are listed in Table 4 by the number of guaranteed years remaining on the contracts of all players in the sample who spent the entire 1980 season in the major leagues. There is a direct relationship between the number of guaranteed years remaining on the players' contracts and the average number of days which players spent on a major league club's disabled list in 1980. On average, each additional guaranteed year remaining on the player's contract is associated with a 25 percent increase in the average number of days spent on the disabled list. Players with three or more guaranteed years remaining on their contract spent, on average, 79 percent more time on the disabled list than players with one or two guaranteed years remaining on their contract.[32]

In order to control for some of the other factors which frequently are cited as determinants of baseball's disability rate, we also estimate a logit model in which the dependent variable is *LNDL*, the log of the odds that a player spent time on the disabled list in 1980. Among the independent variables in the model is *GUARYEARS*, the number of guaranteed years remaining on the player's contract. Our hypothesis predicts a positive estimated coefficient for this variable. The other independent variables are: (*a*) *AGE*, the player's age in 1980; (*b*) *ARTITURF*, the percentage of games which the player's club played on artificial turf in 1980;[33] (*c*)

[29] The following twenty-one players are excluded from the sample because they were released by a major league club during 1980: Larvell Blanks, Ted Sizemore, Ralph Garr, Steve Ontiveros, Ken Henderson, Dave Tomlin, Jack Billingham, Steve Busby, Steve Braun, Mike Marshall, Dale Murray, Jose Cardenal, Lerrin LaGrow, Darold Knowles, Bernie Carbo, Fred Kendall, Von Joshua, Roger Metzger, Bob Stinson, Tom Buskey, and Balor Moore.

[30] The following eight players are excluded from the sample because they were suspended or placed on the disqualified list in 1980: Joe Nolan, Bob Horner, Al Cowens, Rick Auerbach, Bill Almon, Bert Blyleven, Mike Ivie, and Ferguson Jenkins.

[31] Two players, John Hiller and Willie McCovey, are excluded from the sample because they voluntarily retired during the 1980 season. Only four of the fifty players who are excluded from the sample for this test spent time on the disabled list in 1980 (for a total of 106 days). Thus, we have not biased the sample by excluding players who were sent to the minor leagues or released because of disabling injuries.

[32] The evidence presented in Table 4 is relevant for the hypothesis that the increase in baseball's disability rate is accounted for by a growing sophistication in sports medicine. The evidence in Table 4 does not refute this hypothesis. However, this hypothesis does not predict that at a point in time there should be a significant difference in the average number of days spent on the disabled list by players with guaranteed long-term contracts and the average number of days spent on the disabled list by players with short-term contracts.

[33] Twenty-three players in the sample of 526 played for more than one club in 1980 and were deleted from the sample for this estimate because of computational difficulties with respect to this variable.

TABLE 4
AVERAGE NUMBER OF DAYS SPENT ON DISABLED LIST IN 1980 AND OTHER SUMMARY STATISTICS FOR 526 PLAYERS WHO SPENT ENTIRE 1980 SEASON IN MAJOR LEAGUES

Number of Guaranteed Years Remaining on Contract in 1980	*N*	Average Number of Days Spent by All Players on Disabled List in 1980	SD	Minimum	Maximum	Coefficient of Variation
0–1	328	9.424	25.973	.000	201.000	275.605
2	60	14.683	31.853	.000	158.000	216.938
3	43	18.116	37.815	.000	192.000	208.744
4	42	15.024	34.826	.000	132.000	231.803
5+	53	21.189	42.313	.000	179.000	199.693
0–2	388	10.237	26.987	.000	201.000	263.622
3+	138	18.355	38.568	.000	192.000	210.123

TABLE 5
LOGIT ESTIMATE OF ODDS THAT PLAYER SPENT TIME ON DISABLED LIST IN 1980 FOR 503 PLAYERS IN 1980

Variable	Logit Model (Dependent Variable = *LNDL*)
INTERCEPT	−1.710
	(3.31)
GUARYEARS	.125
	(3.46)
AGE	.005
	(.03)
ARTITURF	−.057
	(.01)
PITCHER	.363
	(1.36)
AL	.269
	(.72)
ALPITCH	−.838
	(3.45)
N	503
D-statistic	.014
Model χ^2 statistic	7.29 (6 df)

NOTE.—χ^2 statistics are shown in parentheses.

PITCHER, which takes on the value of 1 if the player is a pitcher and 0 otherwise; (*d*) *AL*, which takes on the value of 1 if the player performed in the American League for the entire season in 1980 and 0 otherwise; (*e*) *ALPITCH*, which takes on the value of 1 if the player was a pitcher in the American League in 1980 and 0 otherwise.

Results from estimation of this model are reported in Table 5. The variable *GUARYEARS* has an anticipated positive coefficient, and it is statistically significant. The only other independent variable that has a statistically significant coefficient in this equation is the dummy variable that standardizes for whether the player is a pitcher in the American League. Counter to the theory that the designated-hitter rule is in part responsible for the increase in player disability, American League pitchers were less likely to be injured in 1980 than other players.

Tables 4 and 5 contain cross-sectional evidence which supports the hypothesis that changes in contractual incentives are, in part, responsible for the recent increase in baseball's disability rate. Some longitudinal analysis is also possible: the contract data can be used to test directly the hypothesis that players spend more time on the disabled list after signing

TABLE 6
AVERAGE AGE, PRECONTRACT AND POSTCONTRACT AVERAGE NUMBER OF DAYS SPENT ON DISABLED LIST, AND POSTCONTRACT CHANGE IN DISABILITY BY NUMBER OF GUARANTEED YEARS ON CONTRACT FOR 249 ELIGIBLE PLAYERS IN SAMPLE

Guaranteed Years on Contract (*N*)	*N*	Average Age When Signed Contract	Average Number of Days Spent on Disabled List per Season in Three Seasons Prior to Signing Contract	Average Number of Days Spent on Disabled List per Season in All Seasons after Signing Contract	Change in Average Number of Days Spent on Disabled List (%)
0	53	31.019	7.987	5.977	−25.17
1	18	34.722	5.333	.913	−82.88
2	23	34.652	5.841	5.833	−.13
3	36	32.278	5.009	12.206	143.67
4	29	31.379	3.483	8.972	157.60
5+	90	30.056	5.019	13.849	175.92
0–2	94	32.617	6.939	5.171	−25.48
3+	155	30.819	4.729	12.551	165.40

guaranteed multiyear contracts than they do before signing these contracts. The sample for this test is the set of 249 players who either were reentrants when they signed their contract or who would have been eligible for the next reentry draft at the time that they signed a multiyear contract with their current club. This group of players is selected since they had a well-established disability record before signing their contract.

For each eligible player, the total number of days spent on the disabled list is calculated in the three seasons before and in all seasons after signing his contract. Players are then classified by the number of years in which their contract is guaranteed against disability. For each category, the average number of days spent on the disabled list per season by this group of players in the three seasons before, and in all seasons after, they signed their respective contracts is calculated. These averages are listed by the number of guaranteed years on the players' contracts in Table 6.

It is seen that there is a significant increase in the number of days spent on the disabled list after players sign a guaranteed contract of more than two years in length. The per season average number of days spent on the disabled list decreases from 6.939 to 5.171 for ninety-four players who sign contracts which are guaranteed from zero to two years. For the 155 players who signed contracts which were guaranteed for three or more years, the corresponding average increases from 4.729 days to 12.551

TABLE 7

AVERAGE NUMBER OF DAYS SPENT ON DISABLED LIST IN PRECONTRACT AND POSTCONTRACT PERIODS FOR PLAYERS WITH GUARANTEED CONTRACTS OF AT LEAST THREE YEARS IN LENGTH BY WHETHER THE CONTRACTS CONTAINED INCENTIVE BONUSES

	N	Average Number of Days Spent on Disabled List per Season in Three Seasons Prior to Signing Contract	Average Number of Days Spent on Disabled List per Season after Signing Contract	Change in Average Number of Days Spent on Disabled List (%)
Without incentive bonuses	117	4.717	14.445	206.23
With incentive bonuses	38	4.763	6.061	27.25

days. This represents a 165 percent increase in postcontract disability for players who sign guaranteed contracts which were more than two years in length.[34]

Of the 155 players who signed contracts which were guaranteed for three or more years, thirty-eight (approximately 25 percent) had contracts which contained bonuses related to the frequency with which they were to perform, the number of awards that they were to win, and/or the judgment of the general manager of the club for which the players were to perform. In Table 7 the average number of days spent on the disabled list by this group of players in both the precontract period and the postcontract period is listed. These averages are also listed for the 117 players who had guaranteed multiyear contracts which did not contain incentive bonuses. Among the former group of players, the average number of days spent on the disabled list increased by 27.25 percent, from 4.763 days in the precontract period to 6.061 days in the postcontract period. Among the latter group of players, the corresponding increase was 206.23 percent, from 4.717 days in the precontract period to 14.445 days in the postcontract period. Thus, it appears that the disincentive effects of guaranteed multiyear player contracts can be mitigated considerably by the inclusion of incentive bonuses in the players' contracts.

IV. Conclusion

Adopting the perspective that contracts serve as a conduit through which performance is affected by rules governing contracting rights, this study has examined empirically some effects that a change in the assignment of ownership rights to players' services has had on players' contracts in major league baseball. An unambiguous relationship has been found among the assignment of the right to players' services, the alloca-

[34] One hypothesis is that, with one-year contracts, clubs are more willing to release disabled players than they are to release players who have guaranteed, multiyear contracts. Thus, the argument goes, players who previously would be released now show up on the disabled lists because of their multiyear contracts. To test this hypothesis, we calculated the average number of days spent on the disabled list in the first season after signing their contract for the 249 players in Table 6. Since all of these players are established players, it is not likely that they would be released during the first year of their contracts, regardless of their disability status (that is, it is likely that they would show up in the disability statistics even if they had a one-year contract). Among the 94 players who had less than three guaranteed years on their contract the average number of days on the disabled list decreased from 6.939 days before signing the contract to 4.596 days in the first season after signing the contract. Among the 155 players whose contracts were guaranteed for at least three years, the corresponding average increased from 4.729 days before signing the contract to 10.323 days in the first season after signing the contract, an increase of approximately 116 percent. These results refute the argument that the relationship between guaranteed multiyear contracts and player disability can be explained by sample bias.

tion of risk bearing between players and club owners, and player disability. These results suggest that, in addition to affecting the distribution of rents between players and club owners, the assignment of the right to players' services also affects the nature of what is produced in major league baseball.

One interpretation of these results is that the 1975 arbitration decision changed the property rights in the market for players' services so dramatically that it is unlikely that there has been an instantaneous adjustment to a new equilibrium contractual form. During the past five years information has been obtained regarding the incentive effects of different contractual forms.[35] If the results on player disability were unanticipated by the club owners, then in the future it is expected that the risk associated with the value of a player's performance will be reallocated, at least in part, to the players, in the form of fewer guaranteed multiyear contracts and more incentive contracts.

[35] The following passage, which is an attachment to the Basic Agreement, supports the view that there has not been an instantaneous adjustment to a new equilibrium contractual form during the Basic Agreement: "The Parties recognize that the provisions of the Agreement concerning player control establish a new dimension in their collectively bargained relationship and, therefore, to a degree must be regarded as experimental."

The Nature of the Firm

By R. H. COASE

ECONOMIC theory has suffered in the past from a failure to state clearly its assumptions. Economists in building up a theory have often omitted to examine the foundations on which it was erected. This examination is, however, essential not only to prevent the misunderstanding and needless controversy which arise from a lack of knowledge of the assumptions on which a theory is based, but also because of the extreme importance for economics of good judgment in choosing between rival sets of assumptions. For instance, it is suggested that the use of the word "firm" in economics may be different from the use of the term by the "plain man."[1] Since there is apparently a trend in economic theory towards starting analysis with the individual firm and not with the industry,[2] it is all the more necessary not only that a clear definition of the word "firm" should be given but that its difference from a firm in the "real world," if it exists, should be made clear. Mrs. Robinson has said that "the two questions to be asked of a set of assumptions in economics are: Are they tractable? and: Do they correspond with the real world?"[3] Though, as Mrs. Robinson points out, "more often one set will be manageable and the other realistic," yet there may well be branches of theory where assumptions may be both manageable and realistic. It is hoped to show in the following paper that a definition of a firm may be obtained which is not only realistic in that it corresponds to what is meant by a firm in the real world, but is tractable by two of the most powerful instruments of economic analysis developed by Marshall, the idea of the margin and that of substitution, together giving the idea of substitution at

[1] Joan Robinson, *Economics is a Serious Subject*, p. 12.
[2] See N. Kaldor, "The Equilibrium of the Firm," *Economic Journal*, March, 1934.
[3] Op. cit., p. 6.

the margin.[1] Our definition must, of course, "relate to formal relations which are capable of being *conceived* exactly."[2]

I

It is convenient if, in searching for a definition of a firm, we first consider the economic system as it is normally treated by the economist. Let us consider the description of the economic system given by Sir Arthur Salter.[3] "The normal economic system works itself. For its current operation it is under no central control, it needs no central survey. Over the whole range of human activity and human need, supply is adjusted to demand, and production to consumption, by a process that is automatic, elastic and responsive." An economist thinks of the economic system as being co-ordinated by the price mechanism and society becomes not an organisation but an organism.[4] The economic system "works itself." This does not mean that there is no planning by individuals. These exercise foresight and choose between alternatives. This is necessarily so if there is to be order in the system. But this theory assumes that the direction of resources is dependent directly on the price mechanism. Indeed, it is often considered to be an objection to economic planning that it merely tries to do what is already done by the price mechanism.[5] Sir Arthur Salter's description, however, gives a very incomplete picture of our economic system. Within a firm, the description does not fit at all. For instance, in economic theory we find that the allocation of factors of production between different uses is determined by the price mechanism. The price of factor A becomes higher in X than in Y. As a result, A moves from Y to X until the difference between the prices in X and Y, except in so far as it compensates for other differential advantages, disappears. Yet in the real world, we find that there are many areas where this does not apply. If a workman moves from department Y to department X, he does not go because of a change in relative prices, but because he is ordered to do so. Those who

[1] J. M. Keynes, *Essays in Biography*, pp. 223–4.

[2] L. Robbins, *Nature and Significance of Economic Science*, p. 63.

[3] This description is quoted with approval by D. H. Robertson, *Control of Industry*, p. 85, and by Professor Arnold Plant, "Trends in Business Administration," ECONOMICA, February, 1932. It appears in *Allied Shipping Control*, pp. 16-17.

[4] See F. A. Hayek, "The Trend of Economic Thinking," ECONOMICA, May, 1933.

[5] See F. A. Hayek, op. cit.

object to economic planning on the grounds that the problem is solved by price movements can be answered by pointing out that there is planning within our economic system which is quite different from the individual planning mentioned above and which is akin to what is normally called economic planning. The example given above is typical of a large sphere in our modern economic system. Of course, this fact has not been ignored by economists. Marshall introduces organisation as a fourth factor of production; J. B. Clark gives the co-ordinating function to the entrepreneur; Professor Knight introduces managers who co-ordinate. As D. H. Robertson points out, we find "islands of conscious power in this ocean of unconscious co-operation like lumps of butter coagulating in a pail of buttermilk."[1] But in view of the fact that it is usually argued that co-ordination will be done by the price mechanism, why is such organisation necessary? Why are there these "islands of conscious power"? Outside the firm, price movements direct production, which is co-ordinated through a series of exchange transactions on the market. Within a firm, these market transactions are eliminated and in place of the complicated market structure with exchange transactions is substituted the entrepreneur-co-ordinator, who directs production.[2] It is clear that these are alternative methods of co-ordinating production. Yet, having regard to the fact that if production is regulated by price movements, production could be carried on without any organisation at all, well might we ask, why is there any organisation?

Of course, the degree to which the price mechanism is superseded varies greatly. In a department store, the allocation of the different sections to the various locations in the building may be done by the controlling authority or it may be the result of competitive price bidding for space. In the Lancashire cotton industry, a weaver can rent power and shop-room and can obtain looms and yarn on credit.[3] This co-ordination of the various factors of production is, however, normally carried out without the intervention of the price mechanism. As is evident, the amount of "vertical" integration, involving as it does

[1] Op. cit., p. 85.

[2] In the rest of this paper I shall use the term entrepreneur to refer to the person or persons who, in a competitive system, take the place of the price mechanism in the direction of resources.

[3] *Survey of Textile Industries*, p. 26.

the supersession of the price mechanism, varies greatly from industry to industry and from firm to firm.

It can, I think, be assumed that the distinguishing mark of the firm is the supersession of the price mechanism. It is, of course, as Professor Robbins points out, " related to an outside network of relative prices and costs,"[1] but it is important to discover the exact nature of this relationship. This distinction between the allocation of resources in a firm and the allocation in the economic system has been very vividly described by Mr. Maurice Dobb when discussing Adam Smith's conception of the capitalist: " It began to be seen that there was something more important than the relations inside each factory or unit captained by an undertaker; there were the relations of the undertaker with the rest of the economic world outside his immediate sphere . . . . the undertaker busies himself with the division of labour inside each firm and he plans and organises consciously," but " he is related to the much larger economic specialisation, of which he himself is merely one specialised unit. Here, he plays his part as a single cell in a larger organism, mainly unconscious of the wider rôle he fills."[2]

In view of the fact that while economists treat the price mechanism as a co-ordinating instrument, they also admit the co-ordinating function of the " entrepreneur," it is surely important to enquire why co-ordination is the work of the price mechanism in one case and of the entrepreneur in another. The purpose of this paper is to bridge what appears to be a gap in economic theory between the assumption (made for some purposes) that resources are allocated by means of the price mechanism and the assumption (made for other purposes) that this allocation is dependent on the entrepreneur-co-ordinator. We have to explain the basis on which, in practice, this choice between alternatives is effected.[3]

[1] Op. cit., p. 71.

[2] *Capitalist Enterprise and Social Progress*, p. 20. Cf., also, Henderson, *Supply and Demand*, pp. 3–5.

[3] It is easy to see when the State takes over the direction of an industry that, in planning it, it is doing something which was previously done by the price mechanism. What is usually [illegible] realised is that any business man in organising the relations between his departments i[illegible] doing something which could be organised through the price mechanism. There is ther[illegible]e point in Mr. Durbin's answer to those who emphasise the problems involved in economic planning that the same problems have to be solved by business men in the competitive system. (See " Economic Calculus in a Planned Economy," *Economic Journal*, December, 1936.) The important difference between these two cases is that economic planning is imposed on industry while firms arise voluntarily because they represent a more efficient method of organising production. In a competitive system, there is an " optimum " amount of planning!

II

Our task is to attempt to discover why a firm emerges at all in a specialised exchange economy. The price mechanism (considered purely from the side of the direction of resources) might be superseded if the relationship which replaced it was desired for its own sake. This would be the case, for example, if some people preferred to work under the direction of some other person. Such individuals would accept less in order to work under someone, and firms would arise naturally from this. But it would appear that this cannot be a very important reason, for it would rather seem that the opposite tendency is operating if one judges from the stress normally laid on the advantage of "being one's own master."[1] Of course, if the desire was not to be controlled but to control, to exercise power over others, then people might be willing to give up something in order to direct others; that is, they would be willing to pay others more than they could get under the price mechanism in order to be able to direct them. But this implies that those who direct pay in order to be able to do this and are not paid to direct, which is clearly not true in the majority of cases.[2] Firms might also exist if purchasers preferred commodities which are produced by firms to those not so produced; but even in spheres where one would expect such preferences (if they exist) to be of negligible importance, firms are to be found in the real world.[3] Therefore there must be other elements involved.

The main reason why it is profitable to establish a firm would seem to be that there is a cost of using the price mechanism. The most obvious cost of "organising" production through the price mechanism is that of discovering what the relevant prices are.[4] This cost may be reduced but it will not be eliminated by the emergence of specialists who will sell this information. The costs of negotiating and

[1] Cf. Harry Dawes, "Labour Mobility in the Steel Industry," *Economic Journal*, March, 1934, who instances "the trek to retail shopkeeping and insurance work by the better paid of skilled men due to the desire (often the main aim in life of a worker) to be independent" (p. 86).

[2] None the less, this is not altogether fanciful. Some small shopkeepers are said to earn less than their assistants.

[3] G. F. Shove, "The Imperfection of the Market: a Further Note," *Economic Journal*, March, 1933, p. 116, note 1, points out that such preferences may exist, although the example he gives is almost the reverse of the instance given in the text.

[4] According to N. Kaldor, "A Classificatory Note of the Determinateness of Equilibrium," *Review of Economic Studies*, February, 1934, it is one of the assumptions of static theory that "All the relevant prices are known to all individuals." But this is clearly not true of the real world.

concluding a separate contract for each exchange transaction which takes place on a market must also be taken into account.[1] Again, in certain markets, e.g., produce exchanges, a technique is devised for minimising these contract costs; but they are not eliminated. It is true that contracts are not eliminated when there is a firm but they are greatly reduced. A factor of production (or the owner thereof) does not have to make a series of contracts with the factors with whom he is co-operating within the firm, as would be necessary, of course, if this co-operation were as a direct result of the working of the price mechanism. For this series of contracts is substituted one. At this stage, it is important to note the character of the contract into which a factor enters that is employed within a firm. The contract is one whereby the factor, for a certain remuneration (which may be fixed or fluctuating), agrees to obey the directions of an entrepreneur *within certain limits*.[2] The essence of the contract is that it should only state the limits to the powers of the entrepreneur. Within these limits, he can therefore direct the other factors of production.

There are, however, other disadvantages—or costs—of using the price mechanism. It may be desired to make a long-term contract for the supply of some article or service. This may be due to the fact that if one contract is made for a longer period, instead of several shorter ones, then certain costs of making each contract will be avoided. Or, owing to the risk attitude of the people concerned, they may prefer to make a long rather than a short-term contract. Now, owing to the difficulty of forecasting, the longer the period of the contract is for the supply of the commodity or service, the less possible, and indeed, the less desirable it is for the person purchasing to specify what the other contracting party is expected to do. It may well be a matter of indifference to the person supplying the service or commodity which of several courses of action is taken, but not to the purchaser of that service or commodity. But the purchaser will not know which of these several courses he will want the supplier to take. Therefore,

[1] This influence was noted by Professor Usher when discussing the development of capitalism. He says: "The successive buying and selling of partly finished products were sheer waste of energy." (*Introduction to the Industrial History of England*, p. 13). But he does not develop the idea nor consider why it is that buying and selling operations still exist.

[2] It would be possible for no limits to the powers of the entrepreneur to be fixed. This would be voluntary slavery. According to Professor Batt, *The Law of Master and Servant*, p. 18, such a contract would be void and unenforceable.

the service which is being provided is expressed in general terms, the exact details being left until a later date. All that is stated in the contract is the limits to what the persons supplying the commodity or service is expected to do. The details of what the supplier is expected to do is not stated in the contract but is decided later by the purchaser. When the direction of resources (within the limits of the contract) becomes dependent on the buyer in this way, that relationship which I term a " firm " may be obtained.[1] A firm is likely therefore to emerge in those cases where a very short term contract would be unsatisfactory. It is obviously of more importance in the case of services—labour—than it is in the case of the buying of commodities. In the case of commodities, the main items can be stated in advance and the details which will be decided later will be of minor significance.

We may sum up this section of the argument by saying that the operation of a market costs something and by forming an organisation and allowing some authority (an " entrepreneur ") to direct the resources, certain marketing costs are saved. The entrepreneur has to carry out his function at less cost, taking into account the fact that he may get factors of production at a lower price than the market transactions which he supersedes, because it is always possible to revert to the open market if he fails to do this.

The question of uncertainty is one which is often considered to be very relevant to the study of the equilibrium of the firm. It seems improbable that a firm would emerge without the existence of uncertainty. But those, for instance, Professor Knight, who make the *mode of payment* the distinguishing mark of the firm—fixed incomes being guaranteed to some of those engaged in production by a person who takes the residual, and fluctuating, income—would appear to be introducing a point which is irrelevant to the problem we are considering. One entrepreneur may sell his services to another for a certain sum of money, while the payment to his employees may be mainly or wholly a share in profits.[2] The significant question would

[1] Of course, it is not possible to draw a hard and fast line which determines whether there is a firm or not. There may be more or less direction. It is similar to the legal question of whether there is the relationship of master and servant or principal and agent. See the discussion of this problem below.

[2] The views of Professor Knight are examined below in more detail.

appear to be why the allocation of resources is not done directly by the price mechanism.

Another factor that should be noted is that exchange transactions on a market and the same transactions organised within a firm are often treated differently by Governments or other bodies with regulatory powers. If we consider the operation of a sales tax, it is clear that it is a tax on market transactions and not on the same transactions organised within the firm. Now since these are alternative methods of "organisation"—by the price mechanism or by the entrepreneur—such a regulation would bring into existence firms which otherwise would have no *raison d'être*. It would furnish a reason for the emergence of a firm in a specialised exchange economy. Of course, to the extent that firms already exist, such a measure as a sales tax would merely tend to make them larger than they would otherwise be. Similarly, quota schemes, and methods of price control which imply that there is rationing, and which do not apply to firms producing such products for themselves, by allowing advantages to those who organise within the firm and not through the market, necessarily encourage the growth of firms. But it is difficult to believe that it is measures such as have been mentioned in this paragraph which have brought firms into existence. Such measures would, however, tend to have this result if they did not exist for other reasons.

These, then, are the reasons why organisations such as firms exist in a specialised exchange economy in which it is generally assumed that the distribution of resources is "organised" by the price mechanism. A firm, therefore, consists of the system of relationships which comes into existence when the direction of resources is dependent on an entrepreneur.

The approach which has just been sketched would appear to offer an advantage in that it is possible to give a scientific meaning to what is meant by saying that a firm gets larger or smaller. A firm becomes larger as additional transactions (which could be exchange transactions co-ordinated through the price mechanism) are organised by the entrepreneur and becomes smaller as he abandons the organisation of such transactions. The question which arises is whether it is possible to study the forces which determine the size of the firm. Why does the entrepreneur not organise one less transaction or one more? It is interesting to note that Professor Knight considers that:

> "the relation between efficiency and size is one of the most serious problems of theory, being, in contrast with the relation for a plant, largely a matter of personality and historical accident rather than of intelligible general principles. But the question is peculiarly vital because the possibility of monopoly gain offers a powerful incentive to *continuous and unlimited* expansion of the firm, which force must be offset by some equally powerful one making for decreased efficiency (in the production of money income) with growth in size, if even boundary competition is to exist."[1]

Professor Knight would appear to consider that it is impossible to treat scientifically the determinants of the size of the firm. On the basis of the concept of the firm developed above, this task will now be attempted.

It was suggested that the introduction of the firm was due primarily to the existence of marketing costs. A pertinent question to ask would appear to be (quite apart from the monopoly considerations raised by Professor Knight), why, if by organising one can eliminate certain costs and in fact reduce the cost of production, are there any market transactions at all?[2] Why is not all production carried on by one big firm? There would appear to be certain possible explanations.

First, as a firm gets larger, there may be decreasing returns to the entrepreneur function, that is, the costs of organising additional transactions within the firm may rise.[3] Naturally, a point must be reached where the costs of organising an extra transaction within the firm are equal to the costs involved in carrying out the transaction in the open market, or, to the costs of organising by another entrepreneur. Secondly, it may be that as the transactions which are organised increase, the entrepreneur fails to place the factors of production in the uses where their value

[1] *Risk, Uncertainty and Profit*, Preface to the Re-issue London School of Economics Series of Reprints, No. 16, 1933.

[2] There are certain marketing costs which could only be eliminated by the abolition of "consumers' choice" and these are the costs of retailing. It is conceivable that these costs might be so high that people would be willing to accept rations because the extra product obtained was worth the loss of their choice.

[3] This argument assumes that exchange transactions on a market can be considered as homogeneous; which is clearly untrue in fact. This complication is taken into account below.

is greatest, that is, fails to make the best use of the factors of production. Again, a point must be reached where the loss through the waste of resources is equal to the marketing costs of the exchange transaction in the open market or to the loss if the transaction was organised by another entrepreneur. Finally, the supply price of one or more of the factors of production may rise, because the "other advantages" of a small firm are greater than those of a large firm.[1] Of course, the actual point where the expansion of the firm ceases might be determined by a combination of the factors mentioned above. The first two reasons given most probably correspond to the economists' phrase of "diminishing returns to management."[2]

The point has been made in the previous paragraph that a firm will tend to expand until the costs of organising an extra transaction within the firm become equal to the costs of carrying out the same transaction by means of an exchange on the open market or the costs of organising in another firm. But if the firm stops its expansion at a point below the costs of marketing in the open market and at a point equal to the costs of organising in another firm, in most cases (excluding the case of "combination"[3]), this will imply that there is a market transaction between these two producers, each of whom could organise it at less than the actual marketing costs. How is the paradox to be resolved? If we consider an example the reason for this will become clear. Suppose *A* is buying a product from *B* and that both *A* and *B* could organise this marketing transaction at less than its present cost. *B*, we can assume, is not organising one process or stage of production, but several. If *A* therefore wishes to avoid a market transaction, he will have to take over all the processes of production controlled by *B*. Unless *A* takes over all the processes of

[1] For a discussion of the variation of the supply price of factors of production to firms of varying size, see E. A. G. Robinson, *The Structure of Competitive Industry*. It is sometimes said that the supply price of organising ability increases as the size of the firm increases because men prefer to be the heads of small independent businesses rather than the heads of departments in a large business. See Jones, *The Trust Problem*, p. 531, and Macgregor, *Industrial Combination*, p. 63. This is a common argument of those who advocate Rationalisation. It is said that larger units would be more efficient, but owing to the individualistic spirit of the smaller entrepreneurs, they prefer to remain independent, apparently in spite of the higher income which their increased efficiency under Rationalisation makes possible.

[2] This discussion is, of course, brief and incomplete. For a more thorough discussion of this particular problem, see N. Kaldor, "The Equilibrium of the Firm," *Economic Journal*, March, 1934, and E. A. G. Robinson, "The Problem of Management and the Size of the Firm," *Economic Journal*, June, 1934.

[3] A definition of this term is given below.

production, a market transaction will still remain, although it is a different product that is bought. But we have previously assumed that as each producer expands he becomes less efficient; the additional costs of organising extra transactions increase. It is probable that *A*'s cost of organising the transactions previously organised by *B* will be greater than *B*'s cost of doing the same thing. *A* therefore will take over the whole of *B*'s organisation only if his cost of organising *B*'s work is not greater than *B*'s cost by an amount equal to the costs of carrying out an exchange transaction on the open market. But once it becomes economical to have a market transaction, it also pays to divide production in such a way that the cost of organising an extra transaction in each firm is the same.

Up to now it has been assumed that the exchange transactions which take place through the price mechanism are homogeneous. In fact, nothing could be more diverse than the actual transactions which take place in our modern world. This would seem to imply that the costs of carrying out exchange transactions through the price mechanism will vary considerably as will also the costs of organising these transactions within the firm. It seems therefore possible that quite apart from the question of diminishing returns the costs of organising certain transactions within the firm may be greater than the costs of carrying out the exchange transactions in the open market. This would necessarily imply that there were exchange transactions carried out through the price mechanism, but would it mean that there would have to be more than one firm? Clearly not, for all those areas in the economic system where the direction of resources was not dependent directly on the price mechanism could be organised within one firm. The factors which were discussed earlier would seem to be the important ones, though it is difficult to say whether "diminishing returns to management" or the rising supply price of factors is likely to be the more important.

Other things being equal, therefore, a firm will tend to be larger:

(*a*) the less the costs of organising and the slower these costs rise with an increase in the transactions organised.

(*b*) the less likely the entrepreneur is to make mistakes and the smaller the increase in mistakes with an increase in the transactions organised.

(*c*) the greater the lowering (or the less the rise) in the supply price of factors of production to firms of larger size.

Apart from variations in the supply price of factors of production to firms of different sizes, it would appear that the costs of organising and the losses through mistakes will increase with an increase in the spatial distribution of the transactions organised, in the dissimilarity of the transactions, and in the probability of changes in the relevant prices.[1] As more transactions are organised by an entrepreneur, it would appear that the transactions would tend to be either different in kind or in different places. This furnishes an additional reason why efficiency will tend to decrease as the firm gets larger. Inventions which tend to bring factors of production nearer together, by lessening spatial distribution, tend to increase the size of the firm.[2] Changes like the telephone and the telegraph which tend to reduce the cost of organising spatially will tend to increase the size of the firm. All changes which improve managerial technique will tend to increase the size of the firm.[3-4]

It should be noted that the definition of a firm which was given above can be used to give more precise meanings to the terms " combination " and " integration."[5] There is a combination when transactions which were previously

[1] This aspect of the problem is emphasised by N. Kaldor. op. cit. Its importance in this connection had been previously noted by E. A. G. Robinson, *The Structure of Competitive Industry*, pp. 83–106. This assumes that an increase in the probability of price movements increases the costs of organising within a firm more than it increases the cost of carrying out an exchange transaction on the market—which is probable.

[2] This would appear to be the importance of the treatment of the technical unit by E. A. G. Robinson, op. cit., pp. 27–33. The larger the technical unit, the greater the concentration of factors and therefore the firm is likely to be larger.

[3] It should be noted that most inventions will change both the costs of organising and the costs of using the price mechanism. In such cases, whether the invention tends to make firms larger or smaller will depend on the relative effect on these two sets of costs. For instance, if the telephone reduces the costs of using the price mechanism more than it reduces the costs of organising, then it will have the effect of reducing the size of the firm.

[4] An illustration of these dynamic forces is furnished by Maurice Dobb, *Russian Economic Development*, p. 68. " With the passing of bonded labour the factory, as an establishment where work was organised under the whip of the overseer, lost its *raison d'être* until this was restored to it with the introduction of power machinery after 1846." It seems important to realise that the passage from the domestic system to the factory system is not a mere historical accident, but is conditioned by economic forces. This is shown by the fact that it is possible to move from the factory system to the domestic system, as in the Russian example, as well as *vice versa*. It is the essence of serfdom that the price mechanism is not allowed to operate. Therefore, there has to be direction from some organiser. When, however, serfdom passed, the price mechanism was allowed to operate. It was not until machinery drew workers into one locality that it paid to supersede the price mechanism and the firm again emerged.

[5] This is often called " vertical integration," combination being termed " lateral integration."

organised by two or more entrepreneurs become organised by one. This becomes integration when it involves the organisation of transactions which were previously carried out between the entrepreneurs on a market. A firm can expand in either or both of these two ways. The whole of the "structure of competitive industry" becomes tractable by the ordinary technique of economic analysis.

III

The problem which has been investigated in the previous section has not been entirely neglected by economists and it is now necessary to consider why the reasons given above for the emergence of a firm in a specialised exchange economy are to be preferred to the other explanations which have been offered.

It is sometimes said that the reason for the existence of a firm is to be found in the division of labour. This is the view of Professor Usher, a view which has been adopted and expanded by Mr. Maurice Dobb. The firm becomes "the result of an increasing complexity of the division of labour . . . . The growth of this economic differentiation creates the need for some integrating force without which differentiation would collapse into chaos; and it is as the integrating force in a differentiated economy that industrial forms are chiefly significant."[1] The answer to this argument is an obvious one. The "integrating force in a differentiated economy" already exists in the form of the price mechanism. It is perhaps the main achievement of economic science that it has shown that there is no reason to suppose that specialisation must lead to chaos.[2] The reason given by Mr. Maurice Dobb is therefore inadmissible. What has to be explained is why one integrating force (the entrepreneur) should be substituted for another integrating force (the price mechanism).

The most interesting reasons (and probably the most widely accepted) which have been given to explain this fact are those to be found in Professor Knight's *Risk, Uncertainty and Profit.* His views will be examined in some detail.

[1] Op. cit., p. 10. Professor Usher's views are to be found in his *Introduction to the Industrial History of England*, pp. 1–18.

[2] Cf. J. B. Clark, *Distribution of Wealth*, p. 19, who speaks of the theory of exchange as being the "theory of the organisation of industrial society."

Professor Knight starts with a system in which there is no uncertainty:

> "acting as individuals under absolute freedom but without collusion men are supposed to have organised economic life with the primary and secondary division of labour, the use of capital, etc., developed to the point familiar in present-day America. The principal fact which calls for the exercise of the imagination is the internal organisation of the productive groups or establishments. With uncertainty entirely absent, every individual being in possession of perfect knowledge of the situation, there would be no occasion for anything of the nature of responsible management or control of productive activity. Even marketing transactions in any realistic sense would not be found. The flow of raw materials and productive services to the consumer would be entirely automatic."[1]

Professor Knight says that we can imagine this adjustment as being "the result of a long process of experimentation worked out by trial-and-error methods alone," while it is not necessary "to imagine every worker doing exactly the right thing at the right time in a sort of 'pre-established harmony' with the work of others. There might be managers, superintendents, etc., for the purpose of co-ordinating the activities of individuals," though these managers would be performing a purely routine function, "without responsibility of any sort."[2]

Professor Knight then continues:

> "With the introduction of uncertainty—the fact of ignorance and the necessity of acting upon opinion rather than knowledge—into this Eden-like situation, its character is entirely changed . . . . With uncertainty present doing things, the actual execution of activity, becomes in a real sense a secondary part of life; the primary problem or function is deciding what to do and how to do it."[3]

This fact of uncertainty brings about the two most important characteristics of social organisation.

> "In the first place, goods are produced for a market, on the basis of entirely impersonal prediction of wants, not for the satisfaction of the wants of the producers themselves. The producer takes the responsibility of

[1] *Risk, Uncertainty and Profit*, p. 267.

[2] Op. cit., pp. 267–8.

[3] Op. cit., p. 268.

forecasting the consumers' wants. In the second place, the work of forecasting and at the same time a large part of the technological direction and control of production are still further concentrated upon a very narrow class of the producers, and we meet with a new economic functionary, the entrepreneur. . . . . When uncertainty is present and the task of deciding what to do and how to do it takes the ascendancy over that of execution the internal organisation of the productive groups is no longer a matter of indifference or a mechanical detail. Centralisation of this deciding and controlling function is imperative, a process of 'cephalisation' is inevitable."[1]

The most fundamental change is:

"the system under which the confident and venturesome assume the risk or insure the doubtful and timid by guaranteeing to the latter a specified income in return for an assignment of the actual results. . . . With human nature as we know it it would be impracticable or very unusual for one man to guarantee to another a definite result of the latter's actions without being given power to direct his work. And on the other hand the second party would not place himself under the direction of the first without such a guarantee. . . . The result of this manifold specialisation of function is the enterprise and wage system of industry. Its existence in the world is the direct result of the fact of uncertainty."[2]

These quotations give the essence of Professor Knight's theory. The fact of uncertainty means that people have to forecast future wants. Therefore, you get a special class springing up who direct the activities of others to whom they give guaranteed wages. It acts because good judgment is generally associated with confidence in one's judgment.[3]

Professor Knight would appear to leave himself open to criticism on several grounds. First of all, as he himself points out, the fact that certain people have better judgment or better knowledge does not mean that they can only get an income from it by themselves actively taking part in production. They can sell advice or knowledge. Every business buys the services of a host of advisers. We can imagine a system where all advice or knowledge was bought

[1] Op. cit., pp. 268–95. [2] Op. cit., pp. 269–70.
[3] Op. cit., p. 270.

as required. Again, it is possible to get a reward from better knowledge or judgment not by actively taking part in production but by making contracts with people who are producing. A merchant buying for future delivery represents an example of this. But this merely illustrates the point that it is quite possible to give a guaranteed reward providing that certain acts are performed without directing the performance of those acts. Professor Knight says that "with human nature as we know it it would be impracticable or very unusual for one man to guarantee to another a definite result of the latter's actions without being given power to direct his work." This is surely incorrect. A large proportion of jobs are done to contract, that is, the contractor is guaranteed a certain sum providing he performs certain acts. But this does not involve any direction. It does mean, however, that the system of relative prices has been changed and that there will be a new arrangement of the factors of production.[1] The fact that Professor Knight mentions that the "second party would not place himself under the direction of the first without such a guarantee" is irrelevant to the problem we are considering. Finally, it seems important to notice that even in the case of an economic system where there is no uncertainty Professor Knight considers that there would be co-ordinators, though they would perform only a routine function. He immediately adds that they would be "without responsibility of any sort," which raises the question by whom are they paid and why? It seems that nowhere does Professor Knight give a reason why the price mechanism should be superseded.

IV

It would seem important to examine one further point and that is to consider the relevance of this discussion to the general question of the "cost-curve of the firm."

It has sometimes been assumed that a firm is limited in size under perfect competition if its cost curve slopes upward,[2] while under imperfect competition, it is limited

[1] This shows that it is possible to have a private enterprise system without the existence of firms. Though, in practice, the two functions of enterprise, which actually influences the system of relative prices by forecasting wants and acting in accordance with such forecasts, and management, which accepts the system of relative prices as being given, are normally carried out by the same persons, yet it seems important to keep them separate in theory. This point is further discussed below.

[2] See Kaldor, op. cit., and Robinson, *The Problem of Management and the Size of the Firm.*

in size because it will not pay to produce more than the output at which marginal cost is equal to marginal revenue.[1] But it is clear that a firm may produce more than one product and, therefore, there appears to be no *prima facie* reason why this upward slope of the cost curve in the case of perfect competition or the fact that marginal cost will not always be below marginal revenue in the case of imperfect competition should limit the size of the firm.[2] Mrs. Robinson[3] makes the simplifying assumption that only one product is being produced. But it is clearly important to investigate how the number of products produced by a firm is determined, while no theory which assumes that only one product is in fact produced can have very great practical significance.

It might be replied that under perfect competition, since everything that is produced can be sold at the prevailing price, then there is no need for any other product to be produced. But this argument ignores the fact that there may be a point where it is less costly to organise the exchange transactions of a new product than to organise further exchange transactions of the old product. This point can be illustrated in the following way. Imagine, following von Thunen, that there is a town, the consuming centre, and that industries are located around this central point in rings. These conditions are illustrated in the following diagram in which *A*, *B* and *C* represent different industries.

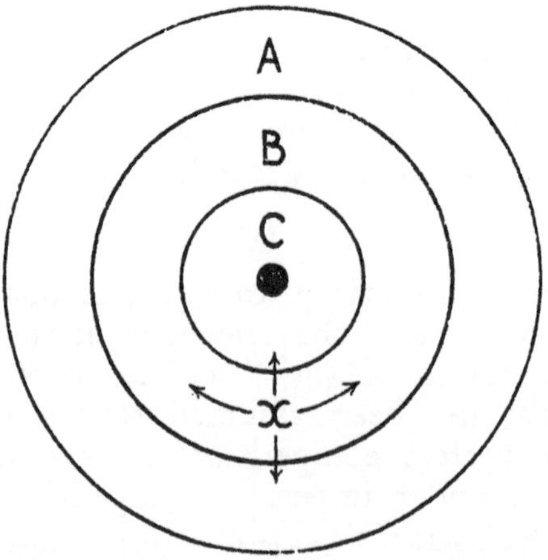

[1] Mr. Robinson calls this the Imperfect Competition solution for the survival of the small firm.

[2] Mr. Robinson's conclusion, op. cit., p. 249, note 1, would appear to be definitely wrong. He is followed by Horace J. White, Jr., "Monopolistic and Perfect Competition," *American Economic Review*, December, 1936, p. 645, note 27. Mr. White states "It is obvious that the size of the firm is limited in conditions of monopolistic competition."

[3] *Economics of Imperfect Competition.*

Imagine an entrepreneur who starts controlling exchange transactions from *x*. Now as he extends his activities in the same product (*B*), the cost of organising increases until at some point it becomes equal to that of a dissimilar product which is nearer. As the firm expands, it will therefore from this point include more than one product (*A* and *C*). This treatment of the problem is obviously incomplete,[1] but it is necessary to show that merely proving that the cost curve turns upwards does not give a limitation to the size of the firm. So far we have only considered the case of perfect competition; the case of imperfect competition would appear to be obvious.

To determine the size of the firm, we have to consider the marketing costs (that is, the costs of using the price mechanism), and the costs of organising of different entrepreneurs and then we can determine how many products will be produced by each firm and how much of each it will produce. It would, therefore, appear that Mr. Shove[2] in his article on "Imperfect Competition" was asking questions which Mrs. Robinson's cost curve apparatus cannot answer. The factors mentioned above would seem to be the relevant ones.

V

Only one task now remains; and that is, to see whether the concept of a firm which has been developed fits in with that existing in the real world. We can best approach the question of what constitutes a firm in practice by considering the legal relationship normally called that of "master and servant" or "employer and employee."[3] The essentials of this relationship have been given as follows:

"(1) the servant must be under the duty of rendering personal services to the master or to others on behalf

[1] As has been shown above, location is only one of the factors influencing the cost of organising.

[2] G. F. Shove, "The Imperfection of the Market," *Economic Journal*, March, 1933, p. 115. In connection with an increase in demand in the suburbs and the effect on the price charged by suppliers, Mr. Shove asks "'. . . . why do not the old firms open branches in the suburbs?" If the argument in the text is correct, this is a question which Mrs. Robinson's apparatus cannot answer.

[3] The legal concept of "employer and employee" and the economic concept of a firm are not identical, in that the firm may imply control over another person's property as well as over their labour. But the identity of these two concepts is sufficiently close for an examination of the legal concept to be of value in appraising the worth of the economic concept.

of the master, otherwise the contract is a contract for sale of goods or the like.

(2) The master must have the right to control the servant's work, either personally or by another servant or agent. It is this right of control or interference, of being entitled to tell the servant when to work (within the hours of service) and when not to work, and what work to do and how to do it (within the terms of such service) which is the dominant characteristic in this relation and marks off the servant from an independent contractor, or from one employed merely to give to his employer the fruits of his labour. In the latter case, the contractor or performer is not under the employer's control in doing the work or effecting the service; he has to shape and manage his work so as to give the result he has contracted to effect."[1]

We thus see that it is the fact of direction which is the essence of the legal concept of "employer and employee," just as it was in the economic concept which was developed above. It is interesting to note that Professor Batt says further:

"That which distinguishes an agent from a servant is not the absence or presence of a fixed wage or the payment only of commission on business done, but rather the freedom with which an agent may carry out his employment."[2]

We can therefore conclude that the definition we have given is one which approximates closely to the firm as it is considered in the real world.

Our definition is, therefore, realistic. Is it manageable? This ought to be clear. When we are considering how large a firm will be the principle of marginalism works smoothly. The question always is, will it pay to bring an extra exchange transaction under the organising authority? At the margin, the costs of organising within the firm will be equal either to the costs of organising in another firm or to the costs involved in leaving the transaction to be "organised" by the price mechanism. Business men will be constantly experimenting, controlling more or less, and in this way, equilibrium will be maintained. This gives the position of equilibrium for static analysis. But

[1] Batt, *The Law of Master and Servant*, p. 6.
[2] Op. cit., p. 7.

it is clear that the dynamic factors are also of considerable importance, and an investigation of the effect changes have on the cost of organising within the firm and on marketing costs generally will enable one to explain why firms get larger and smaller. We thus have a theory of moving equilibrium. The above analysis would also appear to have clarified the relationship between initiative or enterprise and management. Initiative means forecasting and operates through the price mechanism by the making of new contracts. Management proper merely reacts to price changes, rearranging the factors of production under its control. That the business man normally combines both functions is an obvious result of the marketing costs which were discussed above. Finally, this analysis enables us to state more exactly what is meant by the "marginal product" of the entrepreneur. But an elaboration of this point would take us far from our comparatively simple task of definition and clarification.

The theory of economic regulation

George J. Stigler

The University of Chicago

The potential uses of public resources and powers to improve the economic status of economic groups (such as industries and occupations) are analyzed to provide a scheme of the demand for regulation. The characteristics of the political process which allow relatively small groups to obtain such regulation is then sketched to provide elements of a theory of supply of regulation. A variety of empirical evidence and illustration is also presented.

■ The state—the machinery and power of the state—is a potential resource or threat to every industry in the society. With its power to prohibit or compel, to take or give money, the state can and does selectively help or hurt a vast number of industries. That political juggernaut, the petroleum industry, is an immense consumer of political benefits, and simultaneously the underwriters of marine insurance have their more modest repast. The central tasks of the theory of economic regulation are to explain who will receive the benefits or burdens of regulation, what form regulation will take, and the effects of regulation upon the allocation of resources.

Regulation may be actively sought by an industry, or it may be thrust upon it. A central thesis of this paper is that, as a rule, regulation is acquired by the industry and is designed and operated primarily for its benefit. There are regulations whose net effects upon the regulated industry are undeniably onerous; a simple example is the differentially heavy taxation of the industry's product (whiskey, playing cards). These onerous regulations, however, are exceptional and can be explained by the same theory that explains beneficial (we may call it "acquired") regulation.

Two main alternative views of the regulation of industry are widely held. The first is that regulation is instituted primarily for the protection and benefit of the public at large or some large subclass of the public. In this view, the regulations which injure the public—as when the oil import quotas increase the cost of petroleum products to America by $5 billion or more a year—are costs of some social goal (here, national defense) or, occasionally, perversions of the regulatory philosophy. The second view is essentially that the political process defies rational explanation: "politics" is an imponderable, a constantly and unpredictably shifting mixture of forces of the most diverse nature, comprehending acts of great moral virtue (the emancipation of slaves) and of the most vulgar venality (the congressman feathering his own nest).

The author obtained the B.B.A. degree from the University of Washington, the M.B.A. degree from Northwestern, and the Ph.D. degree from the University of Chicago. He is presently Charles R. Walgreen Distinguished Service Professor of American Institutions at the University of Chicago, and has published numerous articles and texts in the field of economics. Dr. Stigler is Vice Chairman of the Securities Investor Protective Commission.

Let us consider a problem posed by the oil import quota system: why does not the powerful industry which obtained this expensive program instead choose direct cash subsidies from the public treasury? The "protection of the public" theory of regulation must say that the choice of import quotas is dictated by the concern of the federal government for an adequate domestic supply of petroleum in the event of war—a remark calculated to elicit uproarious laughter at the Petroleum Club. Such laughter aside, if national defense were the goal of the quotas, a tariff would be a more economical instrument of policy: it would retain the profits of exclusion for the treasury. The non-rationalist view would explain the policy by the inability of consumers to measure the cost to them of the import quotas, and hence their willingness to pay $5 billion in higher prices rather than the $2.5 billion in cash that would be equally attractive to the industry. Our profit-maximizing theory says that the explanation lies in a different direction: the present members of the refining industries would have to share a cash subsidy with all new entrants into the refining industry.[1] Only when the elasticity of supply of an industry is small will the industry prefer cash to controls over entry or output.

This question, why does an industry solicit the coercive powers of the state rather than its cash, is offered only to illustrate the approach of the present paper. We assume that political systems are rationally devised and rationally employed, which is to say that they are appropriate instruments for the fulfillment of desires of members of the society. This is not to say that the state will serve any person's concept of the public interest: indeed the problem of regulation is the problem of discovering when and why an industry (or other group of like-minded people) is able to use the state for its purposes, or is singled out by the state to be used for alien purposes.

1. What benefits can a state provide to an industry?

■ The state has one basic resource which in pure principle is not shared with even the mightiest of its citizens: the power to coerce. The state can seize money by the only method which is permitted by the laws of a civilized society, by taxation. The state can ordain the physical movements of resources and the economic decisions of households and firms without their consent. These powers provide the possibilities for the utilization of the state by an industry to increase its profitability. The main policies which an industry (or occupation) may seek of the state are four.

The most obvious contribution that a group may seek of the government is a direct subsidy of money. The domestic airlines received "air mail" subsidies (even if they did not carry mail) of $1.5 billion through 1968. The merchant marine has received construction and operation subsidies reaching almost $3 billion since World War II. The education industry has long shown a masterful skill in obtaining public funds: for example, universities and colleges have received federal funds exceeding $3 billion annually in recent years, as well as subsidized loans for dormitories and other construction. The veterans of wars have often received direct cash bonuses.

---

[1] The domestic producers of petroleum, who also benefit from the import quota, would find a tariff or cash payment to domestic producers equally attractive. If their interests alone were consulted, import quotas would be auctioned off instead of being given away.

We have already sketched the main explanation for the fact that an industry with power to obtain governmental favors usually does not use this power to get money: unless the list of beneficiaries can be limited by an acceptable device, whatever amount of subsidies the industry can obtain will be dissipated among a growing number of rivals. The airlines quickly moved away from competitive bidding for air mail contracts to avoid this problem.[2] On the other hand, the premier universities have not devised a method of excluding other claimants for research funds, and in the long run they will receive much-reduced shares of federal research monies.

The second major public resource commonly sought by an industry is control over entry by new rivals. There is considerable, not to say excessive, discussion in economic literature of the rise of peculiar price policies (limit prices), vertical integration, and similar devices to retard the rate of entry of new firms into oligopolistic industries. Such devices are vastly less efficacious (economical) than the certificate of convenience and necessity (which includes, of course, the import and production quotas of the oil and tobacco industries).

The diligence with which the power of control over entry will be exercised by a regulatory body is already well known. The Civil Aeronautics Board has not allowed a single new trunk line to be launched since it was created in 1938. The power to insure new banks has been used by the Federal Deposit Insurance Corporation to reduce the rate of entry into commercial banking by 60 percent.[3] The interstate motor carrier history is in some respects even more striking, because no even ostensibly respectable case for restriction on entry can be developed on grounds of scale economies (which are in turn adduced to limit entry for safety or economy of operation). The number of federally licensed common carriers is shown in Figure 1: the immense growth of the freight hauled by trucking common carriers has been associated with a steady secular decline of numbers of such carriers. The number of applications for new certificates has been in excess of 5000 annually in recent years: a rigorous proof that hope springs eternal in an aspiring trucker's breast.

We propose the general hypothesis: every industry or occupation that has enough political power to utilize the state will seek to control entry. In addition, the regulatory policy will often be so fashioned as to retard the rate of growth of new firms. For example, no new savings and loan company may pay a dividend rate higher than that prevailing in the community in its endeavors to attract deposits.[4] The power to limit selling expenses of mutual funds, which is soon to be conferred upon the Securities and Exchange Commission, will serve to limit the growth of small mutual funds and hence reduce the sales costs of large funds.

One variant of the control of entry is the protective tariff (and the corresponding barriers which have been raised to interstate movements of goods and people). The benefits of protection to an industry, one might think, will usually be dissipated by the entry of new domestic producers, and the question naturally arises: Why does the industry not also seek domestic entry controls? In a few industries

[2] See [7], pp. 60 ff.

[3] See [10].

[4] The Federal Home Loan Bank Board is the regulatory body. It also controls the amount of advertising and other areas of competition.

FIGURE 1

CERTIFICATES FOR INTERSTATE MOTOR CARRIERS

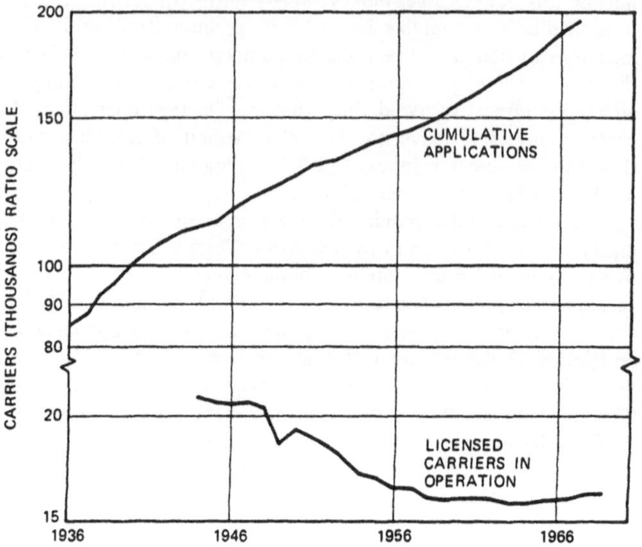

SOURCE: TABLE 5

(petroleum) the domestic controls have been obtained, but not in most. The tariff will be effective if there is a specialized domestic resource necessary to the industry; oil-producing lands is an example. Even if an industry has only durable specialized resources, it will gain if its contraction is slowed by a tariff.

A third general set of powers of the state which will be sought by the industry are those which affect substitutes and complements. Crudely put, the butter producers wish to suppress margarine and encourage the production of bread. The airline industry actively supports the federal subsidies to airports; the building trade unions have opposed labor-saving materials through building codes. We shall examine shortly a specific case of inter-industry competition in transportation.

The fourth class of public policies sought by an industry is directed to price-fixing. Even the industry that has achieved entry control will often want price controls administered by a body with coercive powers. If the number of firms in the regulated industry is even moderately large, price discrimination will be difficult to maintain in the absence of public support. The prohibition of interest on demand deposits, which is probably effective in preventing interest payments to most non-business depositors, is a case in point. Where there are no diseconomies of large scale for the individual firm (e.g., a motor trucking firm can add trucks under a given license as common carrier), price control is essential to achieve more than competitive rates of return.

☐ **Limitations upon political benefits.** These various political boons are not obtained by the industry in a pure profit-maximizing form. The political process erects certain limitations upon the exercise of cartel policies by an industry. These limitations are of three sorts.

TABLE 1

IMPORT QUOTAS OF REFINERIES AS PERCENT OF DAILY INPUT OF PETROLEUM (DISTRICTS I – IV, JULY 1, 1959 – DEC. 31, 1959)

SIZE OF REFINERY (THOUSANDS OF BARRELS)	PERCENT QUOTA
0–10	11.4
10–20	10.4
20–30	9.5
30–60	8.5
60–100	7.6
100–150	6.6
150–200	5.7
200–300	4.7
300 AND OVER	3.8

SOURCE: HEARING, SELECT COMMITTEE ON SMALL BUSINESS, U. S. CONGRESS, 88th CONG., 2nd SESS., AUG. 10 AND 11, 1964, [12] P. 121.

First, the distribution of control of the industry among the firms in the industry is changed. In an unregulated industry each firm's influence upon price and output is proportional to its share of industry output (at least in a simple arithmetic sense of direct capacity to change output). The political decisions take account also of the political strength of the various firms, so small firms have a larger influence than they would possess in an unregulated industry. Thus, when quotas are given to firms, the small firms will almost always receive larger quotas than cost-minimizing practices would allow. The original quotas under the oil import quota system will illustrate this practice (Table 1). The smallest refiners were given a quota of 11.4 percent of their daily consumption of oil, and the percentage dropped as refinery size rose.[5] The pattern of regressive benefits is characteristic of public controls in industries with numerous firms.

Second, the procedural safeguards required of public processes are costly. The delays which are dictated by both law and bureaucratic thoughts of self-survival can be large: Robert Gerwig found the price of gas sold in interstate commerce to be 5 to 6 percent higher than in intrastate commerce because of the administrative costs (including delay) of Federal Power Commission reviews [5].

Finally, the political process automatically admits powerful outsiders to the industry's councils. It is well known that the allocation of television channels among communities does not maximize industry revenue but reflects pressures to serve many smaller communities. The abandonment of an unprofitable rail line is an even more notorious area of outsider participation.

These limitations are predictable, and they must all enter into the calculus of the profitability of regulation of an industry.

☐ **An illustrative analysis.** The recourse to the regulatory process is of course more specific and more complex than the foregoing sketch

[5] The largest refineries were restricted to 75.7 percent of their historical quota under the earlier voluntary import quota plan.

suggests. The defensive power of various other industries which are affected by the proposed regulation must also be taken into account. An analysis of one aspect of the regulation of motor trucking will illustrate these complications. At this stage we are concerned only with the correspondence between regulations and economic interests; later we shall consider the political process by which regulation is achieved.

The motor trucking industry operated almost exclusively within cities before 1925, in good part because neither powerful trucks nor good roads were available for long-distance freight movements. As these deficiencies were gradually remedied, the share of trucks in intercity freight movements began to rise, and by 1930 it was estimated to be 4 percent of ton-miles of intercity freight. The railroad industry took early cognizance of this emerging competitor, and one of the methods by which trucking was combatted was state regulation.

By the early 1930's all states regulated the dimensions and weight of trucks. The weight limitations were a much more pervasive control over trucking than the licensing of common carriers because even the trucks exempt from entry regulation are subject to the limitations on dimensions and capacity. The weight regulations in the early 1930's are reproduced in the appendix (Table 6). Sometimes the participation of railroads in the regulatory process was incontrovertible: Texas and Louisiana placed a 7000-pound payload limit on trucks serving (and hence competing with) two or more railroad stations, and a 14,000-pound limit on trucks serving only one station (hence, not competing with it).

We seek to determine the pattern of weight limits on trucks that would emerge in response to the economic interests of the concerned parties. The main considerations appear to be the following:

(1) Heavy trucks would be allowed in states with a substantial number of trucks on farms: the powerful agricultural interests would insist upon this. The 1930 Census reports nearly one million trucks on farms. One variable in our study will be, for each state, trucks per 1000 of agricultural population.[6]

(2) Railroads found the truck an effective and rapidly triumphing competitor in the shorter hauls and hauls of less than carload traffic, but much less effective in the carload and longer-haul traffic. Our second variable for each state is, therefore, length of average railroad haul.[7] The longer the average rail haul is, the less the railroads will be opposed to trucks.

(3) The public at large would be concerned by the potential damage done to the highway system by heavy trucks. The better the state highway system, the heavier the trucks that would be permitted. The percentage of each state's highways that had a high type surface is the third variable. Of course good highways are more likely to exist where the potential contribution of trucks to a state's economy is greater, so the causation may be looked at from either direction.

[6] The ratio of trucks to total population would measure the product of (1) the importance of trucks to farmers, and (2) the importance of farmers in the state. For reasons given later, we prefer to emphasize (1).

[7] This is known for each railroad, and we assume that (1) the average holds within each state, and (2) two or more railroads in a state may be combined on the basis of mileage. Obviously both assumptions are at best fair approximations.

We have two measures of weight limits on trucks, one for 4-wheel trucks (X_1) and one for 6-wheel trucks (X_2). We may then calculate two equations,

$$X_1 \text{ (or } X_2) = a + bX_3 + cX_4 + dX_5 ,$$

where

X_3 = trucks per 1000 agricultural labor force, 1930 ,
X_4 = average length of railroad haul of freight traffic, 1930,
X_5 = percentage of state roads with high-quality surface, 1930.

(All variables are fully defined and their state values given in Table 7 on page 20.)

The three explanatory variables are statistically significant, and each works in the expected direction. The regulations on weight were less onerous; the larger the truck population in farming, the less competitive the trucks were to railroads (i.e., the longer the rail hauls), and the better the highway system (see Table 2).

☐ The foregoing analysis is concerned with what may be termed the industrial demand for governmental powers. Not every industry will have a significant demand for public assistance (other than money!), meaning the prospect of a substantial increase in the present value of the enterprises even if the governmental services could be obtained gratis (and of course they have costs to which we soon turn). In some economic activities entry of new rivals is extremely difficult to control—consider the enforcement problem in restricting the supply of domestic servants. In some industries the substitute products cannot be efficiently controlled—consider the competition offered to bus lines by private car-pooling. Price fixing is not feasible where every

TABLE 2

REGRESSION ANALYSIS OF STATE WEIGHT LIMITS ON TRUCKS
(T VALUES UNDER REGRESSION COEFFICIENTS)

DEPENDENT VARIABLE	N	CONSTANT	X_3	X_4	X_5	R^2
X_1	48	12.28 (4.87)	0.0336 (3.99)	0.0287 (2.77)	0.2641 (3.04)	0.502
X_2	46	10.34 (1.57)	0.0437 (2.01)	0.0788 (2.97)	0.2528 (1.15)	0.243

X_1 = WEIGHT LIMIT ON 4-WHEEL TRUCKS (THOUSANDS OF POUNDS), 1932-33
X_2 = WEIGHT LIMIT ON 6-WHEEL TRUCKS (THOUSANDS OF POUNDS), 1932-33
X_3 = TRUCKS ON FARMS PER 1,000 AGRICULTURAL LABOR FORCE, 1930
X_4 = AVERAGE LENGTH OF RAILROAD HAUL OF FREIGHT (MILES), 1930
X_5 = PERCENT OF STATE HIGHWAYS WITH HIGH-TYPE SURFACE, DEC. 31, 1930

SOURCES: X_1 AND X_2: THE MOTOR TRUCK RED BOOK AND DIRECTORY [11], 1934 EDITION, P. 85-102, AND U.S. DEPT. OF AGRIC., BUR. OF PUBLIC ROADS, DEC. 1932 [13].

X_3: CENSUS OF AGRICULTURE, 1930, VOL. IV, [14].

X_4: A.A.R.R., BUR. OF RAILWAY ECONOMICS, RAILWAY MILEAGE BY STATES, DEC. 31, 1930 [1] AND U.S.I.C.C., STATISTICS OF RAILWAYS IN THE U.S., 1930 [18].

X_5: STATISTICAL ABSTRACT OF THE U.S., 1932 [16].

unit of the product has a different quality and price, as in the market for used automobiles. In general, however, most industries will have a positive demand price (schedule) for the services of government.

2. The costs of obtaining legislation

■ When an industry receives a grant of power from the state, the benefit to the industry will fall short of the damage to the rest of the community. Even if there were no deadweight losses from acquired regulation, however, one might expect a democratic society to reject such industry requests unless the industry controlled a majority of the votes.[8] A direct and informed vote on oil import quotas would reject the scheme. (If it did not, our theory of rational political processes would be contradicted.) To explain why many industries are able to employ the political machinery to their own ends, we must examine the nature of the political process in a democracy.

A consumer chooses between rail and air travel, for example, by voting with his pocketbook: he patronizes on a given day that mode of transportation he prefers. A similar form of economic voting occurs with decisions on where to work or where to invest one's capital. The market accumulates these economic votes, predicts their future course, and invests accordingly.

Because the political decision is coercive, the decision process is fundamentally different from that of the market. If the public is asked to make a decision between two transportation media comparable to the individual's decision on how to travel—say, whether airlines or railroads should receive a federal subsidy—the decision must be abided by everyone, travellers and non-travellers, travellers this year and travellers next year. This compelled universality of political decisions makes for two differences between democratic political decision processes and market processes.

(1) The decisions must be made simultaneously by a large number of persons (or their representatives): the political process demands simultaneity of decision. If *A* were to vote on the referendum today, *B* tomorrow, *C* the day after, and so on, the accumulation of a majority decision would be both expensive and suspect. (*A* might wish to cast a different vote now than last month.)

The condition of simultaneity imposes a major burden upon the political decision process. It makes voting on specific issues prohibitively expensive: it is a significant cost even to engage in the transaction of buying a plane ticket when I wish to travel; it would be stupendously expensive to me to engage in the physically similar transaction of voting (i.e., patronizing a polling place) whenever a number of my fellow citizens desired to register their views on railroads versus airplanes. To cope with this condition of simultaneity, the voters must employ representatives with wide discretion and must eschew direct expressions of marginal changes in preferences. This characteristic also implies that the political decision does not predict voter desires and make preparations to fulfill them in advance of their realization.

---

[8] If the deadweight loss (of consumer and producer surplus) is taken into account, even if the oil industry were in the majority it would not obtain the legislation if there were available some method of compensation (such as sale of votes) by which the larger damage of the minority could be expressed effectively against the lesser gains of the majority.

(2) The democratic decision process must involve "all" the community, not simply those who are directly concerned with a decision. In a private market, the non-traveller never votes on rail versus plane travel, while the huge shipper casts many votes each day. The political decision process cannot exclude the uninterested voter: the abuses of any exclusion except self-exclusion are obvious. Hence, the political process does not allow participation in proportion to interest and knowledge. In a measure, this difficulty is moderated by other political activities besides voting which do allow a more effective vote to interested parties: persuasion, employment of skilled legislative representatives, etc. Nevertheless, the political system does not offer good incentives like those in private markets to the acquisition of knowledge. If I consume ten times as much of public service A (streets) as of B (schools), I do not have incentives to acquire corresponding amounts of knowledge about the public provision of these services.[9]

These characteristics of the political process can be modified by having numerous levels of government (so I have somewhat more incentive to learn about local schools than about the whole state school system) and by selective use of direct decision (bond referenda). The chief method of coping with the characteristics, however, is to employ more or less full-time representatives organized in (disciplined by) firms which are called political parties or machines.

The representative and his party are rewarded for their discovery and fulfillment of the political desires of their constituency by success in election and the perquisites of office. If the representative could confidently await reelection whenever he voted against an economic policy that injured the society, he would assuredly do so. Unfortunately virtue does not always command so high a price. If the representative denies ten large industries their special subsidies of money or governmental power, they will dedicate themselves to the election of a more complaisant successor: the stakes are that important. This does not mean that every large industry can get what it wants or all that it wants: it does mean that the representative and his party must find a coalition of voter interests more durable than the anti-industry side of every industry policy proposal. A representative cannot win or keep office with the support of the sum of those who are opposed to: oil import quotas, farm subsidies, airport subsidies, hospital subsidies, unnecessary navy shipyards, an inequitable public housing program, and rural electrification subsidies.

The political decison process has as its dominant characteristic infrequent, universal (in principle) participation, as we have noted: political decisions must be infrequent and they must be global. The voter's expenditure to learn the merits of individual policy proposals and to express his preferences (by individual and group representation as well as by voting) are determined by expected costs and returns, just as they are in the private marketplace. The costs of comprehensive information are higher in the political arena because information must be sought on many issues of little or no direct concern to the individual, and accordingly he will know little about most matters before the legislature. The expressions of preferences in voting will be less precise than the expressions of preferences in the

[9] See [2].

marketplace because many uninformed people will be voting and affecting the decision.[10]

The channels of political decision-making can thus be described as gross or filtered or noisy. If everyone has a negligible preference for policy A over B, the preference will not be discovered or acted upon. If voter group X wants a policy that injures non-X by a small amount, it will not pay non-X to discover this and act against the policy. The system is calculated to implement all strongly felt preferences of majorities and many strongly felt preferences of minorities but to disregard the lesser preferences of majorities and minorities. The filtering or grossness will be reduced by any reduction in the cost to the citizen of acquiring information and expressing desires and by any increase in the probability that his vote will influence policy.

The industry which seeks political power must go to the appropriate seller, the political party. The political party has costs of operation, costs of maintaining an organization and competing in elections. These costs of the political process are viewed excessively narrowly in the literature on the financing of elections: elections are to the political process what merchandizing is to the process of producing a commodity, only an essential final step. The party maintains its organization and electoral appeal by the performance of costly services to the voter at all times, not just before elections. Part of the costs of services and organization are borne by putting a part of the party's workers on the public payroll. An opposition party, however, is usually essential insurance for the voters to discipline the party in power, and the opposition party's costs are not fully met by public funds.

The industry which seeks regulation must be prepared to pay with the two things a party needs: votes and resources. The resources may be provided by campaign contributions, contributed services (the businessman heads a fund-raising committee), and more indirect methods such as the employment of party workers. The votes in support of the measure are rallied, and the votes in opposition are dispersed, by expensive programs to educate (or uneducate) members of the industry and of other concerned industries.

These costs of legislation probably increase with the size of the industry seeking the legislation. Larger industries seek programs which cost the society more and arouse more opposition from substantially affected groups. The tasks of persuasion, both within and without the industry, also increase with its size. The fixed size of the political "market," however, probably makes the cost of obtaining legislation increase less rapidly than industry size. The smallest industries are therefore effectively precluded from the political process unless they have some special advantage such as geographical concentration in a sparsely settled political subdivision.

If a political party has in effect a monopoly control over the governmental machine, one might expect that it could collect most of the benefits of regulation for itself. Political parties, however, are

[10] There is an organizational problem in any decision in which more than one vote is cast. If because of economies of scale it requires a thousand customers to buy a product before it can be produced, this thousand votes has to be assembled by some entrepreneur. Unlike the political scene, however, there is no need to obtain the consent of the remainder of the community, because they will bear no part of the cost.

perhaps an ideal illustration of Demsetz' theory of natural monopoly [4]. If one party becomes extortionate (or badly mistaken in its reading of effective desires), it is possible to elect another party which will provide the governmental services at a price more closely proportioned to costs of the party. If entry into politics is effectively controlled, we should expect one-party dominance to lead that party to solicit requests for protective legislation but to exact a higher price for the legislation.

The internal structure of the political party, and the manner in which the perquisites of office are distributed among its members, offer fascinating areas for study in this context. The elective officials are at the pinnacle of the political system—there is no substitute for the ability to hold the public offices. I conjecture that much of the compensation to the legislative leaders takes the form of extra-political payments. Why are so many politicians lawyers?—because everyone employs lawyers, so the congressman's firm is a suitable avenue of compensation, whereas a physician would have to be given bribes rather than patronage. Most enterprises patronize insurance companies and banks, so we may expect that legislators commonly have financial affiliations with such enterprises.

The financing of industry-wide activities such as the pursuit of legislation raises the usual problem of the free rider.[11] We do not possess a satisfactory theory of group behavior—indeed this theory is the theory of oligopoly with one addition: in the very large number industry (e.g., agriculture) the political party itself will undertake the entrepreneurial role in providing favorable legislation. We can go no further than the infirmities of oligopoly theory allow, which is to say, we can make only plausible conjectures such as that the more concentrated the industry, the more resources it can invest in the campaign for legislation.

☐ **Occupational licensing.** The licensing of occupations is a possible use of the political process to improve the economic circumstances of a group. The license is an effective barrier to entry because occupational practice without the license is a criminal offense. Since much occupational licensing is performed at the state level, the area provides an opportunity to search for the characteristics of an occupation which give it political power.

Although there are serious data limitations, we may investigate several characteristics of an occupation which should influence its ability to secure political power:

(1) *The size of the occupation.* Quite simply, the larger the occupation, the more votes it has. (Under some circumstances, therefore, one would wish to exclude non-citizens from the measure of size.)

(2) *The per capita income of the occupation.* The income of the occupation is the product of its number and average income, so this variable and the preceding will reflect the total income of the occupation. The income of the occupation is presumably an index of the probable rewards of successful political action: in the absence of specific knowledge of supply and demand functions, we expect

[11] The theory that the lobbying organization avoids the "free-rider" problem by selling useful services was proposed by Thomas G. Moore [8] and elaborated by Mancur Olson [9]. The theory has not been tested empirically.

licensing to increase each occupation's equilibrium income by roughly the same proportion. In a more sophisticated version, one would predict that the less the elasticity of demand for the occupation's services, the more profitable licensing would be. One could also view the income of the occupation as a source of funds for political action, but if we view political action as an investment this is relevant only with capital-market imperfections.[12]

The average income of occupational members is an appropriate variable in comparisons among occupations, but it is inappropriate to comparisons of one occupation in various states because real income will be approximately equal (in the absence of regulation) in each state.

(3) *The concentration of the occupation in large cities.* When the occupation organizes a campaign to obtain favorable legislation, it incurs expenses in the solicitation of support, and these are higher for a diffused occupation than a concentrated one. The solicitation of support is complicated by the free-rider problem in that individual members cannot be excluded from the benefits of legislation even if they have not shared the costs of receiving it. If most of the occupation is concentrated in a few large centers, these problems (we suspect) are much reduced in intensity: regulation may even begin at the local governmental level. We shall use an orthodox geographical concentration measure: the share of the occupation of the state in cities over 100,000 (or 50,000 in 1900 and earlier).

(4) *The presence of a cohesive opposition to licensing.* If an occupation deals with the public at large, the costs which licensing imposes upon any one customer or industry will be small and it will not be economic for that customer or industry to combat the drive for licensure. If the injured group finds it feasible and profitable to act jointly, however, it will oppose the effort to get licensure, and (by increasing its cost) weaken, delay, or prevent the legislation. The same attributes—numbers of voters, wealth, and ease of organization—which favor an occupation in the political arena, of course, favor also any adversary group. Thus, a small occupation employed by only one industry which has few employers will have difficulty in getting licensure; whereas a large occupation serving everyone will encounter no organized opposition.

An introductory statistical analysis of the licensing of select occupations by states is summarized in Table 3. In each occupation the dependent variable for each state is the year of first regulation of entry into the occupation. The two independent variables are

(1) the ratio of the occupation to the total labor force of the state in the census year nearest to the median year of regulation,

(2) the fraction of the occupation found in cities over 100,000 (over 50,000 in 1890 and 1900) in that same year.

---

[12] Let n = the number of members of the profession and y = average income. We expect political capacity to be in proportion to (ny) so far as benefits go, but to reflect also the direct value of votes, so the capacity becomes proportional to $(n^a y)$ with $a > 1$.

TABLE 3

INITIAL YEAR OF REGULATION AS A FUNCTION OF RELATIVE SIZE OF OCCUPATION AND DEGREE OF URBANIZATION

OCCUPATION	NUMBER OF STATES LICENSING	MEDIAN CENSUS YEAR OF LICENSING	REGRESSION COEFFICIENTS (AND T-VALUES)		R^2
			SIZE OF OCCUPATION (RELATIVE TO LABOR FORCE)	URBANIZATION (SHARE OF OCCUPATION IN CITIES OVER 100,000*)	
BEAUTICIANS	48	1930	−4.03 (2.50)	5.90 (1.24)	0.125
ARCHITECTS	47	1930	−24.06 (2.15)	−6.29 (0.84)	0.184
BARBERS	46	1930	−1.31 (0.51)	−26.10 (2.37)	0.146
LAWYERS	29	1890	−0.26 (0.08)	−65.78 (1.70)	0.102
PHYSICIANS	43	1890	0.64 (0.65)	−23.80 (2.69)	0.165
EMBALMERS	37	1910	3.32 (0.36)	−4.24 (0.44)	0.007
REGISTERED NURSES	48	1910	−2.08 (2.28)	−3.36 (1.06)	0.176
DENTISTS	48	1900	2.51 (0.44)	−22.94 (2.19)	0.103
VETERINARIANS	40	1910	−10.69 (1.94)	−37.16 (4.20)	0.329
CHIROPRACTORS	48	1930	−17.70 (1.54)	11.69 (1.25)	0.079
PHARMACISTS	48	1900	−4.19 (1.50)	−6.84 (0.80)	0.082

SOURCES: THE COUNCIL OF STATE GOVERNMENTS, "OCCUPATIONAL LICENSING LEGISLATION IN THE STATES", 1952 [3], AND U.S. CENSUS OF POPULATION [15], VARIOUS YEARS.

* 50,000 IN 1890 AND 1900.

We expect these variables to be negatively associated with year of licensure, and each of the nine statistically significant regression coefficients is of the expected sign.

The results are not robust, however: the multiple correlation coefficients are small, and over half of the regression coefficients are not significant (and in these cases often of inappropriate sign). Urbanization is more strongly associated than size of occupation with licensure.[13] The crudity of the data may be a large source of these disappointments: we measure, for example, the characteristics of the barbers in each state in 1930, but 14 states were licensing barbers by 1910. If the states which licensed barbering before 1910 had relatively more barbers, or more highly urbanized barbers, the predictions

[13] We may pool the occupations and assign dummy variables for each occupation; the regression coefficients then are:

size of occupation relative to labor force: -0.450 ($t = 0.59$)
urbanization : -12.133 ($t = 4.00$).

Thus urbanization is highly significant, while size of occupation is not significant.

would be improved. The absence of data for years between censuses and before 1890 led us to make only the cruder analysis.[14]

In general, the larger occupations were licensed in earlier years.[15] Veterinarians are the only occupation in this sample who have a well-defined set of customers, namely livestock farmers, and licensing was later in those states with large numbers of livestock relative to rural population. The within-occupation analyses offer some support for the economic theory of the supply of legislation.

A comparison of different occupations allows us to examine several other variables. The first is income, already discussed above. The second is the size of the market. Just as it is impossible to organize an effective labor union in only one part of an integrated market, so it is impossible to regulate only one part of the market. Consider an occupation—junior business executives will do—which has a national market with high mobility of labor and significant mobility of employers. If the executives of one state were to organize, their scope for effective influence would be very small. If salaries were raised above the competitive level, employers would often recruit elsewhere so the demand elasticity would be very high.[16] The third variable is stability of occupational membership: the longer the members are in the occupation, the greater their financial gain from control of entry. Our regrettably crude measure of this variable is based upon the number of members aged 35–44 in 1950 and aged 45–54 in 1960: the closer these numbers are, the more stable the membership of the occupation. The data for the various occupations are given in Table 4.

The comparison of licensed and unlicensed occupations is consistently in keeping with our expectations:

(1) the licensed occupations have higher incomes (also before licensing, one may assume),

(2) the membership of the licensed occupations is more stable (but the difference is negligible in our crude measure),

(3) the licensed occupations are less often employed by business enterprises (who have incentives to oppose licensing),

(4) all occupations in national markets (college teachers, engineers, scientists, accountants) are unlicensed or only partially licensed.

---

[14] A more precise analysis might take the form of a regression analysis such as:

$$\text{Year of licensure} = \text{constant} + b_1 \text{ (year of critical size of occupation)} + b_2 \text{ (year of critical urbanization of occupation)},$$

where the critical size and urbanization were defined as the mean size and mean urbanization in the year of licensure.

[15] Lawyers, physicians, and pharmacists were all relatively large occupations by 1900, and nurses also by 1910. The only large occupation to be licensed later was barbers; the only small occupation to be licensed early was embalmers.

[16] The regulation of business in a partial market will also generally produce very high supply elasticities within a market: if the price of the product (or service) is raised, the pressure of excluded supply is very difficult to resist. Some occupations are forced to reciprocity in licensing, and the geographical dispersion of earnings in licensed occupations, one would predict, is not appreciably different than in unlicensed occupations with equal employer mobility. Many puzzles are posed by the interesting analysis of Arlene S. Holen in [6], pp. 492-98.

TABLE 4

CHARACTERISTICS OF LICENSED AND UNLICENSED PROFESSIONAL OCCUPATIONS, 1960

OCCUPATION	MEDIAN AGE (YEARS)	MEDIAN EDUCATION (YEARS)	MEDIAN EARNINGS (50-52 WKS.)	INSTABILITY OF MEMBERSHIP*	PERCENT NOT SELF-EMPLOYED	PERCENT IN CITIES OVER 50,000	PERCENT OF LABOR FORCE
LICENSED:							
ARCHITECTS	41.7	16.8	$ 9,090	0.012	57.8%	44.1%	0.045%
CHIROPRACTORS	46.5	16.4	6,360	0.053	5.8	30.8	0.020
DENTISTS	45.9	17.3	12,200	0.016	9.4	34.5	0.128
EMBALMERS	43.5	13.4	5,990	0.130	52.8	30.2	0.055
LAWYERS	45.3	17.4	10,800	0.041	35.8	43.1	0.308
PROF. NURSES	39.1	13.2	3,850	0.291	91.0	40.6	0.868
OPTOMETRISTS	41.6	17.0	8,480	0.249	17.5	34.5	0.024
PHARMACISTS	44.9	16.2	7,230	0.119	62.3	40.0	0.136
PHYSICIANS	42.8	17.5	14,200	0.015	35.0	44.7	0.339
VETERINARIANS	39.2	17.4	9,210	0.169	29.5	14.4	0.023
AVERAGE	43.0	16.3	8,741	0.109	39.7	35.7	0.195
PARTIALLY LICENSED:							
ACCOUNTANTS	40.4	14.9	6,450	0.052	88.1	43.5	0.698
ENGINEERS	38.3	16.2	8,490	0.023	96.8	31.6	1.279
ELEM. SCHOOL TEACHERS	43.1	16.5	4,710	(a)	99.1	18.8	1.482
AVERAGE	40.6	15.9	6,550	0.117(b)	94.7	34.6	1.153
UNLICENSED:							
ARTISTS	38.0	14.2	5,920	0.103	77.3	45.7	0.154
CLERGYMEN	43.3	17.0	4,120	0.039	89.0	27.2	0.295
COLLEGE TEACHERS	40.3	17.4	7,500	0.085	99.2	36.0	0.261
DRAFTSMEN	31.2	12.9	5,990	0.098	98.6	40.8	0.322
REPORTERS & EDITORS	39.4	15.5	6,120	0.138	93.9	43.3	0.151
MUSICIANS	40.2	14.8	3,240	0.081	65.5	37.7	0.289
NATURAL SCIENTISTS	35.9	16.8	7,490	0.264	96.3	32.7	0.221
AVERAGE	38.3	15.5	5,768	0.115	88.5	37.6	0.242

(*) 1-R, WHERE R = RATIO: 1960 AGE 45-54 TO 1950 AGE 35-44.

(a) NOT AVAILABLE SEPARATELY; TEACHERS N.E.C. (INCL. SECONDARY SCHOOL AND OTHER) = 0.276

(b) INCLUDES FIGURE FOR TEACHERS N.E.C. IN NOTE (a)

SOURCE: U.S. CENSUS OF POPULATION, [15], 1960.

The size and urbanization of the three groups, however, are unrelated to licensing. The inter-occupational comparison therefore provides a modicum of additional support for our theory of regulation.

3. Conclusion

■ The idealistic view of public regulation is deeply imbedded in professional economic thought. So many economists, for example, have denounced the ICC for its pro-railroad policies that this has become a cliché of the literature. This criticism seems to me exactly as appropriate as a criticism of the Great Atlantic and Pacific Tea Company for selling groceries, or as a criticism of a politician for currying popular support. The fundamental vice of such criticism is that it misdirects attention: it suggests that the way to get an ICC which is not subservient to the carriers is to preach to the commissioners or to the people who appoint the commissioners. The only way to get a different commission would be to change the political support for the Commission, and reward commissioners on a basis unrelated to their services to the carriers.

Until the basic logic of political life is developed, reformers will be ill-equipped to use the state for their reforms, and victims of the pervasive use of the state's support of special groups will be helpless to protect themselves. Economists should quickly establish the license to practice on the rational theory of political behavior.

Appendix

TABLE 5

COMMON, CONTRACT AND PASSENGER MOTOR CARRIERS, 1935–1969[1]

YEAR ENDING	CUMULATIVE APPLICATIONS			OPERATING CARRIERS	
	GRAND-FATHER	NEW	TOTAL	APPROVED APPLICATIONS[3]	NUMBER IN OPERATION[2]
OCT. 1936	82,827	1,696	84,523	–	–
1937	83,107	3,921	87.028	1;114	–
1938	85,646	6,694	92,340	20,398	–
1939	86,298	9,636	95,934	23,494	–
1940	87,367	12,965	100,332	25,575	–
1941	88,064	16,325	104,389	26,296	–
1942	88,702	18,977	107,679	26,683	–
1943	89,157	20,007	109,164	27,531	–
1944	89,511	21,324	110,835	27,177	21,044
1945	89,518	22,829	112,347		20,788
1946	89,529	26,392	115,921		20,632
1947	89,552	29,604	119,156		20,665
1948	89,563	32,678	122,241		20,373
1949	89,567	35,635	125,202		18,459
1950	89,573	38,666	128,239		19,200
1951	89,574	41,889	131,463		18,843
1952	(89,574)[4]	44,297	133,870		18,408
1953	"	46,619	136,192		17,869
1954	"	49,146	138,719		17,080
1955	"	51,720	141,293		16,836
JUNE 1956	"	53,640	143,213		16,486
1957	"	56,804	146,377		16,316
1958	"	60,278	149,851		16,065
1959	"	64,171	153,744		15,923
1960	"	69,205	158,778		15,936
1961	"	72,877	162,450		15,967
1962	"	76,986	166,559		15,884
1963	"	81,443	171,016		15,739
1964	"	86,711	176,284		15,732
1965	"	93,064	182,637		15,755
1966	"	101,745	191,318		15,933
1967	"	106,647	196,220		16,003
1968	"	(6)	(6)		16,230[5]
1969	"	(6)	(6)		16,318[5]

SOURCE: U.S. INTERSTATE COMMERCE COMMISSION ANNUAL REPORTS [17].

1 EXCLUDING BROKERS AND WITHIN-STATE CARRIERS.

2 PROPERTY CARRIERS WERE THE FOLLOWING PERCENTAGES OF ALL OPERATING CARRIERS: 1944–93.4%; 1950–92.4%; 1960–93.0%; 1966–93.4%.

3 ESTIMATED.

4 NOT AVAILABLE; ASSUMED TO BE APPROXIMATELY CONSTANT.

5 1968 AND 1969 FIGURES ARE FOR NUMBER OF CARRIERS REQUIRED TO FILE ANNUAL REPORTS.

6 NOT AVAILABLE COMPARABLE TO PREVIOUS YEARS; APPLICATIONS FOR PERMANENT AUTHORITY DISPOSED OF (I.E., FROM NEW AND PENDING FILES) 1967-69 ARE AS FOLLOWS: 1967–7,049; 1968–5,724; 1969–5,186.

TABLE 6

WEIGHT LIMITS ON TRUCKS, 1932-33*, BY STATES (BASIC DATA FOR TABLE 2).

STATE	MAXIMUM WEIGHT (IN LBS.)		STATE	MAXIMUM WEIGHT (IN LBS.)	
	4-WHEEL[1]	6-WHEEL[2]		4-WHEEL[1]	6-WHEEL[2]
ALABAMA	20,000	32,000	NEBRASKA	24,000	40,000
ARIZONA	22,000	34,000	NEVADA	25,000	38,000
ARKANSAS	22,200	37,000	NEW HAMPSHIRE	20,000	20,000
CALIFORNIA	22,000	34,000	NEW JERSEY	30,000	30,000
COLORADO	30,000	40,000	NEW MEXICO	27,000	45,000
CONNECTICUT	32,000	40,000	NEW YORK	33,600	44,000
DELAWARE	26,000	38,000	NO. CAROLINA	20,000	20,000
FLORIDA	20,000	20,000	NO. DAKOTA	24,000	48,000
GEORGIA	22,000	39,600	OHIO	24,000	24,000
IDAHO	24,000	40,000	OKLAHOMA	20,000	20,000
ILLINOIS	24,000	40,000	OREGON	25,500	42,500
INDIANA	24,000	40,000	PENNSYLVANIA	26,000	36,000
IOWA	24,000	40,000	RHODE ISLAND	28,000	40,000
KANSAS	24,000	34,000	SO. CAROLINA	20,000	25,000
KENTUCKY	18,000	18,000	SO. DAKOTA	20,000	20,000
LOUISIANA	13,400	N. A.	TENNESSEE	20,000	20,000
MAINE	18,000	27,000	TEXAS	13,500	N. A.
MARYLAND	25,000	40,000	UTAH	26,000	34,000
MASSACHUSETTS	30,000	30,000	VERMONT	20,000	20,000
MICHIGAN	27,000	45,000	VIRGINIA	24,000	35,000
MINNESOTA	27,000	42,000	WASHINGTON	24,000	34,000
MISSISSIPPI	18,000	22,000	WEST VA.	24,000	40,000
MISSOURI	24,000	24,000	WISCONSIN	24,000	36,000
MONTANA	24,000	34,000	WYOMING	27,000	30,000

RED BOOK [1] FIGURES ARE REPORTED (P. 89) AS "BASED ON THE STATE'S INTERPRETATIONS OF THEIR LAWS [1933] AND ON PHYSICAL LIMITATIONS OF VEHICLE DESIGN AND TIRE CAPACITY." *PUBLIC ROADS* [13] FIGURES ARE REPORTED (P. 167) AS "AN ABSTRACT OF STATE LAWS, INCLUDING LEGISLATION PASSED IN 1932."

1. *4-WHEEL*: THE SMALLEST OF THE FOLLOWING 3 FIGURES WAS USED:

   (A) MAXIMUM GROSS WEIGHT (AS GIVEN IN *RED BOOK*, P. 90-91).

   (B) MAXIMUM AXLE WEIGHT (AS GIVEN IN *RED BOOK*, P. 90-91), MULTIPLIED BY 1.5 (SEE *RED BOOK*, P. 89).

   (C) MAXIMUM GROSS WEIGHT (AS GIVEN IN *RED BOOK*, P. 93).

EXCEPTIONS: TEXAS AND LOUISIANA—SEE *RED BOOK*, P. 91.

2. *6-WHEEL*: MAXIMUM GROSS WEIGHT AS GIVEN IN *PUBLIC ROADS*, P. 167. THESE FIGURES AGREE IN MOST CASES WITH THOSE SHOWN IN *RED BOOK*, P. 93, AND WITH *PUBLIC ROADS* MAXIMUM AXLE WEIGHTS MULTIPLIED BY 2.5 (SEE *RED BOOK*, P. 93). TEXAS AND LOUISIANA ARE EXCLUDED AS DATA ARE NOT AVAILABLE TO CONVERT FROM PAYLOAD TO GROSS WEIGHT LIMITS.

TABLE 7

INDEPENDENT VARIABLES
(BASIC DATA FOR TABLE 2 – CONT'D)

STATE	TRUCKS ON FARMS PER 1,000 AGRICULTURAL LABOR FORCE	AVERAGE LENGTH OF RAILROAD HAUL OF FREIGHT (MILES)	PERCENT OF STATE HIGHWAYS WITH HIGH-TYPE SURFACE
ALABAMA	26.05	89.4	1.57
ARIZONA	79.74	212.2	2.60
ARKANSAS	28.62	238.1	1.72
CALIFORNIA	123.40	261.6	13.10
COLORADO	159.50	241.7	0.58
CONNECTICUT	173.80	131.6	7.98
DELAWARE	173.20	202.7	21.40
FLORIDA	91.41	184.1	8.22
GEORGIA	32.07	165.7	1.60
IDAHO	95.89	241.6	0.73
ILLINOIS	114.70	2079	9.85
INDIANA	120.20	2028	6.90
IOWA	98.73	2333	3.39
KANSAS	146.70	2815	0.94
KENTUCKY	20.05	2275	1.81
LOUISIANA	31.27	20.0	1.94
MAINE	209.30	12.4	1.87
MARYLAND	134.20	18.1	12.90
MASSACHUSETTS	172.20	14.7	17.70
MICHIGAN	148.40	16.0	6.68
MINNESOTA	120.40	25.6	1.44
MISSISSIPPI	29.62	14.9	1.14
MISSOURI	54.28	29.7	2.91
MONTANA	183.80	25.5	0.09
NEBRASKA	132.10	26.9	0.41
NEVADA	139.40	273.[illegible]	0.39
NEW HAMPSHIRE	205.40	129.0	3.42
NEW JERSEY	230.20	137.6	23.30
NEW MEXICO	90.46	279.0	0.18
NEW YORK	220.50	163.3	21.50
NO. CAROLINA	37.12	171.5	8.61
NO. DAKOTA	126.40	255.1	0.01
OHIO	125.80	194.2	11.20
OKLAHOMA	78.18	223.3	1.42
OREGON	118.90	246.2	3.35
PENNSYLVANIA	187.60	166.5	9.78
RHODE ISLAND	193.30	131.0	20.40
SO. CAROLINA	20.21	169.8	2.82
SO. DAKOTA	113.40	216.6	0.04
TENNESSEE	23.98	191.9	3.97
UTAH	101.70	235.7	1.69
VERMONT	132.20	109.7	2.26
VIRGINIA	71.88	229.8	2.86
WASHINGTON	180.90	254.4	4.21
WEST VIRGINIA	62.88	218.7	8.13
WISCONSIN	178.60	195.7	4.57
WYOMING	133.40	286.7	0.08

(1) AVERAGE LENGTH OF RR HAUL OF (REVENUE) FREIGHT = AVERAGE DISTANCE IN MILES EACH TON IS CARRIED = RATIO OF NUMBER OF TON-MILES TO NUMBER OF TONS CARRIED. FOR EACH STATE, AVERAGE LENGTH OF HAUL WAS OBTAINED BY WEIGHTING AVERAGE LENGTH OF HAUL OF EACH COMPANY BY THE NUMBER OF MILES OF LINE OPERATED BY THAT COMPANY IN THE STATE (ALL FOR CLASS I RR'S).

(2) PERCENTAGE OF STATE ROADS WITH HIGH-QUALITY SURFACE: WHERE HIGH-QUALITY (HIGH-TYPE) SURFACE CONSISTS OF BITUMINOUS MACADAM, BITUMINOUS CONCRETE, SHEET ASPHALT, PORTLAND CEMENT CONCRETE, AND BLOCK PAVEMENTS. ALL STATE RURAL ROADS, BOTH LOCAL AND STATE HIGHWAYS SYSTEMS, ARE INCLUDED.

References

1. Association of American Railroads, Bureau of Railway Economics. *Railway Mileage by States.* Washington, D. C.: December 31, 1930.
2. Becker, G. S. "Competition and Democracy." *Journal of Law and Economics*, October 1958.
3. The Council of State Governments. "Occupational Licensing Legislation in the States." 1952.
4. Demsetz, H., "Why Regulate Utilities?" *Journal of Law and Economics*, April 1968.
5. Gerwig, R. W. "Natural Gas Production: A Study of Costs of Regulation." *Journal of Law and Economics*, October 1962, pp. 69-92.
6. Holen, A. S. "Effects of Professional Licensing Arrangements on Interstate Labor Mobility and Resource Allocation." *Journal of Political Economy*, Vol. 73 (1915), pp. 492-98.
7. Keyes, L. S. *Federal Control of Entry into Air Transportation.* Cambridge, Mass.: Harvard University Press, 1951.
8. Moore, T. G. "The Purpose of Licensing." *Journal of Law and Economics*, October 1961.
9. Olson, M. *The Logic of Collective Action.* Cambridge, Mass.: Harvard University Press, 1965.
10. Peltzman, S. "Entry in Commercial Banking." *Journal of Law and Economics*, October 1965.
11. *The Motor Truck Red Book and Directory*, 1934 Edition, pp. 85–102.
12. U. S. Congress, Select Committee on Small Business. *Hearings*, 88th Congress, 2nd Session, August 10 and 11, 1964.
13. U. S. Department of Agriculture, Bureau of Public Roads. *Public Roads.* Washington, D. C.: U. S. Government Printing Office, December 1932.
14. U. S. Department of Commerce, Bureau of the Census. *United States Census of Agriculture, 1930*, Vol. 4. Washington, D. C.: U. S. Government Printing Office, 1930.
15. ———. *United States Census of Population.* Washington, D. C.: U. S. Government Printing Office, appropriate years.
16. ———, Bureau of Foreign and Domestic Commerce. *Statistical Abstract of the U. S., 1932.* Washington, D. C.: U. S. Government Printing Office, 1932.
17. U. S. Interstate Commerce Commission. *Annual Report.* Washington, D. C.: U. S. Government Printing Office, appropriate years.
18. ———. *Statistics of Railways in the United States, 1930.* Washington, D. C.: U. S. Government Printing Office, 1930.

The Journal of

LAW & ECONOMICS

VOLUME V OCTOBER 1962

WHAT CAN REGULATORS REGULATE? THE CASE OF ELECTRICITY

GEORGE J. STIGLER and CLAIRE FRIEDLAND
University of Chicago

THE literature of public regulation is so vast that it must touch on everything, but it touches seldom and lightly on the most basic question one can ask about regulation: Does it make a difference in the behavior of an industry?

This impertinent question will strike anyone connected with a regulated industry as palpably trivial. Are not important prices regulated? Are not the routes of a trucker and an airline prescribed? Is not entry into public utility industries limited? Is not an endless procession of administrative proceedings aging entrepreneurs and enriching lawyers?

But the innumerable regulatory actions are conclusive proof, not of effective regulation, but of the desire to regulate. And if wishes were horses, one would buy stock in a harness factory.

The question of the influence of regulation can never be answered by an enumeration of regulatory policies. A thousand statutes now forbid us to do things that we would not dream of doing even if the statutes were repealed: we would not slay our neighbor, or starve our children, or burn our house for the insurance, or erect an abattoir in the back yard. Whether the statutes really have an appreciable effect on actual behavior can only be determined by examining the behavior of people not subject to the statutes.

An order to a trucker not to haul goods between cities A and B is even more difficult to assess. He may not wish to have this route, in analogy to the laws governing our personal behavior. But let him wish with all his heart to have it, and be denied; there still will be no economic effect of the regulation if others are allowed, in adequate number, to have the desired route.

The point at issue may be restated in the language of economics. An industry's output and price are normally governed primarily by the basic economic and technological determinants of supply and demand: by whether the demand curve is D_1 or D_2, and the supply curve S_1 or S_2 (see Fig. 1). Regulation will affect price and output only if it shifts the curves or the point on a curve where the industry operates. Does regulation introduce shifts in curves

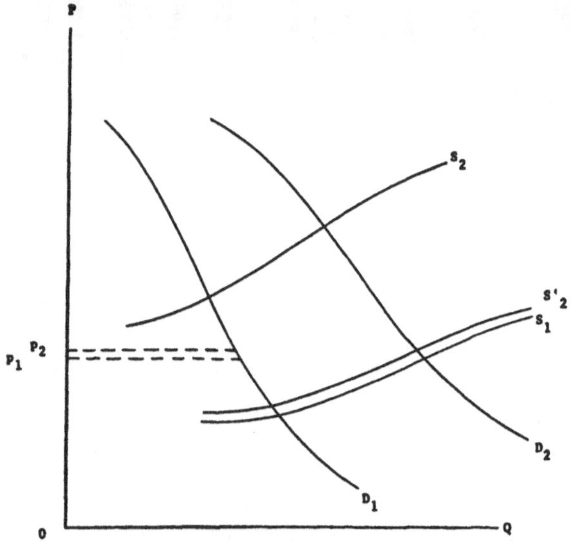

FIG. 1

of the magnitude of S_1 to S_2 or S_1 to S'_2? Then its effect will be negligible. Does regulation shift the effective operating point from p_1 to p_2? Then its effect will again be negligible.

The test of the economic effect of regulation is essentially independent of the content of the formal regulations. No degree of care in analyzing the regulations, or even their administration, will tell us whether they rubber-stamp or slightly heckle the state of affairs or substantially alter it.

What does one mean in saying that regulation has had large or small effects? He means that of the observed economic behavior in a cetrain industrial sector, a large or small part can be explained only by recourse to regulation. Consider these examples:

1. Is the decline of railroading due in any important part to ICC regulations? If in other economies with rising incomes and extensive adoption of automobiles

and trucks the railroad traffic shows a pattern similar to ours, then regulation has not been the primary influence.

2. Do utility commissions reduce the differential in prices of utility services to large and small buyers? If in a group of unregulated markets we observe a mean ratio of rates of large to small buyers of m_{nr}, and in regulated markets a ratio of m_r, do m_{nr} and m_r differ significantly? If of the total variance among markets in the ratio of rates of large to small buyers only 2 per cent can be explained by regulation, the regulations have negligible impact.
3. Do regulatory bodies succeed in preventing monopoly profits? We take it that they will usually prevent such profits from appearing explicitly in accounting statements. Whether they go beyond this may be judged, for example, by the fortunes of investors in stocks of regulated companies over periods extending from pre-regulation on, compared with those of investors in similar but unregulated enterprises.

These summary remarks will deceive no informed person as to the analytical and empirical complexity of the task of isolating the effects of regulation. They are intended only to suggest why one does not read the regulations to reach the answer.

We propose now to make an investigation of one regulated industry to explore techniques and hopefully reach tentative results. This is the electric utility industry. Here we face three major problems: (1) What firms are regulated? (2) What effects of regulation shall we study, and how shall we measure them? (3) How do we explain our findings?

I. When Is a Firm Regulated?

Every enterprise producing and distributing electricity has been regulated since its founding by way of charter limitations and franchises; its use of public thoroughfares was enough to insure this. It would therefore be possible to say that there is no unregulated sector to provide a base for judging the effects of regulation. This statement would not be acceptable to the professional writers on public utilities: they hail the beginnings of effective regulation with the establishment of the public service commissions in New York and Wisconsin in 1907.[1]

Yet these specialists have assuredly not faced the problem of measuring the effects of regulation, so their judgments are suspect. Indeed, if we accepted their judgments our problem would be solved, for they never question the importance of (effective!) regulation.

There is no substitute for an objective measure of regulation, and the one we choose is the creation of a special state commission endowed with the

[1] 2 L. S. Lyon and V. Abramson, Government and Economic Life 636 (1940); Twentieth Cent. Fund, Electric Power and Government Policy 65, 235 (1948).

power to regulate rates of electric utilities.[2] It may be complained that some of these commissions were long ineffective, or that municipal regulation was effective earlier in some states. Such assertions can only be tested by a study invoking another criterion of the existence of regulation: the year the commission issued its first rate order upheld by the courts, the year the commission first spent $100,000 or published 100 pages of orders, etc. But it is intrinsic to the problem that there be an independent criterion of regulation, and that findings on effectiveness be conditional on acceptance of that criterion. There is a strict analogy with the problem of estimating the influence of monopoly, where the result is conditioned by the criterion of monopoly (concentration ratio, number of firms, etc.).

The classification of states by the existence of regulatory commissions with jurisdiction over electric utilities is given in the Appendix in Table A1. The beginning of regulation by this criterion varied as shown in the accompanying tabulation. Two-thirds of the states had commissions by 1915, three-quarters by 1922.

	States
Before 1910	6
1910–20	29
1920–30	1
1930–40	3
1940–50	2
1950–60	2

II. The Effects of Regulation on Rates and Returns

There are two basic purposes of the public regulation of prices: the curtailment of the exercise of monopoly power and the elimination of certain forms of price discrimination. There will no doubt be other effects on prices, including unintended effects such as the short term rigidity of price commonly associated with regulation, but we shall concentrate upon these basic purposes. Our analysis of effects will be limited to the period up to 1937, simply because by that time 39 states had regulating commissions. By that date every unregulated state had at least two adjoining states with regulatory commissions, and even a showing of no difference in rates thereafter would be ambiguous: it could be argued that the threat of regulation was always latent in the unregulated states. This position does not seem wholly convincing to us—in a sense the threat of regulation was operative as soon as the Interstate Commerce Commission was created—but the small number of unregulated states after 1937 offers statistical support for this terminus.

[2] In our statistical work we measure regulation from three years after the creation of the commission, on impressionistic evidence of the lag involved in organizing the commission, hence all statements regarding, for example, states regulating in 1917 should be interpreted to refer to states initiating regulation no later than 1914.

THE LEVEL OF RATES

We shall make little use of the direct comparison of the average level of rates in regulated and unregulated states, of which a sample summary is given in Table 1.[3] The ambiguity of simple differences may be illustrated by the data for 1917. In this year the average revenue per KWH was 1.88 cents in regulated states and 3.20 cents in unregulated states, which might suggest that regulation lowered rates by almost 40 per cent. But we can classify the rates of these states in several years (see Table 2). This classification makes clear the fact that rates were lower on average in the regulating states, not only *after* but also *before* regulation.

TABLE 1

AVERAGE REVENUE PER KWH, STATES WITH AND WITHOUT REGULATION, 1912–37*

Year	Regulated		Unregulated	
	States	Revenue (Cents)	States	Revenue (Cents)
1912	6	2.30	41	2.99
1917	31	1.88	16	3.20
1922	33	2.44	12	3.87
1927	35	2.85	10	4.21
1932	34	2.91	8	3.69
1937	34	2.32	6	3.04

* A state is considered regulated in a given year if commission regulation was established three years previously.

TABLE 2

	Number of States	Average Rate		
		1917	1912	1907
States instituting regulation before 1912	6	1.88	2.30	2.76
States instituting regulation from 1912 to 1917	25	1.88	2.30	2.93
States not regulating before 1917	16	3.20	4.07	4.34

[3] The complete average rates are reported in the Appendix in Table A2. These average revenues per kilowatt hour involve the following adjustments of census data: for 1907 to 1922 revenues include sales by private electric companies to ultimate consumers, domestic and industrial, plus net sales to out-of-state electric companies, municipal electric companies, and electric railroads, but exclude intercompany sales within states. KWH figures are for KWH's generated by private electric companies plus net purchases of KWH's from electric railroads or out-of-state electric companies. For 1927 to 1937 revenue and KWH data are for current sold to ultimate consumers, including gross sales to electric railroads but excluding all sales to other electric companies.

The basic fact is, of course, that regulation is associated with economic characteristics which also exert direct, independent influences on rates—the size and urbanization of the population, the extent of industrialization, etc. To isolate the effects of regulation we must take direct account of these economic factors. We do so by the following procedure.

The main determinants of the level of rates for an unregulated monopolist would be the size of the market and its density (which affect both production and distribution costs), the price of fuel, and the incomes of consumers. We approximate the market size and density by the population in cities with

TABLE 3

REGRESSION EQUATIONS OF AVERAGE REVENUE PER KWH AND OUTPUT ON URBAN POPULATION, COST OF FUEL, PER CAPITA INCOME, PROPORTION OF HP FROM HYDROELECTRIC, AND REGULATION, 47 STATES, 1922

Dependent Variable	Constant Term	Regression Coefficients and Their Standard Errors					R^2	
		Urban Population	Cost of Fuel	Per Capita Income*	Proportion of HP from Hydroelectric	Regulation	Including Regulation	Excluding Regulation
Average revenue per KWH.....	.0918	−.0592 (.0248)	.0604 (.1665)	.230 (.204)	−.498 (.083)	−.0109 (.0068)	.567	.540
Output......	−.166	.395 (.052)	−.577 (.349)	.718 (.428)	.491 (.174)	.0172 (.0143)	.694	.684

* Linear interpolations between averages for the following years: 1919–21—Source: Maurice Leven, *Income in the Various States* (1925); 1929–31—Source: U.S. Office of Business Economics, *Personal Income by States since 1929*, Supplement to the Survey of Current Business, 1956.

25,000 or more population; the fuel costs by an equivalent BTU cost and by the proportion of power derived from hydroelectric sources; and consumer incomes by per capita state income. We fit the equation,

$$\log p = a + b \log U + c \log p_F + dH + e \log Y + fR,$$

where

p = average revenue per KWH, in cents;
U = population in cities over 25,000 (in thousands);
p_F = price of fuel (in dollars per BTU equivalent ton of bituminous coal);
H = proportion of power from hydroelectric sources;
Y = per capita state income, in dollars;
R = dummy variable, 0 if an unregulated state, 1 if a regulated state.

The results of fitting this equation to 1922 data are presented in Table 3. The regression of millions of KW's of output, in logarithms, on these variables is also added.

The effects of regulation may be expressed in two ways: by the regression coefficient of the dummy variable representing regulation or by the difference in the coefficient of multiple determination including and excluding regulation. By either standard, regulation had no effect upon the level of rates in 1922.

For the other census years we use the abbreviated regression equations summarized in Table 4. No effect of regulation is observable through 1932. The 1937 equation does display a regulation effect, but it is localized in the

TABLE 4

REGRESSION EQUATION OF AVERAGE REVENUE PER KWH ON URBAN POPULATION, PER CAPITA INCOME, PROPORTION OF HYDROELECTRIC POWER AND REGULATION, 1912–1937

Year	Number of States	Constant Term	Regression Coefficients and Their Standard Errors				R^2	
			Urban Population	Per Capita Income*	Proportion Hydro-electric†	Regulation	Including Regulation	Excluding Regulation
			I. All Sales					
1912.....	47	.663	−.0291 (.0134)	....	−.552 (.062)	.0028 (.0590)	.654	.654
1922.....	47	.730	−.0533 (.0240)	....	−.508 (.081)	−.0708 (.0596)	.546	.531
1932.....	42	.380	−.0478 (.0144)	.141 (.090)	−.336 (.058)	−.0630 (.0409)	.580	.554
1937.....	39	.323	−.0486 (.0157)	.123 (.121)	−.257 (.059)	−.102 (.043)	.496	.413
			II. Sales to Domestic Customers					
1932.....	42	1.036	−.0044 (.0125)	−.0804 (.0781)	−.132 (.050)	−.0371 (.0358)	.286	.266
1937.....	39	.726	−.0223 (.0130)	.0187 (.1002)	−.146 (.409)	−.0337 (.0358)	.271	.251
			III. Sales to Commercial and Industrial Customers					
1932.....	42	.622	−.0496 (.0149)	....	−.349 (.059)	−.0306 (.0391)	.546	.539
1937.....	39	.572	−.0520 (.0159)	....	−.262 (.061)	−.0925 (.0417)	.493	.422

* Per capita income variable introduced only in years in which annual data are available.

† In 1912 and 1922, ratio of HP capacity of water wheels and turbines to HP capacity of all prime movers; in 1932 and 1937, ratio of KW capacity of hydroelectric to KW capacity of all generators.

sales to commercial and industrial consumers—the class of consumers that regulation was *not* designed to protect. We believe even this modest 1937 effect would be eliminated by a fuller statistical analysis.[4]

We conclude that no effect of regulation can be found in the average level of rates.

THE RATE STRUCTURE

We have examined two aspects of the rate structure for possible influences of regulation. The first is the ratio of monthly bills of domestic consumers for

TABLE 5

DIFFERENTIALS BY SIZE OF MONTHLY CONSUMPTION 1924 AND 1936

Year	Class of States	Number of States	Average Ratio of Larger to Smaller Monthly Bills
	A. 100 and 25 KWH per Month		
1924	Regulated	29	3.02
	Unregulated	10	3.25
1936	Regulated	30	2.79
	Unregulated	9	2.86
	B. 250 and 100 KWH per Month		
1924	Regulated	29	1.90
	Unregulated	10	2.15
1936	Regulated	30	1.83
	Unregulated	9	1.82

Source: U.S. Federal Power Commission, "Trends in Residential Rates from 1924 to 1936" (Washington, D.C.: 1937), Table 11. The observations are unweighted average rates for cities of over 50,000 population in each state.

larger amounts of electricity relative to smaller amounts. Here our expectation was that the regulatory bodies would recognize the greater potential political popularity of low rates for the numerous consumers who buy small quantities. The evidence is essentially negative (Table 5): in only one of four comparisons was the ratio of monthly bills significantly different in regulated

[4] The regression coefficient of regulation becomes non-significant if we shift from measuring urban population by the logarithm of population in cities over 25,000. A set of alternative regressions, reported in Tables A4 and A5, are also relevant; these equations employ total output and output per customer as independent variables, and thus raise identification questions which led to their replacement by those in the text, but seem worth reporting.

states from unregulated states.[5] The quantity rate structure for domestic consumers seems independent of the existence of regulation.

A second aspect of the rate structure where regulation might be expected to be influential is in the comparative charges to domestic and industrial buyers. The regulatory bodies would reduce domestic rates relative to industrial rates if they sought to reduce discrimination; the industrial users presumably have better alternative power sources and therefore more elastic demands. Or, again as a political matter, the numerous domestic users might be favored relative to the industrial users. To test this expectation, the average ratio of charges per KWH to domestic users to charges to industrial users was calculated for two years (see Table 6). The ratios are therefore directly opposite to those which were expected.[6] But a scatter diagram analysis reveals that the ratio of domestic to industrial rates depends primarily upon the average number of KWH sold to domestic customers divided by the

TABLE 6

AVERAGE RATIO OF DOMESTIC TO INDUSTRIAL PRICE PER KWH

	1917	1937
Regulated states.......	1.616 (29 states)	2.459 (32 states)
Unregulated states.....	1.445 (16 states)	2.047 (7 states)

average number of KWH sold to industrial customers, and the relationship does not differ between regulated and unregulated states.[7] Again no effect of regulation is detectable.

STOCKHOLDER EXPERIENCE

The final area to which we look for effects of regulation is investors' experience. Our basic test is this: Did investors in companies which were not regulated, or were regulated for only a few years, do better than investors in companies which were regulated from an early date?

To answer this question, we invest $1,000 in each electrical utility in 1907, reinvest all dividends and cash value of rights, and calculate the accumulated investment in 1920.[8] The year 1907 was chosen as the first date to reduce the

[5] In 1924 the ratio of bills for 250 and 100 KWH is barely significant at the 5 per cent level; the difference is opposite to that predicted as resulting from regulation.

[6] The 1917 difference is significantly different from zero at the 5 per cent level; the 1937 difference at the 10 per cent level.

[7] In 1937, 6 of 7 unregulated states had KWH per domestic buyer divided by KWH per industrial buyer above the mean of all states, but only 7 of 29 regulated states had ratios above the mean.

[8] A separate termination in 1918 yields the same results.

TABLE 7

MARKET VALUE IN 1920 OF INVESTMENT OF $1,000 IN 1907

(20 Electric Companies)

Year of Regulation	Company	Market Value in 1920	Relative Change in Sales, 1907–20 (Per Cent)
1887	*Massachusetts:*		
	Edison Electric Illuminating Co. of Boston	$1,689	246
	Lowell Electric Light Corporation	1,485	295
	New Bedford Gas & Edison Light Co.	1,528	164
	Edison Electric Illuminating Co. of Brockton	2,310	558
1907	*New York:*		
	Buffalo General Electric Co.	2,632	718
	Kings County Electric Light & Power Co.	2,356	279
	N.Y. and Queens Electric Light & Power Co.	1,059	225
1909	*Michigan:*		
	Detroit Edison Co.	4,273	1,412
	Houghton County Electric Light Co.	1,959	130
1910	*Maryland:*		
	Consolidated Gas, Electric Light & Power Co. (Baltimore)	6,547	286
	New Jersey:		
	Public Service Corp. of New Jersey	1,546	206
1911	*Ohio:*		
	Columbia Gas and Electric Co.	3,952	999
	Connecticut:		
	Hartford Electric Light Co.	2,028	728
	California:		
	Pacific Gas and Electric Co.	2,051	212
1913	*Illinois:*		
	Commonwealth Edison Co.	2,179	299
1914	*Pennsylvania:*		
	Philadelphia Electric Co.	4,254	296
Not regulated in 1920	Galveston-Houston Electric Co.	1,001	262
	Northern Texas Electric Co.	4,861	272
	El Paso Electric Co.	4,046	281
	Tampa Electric Co.	2,830	183

TABLE 8

REGRESSION EQUATIONS OF MARKET VALUE IN 1918 AND 1920 OF $1,000 INVESTMENT IN 1907, ON GROWTH IN SALES AND REGULATION*

(20 Electric Companies)

Terminal Year (t)	Constant Term	Growth in Sales	Regulation	R^2
1918	3.28	.332 (.227)	−.015 (.010)	.16
1920	3.27	.395 (.232)	−.017 (.010)	.21

* Market values in logarithms; growth in sales = log ($sales_t/sales_{1907}$).

possible impact of expectations of regulation, and even this date—which is later than we should like—reduced the number of companies we could trace to 20. The basic data are given in Table 7.

The pattern of increases in market values appears erratic. A simple regression of market value as a function of the increase in dollar sales of the utility system and the number of years of regulation is presented in Table 8. There is thus a slight, statistically insignificant effect of regulation on market values.[9]

III. Conclusion

Our study was undertaken primarily to investigate the feasibility of measuring the effects of regulation, but our inability to find any significant effects of the regulation of electrical utilities calls for some explanation. This finding is contingent upon our criteria of regulation and of the areas in which we sought effects, but both of these criteria are accepted by much of the literature of public utility economics.

The ineffectiveness of regulation lies in two circumstances. The first circumstance is that the individual utility system is not possessed of any large amount of long run monopoly power. It faces the competition of other energy sources in a large proportion of its product's uses, and it faces the competition of other utility systems, to which in the long run its industrial (and hence many of its domestic) users may move. Let the long run demand elasticity of one utility system be on the order of —8; then the system faces demand and marginal revenue curves such as those displayed in Figure 2. Given the cost curves we sketch, price will be *MP*.[10]

The second circumstance is that the regulatory body is incapable of forcing the utility to operate at a specified combination of output, price, and cost. As we have drawn the curves, there is no market price that represents the announced goal of competitive profits; let us assume that the commission would set a price equal to average cost at some output moderately in excess of output *OM*, say at *R*. Since accounting costs are hardly unique, there is a real question whether the regulatory body can even distinguish between costs of *MS* and *MP*. Let the commission be given this knowledge; then the utility can reduce costs below *MS* by reducing one or more dimensions of the services which are really part of its output: peak load capacity, constancy of current, promptness of repairs, speed of installation of service. It can also manipulate its average price by suitable changes in the complex rate structure (also

[9] An analysis of variance was also made of Table 7, grouping states into four classes, by year of regulation: 1887, 1907–1910, 1911–1914, not regulated in 1920. No significant effect of regulation was found.

[10] An elasticity of —8 implies that a utility will set prices 14 per cent above marginal cost. In the constant cost case, given a capital/sales ratio of 4, rates of return will exceed the competitive level by 3½ per cent.

with effects on costs). Finally, recognize that the cost curve falls through time, and recognize also the inevitable time lags of a regulatory process, and the possibility becomes large that the commission will proudly win each battlefield that its protagonist has abandoned except for a squad of lawyers. Since a regulatory body cannot effectively control the daily detail of business operations, it cannot deal with variables whose effect is of the same order of

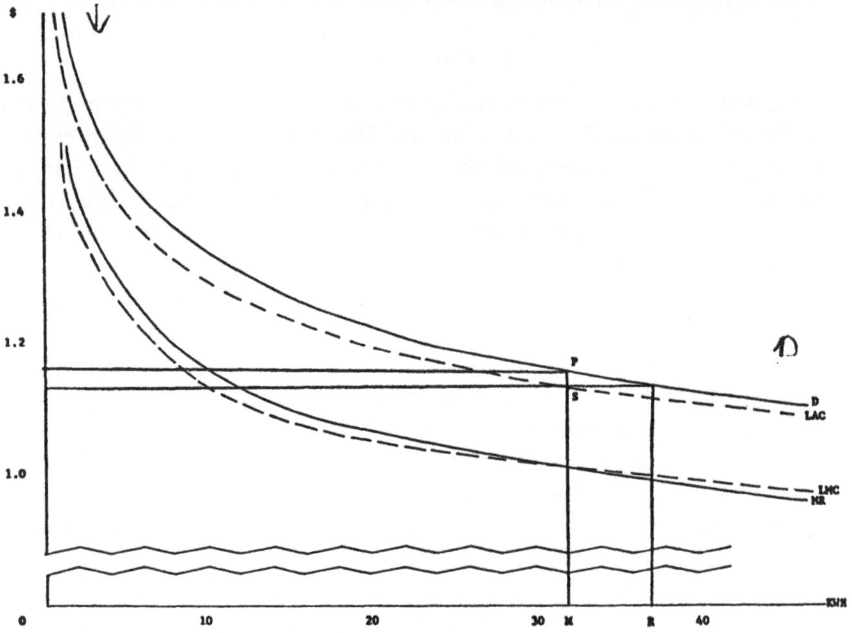

FIG. 2

magnitude in their effects on profits as the variables upon which it does have some influence.

The theory of price regulation must, in fact, be based upon the tacit assumption that in its absence a monopoly has exorbitant power. If it were true that pure monopoly profits in the absence of regulation would be 10 or 20 per cent above the competitive rate of return, so prices would be on the order of 40 or 80 per cent above long run marginal cost, there might indeed be some possibility of effective regulation. The electrical utilities do not provide such a possibility.

possible impact of expectations of regulation, and even this date—which is later than we should like—reduced the number of companies we could trace to 20. The basic data are given in Table 7.

The pattern of increases in market values appears erratic. A simple regression of market value as a function of the increase in dollar sales of the utility system and the number of years of regulation is presented in Table 8. There is thus a slight, statistically insignificant effect of regulation on market values.[9]

III. Conclusion

Our study was undertaken primarily to investigate the feasibility of measuring the effects of regulation, but our inability to find any significant effects of the regulation of electrical utilities calls for some explanation. This finding is contingent upon our criteria of regulation and of the areas in which we sought effects, but both of these criteria are accepted by much of the literature of public utility economics.

The ineffectiveness of regulation lies in two circumstances. The first circumstance is that the individual utility system is not possessed of any large amount of long run monopoly power. It faces the competition of other energy sources in a large proportion of its product's uses, and it faces the competition of other utility systems, to which in the long run its industrial (and hence many of its domestic) users may move. Let the long run demand elasticity of one utility system be on the order of —8; then the system faces demand and marginal revenue curves such as those displayed in Figure 2. Given the cost curves we sketch, price will be *MP*.[10]

The second circumstance is that the regulatory body is incapable of forcing the utility to operate at a specified combination of output, price, and cost. As we have drawn the curves, there is no market price that represents the announced goal of competitive profits; let us assume that the commission would set a price equal to average cost at some output moderately in excess of output *OM*, say at *R*. Since accounting costs are hardly unique, there is a real question whether the regulatory body can even distinguish between costs of *MS* and *MP*. Let the commission be given this knowledge; then the utility can reduce costs below *MS* by reducing one or more dimensions of the services which are really part of its output: peak load capacity, constancy of current, promptness of repairs, speed of installation of service. It can also manipulate its average price by suitable changes in the complex rate structure (also

[9] An analysis of variance was also made of Table 7, grouping states into four classes, by year of regulation: 1887, 1907–1910, 1911–1914, not regulated in 1920. No significant effect of regulation was found.

[10] An elasticity of —8 implies that a utility will set prices 14 per cent above marginal cost. In the constant cost case, given a capital/sales ratio of 4, rates of return will exceed the competitive level by 3½ per cent.

Alcoa: The Influence of Recycling on Monopoly Power

Peter L. Swan

Australian National University

PUZZLE 1: Was Judge Hand correct in his celebrated judicial opinion that Alcoa's monopoly in "virgin" aluminum provided indirect control over "secondary" production?

ANSWER: Estimates based on three models suggest that the "procompetitive" effect of recycling was largely offset by a reduction in virgin production in anticipation of future conversion into secondary. Thus, Hand's judgment appears sound.

PUZZLE 2: Is it in Alcoa's own interests to suppress recycling of scrap aluminum if feasible?

ANSWER: If current users show that they value the future use of the product by selling scrap to merchants, then Alcoa is likely to value the recycling market also. If users discard scrap which is subsequently scavenged, then Alcoa is likely to be harmed by such activity.

I. Introduction

In 1945, Judge Learned Hand ruled against the Aluminum Company of America (Alcoa) in what Adams (1951, p. 917) has called "one of the most celebrated judicial opinions of our time." He concluded that Alcoa constituted an illegal monopoly by virtue of its control over 90 percent of virgin aluminum output, which is produced from bauxite. Sitting in the court of appeals, Judge Hand overturned the 1940 decision of the district court. The judgment of this court had been that, despite Alcoa's domination of virgin production, competition from secondary aluminum, produced by recycling scrap aluminum,

I wish to thank E. Sieper and J. D. Pitchford for most helpful advice during the preparation of this paper. I am also indebted to R. Schmalensee, T. W. Swan, F. Kottke, and two referees for valuable comments on earlier drafts and to R. Albon and R. K. Anstie for assistance with the empirical work. The usual caveat applies.

[*Journal of Political Economy*, 1980, vol. 88, no. 1]

limited the firm's market power. Secondary aluminum is a close or "adequate" substitute for virgin ingot in many uses. Since secondary aluminum made up roughly 30 percent of the total supply of aluminum, and there were a large number of competitive firms engaged in recycling, Alcoa's market share defined in terms of the total output of both virgin and secondary was considerably reduced.

Judge Hand (148 F.2d 416, p. 424; also quoted by Singer [1968], p. 45) summarized the judge's argument from an earlier district court case succinctly: "At any given moment . . . 'secondary' competes with 'virgin' in the ingot market; further, it can, and probably does, set a limit or 'ceiling' beyond which the price of 'virgin' cannot go, for the cost of its production will in the end depend only upon the expense of scavenging and reconditioning. It might seem for this reason that in estimating 'Alcoa's' control over the ingot market, we ought to include the supply of 'secondary,' as the judge did." He then rejected this earlier judge's contention with his own argument to the contrary (148 F.2d 416, p. 425): " 'Alcoa' always knew that the future supply of ingot would be made up in part of what it produced at the time, and, if it was far sighted, as it proclaims itself, that consideration must have had its share in determining how much to produce. . . . The competition of 'secondary' must therefore be disregarded, as soon as we consider the position of 'Alcoa' over a period of years; it was as much within 'Alcoa's' control as was the production of the 'virgin' from which it had been derived." Thus, his decision was justified on the grounds that all secondary aluminum is ultimately derived from virgin aluminum with scrap as an intermediate product. By this means, Alcoa indirectly controlled the output of recycled secondary ingot via its effective control of virgin production.

Hand backed up his ingenious argument by drawing an analogy between Alcoa's situation and that of a lawful monopoly, for example, a patent or a copyright (148 F.2d 416, p. 425): "The monopolist cannot prevent those to whom he sells from reselling at whatever prices they please. . . . Nor can he prevent their reconditioning articles worn by use, unless they in fact make a new article. . . . At any moment his control over the market will therefore be limited by that part of what he has formerly sold, which the price he now charges may bring upon the market, as second hand or reclaimed articles. Yet no one would think of saying that for this reason the patent or copyright did not confer a monopoly."

To accept this analogy as valid may help solve a legal puzzle, but it does not really answer the relevant economic question. It is feasible that the operation of a competitive secondhand or reconditioning market could prevent a legal monopoly from earning economic rents.

Milton Friedman (1976, pp. 337–38) has emphasized both the

importance of the issue and its intrinsic interest in a "mock" problem based on the Alcoa case in which he indicates that Hand's judgment was not strictly correct since output, and hence price, will differ between what I shall call the "Alcoa" case with a single seller of virgin ingot and competitive recycling and the "complete monopoly" case in which the virgin supplier is integrated with the recycling sector and has direct control over the production of secondary ingot. Unfortunately, Friedman is silent on the question of the magnitude of the output discrepancy between the two cases and even its direction: Will a change to complete monopoly expand or contract total sales of virgin plus secondary?

Viewed in this light, it is somewhat surprising that Gaskins (1974, p. 254), in his study of the Alcoa problem, cites Friedman's mock problem in support of the view that "conventional economic wisdom . . . contends that the existence of a competitive secondhand market constitutes a major long-run restraint on monopoly in a primary market."[1] Clearly, it is not the existence of a secondhand market per se which need imply any restraint on the profitability, or the pricing decision, of the monopolist. To see this, and for the sake of argument, suppose that scrap is sold by the original owners to scrap merchants and that the proportion of scrap recycled is entirely fixed by technical conditions anywhere between zero and complete recovery. Alcoa would then be analogous with a monopoly selling a durable item which cannot be repaired, or its life extended, once it has left the factory. The analogy arises because the virgin producer captures in price the present value of the stream of services yielded by aluminum as it is recycled for subsequent use time and time again, net naturally of the actual recycling costs, just as the buyer is reimbursed for the future use to which aluminum is put when he sells some product made of the metal to the scrap merchant. Similarly, the pure monopolist selling such a durable item as an automobile is paid an amount which reflects the net present value of the stream of automobile services to possibly a whole host of future owners. Competitive secondhand auto dealers (or scrap merchants and recyclers in the case of aluminum) can then buy and sell the item indefinitely without in any way restricting the power of the monopolist as the original seller.

Section II develops a model of the competitive recycling sector which recognizes that scrap is not the only input into the finished product, secondary aluminum. In general, one expects substitution possibilities to exist between scrap and all other inputs—"recycling

[1] The literature on the effect of secondhand markets on a monopoly includes Swan (1972), Benjamin and Kormendi (1974), and Miller (1974). None of these authors would appear to support Gaskins's contention.

effort"—such that the greater is the effort in response to a higher price of secondary aluminum, the greater will be the proportion of secondary recovered from any given stock of scrap. Under the reasonable assumption of diminishing returns to effort and hence rising marginal recycling costs, a social loss on the production side is induced in the Alcoa case as competitive recyclers seek the monopoly rents accruing to Alcoa as it raises the price of aluminum above the marginal cost of virgin production. High-cost recycled aluminum thus replaces low-cost virgin, but there is a possible social gain on the consumption side if the expansion in secondary aluminum output is not offset, or more than offset, by a contraction in Alcoa's production of virgin ingot.

In Section III it is assumed that scrap aluminum is discarded by the original owners, as is likely to be the case for a number of uses to which aluminum is put, including foil, bottle tops, and beer and soft-drink cans. Specialized scavengers who place a relatively low value on their time—boy scouts!—may then collect and sell scrap to merchants. The first model to be developed, model i, permits Alcoa to undertake a form of intertemporal price discrimination, and a limiting result is obtained in which price is equated to virgin cost in the long-run equilibrium. Gaskins (1974) makes the assumption of zero scrap value and obtains results somewhat similar to those of model i. Model ii is similar but constrains Alcoa to setting a uniform price over time which results in a price which exceeds virgin cost. Thus, the inability to price discriminate leads, not only to an inferior profit position compared with the unconstrained case, but to a higher, noncompetitive price in the long run as well. Gaskins (1974) appears to be mistaken in attributing equality of price and cost in the long run to competition from secondary when the true explanation is monopoly price discrimination.

Model iii in Section IV examines the case neglected by Gaskins (1974) in which there is no scavenging, for scrap is sold directly by the original owner to the scrap merchant. Obvious examples include the routine factory waste from aluminum fabrication plants, that is, "new scrap," for which the recycling delay is relatively short, to products used in buildings and airplanes which are eventually smelted down after a considerable delay. In such cases the scrap price has an important function in linking past and future uses for aluminum.

It has long been recognized that where substitution possibilities exist the firm with monopoly power has an incentive to integrate with the competitive sector.[2] Vertical integration and control eliminate the

[2] See McKenzie 1951; Burstein 1960; Vernon and Graham 1971; Schmalensee 1973; Hay 1973; Warren-Boulton 1974, 1977; Perry 1978; and Mallela and Nahata 1978.

social loss on the production side which results because competitive firms face a price in excess of marginal cost. An efficient cost-minimizing outcome requires that marginal costs in virgin and secondary production be equated. In Section V it is shown that such an efficient outcome would occur if Alcoa had a pure monopoly with direct control over the recycling sector as well. Surprisingly, consumers might also prefer a pure monopoly solution to the Alcoa solution. This would be the case if the elimination of the production inefficiency under pure monopoly lowered the cost of aluminum sufficiently to induce the monopolist to produce a greater total output of aluminum than would be the case with mixed monopoly and competitive elements. Although such a result can occur, the empirical findings in Section VI suggest that the existence of the competitive recycling sector has brought a slight gain to consumers compared with the pure monopoly solution. While the pure monopoly and Alcoa solutions are barely distinguishable, there is a considerable discrepancy between Alcoa's apparent behavior and the purely competitive result. Thus, the empirical findings tend to support Hand's judgment.

II. Competitive Supply of Secondary Aluminum

In order to develop the simplest possible model of the recycling sector, it is assumed that products made of aluminum all have the same lifetime before becoming "scrap" and therefore available for recycling. Moreover, scrap is assumed to be homogeneous and is combined with other resources, labor, heat, etc., to the value of $\$z$ per unit of scrap input to produce secondary aluminum, s. The unit of time is chosen so as to equal the "average" period of delay between production of virgin and its subsequent conversion into secondary aluminum.[3] This implies that the total output of aluminum, q, consisting of virgin, v, plus secondary, s, produced in one period will be available as a given supply of scrap, $\bar{q}$, in the next.

Competitive recycling of scrap takes place at the end of each period and depends on the price, p, of secondary which is (correctly) anticipated to rule at the beginning of the subsequent period. Gross revenue per unit of scrap processed is represented by $p\gamma(z)$, since $0 \leqq \gamma(z)$

[3] Obviously, aluminum aircraft at one end of the spectrum and foil or soft-drink cans at the other have quite different lives, and the nature of the scrap may be quite different as well. This suggests a possible means of obtaining the average period of delay between sale of ingot and its ultimate availability as scrap, requiring average lives of different aluminum products and a breakdown of the uses to which aluminum is put. Data limitation has prevented pursuit of this method for the interwar period in Section VI below. The models themselves abstract from the composition of scrap except insofar as it may affect whether models i and ii on the one hand, or model iii on the other, is empirically relevant.

$= s/\bar{q} \leqq 1$ is the survival function which determines the recovery of secondary from any given amount of scrap as a function of the expenditure on recycling, z, per unit of scrap.[4] The greater the resources devoted to scrap dealing and refining, the greater the recovery; hence, $\gamma(0) = 0$ and $\gamma'(z) > 0$ for $z < \bar{z}$ if there exists a technically determined maximum for z, $\bar{z}$, defined by max $\gamma(\bar{z}) \leqq 1$. There are also diminishing returns as other inputs are combined with any given amount of scrap so that $\gamma''(z) < 0$ reflects rising marginal costs.

Competitive recycling-industry profits,

$$\pi(z) = [p\gamma(z) - z - \phi]\bar{q}, \tag{1}$$

represent the difference between receipts, $p\gamma(z)\bar{q}$, and the outlay on resources $z\bar{q}$ plus the value of scrap aluminum $\phi\bar{q}$ used, where ϕ is the scrap (i.e., secondhand) price of aluminum paid by merchants to former owners of aluminum products or to scavengers (e.g., boy scouts) of discarded scrap.

The first-order condition for a maximum of (1) requires that

$$\pi'(z) = [p\gamma'(z) - 1]\bar{q} \leqq 0, \tag{2}$$

since input and output prices are treated parametrically. For an interior solution, with which we will largely be concerned, $z < \bar{z}$, and $\pi'(z) = 0$ so that $\gamma'(z) = 1/p$, which defines the cost outlay as an implicit function of price. In explicit form, the solution is denoted by $z = z(p)$ with $z'(p) \equiv -1/[p^2\gamma''(z)] > 0$. A corner solution may also occur in which $\pi'(z) < 0$ for $z \leqq \bar{z}$ with the optimal value of $z = \bar{z}$. For example, both the square-root survival function,

$$\gamma(z) = 2(0.5kz)^{0.5};\ \bar{z} = 0.5k, \tag{3}$$

and the quadratic function,

$$\gamma(z) = kz(1 - 0.25kz);\ \bar{z} = 2k, \tag{3'}$$

are capable of generating a corner solution at $\gamma(\bar{z}) = 1$; whereas a corner solution with the exponential function,

$$\gamma(z) = 1 - e^{-kz}, \tag{3''}$$

is impossible for a finite price $p > 1$ since $\gamma(z) \to 1$ as $z \to \infty$. In each expression, the coefficient $k > 0$.

Free entry of competitive firms drives profit, $\pi(z)$, to zero. Hence, for an interior solution the price of scrap is

$$\phi(p) = p\gamma[z(p)] - z(p), \tag{4}$$

[4] Here there is an analogy with Schmalensee (1974), who makes the decay rate a function of maintenance expenditure in his model of a single seller subject to a competitive repair sector. See also Su (1975) for a model with some similarity to Schmalensee's.

and for a corner solution,

$$\phi(p) = p\gamma(\bar{z}) - \bar{z}, \tag{4'}$$

with both equations obtained from (1). In the case in which scrap aluminum is discarded and subsequently scavenged, the price of scrap is of no great significance for the model except insofar as a positive price, $\phi > 0$, is necessary to induce scavenging. However, in a more general model it plays a more crucial role in that buyers of aluminum products may anticipate the recovery of some portion of the initial purchase price with sale of the inevitable by-product, scrap aluminum, and this in turn will influence the initial purchase.

III. A Relatively "Simplistic" Model of the Alcoa Problem

In this section I adopt a relatively simplistic approach to secondhand markets and assume that scrap is discarded by users and collected by a group specializing in collection (scavengers) for reprocessing. Such a model implicitly places a low upper bound on the price of scrap relative to transactions costs, to explain why the product should be discarded in the first place, and also presupposes the existence of scavengers who place a lower value on their time relative to users, or have some other distinguishing feature, for whom a low but nonetheless positive price of scrap provides adequate incentive for scavenging.[5]

Model i

Denote the time-stationary negatively sloped inverse demand function for aluminum by $p(q), p'(q) < 0$, and the constant level of average total costs in production of virgin by c so that Alcoa's long-run-equilibrium profit on sales of virgin aluminum, v, is $\pi(q) = [p(q) - c]v$. Recalling that one time period corresponds to one life cycle of aluminum, and that by definition virgin sales equal total sales minus the secondary supply generated by the previous period's production, it is clear from (2) above that virgin sales at time t,

$$v_t \equiv q_t - s_t = q_t - \gamma(q_t)q_{t-1}, \tag{5}$$

[5] Gaskins (1974, p. 256) has a pragmatic justification for making the assumption of a zero scrap price: "The fact that we observe discarded newspapers, beer cans and automobiles indicates that scrap aluminum, steel and newsprint may have a very low value in certain forms." However, one cannot argue logically from a special limiting case which may represent a particular *equilibrium* solution to one in which the zero scrap price must hold for every ingot price no matter how high and regardless of the ease of recovery. The assumption of a negligible scrap price is relaxed in Section IV below.

where for simplicity the survival function, $\gamma\{z[p(q_t)]\}$, has been abbreviated to $\gamma(q_t)$ with derivative $\gamma'(q_t) \equiv \gamma'(z)z'(p)p'(q_t) < 0$ by the chain rule. Thus, the rate at which aluminum is recovered from the recycling process falls as total sales increase since the lower price of the final product induces a reduction in the value, z, of other inputs into recycling.

Now long-run-equilibrium virgin sales, $v = [1 - \gamma(q)]q$, obtained from (5), can be subdivided into components which are subject to the firm's control and the remainder which represent initial conditions on the problem:[6]

$$v = [1 - \delta\gamma(q)]q - (1 - \delta)\gamma(q)\bar{q}, \tag{6}$$

where the bar indicates that output is constrained by the fact that the firm is in long-run equilibrium and $\delta = 1/(1 + r)$ is the discount factor with interest rate r. The stationary-state profit-maximizing solution becomes

$$p(q)\left(1 - \frac{\eta_v}{\eta_p}\right) = c, \tag{7}$$

where the elasticity of total sales with respect to virgin sales in long-run equilibrium, $\eta_v = (dq/dv)(v/q) = [1 - \gamma(q)]/[1 - \delta\gamma(q) - q\gamma'(q)] \gtreqq 0$, which is obtained from (6) using the implicit function rule, given that $\bar{q}$ is unalterable and $\eta_p = -(dq/dp)(p/q) > 0$ is the conventional price elasticity of total sales.

Equation (7) is a most interesting one in that it is just the standard marginal revenue = marginal cost (MR = MC) condition for a nonrecyclable good, except that the ratio of elasticities, η_v/η_p, has replaced the usual elasticity term $1/\eta_p$. There is, however, a disturbing counterintuitive aspect to this result for, not only do we have $\eta_v = 1$ when the rate of recovery γ is technically or legally fixed at zero, $\gamma = \bar{\gamma} = 0$, so that the standard result for a nonrecyclable product is obtained, but also when technical conditions promote complete recovery, so that $\gamma \rightarrow \bar{\gamma} = 1$ and $\gamma'(q) \rightarrow 0$, the elasticity term $\eta_v \rightarrow 0$, and price approaches marginal cost, $p(q) \rightarrow c$.

[6] Following an approach suggested by Sieper and Swan (1973), the discounted summation of both sides of (5) yields

$$\sum_{t=0}^{\infty} v_t \delta^t = \sum_{t=0}^{\infty} q_t \delta^t - \delta \sum_{t=0}^{\infty} [\gamma(q_{t+1})q_t\delta^t - \gamma(q_0)q_{-1}].$$

In a long-run equilibrium with $q_t = q_{t+1} = q_{-1} = q_{-\infty}$, etc.,

$$\frac{v}{1-\delta} = \frac{q}{1-\delta} - \frac{\delta\gamma(q)q}{1-\delta} - \gamma(q)q_{-1},$$

and, on simplifying, eq. (6) in the text is obtained. Note that $\bar{q}$ in (6) has been used to denote the initial condition at time $t = 0$ represented by q_{-1}.

This limiting long-run solution to what in essence is a monopoly problem is surprising because it would appear to give rise to a purely competitive result with absence of supernormal profits. One might even be forgiven for a suggestion that, in this case at least, the virgin producer is forced to compete against itself by the existence of the secondhand recycling market.[7] This conclusion would be premature, however, for, while marginal cost pricing may be consistent with perfect competition, it does not imply it. In fact, it may be equally consistent with precisely the contrary result of a perfectly discriminating monopolist. This happens to be the situation here, although the fact that it is a form of dynamic price discrimination makes it more difficult to recognize. Take as the starting point a situation in which the initial supply of scrap is small or nonexistent. The initial price charged is high, and the monopolist sweeps out an area under the demand curve but above marginal cost.[8] The orginal seller will clearly do better under this scenario than if the firm is constrained to keep the price of the product the same in each period so as to rule out dynamic price discrimination.

Model ii

Suppose, initially, there is no scrap, and a ban is instituted on dynamic price discrimination so that $p(q_0) = p(q_t) = p(q)$. The original supplier must sell an amount of virgin $v = q$ in the initial period plus an amount $q - s = q - \gamma(q)\bar{q}$ in each subsequent period, once an amount of scrap $q = \bar{q}$ is available for reprocessing, so as to maintain a uniform product price over time. The net present value of profits at time zero,

$$V_0(q) = [p(q) - c][q + v\delta(1 + \delta + \delta^2 + \ldots + \ldots)]$$
$$= [p(q) - c]\{1 + [1 - \gamma(q)]\delta/(1 - \delta)\}q,$$

[7] Gaskins (1974) obtains an equivalent result as a limiting case in a model somewhat similar to model i and remarks (p. 255) that "if . . . the competitive supply of secondary aluminum inexorably drives the price toward the competitive level, the court was wrong in its finding." In his simulations Gaskins does not, in fact, obtain a price close to the competitive level in the long-run equilibrium. Rather, if demand grows at some appropriate rate over time, his model generates a price close to the observed price. This suggests that it may be unfair to criticize his model on the basis of a limiting case. As a counter to this, a sound model should be robust with respect to a change in some parameter, such as the growth rate, and still give sensible results. Moreover, no aspect of Hand's argument depends on an artificial condition such as perpetual growth. A model in which the growth rate is of such vital importance may be of little use in evaluating the soundness or otherwise of Hand's judgment.

[8] Gaskins (1974, p. 255) notes the high initial price and concludes that "the existence of a competitive secondhand market makes things worse in the short run." It is, of course, not so much the existence of the secondhand market but rather the ability to intertemporally price discriminate which makes for the relatively high initial price. In my opinion, Gaskins's (1974) study is open to criticism more for a failure to interpret the results fully than for weaknesses in the model itself.

so that

$$rV_0(q) = [p(q) - c][r + 1 - \gamma(q)]q \tag{8}$$

on simplification.

The constrained profit-maximizing solution obtained from (8) is

$$p(q)\left(1 - \frac{1}{\eta_p}\right) = c + \frac{[p(q) - c]q\gamma'(q)}{r + 1 - \gamma(q)}, \tag{9}$$

which is just the usual MR = MC condition for a nonrecyclable good plus a negative term on the RHS which tends to lower the equilibrium price. A number of interesting implications follow:

1. It is in the interests of the initial producer (Alcoa) to institute a tying arrangement or promote a law so that other inputs, z, are used in fixed proportion with scrap to produce secondary aluminum. Elimination of substitution possibilities between scrap and other inputs implies that $\gamma'(q) = 0$, so that the entire RHS term in (9) due to recycling disappears. Product price is increased to what it would be in the complete absence of recycling, irrespective of whether the survival rate, $\gamma = \bar{\gamma}$, is fixed at zero, unity, or in between. Clearly, consumers would wish to oppose elimination of substitution possibilities because of the higher price that results.

2. It follows that, so long as $\gamma = \bar{\gamma}$ and is therefore fixed, consumers are indifferent as to the existence or otherwise of the recycling sector, as price is independent of $\bar{\gamma}$. A larger recycling sector is precisely offset by a reduction in the steady-state output of the initial producer.

3. If the initial producer has a choice in setting the fixed survival rate, $\bar{\gamma}$, via legal restriction or other means, it will prefer to set $\bar{\gamma} = 0$ so as to eliminate the recycling sector entirely, for example, by invention of "self-destruct after use" aluminum cans. This follows from the fact that for any given $\gamma = \bar{\gamma}$, profits per unit of virgin sales, $p(q) - c$, are fixed and reach a maximum when $v = q$ in every period, as can be seen from (8). While dislike of secondhand markets, that is, recycling, by the initial producer is in accord with what Gaskins (1974) sees as the conventional economic wisdom, it should be realized that this conclusion is entirely the artifact of the basic assumption underlying this model; namely, that consumers of the firm's products also place no value, or perhaps even a negative valuation when disposal costs are taken account of, on the future use of the good. The consumer's implicit valuation is revealed by the decision to discard the good after use.

4. Long-run-equilibrium output without price discrimination is less than in model i with price discrimination. This can be seen by rearranging the latter, (7) above, as

$$p(q)\left(1-\frac{1}{\eta_p}\right)=c+\frac{[p(q)-c]q\gamma'(q)}{r+1-\gamma(q)}$$
$$+\frac{r\{[p(q)-c]\gamma'(q)+\gamma(q)p'(q)\}q}{r+1-\gamma(q)},$$

for $\gamma(q) < 1$, which differs from the constrained solution, (9), by only the final negative term on the RHS. The sign of this term ensures that quantity is expanded further, and that price is lower, in model i. Those who would believe that pricing at or close to marginal cost in the unconstrained case is due to unavoidable competition from the secondhand recycled product would presumably expect price to be the same, or even lower, once a uniform intertemporal pricing constraint is placed on the original seller.

IV. A More Sophisticated Model

Model iii

In this section the restrictive assumption that consumers discard the product after use is relaxed. This implies that if a consumer purchases a unit of the good for the purchase price p and sells it a period later as scrap for ϕ, the net present value cost to the consumer is not p, as in the previous section, but rather p net of the discounted price of scrap, $\delta\phi$. But the price of scrap itself depends on the purchase price, as is shown by (4) or (4′), so that the actual cost incurred by the user of the product, $\rho(q)$, that is, what one can think of as the inverse demand function for the services yielded by the product, becomes[9]

$$\rho(q) \equiv [p - \delta\phi(p)]/\delta \equiv p\{r + 1 - \gamma[z(p)]\} + z(p), \qquad (10)$$

in the stationary state, on substitution from the interior solution to ϕ given by (4). Thus, the service price has a sensible interpretation as the opportunity cost of funds tied up in the good, rp, plus the mortality or depreciation cost, $1 - \gamma[z(p)]$, plus the actual recycling cost, $z(p)$.

In the previous section it was found that, if the initial producer is not constrained to establish the same product price in each period, the outcome is affected by intertemporal price discrimination. Even more serious problems emerge in the present model since the firm has yet another method to influence demand for its product via the price which is established for scrap. Thus, for example, if a consumer buys a certain amount of the product on the basis that the current price of scrap will persist, the producer can exploit this myopic foresight by an

[9] The service price $\rho(q)$ is measured at the end of the period in question, so that the net present value cost in (10) has been divided by the discount factor δ.

unanticipated sales expansion, which leaves the consumer unpleasantly surprised by the now lower price of scrap. Had he foreseen this price decline, the consumer's initial purchase would have been lower. This is but one instance of the kind of game-theoretic problems which can arise between a monopolist selling what is de facto a durable good and the consumer who lacks perfect foresight.

This kind of problem can be overcome if the seller is precommitted to a particular pricing policy, such as a stable price.[10] In an assumed absence of fixed costs in production, the stationary-state solution is reached immediately from an initial situation in which there is no scrap available for processing. As in the case of model ii in the previous section, the net present value of profits at time zero, from an initial sale of $v = q$ units followed by subsequent sales of $v = \{1 - \gamma[z(p)]\}q$ units, is

$$rV_0 = (p - c)\{r + 1 - \gamma[z(p)]\}q, \tag{11}$$

as in (8) above. On replacing the initial p in (11) by its equivalent, $p = [\rho(q) - z(p)]/\{r + 1 - \gamma[z(p)]\}$, obtained from (10), the maximand (11) becomes

$$rV_0 = [\rho(q) - (c\{r + 1 - \gamma[z(p)]\} + z(p))]q. \tag{11'}$$

Equation (10) expresses the purchase price, p, as an indirect function of the service price, ρ, such that

$$p'(\rho) = 1/\{r + 1 - \gamma[z(p)]\} \tag{12}$$

on simplifying using (2). Since ρ is itself a function of q, p can be expressed in direct form as a function of q, that is, $p = p[\rho(q)]$ and likewise z and γ. So as to distinguish these functions from those appearing in the previous section, the abbreviation becomes $p[\rho(q)] = p^*(q)$, $z\{p[\rho(q)]\} = z^*(q)$, etc. It is interesting to observe that the elasticity of the demand function with respect to the purchase price,

[10] These game-theoretic problems arise with the sale of any durable good or asset by a monopolist because the price the consumer is willing to pay depends on the anticipated future price of the good. If the seller can help generate a particular set of expectations in the buyer and subsequently lower the price to a new purchaser in a way which was not anticipated by the original purchaser, then the original buyer suffers a windfall capital loss. In this way, the monopolist may be able to gain through a form of price discrimination, but it presupposes an ability to go on fooling consumers. In effect, pricing policy becomes a game played between the seller and a collection of buyers. Several such pricing strategies are investigated in Sieper and Swan (1973). A strategy of precommitment to a particular pricing policy, or a form of "locking-in" of future options, may be the most effective way of ensuring "perfect foresight" on the part of consumers at all times. It is similar in effect to a form of repurchase guarantee at some specified price.

η_p^*, is lower than the elasticity with respect to the service price, $\eta_\rho = -(dq/d\rho)(\rho/q)$, since

$$\eta_p^* = -(dq/d\rho)(\rho - z)/q = \eta_\rho(\rho - z)/\rho < \eta_\rho, \tag{13}$$

based on (12) and (10).

With the aid of this new terminology, the maximand, (11′), becomes the difference between revenue, $\rho(q)q$, and total cost, $C(q)$:

$$rV_0^*(q) = \rho(q)q - C(q), \tag{14}$$

where $C(q) = \{c[r + 1 - \gamma^*(q)] + z^*(q)\}q$. The average cost term in braces, $AC(z\{p[\rho(q)]\}) \equiv AC(q)$, consists of the opportunity cost of funds tied up in virgin production, rc, plus the cost of virgin production, $c(1 - \gamma)$, necessary to allow for mortality, $1 - \gamma$, in the recycling process plus, finally, the recycling cost, z, itself. It clearly encompasses not only the initial producer's own costs but also those incurred by the competitive recycling sector as well. It therefore represents industrywide costs. Thus, a remarkable transformation of the firm's maximand from one involving virgin production and costs only has occurred. Although the initial producer has no direct concern with costs incurred in competitive recycling, the link provided by the price of scrap, ϕ, between the two markets ensures that the firm must act as if it were bearing the entire costs of the competitive sector on its own account.

The condition for a maximum present value of the firm is simply that marginal revenue be equated to industrywide marginal costs:

$$\rho(q)\left(1 - \frac{1}{\eta_\rho}\right) = C'(q); \tag{15}$$

and, if marginal cost is falling, it must not be falling more rapidly than marginal revenue at the optimal point. Equation (15) is the solution to a Bertrand-Edgeworth type "duopoly" problem of the leader-follower variety in which the "follower" is the competitive recycling sector which takes the purchase price of the product as given and determines its output accordingly. The "leader" is the initial producer (Alcoa), and the firm's revenue function is determined by subtracting the known competitive supply from total industry demand. The interaction between the firm's production decision and that of the competitive sector is incorporated into the marginal cost term, $C'(q)$.

Several cases can now be examined. For example, if the proportion recovered is fixed by technical or legal restriction at $\gamma = \bar{\gamma}$ and z at $\bar{z}$, marginal cost becomes a horizontal line, $C'(q) = c(r + 1 - \bar{\gamma}) + \bar{z}$, and the initial producer acts as a complete monopolist with no competition from the recycling sector at all. In this case, the initial producer will wish to preserve the competitive recycling sector as long as marginal costs are less than they would be with no recycling ($\bar{\gamma} = 0, \bar{z} = 0$), that is, $c(r + 1 - \bar{\gamma}) + \bar{z} < c$. Both the initial producer and consumers stand to gain by the existence of the recycling sector since industry costs are lowered. This is in contrast to model ii, in the previous section, in which consumers could be indifferent to the size of the competitive sector because they chose to discard the product.

The general solution to (15) in which recovery, γ, is endogenous is more complex because the initial producer must take account of the degree of substitutability between scrap and other inputs into the recycling process. The solution is shown in figure 1. Marginal revenue cuts Alcoa's marginal cost, $C'(q)$, from above at industry output level q^a (for Alcoa). The average cost curve, $AC(q)$, is downward sloping for a purchase price, p, in excess of virgin cost, c, since

$$AC'(q) = [1 - c\gamma'(z)]z'(p)p'(\rho)\rho'(q) < 0, \tag{16}$$

and $1 - c\gamma'(z) > 0$ if $p > c$, as implied by the recycling condition (2). At the point $p = c$, below which purchase price cannot fall, $1 - c\gamma'(z) = 1 - p\gamma'(z) = 0$, according to the competitive recycling condition (2), so that average cost is at a minimum given by

$$AC[z(c)] = c\{r + 1 - \gamma[z(c)]\} + z(c), \tag{17}$$

shown as the horizontal line in the diagram.

Points along $AC[z(c)]$ are Pareto efficient in that industry costs are minimized, with the marginal cost of virgin, c, equated to $1/\gamma'(z)$, which has an interpretation as the marginal cost of secondary aluminum. Paradoxically, it is the very fact that marginal recycling costs are rising, $-1/\gamma''(z) > 0$, which brings about Alcoa's falling average cost curve, since an expansion in q lowers p and in turn reduces the proportion of industry output emanating from the high-cost, overextended competitive recycling sector. This lowers cost averaged over both virgin and secondary production. Of course, the assumption underlying the model is that both the initial producer and the recycling sector are efficient in a purely *technical* sense. The difficulty is that control of virgin production by a single seller implies that $p > c$, and hence competitive recycling firms are conveyed the wrong price signal from the point of view of *economic* efficiency. If there was also perfect competition in the supply of virgin aluminum so that $p = c$, the correct price signal would be conveyed with $AC[z(c)]$ as the relevant average cost curve.

Let industry output for which $p = c$ be denoted q^c (for competition); then it must be true that Alcoa's average cost evaluated at q^c equals the minimum cost level, that is, $AC(q^c) = AC[z(c)]$. Under perfectly competitive conditions industrywide, the service price, $\rho(q)$, is driven down to the constant level of average (and marginal) cost, $AC[z(c)]$, so

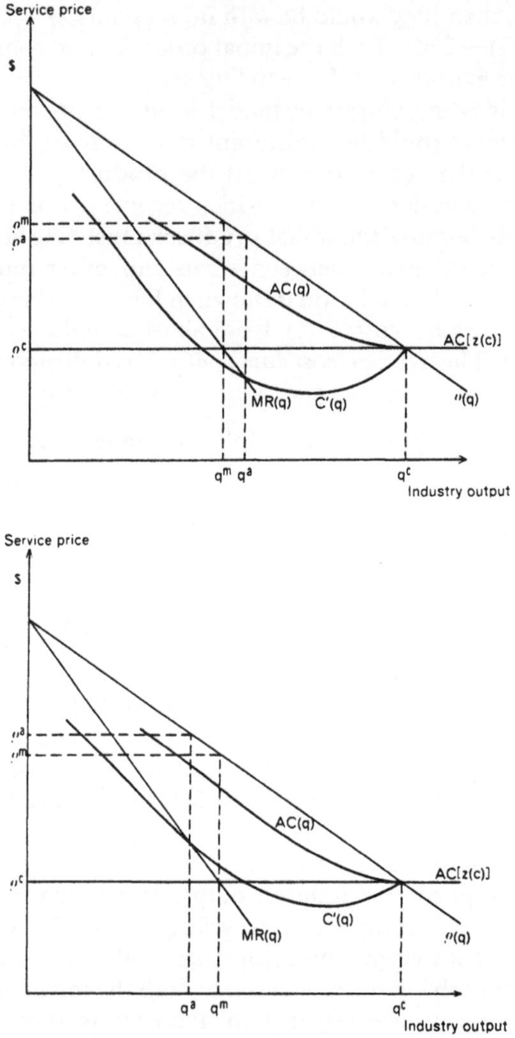

FIG. 1.—Alcoa and pure monopoly solutions

that the service demand curve must cut $AC[z(c)]$ at $AC(q^c)$, as shown in figure 1.[11]

V. Alcoa versus Pure Monopolist

The question is posed in the context of model iii: How would Alcoa's behavior differ if by some means, such as a patent or government

[11] Since it is unusual to have demand conditions included in a cost term, one should note that $AC(q)$ is itself dependent on demand conditions which affect the relative shares going to low-cost virgin and high-cost secondary aluminum.

license, it could obtain a complete monopoly with control of recycling of scrap, in addition to its dominant position in virgin, so as to maximize joint profits in both virgin and secondary aluminum?[12] The same situation would arise if a rental policy could be adopted and property rights retained in scrap aluminum.

The optimal unconstrained profit-maximizing strategy for the pure monopolist is to produce the stationary-state industry output, q, in the initial period and then to maintain that output by producing the cost-minimizing combination of virgin and secondary at the point where marginal virgin cost equals marginal recycling cost, $c = 1/\gamma'(z)$. The Alcoa solution (15) is now modified to yield the MR = MC condition,[13]

$$\rho(q)\left(1 - \frac{1}{\eta_\rho}\right) = AC[z(c)], \qquad (18)$$

where average cost (17) on the RHS is the horizontal minimum cost line shown in figure 1. This pure monopoly solution is depicted at $q = q^m$ (m for monopoly).

Figure 1, top, shows a solution for which $q^a > q^m$, so that the consumer gains by competition in the recycling sector in the form of a lower price, $\rho(q^a) < \rho(q^m)$, compared with the pure monopoly solution. Figure 1, bottom, on the other hand, shows a solution in which $q^m > q^a$, so that the consumer would gain if competition were suppressed in the recycling sector, given the lack of competition in virgin aluminum. Obviously, competition in both markets is the ideal solution in which the consumer unambiguously gains, with solution depicted by q^c.

[12] Gaskins's comparison (1974, p. 258) between the Alcoa case and a monopolist is different from the one made here since it is between Alcoa subject to a competitive recycling sector and the firm's behavior if recycling was either technically impossible or had been declared illegal. Hence, he is really concerned with the effect of the existence of a secondhand market, whereas the present paper, and Section V in particular, is concerned with control of the secondhand market. The existence question can be regarded as a special case of the control question by constraining the recovery factor, γ, to zero in the pure monopoly case. On some occasions, legal or political constraints may be such that it is a question of having an unfettered secondhand market or doing without it. Examples of controls on secondhand markets include the cooperage industry (see Urban and Mancke 1972) and the uranium industry for which several producer countries (including the United States and Australia) desire strict controls, or even a ban on reprocessing, of spent nuclear fuel. The ostensible reason for controls is to hinder nuclear arms proliferation, since plutonium for bomb manufacture can be obtained via the recycling process. The present paper suggests reasons why producer interests might be in favor of some type of control over reprocessing.

[13] In marked contrast to the "Alcoa" solution, the price of scrap ϕ, and by implication the purchase price p, are immaterial to the monopoly and have no bearing on the solution. A higher purchase price which is exactly offset by increased payments for scrap metal is of no consequence since the monopolist directly controls the recycling activity. This would be immediately obvious if a rental policy could be adopted since the price of scrap would play no role at all, unless it took the form of a deposit as on soft-drink bottles (see Massel and Parish 1968).

It is clear from figure 1 that the consumer gains from competitive recycling if, and only if, Alcoa's marginal cost curve, $C'(q)$, lies below the pure monopolist's marginal cost curve, $AC[z(c)]$, at the point where marginal revenue cuts marginal cost from above, that is, $q^a \gtreqless q^m$ as $AC[z(c)] \gtreqless C'(q^a)$. It is only the downward-sloping demand curve facing Alcoa that permits equilibrium to occur on the downward sloping, as well as the positively sloped, portion of the marginal cost curve. In a more fundamental sense, the ambiguity in outcome is a reflection of the theory of the second best: Given that a monopoly exists in one market (virgin aluminum), and is to remain, then the socially optimal response is not necessarily perfect competition in a closely related (secondary aluminum) market. In fact, monopoly control of recycling must not only lead to a Pareto improvement on the cost side via substitution of low-cost virgin for high-cost secondary, with a consequent rise in monopoly profits, but in addition these savings may be so great that it pays the monopolist to lower price into the bargain.[14] Paradoxically, model ii of Section III showed that the consumer could not lose, and may gain, from recycling, although the consumer demonstrated by discarding the product that he placed no explicit value on the existence of a competitive recycling market. Once the consumer no longer discards the item, he may actually be made worse off by the operation of the competitive recycling market.

VI. Empirical Results: 1923–40

The aim of this section is to obtain independent estimates of recycling recovery, $\gamma(z)$, virgin cost, c, and demand, $p(q)$, for the interwar period 1923–40 relevant to Hand's judgment, so as to make predictions on the basis of the three models of Alcoa's optimal price for aluminum ingot. These predictions can then be compared with Alcoa's mean price actually ruling over this period. Close correspondence between these predictions and the observed value would not only provide support for the models but also would provide indirectly a check on Hand's reasoning since the models incorporate his insight into the functioning of the overall market. Ideally, and with sufficient optimism, the test may show which of the three models performs best from an empirical standpoint.

[14] A simple numerical example is all that is required to establish this logical possibility. Let the survival function take the exponential form given by (3″) above, so as to exclude the possibility of a corner solution. It is easy to establish that $z(p) = (\ln kp)/k$ and $z'(p) = 1 - \gamma[z(p)] = 1/(kp)$. A linear inverse service-demand function, $\rho(q) = \alpha_0 - \alpha_1 q$, is assumed, where the parameter $\alpha_0 = 14.6556$ and $\alpha_1 > 0$. Parameter values $c = 1, k = 1$, and $r = 0.5$ are assumed. Equations (10) and (15) can be solved to obtain $p(q^a) = 10$ and $\rho(q^a) = 8.3026$, while the pure monopoly equation (18) implies that $\rho(q^m) = \{\alpha_0 + AC[z(c)]\}/2 = 8.0778 < \rho(q^a)$. This example is obviously not intended to be realistic.

For simplicity, the square-root survival function, equation (3) above, is assumed. This implies that $\gamma[z(p)] = kp$ is proportional to price and that cost outlay $z(p) = 0.5kp^2$ is proportional to the square of price. The recycling coefficient k is estimated for the period 1925–40, inclusive,[15] from the linear secondary-supply equation,

$$\gamma[z(p)] = s_t/q_{t-1} = \beta_0 + \beta_1 p_t^s = \underset{(0.8544)}{0.0751} + \underset{(3.4754)}{0.0242} p_t^s, \qquad (19)$$

$$F = 12.078, R^2 = .462, d = 0.647$$

where s_t is the output of secondary aluminum in t; q_{t-1} is the available stock of scrap aluminum in t (proxied by output in the previous year); s_t/q_{t-1} is the proportion of scrap recovered; p_t^s is the price of secondary aluminum deflated by the wholesale price index, and the student t value is in parentheses. While the coefficient on the price variable is significant, the Durbin-Watson d-statistic indicates serial correlation of the residuals which may be due to specification error.

The equation was reestimated, using a Cochrane-Orcutt type procedure,[16] to give

$$s_t/q_{t-1} = \underset{(0.0077)}{0.00093} + \underset{(3.3996)}{0.0286} p_t^s, \qquad (19')$$

$$F = 16.229, R^2 = .714, d = 1.398, \rho = -0.71$$

which appears satisfactory in that there is no longer evidence of serial correlation, and the coefficient of the price variable, which has increased slightly on the previous equation, is significant at the 1 percent level. The constant term is insignificantly different from zero and is therefore assumed equal to zero. A correction needs to be made to the coefficient of secondary price, p_t^s, to make allowance for a price discrepancy which existed between secondary and virgin ingot. The mean price of virgin for the entire sample period 1923–40, $\bar{p}$, is 24.886 cents/lb, once the series of virgin ingot prices has been deflated by the Bureau of Labor Statistics (BLS) Index of Metals and Metal Products.[17] Since the mean price of secondary $\bar{p}^s = 12.116$, a correction factor of $\bar{p}^s/\bar{p} = 0.4868$ needs to be applied to the coefficient of p_t^s to obtain $\gamma[z(p)] = kp = 0.01395p$, where p is the price of virgin.[18] The

[15] The data series for the sample period is contained in Engle et al. (1945, p. 164).

[16] The method used for dealing with the problem of autocorrelation is based on Pagan (1974) and is described in the notes accompanying his program AUTREGAL.

[17] The mean real price of virgin is obtained from data presented by Mason (1972, p. 104).

[18] A further adjustment could have been made in obtaining k to allow for the fact that in value terms a pound of secondary is not equivalent to a pound of virgin ingot. Since all the demand studies and the various legal judgments have treated them as equivalent, no additional correction was made.

implied share of secondary in the total is $\gamma = k\bar{p} = 0.3472$, which is not far off the mean share of secondary in total production of around 32 percent.[19]

Fortunately, a great deal is known about virgin aluminum production in the interwar period, due largely to Alcoa's evidence on production costs and other matters presented at various antitrust suits. Mason (1972, p. 161) has constructed a series for Alcoa's average total costs of virgin for the period 1923–40 from this source. When deflated by the BLS metals index, a figure of c = 13.63 cents/lb is obtained.[20] The interest rate, r, is assumed to be 10 percent.

The remaining information required relates to demand. There have been a number of U.S. studies of demand for aluminum. Fisher (1962) carried out some of the pioneering econometric work, and his results were relied on by Gaskins (1974). The elasticity value Fisher (p. 100) obtained, however, does not statistically differ significantly from zero and seems implausibly low. In contrast, Peck (1961, pp. 31–33) obtained significant elasticity values ranging from 1.15 to 2.07. More recently, Mason (1972, p. 132) fitted a linear equation to both interwar and postwar data to obtain a mean long-run price elasticity of $\bar{\eta}_p$ = 2.322 for the interwar period 1923–40 and a much lower elasticity of 0.889 in the postwar period. Since Mason's study applies specifically to our sample period, his estimate will be accepted.

In keeping with Mason's (1972) specification, a linear demand curve is assumed, with intercept on the price axis denoted by α. Knowledge of the mean price and elasticity provides this intercept readily, for it is related to the elasticity by

$$\alpha = p(1 + \eta)/\eta. \tag{20}$$

For models i and ii, the product and service demand are one and the same, so that the implied value of α = 35.6035 is immediately available. For model iii, in which they differ, the elasticity of service demand is not observable directly but is computed from a knowledge of η_p, k, and r, using (13) to give η_ρ = 2.858. Since the mean service

[19] The estimated mortality rate, $1 - \gamma$, includes any shrinkage which takes place when scrap is melted down to form secondary. Wallace (1937, p. 457) reports that, in the early twenties at least, the loss averaged between 10 and 20 percent of the weight of the scrap.

[20] Engle et al. (1945, p. 215) presents comparable figures. The average total cost figure implies a considerable markup on cost of around 83 percent, whereas Alcoa's highest rate of return on investment over the sample period was in 1940 with a return of 19.4 percent (Engle et al. 1945, p. 124). The value of capital per unit of output is such that if the markup is reliable and its only activity is production of ingot, its rate of return should have been higher. Since the basis for the average markup is Alcoa's own records and testimony, a more likely explanation for the discrepancy is the dilution of Alcoa's overall rate of return through its engagement in competitive activities, such as aluminum fabrication, etc., for which a far lower average rate of return could be expected.

TABLE 1

PREDICTED SERVICE PRICES OF ALUMINUM INGOT AND PERCENTAGE DEVIATION FROM ACTUAL PRICES, 1923–40

	MODEL*		
	i	ii	iii
$\eta_p = 2.322$, $c = 13.63$ (1923–40)			
p^c	13.63	13.63	12.45
p^m	24.62	24.62	...
p^a	22.63	23.55	23.42
Deviation of p^a from observed $p = 24.89$ (%)	− 9.07	− 5.37	− 5.89
ρ^c	...	...	13.70
ρ^m	...	...	22.41
ρ^a	...	...	21.94
Deviation of ρ^a from imputed $\rho = 23.055$ (%)	...	...	− 4.84
$.5\eta_p = 1.161$, $c = 13.63$ (1923–40)			
p^m	29.98	29.98	...
p^a	25.96	27.51	27.82
Deviation of p^a from observed $p = 24.89$ (%)	4.31	10.54	11.79
ρ^m	...	...	26.58
ρ^a	...	...	25.20
Deviation of ρ^a from imputed $\rho = 23.055$ (%)	...	...	9.30
$\eta_p = 2.322$, $c = 17.14$ (1934)			
p^m	26.37	26.37	...
p^a	24.51	25.60	25.64
Deviation of p^a from observed $p = 26.81$ (%)	− 8.58	− 4.51	− 4.36
ρ^m	...	...	23.96
ρ^a	...	...	23.62
Deviation of ρ^a from imputed $\rho = 24.48$ (%)	...	...	− 3.51

*Cents/lb.

price $\bar{\rho} = 23.0544$, equation (20) implies that the price intercept of the linear service demand equation is lower at $\alpha = 31.1224$. Solutions to models i and ii are found by solving quadratic equations in product price, p, and to model iii by a cubic equation.[21] The results are presented in table 1.

[21] The coefficients in ascending order of the three models of Alcoa's behavior, based on equations (7), (9), and (15), respectively, are:

i. $a_0 = -[\alpha + c(1 + r)(1 + \alpha k)]$; $a_1 = (2 + r)[1 + k(\alpha + c)]$; $a_2 = -(3 + r)k$.

ii. $a_0 = -[\alpha ck + (1 + r)(\alpha + c)]$; $a_1 = 2[1 + r + (\alpha + c)k]$; $a_2 = -3k$.

iii. $a_0 = -[\alpha(1 + r + ck) + (1 + r)^2 c]$; $a_1 = (1 + r)[2(1 + r) + 3ck] + 2\alpha k$;

$a_2 = -k[1.5ck + 4.5(1 + r)]$; $a_3 = 2k^2$.

The pure monopoly solution to i and ii is given by $p^m = 0.5(\alpha + c)$ so long as the scrap price $\phi = 0.5kc^2$ is just sufficient to cover scavenging cost, while the pure monopoly solution to iii, (18), is $\rho^m = 0.5[\alpha + c(1 + r - 0.5kc^2)]$.

The upper portion of the table takes the best available parameter values for the interwar sample period and shows that the nonprice discriminatory models ii and iii give roughly the same degree of underprediction of Alcoa's mean price with about a 5 percent error. Model i, which permits dynamic price discrimination, predicts an even lower price and therefore does not do as well. A slightly lower elasticity value, η_p, a higher virgin cost, c, or a lower recycling parameter, k, would each have tended to improve the predictive performance of each of the models. In fact, all three models are supportive of Hand's decision in that the predicted price charged by Alcoa, p^a or ρ^a, is only slightly below the predicted pure monopoly price, p^m or ρ^m, but is well above the purely competitive price, p^c or ρ^c, based on the company's own cost records.[22] Virgin's market share in the pure monopoly and purely competitive cases is $1 - kc = 81$ percent and falls to $1 - kp^a = 67.3$ percent on the basis of model iii's predicted price. Thus, starting from a situation of pure monopoly, any procompetitive effect of competitive production of secondary is largely offset by a contraction in the output of virgin with very little reduction in product price.

The middle section of table 1 examines the effect of halving the observed product price elasticity. All three models now overpredict, and, as one would expect, model i displays the least amount of overprediction. The final section of table 1 investigates the ability of all three models to predict individual year values, although being steady-state solutions they are not really designed for this purpose. In 1934 there occurred the highest value of real virgin cost, c, which exceeded the mean value by nearly 26 percent. Model iii performed

[22] Some authors seem to have rejected Hand's reasoning on a priori grounds without need for empirical evidence either for or against. For example, Singer (1968, p. 47) seems to deny the relevance of Hand's argument based on indirect control and instead states that "the proper test . . . should have been whether Alcoa had actual control over the prices or output of the approximately fifty firms on the secondary aluminum market." His failure to entirely endorse Hand's reasoning is perhaps surprising since he, himself, takes an even stronger position when the same problem reappears in a slightly different guise. Singer (1968, pp. 206–8) argues that a monopoly with control over an input into some further process has no incentive to integrate forward in order to extract all the monopoly rents. Had he relaxed his simplifying assumption of a fixed input-output coefficient, he would no doubt have realized that the proposition is false whenever there are input substitution possibilities. Clearly, Singer's direct control is not necessary since indirect control via the supply of virgin is all that is required. Interestingly enough, at one stage Alcoa appears to have tried to obtain direct control. In the years 1922–25, Alcoa purchased considerable quantities of scrap, and some sales of ingot were conditional on the sale of scrap back to the company. In 1923 Alcoa purchased between 10 and 25 percent of available scrap, but subsequently its share was less than 10 percent (see Wallace 1937, pp. 456–57). Perhaps Alcoa came to a realization that a high scrap price was counterproductive in that it would exacerbate the problem of excessive scavenging, and perhaps also the company recognized that competitive recycling posed no real threat to its monopoly position.

marginally better than model ii in its ability to predict the observed price in that year.

The empirical evidence, for what it is worth, suggests that the main effect of the inability of Alcoa to exclude the competitive recycling sector was a bias in industry product mix toward secondary aluminum with a consequent social loss arising from production inefficiency. There is virtually no effect on price or total output, so that the gain to consumers from competitive recycling appears relatively small. The empirical results cannot really enable one to distinguish between the two hypotheses: scrap is discarded as in model ii or scrap is sold directly to merchants as in model iii. However, the results do suggest that the dynamic price-discrimination hypothesis, model i, does relatively poorly; but this may not be a fair test since the results are predicated on the assumption that the aluminum market during the interwar period was in long-run equilibrium.

Conclusion

Many economists as well as lay people are skeptical of the ability, or even the desire, of firms to employ marginal analysis and to maximize profits. If this is true of simple nondurable products, it is ever so much more likely in aluminum where the corresponding aim is to maximize the present value of net cash flows. The nature of the competitive recycling response to Alcoa's price of virgin ingot puts a premium on the firm's ability to plan ahead. Consequently, one is pleasantly surprised when models of Alcoa, which embody extreme assumptions such as perfect foresight, are shown to be capable of conforming to reality reasonably closely with respect to the crucial matter of price. This, however, is just an added bonus to the main theoretical and empirical results which provide some measure of one's confidence in Hand's decision in his famous 1945 judgment. It has required an approach which embodies Hand's insight into the nature of aluminum ingot as a capital asset and also a knowledge of parameter values which are derived from econometric investigation.

One of the most interesting results to emerge is the important role of the price of scrap as the nexus between past and future uses of aluminum, as long as scrap is sold rather than discarded by the original purchaser of aluminum products. A high sale price for scrap increases the price that users of aluminum are willing to pay for the original product, whereas this demand-boosting effect is lacking if scrap is simply discarded. Hence, Alcoa should be more sympathetic toward the competitive recycling market the more likely it is that scrap will be sold by the original purchaser. Thus, one would expect that Alcoa would favor routine reprocessing of "new" scrap from aluminum fabrication plants and elsewhere but would look with disfavor upon collection drives for discarded beer cans, etc.

In the case in which scrap is sold by the original purchasers, Alcoa would prefer controls on the rate of recovery in recycling which would equate marginal recycling costs to virgin costs. In this way, a social loss resulting from an overextended recycling sector is converted, at least partially, into monopoly rents.

If scrap is discarded by the original purchasers and price discrimination is not possible, consumers will be indifferent to any fixed rate of recovery in the recycling sector. Consumers would be in opposition, however, to any move by Alcoa to prevent substitution between scrap and other inputs into secondary aluminum so as to generate a fixed rate of recovery. Once scrap is no longer discarded, the consumer attitude becomes less certain. Although it does not appear to be empirically relevant, it is theoretically possible that consumers could gain if Alcoa dictated to the recycling sector and assumed the mantle of a complete monopolist.

References

Adams, Walter. "The Aluminum Case: Legal Victory, Economic Defeat." *A.E.R.* 41 (December 1951): 915–22.

Benjamin, Daniel K., and Kormendi, Roger C. "Interrelationship between Markets for New and Used Durable Goods." *J. Law and Econ.* 17 (October 1974): 381–401.

Burstein, M. L. "A Theory of Full-Line Forcing." *Northwestern Univ. Law Rev.* 55 (February 1960): 62–95.

Engle, Nathanael H.; Gregory, Homer E.; and Mossé, Robert. *Aluminum: An Industrial Marketing Appraisal.* Chicago: Irwin, 1945.

Fisher, Franklin M. *A Priori Information and Time Series Analysis: Essays in Economic Theory and Measurement.* Amsterdam: North-Holland, 1962.

Friedman, Milton. *Price Theory.* 1st ed., 1962; Chicago: Aldine, 1976.

Gaskins, Darius W., Jr. "Alcoa Revisited: The Welfare Implications of a Secondhand Market." *J. Econ. Theory* 7 (March 1974): 254–71.

Hay, George A. "An Economic Analysis of Vertical Integration." *Indus. Org. Rev.* 1 (1973): 188–98.

McKenzie, Lionel W. "Ideal Output and the Interdependence of Firms." *Econ. J.* 61 (December 1951): 785–803.

Mallela, P., and Nahata, B. "Theory of Vertical Control with Variable Proportions." Mimeographed. DeKalb: Northern Illinois Univ., Dept. Econ., 1978.

Mason, T. "The Effects of Entry: A Study of the American Aluminum Industry." Ph.D. dissertation, Univ. Pittsburgh, 1972.

Massel, Benton F., and Parish, Ross M. "Empty Bottles." *J.P.E.* 76, no. 6 (November/December 1968): 1224–33.

Miller, H. Laurence, Jr. "On Killing Off the Market for Used Textbooks and the Relationship between Markets for New and Secondhand Goods." *J.P.E.* 82, no. 3 (May/June 1974): 612–19.

Pagan, Adrian. "A Generalised Approach to the Treatment of Autocorrelation." *Australian Econ. Papers* 13, no. 23 (December 1974): 267–80.

Peck, Merton J. *Competition in the Aluminum Industry, 1945–1958*. Cambridge, Mass.: Harvard Univ. Press, 1961.

Perry, Martin K. "Vertical Integration: The Monopsony Case." *A.E.R.* 68, no. 4 (September 1978): 561–70.

Schmalensee, Richard. "A Note on the Theory of Vertical Integration." *J.P.E.* 81, no. 2, pt. 1 (March/April 1973): 442–49.

———. "Market Structure, Durability, and Maintenance Effort." *Rev. Econ. Studies* 41 (April 1974): 277–87.

Sieper, E., and Swan, P. L. "Monopoly and Competition in the Market for Durable Goods." *Rev. Econ. Studies* 40 (July 1973): 333–51.

Singer, Eugene M. *Antitrust Economics: Selected Legal Cases and Economic Models*. Englewood Cliffs, N.J.: Prentice Hall, 1968.

Su, Teddy T. "Durability of Consumption Goods: Reconsidered." *A.E.R.* 65, no. 1 (March 1975): 148–57.

Swan, Peter L. "Optimum Durability, Second-Hand Markets, and Planned Obsolescence." *J.P.E.* 80, no. 3, pt. 1 (May/June 1972): 575–85.

Urban, Raymond, and Mancke, Richard B. "Federal Regulation of Whisky Labelling: From the Repeal of Prohibition to the Present." *J. Law and Econ.* 15, no. 2 (October 1972): 411–26.

Vernon, John M., and Graham, Daniel A. "Profitability of Monopolization by Vertical Integration." *J.P.E.* 79, no. 4 (July/August 1971): 924–25.

Wallace, Donald H. *Market Control in the Aluminum Industry*. Cambridge, Mass.: Harvard Univ. Press, 1937.

Warren-Boulton, Frederick R. "Vertical Control with Variable Proportions." *J.P.E.* 82, no. 4 (July/August 1974): 783–802.

———. "Vertical Control by Labor Unions." *A.E.R.* 67, no. 3 (June 1977): 309–22.

A Reconsideration of Taxi Regulation

EDWARD C. GALLICK
Federal Trade Commission

DAVID E. SISK
San Francisco State University

In this paper we offer an explanation of how the regulatory enforcement of an average pricing rule for taxi services, which has been frequently observed throughout the history of taxi cabs,[1] can reduce exchange costs and promote efficiency. We further argue that in the modern era, the taxi medallion system became a useful and perhaps necessary institutional arrangement for enforcing average pricing rules. We do not claim that markets for taxi services cannot exist in the absence of regulation and medallions, but only that under certain circumstances, average pricing regulation, enforced by a medallion system, may promote efficiency. Finally, we discuss alternative institutional arrangements for enforcing average pricing.

1. AVERAGE PRICING

Each taxicab ride is a relatively unique service. The cost of providing a ride, ignoring the comfort or style of travel, will be a function of distance, duration,

We would like to thank Ronald Bond, John Hilke, Pauline Ippolito, Robert Mackay, and Douglas Webbink for comments on earlier drafts, and Daniel Alger, Rudy Gonzalez, Edward Mansfield, and Stephen Mehay for helpful discussions on the subject. The editors of this journal have provided us with very helpful suggestions. The analyses and conclusions set forth are those of the authors and do not necessarily reflect the views of the Bureau of Economics, other Commission staff, or the FTC itself.

1. A brief and interesting history of taxicabs is given in Gilbert and Samuels, chap. 2. The remainder of the book provides a survey of taxicabs and regulations in the United States. Interesting episodes of taxi regulation are given in Turvey; Eckert; and Kitch et al.

Journal of Law, Economics, and Organization vol. 3, no. 1 Spring 1987
 ISSN 8756–6222.

and destination. Duration is only partially a function of distance, depending also on road and traffic conditions. Destination is distinct from distance and duration because the probability of obtaining a return fare varies with the location. For example, a thirty-mile trip to a thinly populated suburb has a high probability that the taxi will return empty; whereas a thirty-mile trip to the airport has a low probability that the taxi will return empty. The expected cost to the driver of these two equidistant trips will therefore vary dramatically. Consequently, the competitive price of a particular trip will be difficult to estimate in advance. Riders would have to search out offers from multiple drivers before accepting a ride. Likewise, drivers might search for the most valuable riders, avoiding queues or other situations where riders could cheaply weigh alternative offers. Given that the demand by riders is generally for immediate service, the aggregate search performed by riders and drivers would tend to be extremely costly.

The search requirements of a purely competitive (unregulated) taxi market would clearly limit the extent of exchange. In order to evaluate the efficiency of this search, alternative arrangements must be weighed. We suggest here that the gathering of information in the taxi market described above is highly redundant[2] and that there is at least one possible alternative institutional arrangement which reduces excessive search costs but does not destroy valuable information. We further suggest that observed taxi regulation approximates this arrangement.

Average pricing may be used to reduce redundant search. If price is somehow set on the basis of distance, so that equidistant trips are uniformly priced, then riders could cheaply estimate the price of any particular trip without searching among alternative drivers. However, since trips of equal distance and duration will imply differing probabilities of finding a return fare, trips with the same price will impose different costs on drivers. If all drivers accepted trips randomly, then over the long run all would tend to earn the same rate of return, losing on some high-cost trips and gaining on low-cost trips. As a consequence, even though all drivers might agree to an average pricing arrangement, each has an incentive to cheat, increasing his profits by acquiring a disproportionate share of low-cost trips.[3] Nor would it be possible for a single firm to offer average pricing. In this case, customers would opt for that firm for the high-cost, underpriced trips and turn to other firms, which

2. It is highly redundant, we argue, because drivers will have similar costs for any particular trip and customers have no special preference among different cabs. There would therefore be no social gain from the aggregate search performed by all potential drivers relative to the one search by the driver who ultimately won the trip. While these search activities consume real resources, they represent wealth transfers between drivers and riders with no allocative effects. For a discussion of oversearch activities in the marketing of tuna, see Gallick. Kenney and Klein analyze oversearching in the wholesale marketing of rough uncut diamonds.

3. Such a disproportionate share of low-cost trips could be gained either by queueing or by secret price cutting similar to that occurring under collusive agreements (Stigler). In private contracting situations average pricing combined with block booking arrangements appears to be viable (see Kenney and Klein; and Gallick).

did not use average pricing, for lower-cost trips. The inability of private contracting to effectively establish average pricing leads us to believe that a third-party enforcer or regulatory authority can serve efficiently in the taxi market.[4]

We do not intend to imply that a taxi market cannot exist in the absence of regulatory enforcement of an average pricing scheme, but rather that in some circumstances regulation can increase the number and variety of taxi trips by reducing search costs. Clearly, search costs will vary in importance among different types of trips and different types of customers. Regulation will tend to be more valuable for heterogeneous trips within areas of relatively high density, when time is costly,[5] and when it is easy for taxis to queue for low-cost trips.[6] Also, note that where governmental institutions are less developed or relatively corrupt, intervention is less likely to be successful, customers and drivers are less likely to appeal to government for assistance, and regulation is less likely to be observed.

2. AVERAGE PRICE REGULATION

Regulatory intervention to establish a single price or price schedule appears to be the historical standard in many taxi markets.[7] Prior to the development of the mileage meter, the price was often fixed for some central or downtown area but was negotiable for trips outside this area. Clearly, within the fixed price area, shorter trips would be overpriced and longer trips underpriced; however, such average pricing reduced search costs. As the fixed price area becomes larger, increasing distance and incorporating suburbs of lower density, the disparity in profitability between short and long trips within the area will become greater, causing shorter-distance riders to drop out of the market. This loss of ridership must be weighed against the gains to reduced search costs made possible by a fixed price.

4. For a more elaborate analytical development of the search and sorting costs caused by heterogeneity, see Gallick and Sisk.

5. Kitch et al. (309) reports that while taxis in Chicago were regulated, livery services were exempted. The absence of regulation is understandable, since livery services were arranged in advance, not at the spur of the moment, so time costs provided relatively little constraint on search and negotiation.

6. In 1979 Amtrak, for example, switched from a single franchise taxi service for the railroad station to open entry. Long lines developed, drivers loitered in the station in search of riders, and independent drivers clashed with the lower-priced (major) taxi fleets. More severe problems were observed at the Seattle-Tacoma airport. Customers complained about the differences in rates quoted by competing drivers (Zerbe, 1983a and 1983b). Zerbe (1983b) suggests that protests over the fare discrepancies rather than the amount of the fare indicate that customers would pay a premium to have uniform rates. Yet the market was unable to determine a uniform pricing scheme.

7. The following historical generalizations are based on the literature cited here. We especially recommend Gilbert and Samuels for an introduction into the institutional background and the wide variety of business practices in taxi markets.

After the turn of the nineteenth century, the development and introduction of the mileage meter caused a change in the basis for price regulation from areas to mileage. The meter generally worked to provide a minimum fee for picking up a passenger plus some fee per mile. Modern meters are also adjusted to partially compensate for time so that slower trips have a somewhat higher price per mile. Clearly, this system of average pricing allows a finer sorting of trips. Each distance is in a different category and to some extent the categories are adjusted for time as well. Nonetheless, the problem of destination remains: trips of equal distance and duration are not equally profitable if the destination differs in the probability of obtaining a return rider.

A regulated average price creates two malincentives and requires two complementary regulations that, from historical observation, also appear to be standard. The first malincentive results from the fact that with average pricing some trips are profitable and some unprofitable. This provides an incentive for drivers to reject unprofitable trips and to queue for profitable trips. It is not surprising therefore that one regulation that has generally accompanied taxi regulation is the requirement to haul all customers.[8] A second malincentive arises because regulators must set price based on the average costs of taxi operation. A driver can thus increase profits by lowering the quality of taxi services (for example, employing a small or deteriorated vehicle, reducing insurance coverage, or driving recklessly). This practice will be viable because regulated pricing reduces rider search. If riders were negotiating price on each trip and thus taking alternative bids from multiple taxis, they could simultaneously value some aspects of vehicle quality. Given that regulation reduces the need to search for price, the value of searching solely for vehicle quality is not likely to be worth the cost. As a consequence, vehicle standards regulation must be established to complement average price regulation.

It is important to note that given the two complementary regulations, it was sufficient for the regulatory authority to set a single price. In effect, the

8. The transaction costs of negotiating an alternative agreement whereby the driver promises to accept all trips by the rider within a given time period appear to be prohibitively high. An example where exclusive supply contracts reduce excessive search in the marketing of U.S. landed tuna is provided in Gallick (chap. 2). Each harvest is initially inspected, sorted, and weighed at the processor's dock. The captain is paid on the basis of the weight and specie of the catch. Although larger fish are more valuable because they require less processing time, U.S. landed tuna are not sorted by size (except for unusually small fish, which were also illegal until mid-1970). Rather than sort the catch into numerous size categories (as done in Japanese markets), U.S. harvests are sold as "run-of-the-catch." Exclusive dealing arrangements prevent the captain from searching out the larger, more valuable tunas within each category and offering them to a competing processor. Additional search costs are thereby avoided by determining a single price for each category (specie) based on the average value of all tunas within the category. Similarly in the marketing of rough diamonds, the central selling organization of the De Beers group pays independent mineowners on the basis of the number of stones provided per classification, the variance in value within each category notwithstanding. The exclusive supply requirement (in addition to controlling total supply) prevents the producer from searching out the higher valued stones within each category for sale in the open market (see Kenney and Klein: 500–02).

regulated price serves the function of both a maximum and a minimum. Jointly requiring owners to haul all customers and maintain vehicle quality ensures that, if the average price is regulated at a level that offers a normal rate of return, a taxi service which was priced below the regulated price would be unprofitable. In this sense, the regulated price is a minimum.[9] At the same time, the regulated price is a maximum in the sense that it prohibits drivers from setting fares in excess of cost.

3. THE INTRODUCTION OF MEDALLIONS

Historically, campaigns to introduce medallion systems began after World War I, when the availability of the inexpensive, mass-produced automobile began to wreak havoc on existing taxi regulations. Prior to that time, average pricing rules and requirements to haul were enforced without medallion systems. This has been taken as evidence that medallion systems were introduced solely to blockade entry. However, this view fails to take account of the fact that, prior to medallion systems, occupational licensing restricted entry and average pricing rules were enforced. We believe that it was the technological change in automobiles that necessitated a change in the mechanism of regulatory enforcement from *occupational* licensing to *vehicle* licensing, in the form of medallions.

Coaches and vehicles used as taxis in the earlier era were specialized vehicles. They represented (on an industry level) nonsalvageable production assets designed and built to serve in the taxi trade. The difference between the purchase price and the immediate resale price of the taxi is a sunk cost. This capital element in the production of taxi service appears to be significant since (outside the taxi industry) such vehicles had few alternative uses other than serving as privately chauffered vehicles for the wealthy, a very thin market.[10] It is on this basis that we believe taxis represented industry-specific assets.[11] A substantial reduction in the return to such specialized assets would likely

9. It is not surprising that in the Chicago market, a price minimum was imposed within a few years after the introduction of the medallion system. Although Kitch and his coauthors interpret the enactment of a minimum price regulation as evidence that the medallion system was a monopolizing device, our explanation suggests an efficiency motivation.

10. In addition, the cost of continuing possession could also be substantial. That is, in addition to the initial acquisition (sunk) cost, the difference between the value of the taxicab now and the present value of its resale value in the future (for example, at the end of one year) is likely to be significant. This is based on three underlying factors: (1) taxi drivers are notorious for abusing their taxis; (2) the institution of used-car dealers did not exist; and (3) the market for taxi repairs was not well developed. If the cost of continuing possession falls sharply in the early years and then declines more gradually, the cost of continuing to own a taxi may exceed the depreciation allowance implicit in the (regulated) price of taxi service. Consequently, the taxi owner may incur another cost if he sells his taxi within the first few years of possession.

The distinction between the costs of acquisition, continuing possession, and operating are explained and illustrated by Alchian and Allen (287–90).

11. If the ability of the driver to resell his taxi to another driver is restricted, however, the taxi becomes a firm-specific asset.

result if they were switched to a use outside the taxi industry. It was therefore not a vehicle that could cheaply move in and out of the taxi business, but a driver.

Thus, the specialized nature of the taxi was a necessary but insufficient condition for regulatory enforcement. Although the taxi could not be costlessly moved out of the industry, it could be resold within the industry. Without additional regulations on the taxi or the driver, therefore, the driver could avoid regulation by selling his taxi to another driver and exiting the industry.

Given the industry-specific nature of the taxi in the days prior to the mass production of the automobile, the effectiveness of regulatory enforcement also depended on the ability to penalize drivers who cheated on their contractual commitments with the regulatory authority. Contractual performance on the part of the drivers was assured through the institution of occupational licensing. In some instances, the license required up to one year of study and apprenticeship. Thus, suspension or revocation of the license effectively impounded the investment (implicit in the license) and imposed losses on the driver. Moreover, rules could be enforced because taxi firms were easily identifiable and drivers who continued to work could be easily located.

Consequently, taxi drivers could not enter the business on a short-term basis. If fined by the regulators for infractions of the rules, they would likely pay the fine in order to remain in operation. If serious infractions caused their right to operate to be revoked entirely, they would suffer a nontrivial loss. As long as this loss equalled or exceeded the present value of the gains from violating a regulation, serious infractions were unlikely to occur.

The introduction of the mass-produced automobile and the widespread use of automobiles as a means of personal conveyance seriously undermined the effectiveness of the prevailing system of regulatory enforcement. One consequence of the technological change was to dramatically reduce the degree of nonsalvageable production assets in the provision of taxi service. One principal use of the modern automobile was for personal transportation. Anyone who owned an automobile for personal use could almost costlessly use the vehicle as a taxi. Conversely, the owner of a modern taxi could easily sell the vehicle for personal use. Given the high-valued alternative uses of the modern taxi, it no longer represented an industry-specific asset. Consequently, it became less costly for *unlicensed* drivers to enter the market. If caught by the regulators, the vehicle could be shifted into another use at little, or no, cost.

Thus, the regulatory enforcement problem in the modern period was not that licensed drivers violated taxi regulations more frequently, but rather, the dramatic increase in firms that could cheaply enter or exit any given taxi market. Anyone who owned or who had access to a car could now enter the market surreptitiously. Unless regulators stopped each vehicle and checked identification, it was impossible to tell whether a particular vehicle and its driver were legitimately engaged in the taxi business. Moreover, even if an unauthorized driver were discovered, the regulatory authority could no longer impose a loss by suspending the right to operate: neither the driver nor the vehicle represented a specialized asset. Thus, the technological change reduced the effectiveness of occupational licensure.

The ultimate effect was to increase serious infractions of existing regulations. Vehicles serviceable as taxis were now owned by large numbers of people whose primary source of income was outside the taxi industry. It became possible then for those unlicensed drivers to enter and exit the market rapidly. Such hit-and-run entry could occur at peak hours and on the more profitable routes, undercutting the regulated average price. The likely outcome of this situation was the collapse of the efficiency-based regulations requiring that all customers be served and that a uniform price (a fixed price per mile) be charged. Taxis attempting to obey these rules would now be at a competitive disadvantage relative to the hit-and-run entrants.

The campaigns of professional cab associations for vehicle licensing during the late 1920s were a direct response to the disruption in the market created by hit-and-run entrants. Of course, this does not imply that the campaigns for entry restriction were motivated by concern for the public well-being. No doubt these efforts were an attempt to protect and enhance the wealth of member drivers, but it is a standard economic proposition that selfish efforts may indeed provide net social benefits in some circumstances.

4. HOW MEDALLION SYSTEMS WORK

Contrary to much received economic analysis, the taxi medallion does not represent a perfect private property right to enter the market and operate a taxi but is part of an explicit contract with the regulatory authority. A conditional right to enter and to operate a taxi is granted by the taxi authority in exchange for (1) a commitment from the owner to obey the existing taxi regulations; and (2) the right of the taxi authority to suspend the right of the taxi to be operated if the driver is found in violation of a regulation. If the owner is found in violation, the taxi cannot be operated for a period of time as determined by the regulatory authority. The owner does not have the option to employ another driver and thereby continue to operate the taxi. The medallion system of enforcement therefore restricts the use of the taxi and indirectly limits the behavior of the driver.[12]

Moreover, regulatory authorities generally restrict the number of medallions by issuing new medallions periodically on the basis of ridership, population, profitability, and other demand-related indexes. By maintaining these indexes constant, the quality of service and the real value of the medallion can be held constant over the long run. For example, if ridership increases, so does profitability, and thus the value of owning a medallion increases. By

12. The driver will be assumed to be the owner unless otherwise indicated.

issuing new medallions, ridership and profitability are reduced, and the market value of a medallion declines toward its original level.

The medallion serves as collateral offered by the taxi driver to assure that he will comply with the regulations established within a jurisdiction. In this sense, the medallion is like a brand-name capital asset. The owner of the medallion can expect to earn a normal return on his investment as long as he does not violate his contractual commitments (that is, any of the regulations in the jurisdiction). The competitive return is generated by the higher average price that will prevail due to restricted entry.

Under the medallion system, suspension of the right to operate the taxi imposes a cost on the owner. Consider the following example. Let the current market value of the taxi and the medallion be $15,000 and $50,000, respectively. A one-month suspension without a medallion requirement would simply remove the taxi from the market for the month and the owner could seek to employ the taxi in its next best use. At a 10 percent rate of return, the foregone earnings on the taxi (valued at $15,000) would equal $125 per month.

The cost of the suspension would be somewhat less if the taxi could be employed in another use, as is often the case. However, if a medallion (valued at $50,000) was required to operate a taxi, the additional cost of the one-month suspension would be $417 per month.

In our example, the medallion requirement increased the penalty from $125 to $542 per month, an increase of over 300 percent. Thus, the medallion requirement allows the regulatory authority to appropriate some of the return to the medallion and thereby to impose a larger fine within a given time period.[13]

It is a major feature of the system that the income of medallion owners depends on the number of medallioned taxis in the market. Medallion owners have an incentive to prevent entry by nonmedallioned vehicles and to enforce the suspension of a medallioned taxi, reporting a driver operating a taxi without a valid medallion. If fines were used in place of medallions, enforcement would be more difficult. If operators were fined for violations, it would be difficult for them to pay the fines without operating their taxis to gain the ability to pay the fines. If fined drivers were then legally able to work, other drivers would have no incentive to help the regulatory authority impose sanctions. The medallion system circumvents this issue of ability to pay by attaching the driver's assets rather than by demanding payment out of current income.

13. The alternative of longer suspensions of the taxi from operation may tend to disrupt consumer service and the revocation of the medallion may represent too extreme an action to be utilized as a regular practice. In fact, the emergence of brokers who deal in medallions may act to protect medallion owners from unscrupulous regulators.

5. TWO OTHER REGULATORY SYSTEMS

We have argued that in the modern era medallion systems are useful in assisting regulatory enforcement of average pricing. We do not wish to assert that there are no alternatives to medallion systems. Practical alternatives include the closely related system in London and the zone system of Washington, D.C.

Turvey reports that the London taxi trade regulates fares and requires that all customers be accepted, yet no medallion system exists. However, we think that the requirement that all taxis have a turning radius shorter than that of the standard assembly-line automobile closely approximates a medallion system. The shorter turning radius evidently adds substantially to the cost of the taxi and to the costs of entry into (and exit from) the taxi market. Because there is no demand for this feature outside the industry, an owner whose license is suspended does not have an alternative use for this attribute of his vehicle. The turning-radius regulation appears to have created a nonsalvageable production asset. Earning a normal rate of return on this asset requires that the vehicle be used in the taxi trade. It also serves to identify vehicles in the industry and assists in the exclusion of nonregulated vehicles. That is. it serves the same function as does the medallion. The major difference is that the real resource cost of the medallion is far less than the real resource cost of building a special vehicle. We thus find that the medallion system is superior.

In the Washington, D.C., area, zoning is used instead of the medallion system. The region is divided into geographic zones and the price is set on the basis of the pick-up and drop-off zones (within a zone, a trip is a fixed price and an additional charge may be added each time a zone boundary is crossed). By varying zone size, trips can be finely sorted. For instance, if zones are made smaller for low-density areas, then a driver will cross more zones when taking a rider to such a destination and will be compensated for the lower probability of finding a return fare.

The zone system is a variation of the kind of regulation that existed prior to the introduction of the mileage meter, when the market tended to be divided into two zones: a central area where a single price predominated, regardless of distance covered within the area, and an outer area for which trip price was negotiated. Obviously that was a type of average pricing, since in the central area trips were of different length and therefore of different profitability. The Washington, D.C., zone system simply divides the jurisdiction into additional smaller areas, and within each area a single price prevails. The smaller the single-price area, the smaller will be any differences in trip profitability, and the less incentive there will be for hit-and-run entry by unlicensed taxis or queueing for the more profitable trips by licensed drivers. A medallion system of entry restriction is therefore of relatively less use. Whether or not the zone system is superior to the medallion system is not clear. In the zone system, small deviations in routes may increase the number of zones crossed and thus increase price substantially. For the nonlocal customer such deviations would be difficult to detect. The significance of this problem cannot be determined without further empirical investigation.

6. HYPOTHETICAL ALTERNATIVES

Clearly, if one could discover alternatives to the medallion system which serve the same purpose but do not restrict entry, then the medallion system would be suspect. We will limit our attention to three major alternative arrangements to enforce average pricing: franchising, licensing, and bonding.

In the case of franchising, one can imagine a nationwide service, on the order of McDonald's, providing taxi service in all large cities. Such a franchise operation would allow local providers to operate under a nationally known trademark and to share the reputation of the national firm. Out-of-town riders, unfamiliar with the local area, would recognize competing names and reputations, whereas they would be less knowledgeable about the reputations of strictly local firms. Cheating by local operators would induce customers to withdraw business from the entire chain. Thus the potential loss imposed on the chain by the withdrawal of future business is greater than for a local firm with little or no reputation.[14] While this would undoubtedly induce greater reliability of service in regard to some product attributes,[15] it would not be adequate to assure average pricing. If the firm voluntarily introduced average pricing, and effectively enforced this among its franchisees, customers would simply go to the franchisees for the underpriced trips and go to other firms that did not average price to avoid the franchisees' overpriced trips.

Next, consider the possibility of licensing *all* firms[16] that wanted to enter and suspending or revoking the license for infractions of the average pricing rule. Since in the modern era neither automobiles nor driving skills are specific to the industry, revoking the license of an unbranded firm violating the average price rule could not impose losses equal to the short-run gain from cheating. And fines would be hard to collect from firms that exited, since those firms (or operators) would be difficult to locate and the damages from individual violations would be small relative to the costs of litigation.

14. A model of how a market enforcement mechanism can assure contract performance is presented in Klein and Leffler. The general theory is applied to franchise tie-in contracts in Klein and Saft.

15. Once committed to a particular taxi, the rider may be subject to opportunistic behavior by the driver. During off-peak hours the driver may find it advantageous to reduce waiting time between customers by taking passengers on circuitous routes. Passengers unfamiliar with local routes are more vulnerable to such behavior; hence the advantage of a nationally known reputation (see Klein, Crawford, and Alchian; Klein; and Williamson, chap. 2).

Either franchising or regulation is likely to be superior to litigation, which would be costly relative to the damages involved. Tipping may also have some use in constraining this type of behavior (see Sisk and Gallick).

16. Again, we are assuming that the driver is the owner of a single cab.

Another hypothetical possibility is the requirement that all entrants post a bond. While this would entail a greater capital requirement than entry in a free market, it need not restrict entry. Rather, suppose bonded firms would receive the interest on the bond so long as they conformed to the average pricing rule. Violations of the rule could then be penalized either with temporary suspension of interest payments or loss of the entire bond. If the interest payment were equal to what could be earned elsewhere, there would be no opportunity cost to posting the bond, and entry would thus not be restricted.

The medallion system is very similar to bonding. There is, however, one major difference. Wealth held in the form of a medallion, which serves as collateral to be forfeited for violations, earns no interest. Rather the return to the medallion comes in the form of an increased average fare, brought about by entry restriction. Such a restriction would not be necessary under a bond system, although administering the system might be costly. A fundamental disadvantage of a bond system, however, is that it creates a malincentive for regulators to behave opportunistically by imposing penalties merely to collect the interest accruing on suspended or forfeited bonds.

7. CONCLUDING REMARKS

Most economists have viewed medallions simply as barriers to entry without any socially desirable function. Such a conclusion ignores the importance of average price regulation in taxi markets. We have argued that average price regulation can in some circumstances significantly reduce exchange costs. Indeed, average price regulation has been commonplace throughout the history of taxi services. It appears that the development of the inexpensive, mass-produced automobile led to the breakdown of average price regulation and initiated the campaigns of professional drivers for medallion systems. Such systems, we argue, have served to enforce average price regulation.

Economists have generally recommended the abolition of medallion systems or lamented the impossibility of abolition. Our conclusion leads us to believe that if medallion systems are to be abolished, an alternative mechanism of enforcement should be found. We believe that a bonding arrangement may represent a superior alternative if regulators can be prevented from behaving opportunistically.

REFERENCES

Alchian, Armen A., and William R. Allen. 1969. *Exchange and Production: Theory in Use*. Belmont: Wadsworth.

Eckert, Ross E. 1970. "The Los Angeles Taxi Monopoly: An Economic Inquiry," 43 *University of Southern California Law Review* 407.

Gallick, Edward C. 1984. *Exclusive Dealing and Vertical Integration: The Efficiency of Contracts in the Tuna Industry*. Washington, D.C.: Federal Trade Commission.

———, and David E. Sisk. 1984. *Specialized Assets and Taxi Regulation: An Inquiry into the Possible Efficiency Motivation of Regulation*. Washington, D.C.: Federal Trade Commission.

Gilbert, Gorman, and Robert E. Samuels. 1982. *The Taxicab: An Urban Transportation Survivor*. Chapel Hill: University of North Carolina Press.

Kenney, Roy W., and Benjamin Klein. 1983. "The Economics of Block Booking," 26 *Journal of Law and Economics* 497.

Kitch, Edmund W., Marc Isaacson, and Daniel Kasper. 1971. "The Regulation of Taxicabs in Chicago," 14 *Journal of Law and Economics* 285.

Klein, Benjamin. 1980. "Transaction Cost Determinants of 'Unfair' Contractual Arrangements," 70 *American Economic Review* 356.

———, Robert G. Crawford, and Armen Alchian. 1978. "Vertical Integration, Appropriable Rents, and the Competitive Contracting Process," 21 *Journal of Law and Economics* 297.

———, and Keith B. Leffler. 1981. "The Role of Market Forces in Assuring Contractual Performance," 89 *Journal of Political Economy* 615.

———, and Lester F. Saft. 1985. "The Law and Economics of Franchise Tying Arrangements," 28 *Journal of Law and Economics* 345.

Stigler, George J. 1964. "A Theory of Oligopoly," 72 *Journal of Political Economy* 44.

Sisk, David E., and Edward C. Gallick. 1985. *Tips and Commissions; A Study in Economic Contracting*. Washington, D.C.: Federal Trade Commission.

Turvey, Ralph. 1960. "Some Features of the London Cab Trade," 81 *Economic Journal* 79.

Williamson, Oliver E. 1975. *Markets and Hierarchies: Analysis and Antitrust Implications*. New York: The Free Press.

Zerbe, Richard O. 1983a. "New Trips for Taxicabs: Deregulation in Seattle," *Washington Public Policy Notes II* 1.

——— 1983b. "Seattle Taxis: Deregulation Hits a Pothole," 7 *Regulation* 43.

The Lulling Effect: The Impact of Child-Resistant Packaging on Aspirin and Analgesic Ingestions

By W. KIP VISCUSI*

In 1972 the Food and Drug Administration imposed a protective bottlecap requirement on aspirin and other selected drugs. This regulation epitomizes the technological approach to social regulation. The strategy for reducing children's poisoning risks was to design caps that would make opening containers of hazardous substances more difficult. This engineering approach will be effective provided that children's exposure to hazardous products does not increase. If, however, parents leave protective caps off bottles because they are difficult to open, or increase children's access to these bottles because they are supposedly "child proof," the regulation may not have a beneficial effect.

Indeed, in this case there was no significant impact of the regulation on aspirin poisoning rates, but there has been an alarming, upward shift in the trend of analgesic ingestion rates since 1972. The source of this pattern appears to be attributable to a general reduction in parental caution with respect to such medicines, which has had an adverse spillover effect on unregulated products. The economic mechanisms involved can be best understood by considering the nature of individuals' response to regulatory protection.

I. The Lulling Effect: A Conceptual Analysis

One can distinguish three different mechanisms by which protective packaging requirements can lead to actions on the part of parents and their children that are at least potentially counterproductive. First, regulations will lead to a reduction in safety-related efforts for the affected product. Second, the regulation may produce misperceptions that lead consumers to reduce their safety precautions because they overestimate the product's safety. Finally, if there are indivisibilities in one's actions (for example, choosing whether to keep medicines in a bathroom cabinet or in the kitchen), regulating one product may affect the safety of other products. These effects are quite general and are not restricted to the case of protective bottlecaps.

The existing theoretical literature on individual responses to regulatory protection began with the analysis by Sam Peltzman (1975), who showed that seatbelts would lead to increased driving intensity (for example, less caution or higher speeds). The economic mechanism generating this effect is similar to that which produces adverse incentives or moral hazard problems in the insurance context. As one reduces either the probability of a loss or the size of the loss, individual incentives to take precautionary actions will be reduced. Regulations function much like insurance in this regard, with the only difference being that one need not pay an insurance premium. (There may, however, be an effect of the regulation on the product price.)

In my 1979 article, I derived a similar result for the case of worker safety for quite general classes of risk-averse preferences, where the safety measures also affected the wage rate. Except in the case of very stringently enforced government regulations, firms would not make technological changes in the workplace that were counterproductive. Compliance with policies such as seatbelt and bottlecap requirements is less discretionary, however, so one cannot rule out counter-

*Professor and Director, Center for Study of Business Regulation, Fuqua School of Business, Duke University, Durham, N.C. 27706. This research was supported by a grant from the National Science Foundation to the Center for Study of Business Regulation, Fuqua School of Business, Duke University. I am indebted to Robert Viscusi for insightful comments and to William Evans for able research assistance.

productive regulatory effects in these instances.

To investigate these effects more formally, consider a simple model that captures the essential features of these analyses. Let s be the stringency of the government policy and e be the precautionary effort, where each of these reduces the probability $p(e,s)$ of an accident at a diminishing rate. Alternatively, one can make the mechanism of influence the size of the accident loss L, as in Peltzman, but for purposes of this model I will make L a constant. The individual's effort e generates a disutility $V(e)$, where $V', V'' > 0$. Finally, let the person have an income level I.

The payoff in the case of an accident is $I - V(e) - L$, and the payoff if there is not an accident is $I - V(e)$. The individual's expected utility (assuming risk neutrality) is $I - V(e) - p(e,s)L$. In setting the optimal level of e, one equates the marginal reduction in the loss $p_e L$ to the marginal value of the effort $-V_e$, leading to the optimal point A in Figure 1.

The effect of the regulation on safety effort will be negative, or

$$\frac{de}{ds} = \frac{-p_{es}}{p_{ee}L + V_{ee}} < 0,$$

provided the $p_{es} > 0$ (or $L_{es} > 0$ in Peltzman's loss model). For safety efforts to decline, the safety regulation must reduce the marginal safety benefits from precautionary efforts, that is, the reduction in the expected loss from higher levels of effort is less negative than before. One will then choose a point to the left of point B on the EL_1 curve in Figure 1. This effect should not be particularly controversial. Few would question the opposite relationship where individuals increase their precautions when moving from EL_1 to EL_0. For example, one will drive more carefully on icy streets and reduce cigarette smoking if exposed to synergistic asbestos risks.

What is more problematic is whether the reduction in precautions will be so great that there will be a reduction in safety to a point to the left of point C on EL_1. The conditions

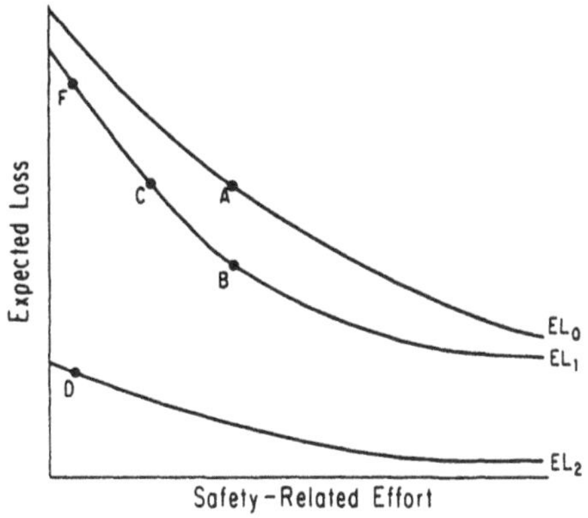

FIGURE 1. PRECAUTIONARY BEHAVIOR AND EXPECTED LOSSES

for this to occur have never been investigated and are quite stringent. It is not sufficient that the marginal expected loss reduction at point C be no greater than at A. The requirement is stronger since the marginal disutility of effort V_e will be lower at lower effort levels. To equate the marginal expected loss reduction $p_e L$ to the marginal effort cost $-V_e$, the loss curve EL_1 must be flatter at point C than EL_0 was at point A. Since there is the additional restriction that EL_1 lie below EL_0, it will be difficult to meet these requirements.

The chance that the impact of protective regulations may be counterproductive may be enhanced if individuals either do not perceive accurately the accident probabilities, or do not fully bear the accident costs. If parents assume "child-resistant" caps are child proof, they may overestimate the safety associated with these products. Similarly, since there is some evidence that individuals tend to set very small probabilities equal to zero, the safety-enhancing properties of caps may reduce the risk so much that parents ignore the poisoning risk. In each case, safety precautions will decline, perhaps to so great an extent that overall safety is reduced. For example, parents may select point D off of their perceived loss curve EL_2 in a situation where the true loss curve is EL_1 and the actual outcome is point F.

A similar effect could occur if parents do not fully value the welfare of their children, or if drivers do not fully internalize the accident costs to pedestrians and other parties. Unlike the case of biased probabilistic beliefs, this modification in the problem need not entail a shift in the relative values of the accident loss in the regulated and unregulated situations. Thus, the EL_0 and EL_1 curves may both simply shift proportionally. In contrast, misperceptions such as those discussed above necessarily lead to a comparatively greater downward shift in the perceived expected loss, increasing the chance of a counterproductive effect.

One's precautionary actions may affect the safety of unregulated products as well as those that are regulated. In the case of child-resistant bottlecaps, parents may make overall decisions regarding the storage of medicines. Should they keep all of the medicines in the bathroom cabinet, on a kitchen shelf, or in a safety-latched drawer? More generally, should they worry about access to medicines or undertake only a mild level of precautions, since the most hazardous products are presumably protected by child-resistant containers?

The analytics of this effort decision parallel that given above, where the only difference is that the EL_0 and EL_1 curves are a weighted average of the component risks, where some products are protected and others are not. A joint risk curve EL_1 will tend to shift downward less in response to a regulation than a comparable curve for a particular regulated product, since the presence of the unregulated product will dampen the response.

There is a clearcut empirical test of whether indivisible actions such as this play a role. If there are such spillover effects, the reduction in safety-enhancing efforts induced by the regulation should increase the risk posed by the unregulated product. In addition, the safety improvement of the regulated product will be reduced at least in part by the reduction in individual precautions. The net effect on safety could be adverse for the regulated product or for both products combined, but one must satisfy fairly stringent conditions for the net effect to be adverse unless misperceptions of the risk play a major role.

II. The Effect of Child-Resistant Bottlecaps

A widely touted product safety regulation success story is child-resistant bottlecaps. The first caps required under this regulation were for aspirin and selected drugs in 1972. Before the advent of protective packaging, manufacturers concentrated their efforts on measures such as decreasing the number of tablets per bottle, warning labels, and educational campaigns. Here I will summarize some of the results from my forthcoming study regarding the effectiveness of safety caps, which provides very strong evidence regarding the role of individual actions that differ in character from the seatbelt case (see Glenn Blomquist, forthcoming, for a review).

In 1971 aspirin was responsible for a fatal poisoning rate of 2.6 per million children under age 5, and by 1980 this rate had dropped to 0.6. The overall aspirin poisoning rate exhibited a similar drop, from 5.0 to 1.7 per 1,000. While these declines were dramatic, after taking into account the trend in aspirin poisonings and the decline in aspirin sales in the 1970's, there is no statistically significant impact of the regulation. This result was obtained using both a regulation dummy variable, which assumed a value of 1 in the 1972–80 period, and a variable that reflected the fraction of aspirin sold with safety cap bottles.

This fraction of capped bottles remained at just over half of all aspirin sold since firms were permitted to market one size of aspirin container without a child-resistant cap. Typically, firms chose the best selling size (the 100-tablet bottle).

Despite the constant sales share of safety capped aspirin, there has been a sharp increase in the proportion of aspirin-related poisonings associated with protective packaging. Whereas 40 percent of all aspirin poisonings in 1972 were from safety cap bottles, this figure rose to 73 percent by 1978. This pattern is noteworthy for two reasons. First, safety cap bottles are by no means risk free, as they account for a majority of the poisonings and a disproportionate amount compared to their sales. Almost half of all aspirin poisonings are from bottles that had been left open. Second, there appears to be an alarming increase in the rate of safety cap poisonings. While each of these effects may be attributable in part to consumers matching their aspirin bottle-type choice (with or without a cap) to whether or not they have young children, another factor may be that there is an increased degree of irresponsibility regarding medicines.

Such irresponsibility is consistent with evidence of an apparent spillover effect on previously unregulated analgesics, which include acetaminophen preparations such as Tylenol. Analgesic poisoning rates for children under age 5 escalated from 1.1 per 1,000 in 1971 to 1.5 per 1,000 in 1980. Even after taking into account increases in analgesic sales, 47 percent of this increase is attributable to an unexplained upward shift in the analgesic poisoning rate beginning in 1972. The coupling of the absence of any shift in the trend of aspirin poisoning rates with an upsurge in analgesic poisoning rates is consistent with the hypothesis that there is a significant indivisibility in safety precautions. Moreover, absence of a significant effect of safety caps on aspirin poisonings and the 47 percent unexplained shift in analgesic poisonings suggests that the impact of the regulation on balance was counterproductive, leading to 3,500 additional poisonings of children under age 5 annually from analgesics.

It is possible but unlikely that such a strong impact could emerge from fully rational consumer decisions. Moreover, this effect is not only large but reasonably widespread, as I have identified a similar pattern for prescription drugs, and for cleaning and polishing agents. A more likely explanation for these dramatic effects is that consumers have been lulled into a less-safety-conscious mode of behavior by the existence of safety caps. The presumed effectiveness of the technological solution may have induced increased parental irresponsibility.

A variety of regulatory efforts have sought to reduce individual risks through mandated technological changes. These measures will be effective if individual actions remain unchanged. In practice, these regulations will produce a lulling effect on consumer behavior because the perceived need for precautions will decline, potentially producing adverse spillover effects on the safety of other products. The strength of these impacts should highlight the importance of taking individual behavior into account when designing regulations intended to promote safety.

REFERENCES

Blomquist, Glenn, *Traffic Safety Regulation by NHTSA*, Washington: American Enterprise Institute, forthcoming.

Peltzman, Sam, "The Effects of Automobile Safety Regulation," *Journal of Political Economy*, August 1975, *83*, 677–725.

Viscusi, W. Kip, "The Impact of Occupational Safety and Health Regulation," *Bell Journal of Economics*, Spring 1979, *10*, 117–40.

______, "An Assessment of the Safety Impacts of Consumer Product Safety Regulations," Center for Study of Business Regulation Working Paper 83-10, Fuqua School of Business, Duke University, 1983.

______, *Regulating Product Safety*, Washington: American Enterprise Institute, forthcoming.

ARE DRIVERS OF AIR-BAG-EQUIPPED CARS MORE AGGRESSIVE? A TEST OF THE OFFSETTING BEHAVIOR HYPOTHESIS*

STEVEN PETERSON, *Virginia Commonwealth University*

GEORGE HOFFER, *Virginia Commonwealth University*

and

EDWARD MILLNER
Virginia Commonwealth University

Abstract

An increasing number of researchers have hypothesized that regulatory attempts to improve automotive safety through product design would be at least partially offset by driver behavioral changes. This article analyzes two independent data sets to test whether differences in driver behavior exist between cars equipped with air bags and those not so equipped. An analysis of an insurance industry generated data set reveals that relative injury claims increase following adoption of an air bag system. Since there is no indication that the increase diminishes over time, the results appear to be attributable to offsetting behavior as opposed to a sorting of auto buyers. Analyses of 1993 Virginia State Police accident reports indicate that air-bag-equipped cars tend to be driven more aggressively and that aggressiveness appears to offset the effect of the air bag for the driver and increases the risk of death to others.

I. Introduction

In the 1970s, Peltzman hypothesized that attempts to improve automobile safety by regulation of product design would be at least partially offset by behavioral changes induced by the mandate.[1] In his model, more recently termed the "offsetting behavior hypothesis," the imposition of mandated safety devices reduces the probability of injury, holding driving

* The authors acknowledge the assistance of Mr. David Mosley and Ms. Cheryl Jablonski of the Virginia Department of Motor Vehicles for supplying data and the constructive comments of an anonymous referee.

[1] Sam Peltzman, The Effects of Automobile Safety Regulation, 83 J. Pol. Econ. 677 (1975); Sam Peltzman, The Effects of Automobile Safety Regulation: A Reply, 8 Accident Analysis & Prevention 139 (1976); Sam Peltzman, A Reply to Robertson, 11 J. Econ. Issues 672 (1977).

[*Journal of Law and Economics*, vol. XXXVIII (October 1995)]

intensity constant. Given a preference for driving intensity and an aversion to injury, one would expect drivers to increase driving intensity relative to the level chosen prior to device imposition. The increase in driving intensity thus induced tends to offset the initial gain in safety for those protected and adversely affects others.

It is the purpose of this article to test whether these expectations can be confirmed. Using the most recent insurance industry generated data, we find that models adopting air bags experience increases in relative personal injury claims and that this increase is not the result of "buyer sorting." Then, using Virginia State Police reports on all fatal crashes involving late model vehicles in the 1993 calendar year, we report a series of tests to ascertain whether driver behavior differences can be found between air-bag- and non-air-bag-equipped cars. We find that air-bag-equipped cars tend to be driven more aggressively than cars without air bags and that the additional aggressiveness appears to offset the effect of the air bag for the driver and increases the risk of death to others.

II. Literature Review

Sparked initially by Lave and Weber, and developed more completely by Peltzman, a sizable body of economic literature focused on the efficacy of government safety regulations has developed over the last 25 years.[2] Initially, most researchers found little or no support for the offsetting behavior hypothesis and concluded that the benefits from various proposed or mandated safety appliances exceeded their costs.[3] By the mid-1980s, slightly more support for the offsetting behavior hypothesis in limited situations is found in a few studies. Evans, as well as Lund and O'Neill, have found some evidence that newly adopted safety devices

[2] Lester B. Lave & Warren E. Weber, A Benefit-Cost Analysis of Auto Safety Features, 2 Applied Econ. 265 (1970); Peltzman, *supra* note 1.

[3] Robert W. Crandall, Theodore Keeler, & Lester B. Lave, The Cost of Automobile Safety and Emissions Regulation to the Consumer: Some Preliminary Results, 72 Am. Econ. Rev. 324 (May 1982); John D. Graham, Technology, Behavior, and Safety: An Empirical Study of Occupant-Protection Regulation, 17 Pol'y Sci. 141 (1984); John D. Graham & Steven Garber, Evaluating the Effects of Automobile Safety Regulation, 3 J. Pol'y Analysis & Mgmt. 206 (1984); Clifford Winston & Fred Mannering, Consumer Demand for Automobile Safety, 74 Am. Econ. Rev. 316 (May 1984); Thomas J. Zlatoper, Regression Analysis of Time Series Data on Motor Vehicle Deaths in the United States, 18 J. Transport Econ. & Pol'y 263 (1984); John D. Graham, Automobile Safety: An Investigation of Occupant Protection Policies (unpublished dissertation, Carnegie-Mellon Univ. 1983); Robert W. Crandall & John D. Graham, Automobile Safety Regulation and Offsetting Behavior: Some New Empirical Estimates, 74 Am. Econ. Rev. 328 (May 1984).

which provide active feedback, such as studded snow tires, may influence driver behavior.[4]

More recently, several researchers have found evidence of substantial offsetting behavior. Blomquist's work both surveyed and contributed to this literature.[5] Subsequently, Chirinko and Harper have concluded that offsetting driver behavior is "quantitatively important to the extent that it has attenuated the effects of safety regulation on automotive fatalities."[6] Most recently, Keeler has interpreted his inability to find that regulation significantly diminishes fatalities as support for the offset hypothesis.[7]

The debate over the efficacy of government safety regulations has been epitomized by the discussion of air bags. No technological innovation has been so opposed initially and later so embraced by the industry as the air bag. Before the National Highway and Traffic Safety Administration (NHTSA) mandated the feature for front-seat occupants for the 1998 model year, the air bag had become the most controversial safety device since passage of the National Traffic and Motor Vehicle Safety Act in 1966. Automotive insurers and consumer advocates lobbied and litigated for their adoption, while domestic automotive manufacturers urged caution and moderation.[8] The latter successfully persuaded the Reagan Administration in 1981 to rescind the passive restraint rule, arguing that they would not be as cost effective as the already mandated three-point belt system. Several years of additional litigation followed the rescission.

By 1990 auto manufacturers began to equip increasing numbers of models with at least one air bag in response to perceived market forces and Federal Motor Vehicle Standard 208 (49 CFR Sec. 571.208). Extensive promotion quickly redefined the state-of-the-art "safe" car as one so equipped. Since air bags are perceived to and do reduce the risk of injury

[4] Leonard Evans, Risk Homeostasis Theory and Traffic Accident Data, 6 Risk Analysis 81 (1986); Adrian K. Lund & Brian O'Neill, Perceived Risks and Driving Behavior, 18 Accident Analysis & Prevention 367 (1986).

[5] Glenn C. Blomquist, The Regulation of Motor Vehicle and Traffic Safety (1988).

[6] Robert S. Chirinko & Edward P. Harper, Jr., Buckle Up or Slow Down? New Estimates of Offsetting Behavior and Their Implications for Automobile Safety Regulation, 12 J. Pol'y Analysis & Mgmt. 270 (1993).

[7] Theodore E. Keeler, Highway Safety, Economic Behavior, and Driving Environment, 84 Am. Econ. Rev. 684 (1994).

[8] Recently, Kneuper and Yandle hypothesize that the insurance industry has supported air bags because insurers can more effectively manage their risks when cars are air-bag-equipped. Robert Kneuper & Bruce Yandle, Auto Insurers and the Air Bag, 61 J. Risk & Ins. 107 (1994).

to protected occupants especially in head-on collisions,[9] the recent widespread manufacturer adoption of air bags as standard equipment provides a new data source for testing the offsetting behavior hypothesis.

Using different tests, but relying on similar data sets, Hoffer and Millner as well as Peterson and Hoffer found that relative injury and absolute collision losses for a model usually increase after the adoption of air bags as standard equipment.[10] The authors noted that while their results are supportive of offsetting behavior, they are also consistent with buyer sorting. In the sorting model, drivers with a greater likelihood of being involved in accidents shift their purchases to air-bag-equipped models. Our task in the present article is to determine which of the competing hypotheses better explains their findings.

III. Analysis of Insurance Loss Data

One of the purposes of the Highway Loss Data Institute (HLDI) is to gather, process, and publish insurance loss experiences for the various makes and models of automobiles and light trucks. Financial support for HLDI is provided by the Insurance Institute for Highway Safety, which in turn is funded by auto insurers directly or through their trade associations. Since the early 1970s, HLDI has published annually series of data on insurer loss experiences, including those on relative injury claim frequencies and collision claims for specific models of cars and light trucks.[11] The "overall injury" statistics reported by HLDI indicate the relative frequencies of occupant personal injury claims under personal injuries protection (PIP) policies for specific vehicle lines and model years. The personal injury results are presented annually in relative terms, with 100 representing the average for all vehicles in that year.[12] Based on vehicle

[9] Insurance Institute for Highway Safety, Airbags in Perspective, 28 Status Rep. 1 (1993); Highway Loss Data Institute, Insurance Special Report: Driver Injury Experience in 1990 Models Equipped with Air Bags or Automatic Belts (Report No. A-38, Highway Loss Data Institute 1991).

[10] George Hoffer & Edward Millner, Are Drivers' Behavioral Changes Negating the Efficacy of Mandated Safety Regulations? 15 Reg. 15 (Summer 1992); George Hoffer & Edward Millner, What Is Driving Behavioral Change? 16 Reg. 5 (1993); Steven P. Peterson & George E. Hoffer, The Impact of Airbag Adoption on Relative Personal Injury and Absolute Collision Insurance Claims, 20 J. Consumer Res. 657 (1994). Lund and Hazelbaker, commenting on Hoffer and Millner, argue that the effectiveness of air bags is overwhelming. Adrian Lund & Kim Hazelbaker, Reviewing the Evidence on Air Bags, 16 Reg. 3 (1993).

[11] For instance, the records of 1991–93 models are found in Highway Loss Data Institute, Injury and Collision Loss Experience by Make and Model (1994).

[12] Over the 1991–93 model years, relative claim frequencies ranged from a low of 28 for the Mercedes SL convertible series to a high of 214 for the Hyundai Scoupe. The score of

identification numbers, the data are adjusted for operator age-group. For any given crash, all claims against whatever policy are counted as a single claim. Therefore, driver fault is not a factor in determining the claim frequencies. For example, if a Mercedes SL collided with a Hyundai Scoupe, all of the personal injury claims for the driver and passengers of the Mercedes would be charged against that vehicle and all personal injury claims for occupants of the Hyundai would be charged against the Hyundai.

Using "Injury and Collision Loss Experience by Make and Model,"[13] we compute the annual change in the relative frequency of injury claims for every non–station wagon, automotive model for which data was available in 1989.[14] This difference is then used as the dependent variable in a series of regression equations. The independent variables include a set of dummy variables indicating if and when air bags were adopted as a standard feature for the model and a dummy variable indicating if the model had been restyled. The restyling dummy variable was included in order to separate the effects of the adoption of air bags and any restyling effects.

Since vehicle size has been determined to be a significant determinant of insurer loss experience under PIP coverages,[15] we assigned a value of unity to the restyling dummy variable if vehicle length increased by at least 2 inches and/or vehicle width increased by at least 1 inch.[16] We anticipated that the estimated coefficient for the restyling dummy variable would be negative.

Omitted explicitly are macroeconomic explanatory variables such as proxies for economic activity and variables which affect the driving envi-

---

28 indicates that the average frequency of personal injury claims filed against 1991–93 Mercedes was 28 percent of the average for the average model. The score for the Hyundai indicates that the average number of claims filed against Scoupes was 114 percent higher than the population average.

[13] Highway Loss Data Institute, *supra* note 11, 1989–94.

[14] Peterson and Hoffer used data for 1989–91 model year cars to examine the impact of air bag adoption on insurance claim histories. Subsequently, two additional years of data have been released.

[15] Robert W. Crandall & John D. Graham, The Effect of Fuel Economy Standards on Automobile Safety, 32 J. Law & Econ. 97 (1989); Insurance Institute for Highway Safety, *supra* note 9; Insurance Institute for Highway Safety, Shopping for a Safer Car (1994).

[16] Peterson and Hoffer's restyling variable did not differentiate between a restyling and an upward resizing. They found for the 1990–91 period that restyled vehicles had significantly lower relative injury claim frequencies. This finding was explained by noting that three of the five restyled models that year had been upsized. See Edward L. Millner & George E. Hoffer, A Re-examination of the Impact of Styling on Demand, 25 Applied Econ. 101 (1993), for definitions and categorizations of styling change.

ronment in general. Examples of the latter variable type would include changes in maximum vehicular speed limits and changes in motor fuel prices. Both variable types have been omitted because the injury measure, claim frequencies relative to the mean, buffer the data set from macroenvironmental changes. For example, decreasing the legal speed limit on interstate highways may decrease the absolute number of claims for all models but would have little effect on relative claim frequencies for a particular model.

We estimated the parameters of the following equation over each time period in question (1989–90, 1990–91, 1991–92, and 1992–93) to test for significant differences in changes in relative personal injury claims for newly equipped air bag models relative to those models without air bags:

$$\Delta \text{PI}_i = \alpha + \beta_1 D_i + \beta_2 R_i + \epsilon_i. \quad (1)$$

The dependent variable is the change in relative personal injury claims. The term D_i equals unity if the model was equipped with an air bag at the beginning of the model year under question.[17] The term R_i is a dummy variable which indicates whether the model was resized.

The intercept, alpha, is the conditional mean of the change in relative claim frequencies for models never equipped with air bags after having controlled for the effect of the dummy variables. The betas measure the impact on the mean of the dependent variable due to the attribute denoted by the dummy variable. The associated t-statistics test statistical significance.

The results are presented in Table 1. The first row contains estimates for the pooled data (1989–93) obtained by combining the data sets for each model year. Subsequent rows break out the estimates by model year. Overall, relative personal injury claims are significantly higher for newly equipped air bag models relative to their non-air-bag-equipped counterparts ($\beta_1 = 3.22$, $t = 1.789$), while those models that are upsized have significantly lower relative personal injury claims ($\beta_2 = -4.944$, $t = -2.343$). Models which received an air bag at the beginning of the 1990 model year subsequently experienced significant increases in relative personal injury claims ($\beta_1 = 6.765$, $t = 2.287$). In contrast, models newly equipped with air bags for 1991 had no significant changes in relative personal injury claims ($\beta_1 = -4.163$, $t = -0.833$).[18] By 1992, however, these claims were once again significantly higher—indeed, higher

[17] Since a driver's side air bag has never been deleted as a standard feature in any automobile line in the U.S. market, all models without air bags in 1993 never had air bags.

[18] Note that three of the five new air bag models for that year were large GM models which had increased in length by up to 10 inches and width by 2 inches.

TABLE 1

CHANGES IN RELATIVE PERSONAL INJURY CLAIMS (PI) BY YEAR FOR NEWLY EQUIPPED AIR BAG MODELS RELATIVE TO NON-AIR-BAG MODELS FOR ALL VEHICLES

$$\Delta PI_i = \alpha + \beta_1 D_i + \beta_2 R_i + \epsilon_i$$

	α	β_1	β_2
All years	.754	3.220	−4.944
	(1.027)	(1.789)*	(−2.343)**
1989–90	1.201	6.765	4.504
	(.889)	(2.287)**	(1.031)
1990–91	−1.339	−4.163	−3.161
	(−.966)	(−.833)	(−.817)
1991–92	2.546	7.784	−10.885
	(1.933)	(2.191)**	(−2.811)**
1992–93	−.364	−.236	−11.067
	(−.301)	(−.084)	(−2.674)**

NOTE.—D = dummy indicating newly equipped with air bag at beginning of model year; R = dummy variable denoting restyling resulting in larger vehicle size. Estimates presented here correspond to eq. (1). t-statistics are given in parentheses.

* Significant at the 5% level (one-tail t-test); 7.5% (two-tail t-test).

** Significant at the 2.5% level (one-tail t-test); 5% (two-tail t-test).

than 2 years previously (β_1 = 7.784, t = 2.191). Furthermore, upsized models experienced significant declines in relative personal injury claims (β_2 = −10.885, t = −2.811). Finally, for 1993, newly equipped air bag models experienced no significant changes in relative personal injury, but, again, upsizing had a significant negative effect on these claims (β_2 = −11.067, t = −2.674).

The results recorded in Table 1 confirm that cars recently equipped with air bags experience increases in relative claim frequencies while resized cars experience decreases. While this finding is inconsistent with the a priori expectations of passive restraint advocates, it is consistent with two competing hypotheses. First, it is completely supportive of offsetting behavior. However, as noted above it is also consistent with a "sorting" hypothesis in which auto buyers who consider themselves at risk gravitate to what they perceive as safer cars. Under the sorting hypothesis, the worsening relative injury claim experience for air-bag-equipped autos is attributed to a changing mix of drivers between the two vehicle groups.

If the sorting hypothesis is correct, then we would expect to find a systematic pattern in the coefficient for the air bag dummy variable. Auto buyers most at risk would have tended to be among the first to gravitate to air-bag-equipped autos. Therefore, if sorting is driving the results, the increase in personal injury claims would be greatest for the first models to adopt air bags. The impact on these claims would subsequently decline as the pool of at-risk drivers have already self-selected.

The data do not support the sorting hypothesis, as the annual pattern displays no systematic trend. Indeed, following the adoption of air bags, claims appear to rise, then stabilize, then rise even higher, and subsequently stabilize again.

Since no systematic pattern can be observed, we reject the sorting hypothesis. But by itself the HLDI data is insufficient to determine whether air-bag-equipped cars are driven more aggressively than otherwise equipped cars. This and other issues are pursued in the next section with a distinctly different micro data set.

IV. Analysis of Traffic Fatality Data

The offsetting behavior hypothesis implies that cars equipped with air bags will be driven more aggressively than cars without air bags. To ascertain whether drivers of air-bag- and non-air-bag-equipped cars have behavioral differences, we use traffic fatality data provided by the Commonwealth of Virginia Department of Motor Vehicles.[19] The data set consisted of 207 motor vehicle crashes resulting in death in the Commonwealth during the 1993 calendar year that met the following criteria: (1) at least one vehicle had to be a post-1989 model year vehicle, and (2) at least one vehicle must have been legally defined as a passenger automobile. (Vans, minivans, sport utility vehicles, and pickup trucks are not considered passenger automobiles.) Thus excluded from the data set are single or multiple vehicle fatal accidents involving exclusively pre-1990 model vehicles and/or post-1989 vehicles not classified as passenger automobiles. Accidents exclusively involving all pre-1990 cars and post-1989 nonautomotive vehicles were excluded because such vehicles were rarely air-bag-equipped. Furthermore, limiting the data set to late model vehicles attenuates problems associated with demographic and socioeconomic differences between drivers of older and newer cars.

The Commonwealth supplied us with copies of the Virginia State Police accident reports after deleting any personal information. We used the

[19] In 1993, traffic fatalities in Virginia represented 2.2 percent of the national total. Traffic fatalities in Virginia increased 4.3 percent over those in 1992, compared to a 2.2 percent increase nationally. On both per capita income and population bases, Virginia ranks twelfth in the nation. Virginia Department of Motor Vehicles, 1993 Virginia Traffic Crash Facts (1994); National Highway Traffic Safety Administration, Final 1993 Traffic Safety Statistics 37–94 (1994).

reports to obtain the make, model, and model year for each vehicle involved. We classified a car as being air-bag-equipped if a driver's side air bag was standard equipment for the model year. The reports allowed us to identify whether an occupant in the vehicle was killed and, if so, the position of the occupant. We could also identify whether the driver of the vehicle initiated the crash when more than one vehicle was involved.

In multiple vehicle crashes, the investigating officer assigns each vehicle an identifying number. The accident reports designated the driver of either vehicle 1 or 2 as the initiator. Vehicles ancillary to the accident were given higher numbers. Since the policy of the Virginia State Police is not to charge deceased drivers with traffic violations, citations could not be used to determine whether the driver was the initiator.

Of the 62 crashes involving cars equipped with air bags, 53 were either single car crashes or multiple vehicle crashes initiated by the driver of the air-bag-equipped car. If drivers in single car crashes and initiators of multiple vehicle crashes are categorized as being at fault,[20] then drivers of air-bag-equipped cars are at fault in 85 percent of the crashes in which they are involved. Such a high percentage suggests that cars equipped with air bags are driven aggressively. In order to determine whether the cars equipped with air bags are driven more aggressively than non-air-bag-equipped cars, we analyze single and multiple vehicle crashes separately.

The analysis was conducted by calculating the probabilities of various combinations of events, for example, the likelihood that 62 of 207 total fatal crashes would involve an air-bag-equipped vehicle given that the relative frequency of vehicles so equipped to all vehicles in the data is no less than 31 percent. If we assume that crashes are independent of each other and that the probability of the existence of an attribute such as an air bag in each crash is a Bernoulli trial with probability p (31 percent, for example), then the appropriate probability distribution for purposes of estimation and testing is the binomial distribution. Thus, in a sample of size n, we calculate the probability of seeing x "successes" (air bags, for example) when the underlying probability of success is p and the probability of "failure" is $(1 - p)$. Using conventional notation,

$$P(x) = \binom{n}{x} p^x (1 - p)^{n-x}, \qquad (2)$$

[20] Classifying all drivers in single car crashes as being at fault may overstate the true percentage. When a single car crash involved a pedestrian or bicyclist, the information in the accident report was often insufficient to determine who actually initiated the crash.

which hereafter will be denoted as bin(n, x, p). The cumulative probability of seeing x or more successes, $P(X \geq x)$, is a simple sum and will be denoted cbin(n, x, p).

A. *Single Car Accidents*

If only one car was involved, it must be a post-1989 model to be included in the data set. The percentage of such cars equipped with air bags is known to be 0.44.[21]

The analysis of single car crashes yields some striking conclusions. Drivers of air-bag-equipped cars do *not* face lower probability of death in spite of being protected and passengers in cars equipped with air bags face higher risks than otherwise.

Rows 1 and 2 of Table 2 contain results for single car crashes in which only the driver was killed. Of the 70 single car crashes, the driver was the sole fatality in 33 instances. Of these 33, 16 were driving cars equipped with air bags. Assuming that drivers with air bags are as likely to die as drivers without air bags and that air-bag-equipped cars account for 44 percent of all post-1989 cars, then the probability of 16 or more such deaths is cbin(33, 16, .44) = 0.363. Here, the number of instances in which the driver alone is killed exceeds the expected value, but not significantly. This finding would be not be unusual assuming the air bag offers no added protection, but does not support a claim that air bags reduce driver deaths.[22] Offsetting behavior can explain the failure to find a significant reduction in the probability of death to drivers.

An even stronger conclusion is reached if one adjusts the binomial probability downward to account for the reduction in risk to individuals protected by an air bag when they are involved in a crash. The Insurance Institute for Highway Safety[23] has found that air bags reduce deaths by 24 percent in front and front-angle crashes over belts alone. Since most single car fatalities involve front-end collisions, fatalities involving models equipped with air bags should not account for 44 percent in single car crashes; rather they should account for 76 percent of 44 percent, or 33 percent when adjusted for the safety advantage of the air bag. This im-

[21] Crain Publications, Automotive News Market Data Book (1991–94).

[22] A similar result was reported by the Insurance Institute for Highway Safety in a recent analysis of the effects of antilock brakes (Antilocks May Not Make the Difference That Many Expected, 29 Status Rep. 2 (1994)). They reported that, despite improved braking abilities, there was no evidence that vehicles equipped with antilock brakes incurred reduced relative insurance losses.

[23] 28 Status Rep. 11 (1993).

TABLE 2

PROBABILITIES OF OBSERVING x OR MORE OCCURRENCES IN A SAMPLE OF n AT PROBABILITY OF x EQUAL TO p UNDER THE BINOMIAL DISTRIBUTION

$$P(X > x) = \Sigma \binom{n}{x} p^x(1 - p)^{n-x}$$

bin(n, x, p)	$P(X = x)$	$P(X \geq x)$*	$E(x)$
(33, 16, .44)†	.120	.363	14.52
(33, 16, .33)	.025	.046	10.89
(13, 9, .44)‡	.043	.050	5.72
(30, 22, .5)§	.005	.008	15.0

* These numbers correspond to conventional p-values.
† Likelihood of 16/33 airbag driver fatalities in single vehicle accidents.
‡ Likelihood of 9 cases in 13 of occupant fatalities involving airbag vehicles.
§ Likelihood of airbag vehicle being the initiator in 22 of 30 multiple vehicle accidents involving airbag vehicles.

plies that cbin(33, 16, .33) = 0.046 is the relevant p-value. One can conclude at the 5 percent level that the proportion of drivers only killed in a single car air bag crashes is greater than 0.33. This conclusion suggests that offsetting behavior negates the added safety afforded by air bags.

Having found evidence of offsetting behavior we now address whether the behavior imposes negative externalities. Unlike pedestrians or bicyclists, occupants rarely initiate crashes. Therefore, we analyzed the probability that an occupant was killed. The third row of Table 2 contains results for single car crashes in which only one or more passengers were killed. There were 13 cases involving single car crashes in which vehicle occupants other than the driver (but not the driver) died, 9 of which involved air-bag-equipped cars. Since few cars in the data set had dual air bags, the a priori probability that a passenger was killed in a car equipped with an air bag equals no more than 0.44, the percentage of 1990–93 cars so equipped. The probability of at least 9 occurrences in 13 is cbin(13, 9, .44) = 0.050.[24] Therefore, when the driver does not die, other occupants in the vehicle die at too high a rate. This finding is consistent with Peltzman's hypothesis that offsetting behavior would impose negative externalities on other parties.

[24] If one allows for the added protection afforded the driver by the air bag, then nine occurrences of passenger-only deaths is not too high; that is, this relative frequency is high because the driver of the air-bag-equipped car is less likely to die. Nevertheless, in the presence of offsetting behavior, passengers are disproportionately at risk, and the adoption of a driver's side air bag imposes a negative externality on unprotected passengers.

B. *Multiple Vehicle Crashes*

Of the 207 fatal crashes, 137 involved two or more vehicles. An analysis of these crashes is also supportive of the offsetting behavior hypothesis. Drivers of air-bag-equipped cars are significantly more likely to be the initiator of a multiple car crash.

To examine whether offsetting behavior imposed externalities on those not in the air-bag-equipped car, we analyzed the probability that the drivers of cars equipped with air bags initiated the multiple vehicle crashes. Of the multiple car crashes, 30 involved crashes where vehicle 1 on the accident report was air-bag-equipped and vehicle 2 was not or vice versa. Since the initiator in each of these could be either equipped with an air bag or not, the a priori binomial probability that a car equipped with air bags is the initiator is 50 percent. However, the air-bag-equipped vehicle was deemed the initiator 22 times. As indicated in row 4 of Table 2, cbin(30, 22, .5) = 0.008. We would, therefore, conclude at the 1 percent level that drivers of air-bag-equipped vehicles are more likely to be the initiator in multiple vehicle crashes than their non-air-bag counterparts, a conclusion strongly supportive of offsetting behavior.

V. Conclusions

Using two independent data sets, we have found strong support for the offsetting behavior hypothesis. Our analysis of the insurance-industry-based HLDI data set indicates that autos newly equipped with an air bag during the 1990–93 model years experience significant increases in relative losses under personal injury protection coverage after controlling for upward resizings. Since these increases do not diminish over time, these results are attributed to offsetting behavior.

Second, we studied 1993 fatal accidents in Virginia. We find that risk to drivers of cars equipped with air bags in single car crashes *is not* diminished, that the percentage of occupants killed in single car air bag crashes *is* unusually high, and that drivers of air-bag-equipped cars initiate an unusually large percentage of such crashes. We conclude that drivers of air-bag-equipped cars tend to be more aggressive than drivers of cars not so equipped, that their added aggressiveness diminishes the protection afforded drivers of cars equipped with air bags and imposes additional risks on occupants and passengers in other vehicles.

Bibliography

Blomquist, Glenn C. *The Regulation of Motor Vehicle and Traffic Safety*. Boston: Kluwer Academic Publishers, 1988.

Chirinko, Robert S., and Harper, Edward P., Jr. "Buckle Up or Slow Down? New Estimates of Offsetting Behavior and Their Implications for Automobile Safety Regulation." *Journal of Policy Analysis and Management* 12 (1993): 270–96.

Crain Publications. *Automotive News Market Data Book.* Detroit: Crain Publications, 1991–94, annual eds.

Crandall, Robert W., and Graham, John D. "The Effect of Fuel Economy Standards on Automobile Safety." *Journal of Law and Economics* 32 (1989): 97–118.

Crandall, Robert W., and Graham, John D. "Automobile Safety Regulation and Offsetting Behavior: Some New Empirical Estimates." *American Economic Review* 74 (May 1984): 328–31.

Crandall, Robert W.; Keeler, Theodore E.; and Lave, Lester B. "The Cost of Automobile Safety and Emissions Regulation to the Consumer: Some Preliminary Results." *American Economic Review* 72 (1982): 324–27.

Evans, Leonard. "Risk Homeostasis Theory and Traffic Accident Data." *Risk Analysis* 6 (1986): 81–94.

Graham, John D. "Automobile Safety: An Investigation of Occupant Protection Policies." Unpublished dissertation, Carnegie-Mellon University, Department of Economics, 1983.

Graham, John D. "Technology, Behavior, and Safety: An Empirical Study of Occupant-Protection Regulation." *Policy Sciences* 17 (1984): 141–51.

Graham, John D., and Garber, Steven. "Evaluating the Effects of Automobile Safety Regulation." *Journal of Policy Analysis and Management* 3 (1984): 206–24.

Highway Loss Data Institute. "Injury and Collision Loss Experience by Make and Model." Report No. I78-93-1. Arlington, Va.: Highway Loss Data Institute, 1979–94.

Highway Loss Data Institute. "Insurance Special Report: Driver Injury Experience in 1990 Models with Airbags or Automatic Belts." Report No. A-38. Arlington, Va.: Highway Loss Data Institute, 1991.

Hoffer, George, and Millner, Edward. "Are Drivers' Behavioral Changes Negating the Efficacy of Mandated Safety Regulations?" *Regulation* 15 (Summer 1992): 15–17.

Hoffer, George, and Millner, Edward. "What Is Driving Behavioral Change?" *Regulation* 16 (Winter 1993): 5.

Insurance Institute for Highway Safety. "Airbags in Perspective." *Status Report* 28 (1993): 1–12.

Insurance Institute for Highway Safety. "Where Is Safety in the Fuel Economy Debate?" *Status Report* 25 (1990): 1–4.

Insurance Institute for Highway Safety. "Antilocks May Not Make the Difference That Many Expected." *Status Report* 29 (1994): 2.

Insurance Institute for Highway Safety. *Shopping for a Safer Car.* Arlington, Va.: Insurance Institute for Highway Safety, 1994.

Keeler, Theodore E. "Highway Safety, Economic Behavior, and Driving Environment." *American Economic Review* 84 (1994): 684–93.

Kneuper, Robert, and Yandle, Bruce. "Auto Insurers and the Air Bag." *Journal of Risk and Insurance* 61 (1994): 107–16.

Lave, Lester B., and Weber, Warren E. "A Benefit-Cost Analysis of Auto Safety Features." *Applied Economics* 2 (1970): 265–75.

Lund, Adrian K., and Hazelbaker, Kim. "Reviewing the Evidence on Air Bags." *Regulation* 16 (1993): 3–5.

Lund, Adrian K., and O'Neill, Brian. "Perceived Risks and Driving Behavior." *Accident Analysis and Prevention* 18 (1986): 367–70.

Millner, Edward L., and Hoffer, George E. "A Re-examination of the Impact of Styling on Demand." *Applied Economics* 25 (1993): 101–10.

Peltzman, Sam. "The Effects of Automobile Safety Regulation." *Journal of Political Economy* 83 (1975): 677–725.

Peltzman, Sam. "The Effects of Automobile Safety Regulation: A Reply." *Accident Analysis and Prevention* 8 (1976): 139–42.

Peltzman, Sam. "A Reply to Robertson." *Journal of Economic Issues* 11 (1977): 672–78.

Peterson, Steven P., and Hoffer, George E. "The Impact of Airbag Adoption on Relative Personal Injury and Absolute Collision Insurance Claims." *Journal of Consumer Research* 20 (1994): 657–62.

Winston, Clifford, and Mannering, Fred. "Consumer Demand for Automobile Safety." *American Economic Review* 74 (May 1984): 316–19.

Zlatoper, Thomas J. "Regression Analysis of Time Series Data on Motor Vehicle Deaths in the United States." *Journal of Transport Economics and Policy* 18 (1984): 263–74.

CRISIS IN THE COCKPIT? THE ROLE OF MARKET FORCES IN PROMOTING AIR TRAVEL SAFETY*

MARK L. MITCHELL *and* *MICHAEL T. MALONEY*
U.S. Securities and Exchange Commission
Clemson University

I. Introduction

This article examines the brand-name effect of airline crashes. These disasters raise several financial issues. A crash represents the loss of a plane, the loss of lives (which the airline indemnifies), the loss of scheduling capacity, higher insurance costs, and the potential loss of consumer goodwill. This article focuses on the last of these. Are consumers reluctant to fly with airlines that have poor safety records or do they treat crashes merely as random events that bear no reflection on the quality of the airline?

The theory of brand names implies the former. Not all crashes affect consumer behavior but some crashes will. Some disasters—and we argue that these are the ones where the carrier is at fault—cause consumers to revise their expectations about the probability of accident. This change in probability will cause travelers to revise their consumption patterns and cause the goodwill value of the carrier to decline.

To test this theory, we examine the abnormal stock market performance of airlines immediately following a crash. Stock market event analysis is useful in studying airline disasters because these accidents can be pinpointed in time, with the effect of the catastrophe incorporated into stock prices at that point. We examine fifty-six crashes between 1964 and 1987. We break the crashes into two groups—those caused by pilot error

* Mitchell is an economist at the U.S. Securities and Exchange Commission (on leave from the Department of Finance at Clemson University); Maloney is a professor of economics at Clemson University. The Center for Policy Studies, Clemson University, and a grant from the Dupont Company to Clemson provided support. Dan Benjamin and Matt Lindsay made useful comments. Bobby McCormick, but for an overly cramped research agenda, would have been a coauthor. We also gratefully acknowledge research assistance by Cyndi Brown. The views expressed here are those of the authors and do not necessarily reflect the views of the Securities and Exchange Commission or the staff of the Commission.

[*Journal of Law & Economics*, vol. XXXII (October 1989)]
 0022-2186/89/3202-0005$01.50

and those in which the carrier was judged by the press or by the Federal Aviation Administration (FAA) not to be at fault. We find that, for crashes caused by pilot error, the carrier experienced significantly negative stock returns but that in the case of other crashes there was no stock market reaction.

The fact that there is no stock market reaction in the case of no-fault crashes suggests that airlines are fully insured against this peril. The cause of the stock market reaction to at-fault crashes must then be due to one or both of the following: the loss of consumer goodwill or increases in the cost of insurance. In fact, if the theory of brand names is correct, an increase in insurance costs should *cause* a loss in consumer goodwill. This is because an increase in insurance costs reflects a change in the probability of accident that will also be taken into account by consumers.

We report an insurance rate function that shows insurance costs do increase consequent to pilot-error crashes and not to disasters caused by forces arguably outside the control of the carrier. And, consistent with the theory, this insurance cost increase adds up to only around 38 percent of the stock market decline. Hence, we conclude that a strong brand name effect is operating in the airline industry to insure quality performance.

This result raises the question, What is the value of regulation in this industry? We could not find any evidence that deregulation caused a change in the stock market response to crashes. Even though more work is warranted, this result interests us because it suggests that regulation had virtually no air-safety effects, a point much in contention today.

II. Airplane Crashes and Brand Name Reputation

In most markets, consumers possess insufficient information about some attributes of products they want to purchase. Acquiring information concerning the intrinsic quality of products prior to purchase is costly. It is commonly believed that in the absence of a government to enforce contracts and sanction stealing, market exchange would be impossible. This is not necessarily true. Brand names and reputations may be enough to prevent cheating by fraudulent firms.

The idea of brand names or reputations as quality assuring devices has formally emerged in the last decade. Klein and Leffler, following the arguments by Klein, Crawford, and Alchian, develop a model in which the presence of firm-specific sunk capital investments, such as those incurred in establishing a brand name, provide a mechanism for assuring contractual performance.[1] Empirical evidence by Jarrell and Peltzman;

[1] Benjamin Klein & Keith Leffler, The Role of Market Forces in Assuring Contractual Performance, 21 J. Pol. Econ. 615 (1981); and Benjamin Klein, Robert G. Crawford, &

Chalk; Mitchell; and Benjamin and Mitchell have recently been accumulated in support of this theory.[2] These studies document wealth losses—in excess of out-of-pocket costs—associated with reduction in product quality.

Air transportation is an industry where almost all companies have well-known brand names. American, Delta, Pan Am, and United are household names. An airline's brand name can be devalued in many ways—delayed or cancelled flights, lost baggage, and unpleasant flight attendants. Arguably, the event most damaging to the brand name capital of an airline is a fatal crash caused by negligence.

Consumers have an expectation about the likelihood of crashes; some crashes will cause consumers to escalate this expectation. When this happens, the theory predicts, consumers will reduce their assessment of the amount of resources the airline devotes to safety. Consumer demand will shift to the left with adverse profit effects. The capital market will recognize this and devalue the goodwill assets of the company.

Airline crashes are caused by a variety of factors including pilot error, improper maintenance, manufacturer error, air traffic control error, and hazardous weather conditions. Theoretically, crashes due to pilot error and improper maintenance are cases where consumers are most likely to reassess the probability of future crashes on that airline. These cases represent a failure to monitor effectively situations directly controllable by the company. Indeed, because airlines are expected to control malfeasance in these important areas, they invariably hire and train their own pilots and maintenance crews, as opposed to subcontracting for these services as they do for meal preparation. Crashes due to causes under the immediate control of an airline will be more likely to affect consumers' expectations about the quality of the airline than are crashes due to what is judged to be bad luck. Consequently, a negligent airline is more likely to suffer a loss in brand name capital than is a nonnegligent carrier in the event of a crash.[3]

Armen A. Alchian, Vertical Integration, Appropriable Rents, and the Competitive Contracting Process, 21 J. Law & Econ. 297 (1978), discuss the notion of a price premium as a bonding device in contract enforcement.

[2] Gregg Jarrell & Sam Peltzman, The Impact of Product Recalls on the Wealth of Sellers, 93 J. Pol. Econ. 512 (1985); Andrew Chalk, Market Forces and Aircraft Safety: The Case of the DC-10, 24 Econ. Inq. 43 (1986), and Market Forces in Commercial Aircraft Safety, 36 J. Indus. Econ. 61 (1987); Mark L. Mitchell, The Impact of External Parties on Brand-Name Capital: The 1982 Tylenol Poisonings and Subsequent Cases, Econ. Inq. (in press); and Daniel Benjamin & Mark L. Mitchell, Quality-Assuring Price Premium: Classic Evidence from the Real Thing (Working paper, U.S. SEC 1989).

[3] Consumers do not have perfect information about the cause of any crash and consumers recognize that the company has an incentive to make itself appear innocent. There is an old

Events that do not change the expectations of future crashes do not affect consumer behavior. In such cases, the stock market reacts only to the airline's out-of-pocket losses. The value of the plane is almost always fully insured, and the liability insurance carried by most airlines would cover the worst imaginable crash: two 747s colliding over New York City. Thus, the only out-of-pocket losses are higher insurance costs, and these should only increase if the probability of future accidents increases, which should also elicit a consumer response.

In other words, a stock market effect attributable to a loss of brand name capital can only occur if there is a revision in the probability of product failure. The experiment reported here tests whether airplane crashes are, on average, associated with a revision of the probability of a crash.[4] Some crashes will change consumer expectations; some will not. But the effect of a crash is asymmetric. We argue that a crash will never cause consumers to lower their expectation of the likelihood of future crashes. Hence, we seek to find a significant effect of those that do change expectations among the noise of those that do not.

Other researchers have approached this problem differently and sometimes, in our opinion, incorrectly. We look for a stock market effect and then examine the other costs in search of a net brand name effect. Others have sought to find a *quantity* effect as a consequence of the stock market reaction.[5] The problem with this approach is that the theory says nothing about quantity. It speaks to price. When a firm depreciates its brand name, the predicted effect is that it must lower price. When it lowers price, because it is offering a lower-quality good, who is to say what happens to quantity? For instance, it is certainly the case that more pieces of cheap jewelry are sold at K-Mart than there are expensive items sold at Tiffany & Co. When a carrier unexpectedly crashes a plane, it moves from the Tiffany class to the K-Mart category.

---

saying, "Sorry don't feed the dog." Hence, consumers may revise upward the probability of crashing even when the news accounts say that the airline was blameless. We argue that the more an airline is judged to have been at fault, the more likely consumers are to reduce their demand.

[4] It is in this sense that we reconcile the results reported in this article with other findings presented in Mitchell, note 2 *supra*. There it is reported that Johnson & Johnson suffered a brand name loss consequent to the 1982 Tylenol poisonings even though that catastrophe was not directly the fault of Johnson & Johnson. We argue that consumers hold companies responsible for all events, but that they have an expectation about performance. When that expectation changes, there will be a stock market reaction that can be used to gauge the brand name value of a company. That the Tylenol disaster represented a revision of consumer expectations is an issue addressed by Mitchell.

[5] Severin Borenstein & Martin B. Zimmerman, Market Incentives for Safe Commercial Airline Operation, 78 Am. Econ. Rev. 913 (1987), approach the problem from this perspective. They conclude that because the consumer response to crashes is quite small in quantity terms, the stock market losses do not reflect a brand name effect.

Interesting evidence on this point has been amassed by Benjamin and Mitchell.[6] They examine the Coca-Cola fiasco with New Coke. They find that Coca-Cola suffered a substantial brand name loss but no market share decline. They then show that both of these results are explainable based on substantial wholesale price cuts by Coca-Cola to its bottlers following the New Coke episode.[7]

Today, direct price cutting in the airline industry is commonplace; however, much of our sample covers the era of airline regulation when price cutting was possible but cumbersome. Even so, we argue that airlines can do many things to fill the price gap created by the loss of consumer goodwill. They can be on time, schedule more flights, offer better food and snacks, provide more numerous and more courteous attendants, and so forth. They can increase the level of maintenance, supervision, and training. They can also increase the commission rate and incentives paid to travel agencies, increase the number of sales representatives calling on these people, increase the number of their own ticketing agents, and increase advertising in general. All of these benefits to consumers can result from depreciated brand name and yet there will be no sign of their effect in the quantity dimension.

III. Airplane Disasters

To examine this theory, we constructed a crash data set. It consists of all fatal airline crashes involving U.S. airlines over the period 1964–87. These crashes meet two criteria. First, the airline must have been registered on either the New York Stock Exchange or the American Stock Exchange at the time of the crash. Second, at least one passenger must have been killed in the crash.[8] The data set contains fifty-six crashes.

We assigned each of the fifty-six crashes to one of two categories: *pilot error* (thirty-four) and *manufacturer error and miscellaneous causes* (twenty-two). Information from the *Brief of Fatal Accidents* and from articles in *Aviation Week and Space Technology* (*AWST*) and the *Wall Street Journal* (*WSJ*) provided the basis for classification.[9] Pilot error

[6] Note 2 *supra*.

[7] Similarly, Mitchell, note 2 *supra*, finds that Johnson & Johnson regained Tylenol's market share within a year following the 1982 cyanide poisonings, but largely at the expense of large price cuts relative to other pain relievers.

[8] Many of the fatal accidents involving U.S. airlines were not crash related. Examples include running over trespassers on the runway, company agents walking into the propeller, and so on. Incidents of this nature are not the focus of this study and hence are excluded.

[9] The crashes are summarized in Briefs of Fatal Accidents, which is compiled from the final reports by the National Transportation Safety Board (NTSB).

represents our at-fault category and manufacturer error and miscellaneous causes represent the no-fault group.[10]

A fortuitous characteristic of the data is that the articles in *AWST* and *WSJ* are rarely in conflict with the information contained in the *Briefs of Fatal Accidents*. This point is essential for the purpose of this study. Many of the articles in *AWST* and *WSJ* were written immediately following the crash, while the National Transportation Safety Board (NTSB) does not typically issue a final report until several months after the crash. If the cause of the crash were not known within a few days after the crash, financial market analysis would be suspect because it would be difficult to determine exactly when the cause of the crash became known to investors. For instance, information about the NTSB investigation could leak out slowly and be spread in trivial proportion across the stock returns of several months. However, since the initial reports from the *AWST* and *WSJ* articles generally prove to be consistent with the *Briefs of Fatal Accidents*, we assume that the cause of the crash was known within a few days after the crash, and on many occasions it was known on the day of or the day after the crash.

The pilot-error category contains those crashes where the pilot (or crew) was the major contributor to the cause of the crash. Thirty-four of the fifty-six crashes belong to this category and are described in Panel A of Table 1. As evident from the "story" column, most of these crashes were due solely to pilot error. For a few of the crashes in Panel A of Table 1, however, a contributing factor may have been hazardous weather conditions, plane malfunctions, or air traffic controller mistakes. Even for those crashes in Panel A of Table 1, the pilot was largely at fault. For example, in the United Airlines crash on December 28, 1978, the plane crashed upon running out of fuel, a crisis that went unnoticed due to the crew's preoccupation with a landing gear malfunction. Undoubtedly, the landing gear malfunction was due either to manufacturer or maintenance error. A plane can make an emergency landing without landing gear, however; consequently, it was the crew's forgetfulness to check the fuel status that led to the crash and eight passenger deaths.[11]

[10] Chalk 1987, note 2 *supra*, uses a similar taxonomy to analyze the effect on the stock price of aircraft manufacturers as a consequence of crashes. He looks at seventy-six crashes, 1966–81. For twenty-three crashes, aircraft design may have been the cause.

[11] According to excerpts from the final report by the NTSB, "the probable cause was the failure of the captain to monitor properly the aircraft's fuel state and to properly respond to the low fuel state and the crew member's advisories regarding fuel state. His inattention resulted from preoccupation with a landing gear malfunction and preparation for a possible emergency landing. Contributing to the accident was the failure of the other two crew members either to fully comprehend the criticality of the fuel state or to successfully communicate their concern to the captain." See Aviation Week and Space Technology, Novem-

Eight of the fifty-six crashes were primarily due to manufacturer error; they are described in Panel B of Table 1. In the well-known American Airlines crash of a McDonnell-Douglas DC-10 in Chicago on May 25, 1979, initial press coverage placed the blame on the manufacturer even though the final NTSB report found the carrier at fault due to improper maintenance procedures. We classify the crash as manufacturer error based on other research.[12] The second part of this category given in Panel B of Table 1 contains fourteen miscellaneous crashes. Six of the crashes had undetermined causes. The remaining eight crashes resulted from a combination of air traffic control error, unavoidable weather conditions (such as wind shear), pilot of another plane at fault, and in one instance, the accident was caused by a bomb in the cargo. Obviously, the carrier could have taken precautions to prevent all of these crashes as well as those attributable to pilot error. We base our argument on the assumption that the costs of reducing the likelihood of pilot-error crashes are lower and that a pilot-error crash is therefore more likey to affect consumers' expectations about future crashes.

IV. Stock Market Event Analysis

There are several methods available to evaluate the stock market effect of an event.[13] The method used in this study estimates the normal market model across the pooled returns of the air carriers involved in each category of crash. The regression includes a dummy variable for the crash event:

$$R_{it} = \alpha_i + \beta_i R_{mt} + \gamma D_t + \epsilon_{it}.$$

ber 5, 1979. A similar incident initiated the Eastern Airlines crash on December 29, 1972. The gear lock indicator failed to come on during the landing approach and the crew tried to determine visually whether the landing gear was extending properly. In their preoccupation with the landing gear none of the crew monitored any of the flight instruments during the final four minutes preceding the crash, failing to detect an uninterrupted descent that led to the crash.

[12] Chalk 1986, note 2 *supra*, estimates the losses suffered by McDonnell-Douglas as a result of the crash. His study shows tht McDonnell-Douglas suffered large losses contemporaneous with the crash, even though the company was eventually cleared by the NTSB.

[13] For a discussion of some of the many choices, see Steve Cantrell, Mark L. Mitchell, & Michael T. Maloney, On Estimating the Variance of Abnormal Stock Market Performance (working paper, U.S. SEC 1989). John Binder, On the Use of the Multivariate Regression Model in Event Studies, 23 J. Acct. Res. 370 (1985); and Michael R. Gibbons, Multivariate Tests of Financial Models: A New Approach, 10 J. Fin. Econ. 3 (1982), discuss an approach very similar to ours. Our approach differs in that we use a pooled estimate of the variance of the residual even though we allow for firm-specific estimates of α and β. We have replicated our results using Binder's model as well as the techniques discussed in Cantrell *et al.* The results we present here are robust.

TABLE 1

DESCRIPTION OF FIFTY-SIX FATAL AIRLINE CRASHES DURING 1964–87
INVOLVING NEW YORK STOCK EXCHANGE OR AMERICAN STOCK EXCHANGE CARRIERS

A: THIRTY-FOUR CRASHES DUE TO PILOT ERROR

Date of Crash	Location	Airline	Aircraft	Passengers Killed	Story
February 8, 1965	Long Island, New York	Eastern	Douglas DC-7	79	Illusion prompted evasive action to avoid collision, placing the plane in an altitude from which it did not recover
September 17, 1965	Monteserrat, British West Indies	Pan Am	Boeing 707	21	Descended too low due to navigational error
November 8, 1965	Constance, Kentucky	American	Boeing 727	53	Failed to arrest an excessive descent rate during landing
November 11, 1965	Salt Lake City, Utah	United	Boeing 727	43	Undershot runway
December 4, 1965	Carmel, New York	Eastern	Lockheed 1049	3	Hit other plane due to misjudgment of altitude separation
August 6, 1966	Falls City, Nebraska	Braniff	British AC	38	Flew too close to avoidable hazardous weather
March 9, 1967	Urbana, Ohio	Trans World	Douglas DC-9	21	Hit other plane due to excessive speed during approach
November 20, 1967	Constance, Kentucky	Trans World	Convair 880	64	Attempted to land without instrument assistance
May 3, 1968	Dawson, Texas	Braniff	Lockheed 188	80	Pilot overloaded wing stress; weather a contributing factor
June 12, 1968	Calcutta, India	Pan Am	Boeing 707	5	Hit trees due to misuse of instruments
October 25, 1968	Hanover, New Hampshire	Northeast	Fairchild 227	30	Premature descent due to misuse of instruments
December 24, 1968	Bradford, Pennsylvania	Allegheny (U.S. Air)	Convair 580	18	Hit trees due to misuse of instruments
November 19, 1969	Glens Falls, New York	Mohawk	Fairchild 227	11	Hit mountain due to misuse of instruments

June 7, 1971	**New Haven, Connecticut**	**Allegheny (U.S. Air)**	**Convair 580**	**26**	**Struck power line due to misuse of instruments**
September 4, 1971	Juneau, Alaska	Alaska	Boeing 727	104	Hit mountain due to misuse of instruments
December 8, 1972	Chicago, Illinois	United	Boeing 737	40	Stalled plane in landing; failed to exercise proper flight management
December 29, 1972	Miami, Florida	Eastern	Lockheed 1011	94	Uninterrupted descent; several deviations from normal operation procedures
July 23, 1973	St. Louis, Missouri	Ozark	Fairchild 227	37	Flew into avoidable thunderstorm
July 31, 1973	Boston, Massachusetts	Delta	McDonnell-Douglas DC-9	82	Hit seawall; failed to note altitude; weather a contributing factor
January 31, 1974	Pago Pago, Samoa	Pan Am	Boeing 707	86	Hit trees due to excessive rate of speed that was uncorrectable
April 22, 1974	Bali, Indonesia	Pan Am	Boeing 707	96	Improper landing; misuse of instruments
September 11, 1974	Charlotte, North Carolina	Eastern	McDonnell-Douglas DC-9	69	Improper landing; lack of altitude awareness due to not following prescribed procedures
December 1, 1974	Berryville, Virginia	Trans World	Boeing 727	85	Hit hill; failed to control an excessive rate of descent; air traffic control procedures partly at fault
April 5, 1976	Ketchikan, Alaska	Alaska	Boeing 727	1	Ran into ditch; misjudged distance necessary to stop on icy runway
April 27, 1976	St. Thomas, Virgin Islands	American	Boeing 727	35	Ran off runway; deviated from prescribed landing techniques
March 27, 1977	Tenerife, Canary Islands	KLM Royal Dutch	Boeing 747	234	Hit other plane; takeoff without clearance
May 8, 1978	Pensacola, Florida	National	Boeing 727	3	Failed to monitor descent rate and altitude
September 25, 1978	San Diego, California	Pacific Southwest	Boeing 727	128	Collided with small plane; failed to comply with a visual separation clearance
December 28, 1978	Portland, Oregon	United	McDonnell-Douglas DC-8	8	Ran out of fuel during preoccupation with a landing gear malfunction
February 12, 1979	Clarksburg, West Virginia	U.S. Air	Frakes M298	1	Failed to deice
October 31, 1979	Mexico City, Mexico	Western	McDonnell-Douglas DC-10	61	Tried to land on closed runway; failed to gain positive visual contact with the open runway

TABLE 1 (*Continued*)

Date of Crash	Location	Airline	Aircraft	Passengers Killed	Story
August 2, 1985	Dallas, Texas	Delta	Lockheed 1011	135	Initiated and continued approach into cloud observed to contain lighting; wind shear also cited
August 16, 1987	Detroit, Michigan	Northwest	McDonnell-Douglas MD80	156	Failed to extend wing flaps in proper position for takeoff
November 15, 1987	Denver, Colorado	Continental	McDonnell-Douglas DC-9	27	Failed to deice after extended wait

B: Twenty-two Crashes in Which Carrier Was Not at Fault

Date of Crash	Location	Airline	Aircraft	Passengers Killed	Story
Manufacturer error:					
February 25, 1964	New Orleans, Louisiana	Eastern	Douglas DC-8	51	Uncontrolled descent due to horizontal stabilization malfunction
November 23, 1964	Rome, Italy	Trans World	Boeing 707	43	Aborted takeoff; power lost on two engines
June 23, 1967	Blossburg, Pennsylvania	Mohawk	British AC 1-11	30	Material failure caused fire in flight
January 18, 1969	Los Angeles, California	United	Boeing 727	32	Inflight electrical failure; weather a contributing factor
March 3, 1972	Albany, New York	Mohawk	Fairchild 227	14	Malfunction of cruise pitch lock system
August 28, 1973	Los Angeles, California	Trans World	Boeing 707	1	Plane porpoised; design defect in control system
March 1, 1978	Los Angeles, California	Continental	McDonnell-Douglas DC-10	2	Skipped off runway; sequential failure of two tires on one landing gear
May 25, 1979	Chicago, Illinois	American	McDonnell-Douglas DC-10	258	Engine fell off on takeoff
Miscellaneous causes:					
July 9, 1964	Parrotsville, Tennessee	United	Viscount 745	35	Exploded in midair; fire in cabin; cause undetermined

August 16, 1965	Lake Michigan, Illinois	United	Boeing 727	24	Crashed in Lake Michigan; cause undetermined
November 6, 1967	Erlanger, Kentucky	Trans World	Boeing 707	1	Aborted takeoff to avoid other plane that lied to tower
December 12, 1968	Caracas, Venezuela	Pan Am	Boeing 707	42	Cause undetermined; possible visual illusion caused by town lights
January 6, 1969	Bradford, Pennsylvania	Allegheny (U.S. Air)	Convair 440	9	Cause undetermined
September 9, 1969	Fairland, Indiana	Allegheny (U.S. Air)	McDonnell-Douglas DC-9	78	Collision with small plane; air traffic control system at fault
July 23, 1973	Papeete, Tahiti	Pan Am	Boeing 707	68	Cause undetermined
September 8, 1974	Cephalomia, Greece	Trans World	Boeing 707	79	Exploded in midair; bomb in cargo
June 24, 1975	Jamaica, New York	Eastern	Boeing 727	106	Wind stream; air traffic control did not advise
March 27, 1977	Tenerife, Canary Islands	Pan Am	Boeing 747	317	Hit by other plane that was taking off without clearance
January 23, 1982	Boston, Massachusetts	World	McDonnell-Douglas DC-10	2	Insufficient information provided by ground control as to runway conditions
July 9, 1982	New Orleans, Louisiana	Pan Am	Boeing 727	153	Wind shear
January 1, 1985	Bolivia	Eastern	Boeing 727	29	Cause undetermined
December 7, 1987	Los Angeles, California	Pacific Southwest	British Aerospace BAe-146	43	Passenger shot crew

The term R_{it} is the return at time t for the ith carrier, R_{mt} is the market return at that date, and the slope and intercept parameters of the market model are allowed to vary for each airline. The dummy variable, D_t, takes a value of one during the event window for each crash in the sample and zero the rest of the time. It directly tests the effects of the event on the stock returns of all companies experiencing this type of crash. In this way, γ is the expected stock market reaction to a crash of this type by any airline.[14]

The window of time used to capture the stock market reaction to the crash is arbitrary. The first day of the crash event window will either be the day of the crash or the day thereafter, depending on whether the stock market was open at the time of the crash.[15] Recall from the previous section that in examining the *Briefs of Fatal Accidents,* which summarizes the NTSB's final reports, and the articles from *AWST* and *WSJ*—many of which were written immediately following the crashes—there was conflict between the initial news accounts and the final reports in only one case. It seems likely that for most of the crashes, the probable cause is known immediately after the crash and, therefore, a short event window should accurately measure the full effect of the crashes. For all models in this article, we present crash event windows ranging from one to ten trading days. Ten trading days (two weeks) should allow more than enough time for investors to accurately forecast the effect of the crashes.

A. *Pilot Error*

We first estimated variations of the pooled, modified market model for the pilot-error category. The estimation periods are 50, 100, and 150 trading days, respectively, and the event window ranges from one to ten trading days.[16] Rather than reporting the estimates of (α_i, β_i) for each

[14] When an airline has more than one crash of a given type, we estimated different sets of $\{\alpha_i, \beta_i\}$ for each crash. In some cases the groupings overlap. Our technique for handling this is discussed in note 19 *infra*.

[15] For crashes that occurred while the stock market was open, the day of the crash is counted as the first day of the crash event window even though the stock market might have been open only thirty minutes after the crash. The first trading day after the crash is used as the first day of the crash event window if the stock market was closed when the crash occurred.

[16] In the pilot-error category, Pan American Airlines had a crash on January 31, 1974, followed by another crash on April 22 during the same year. There are only fifty-five trading days separating the two crashes. The problem here is that if the estimation period is 100 trading days (preceding the crash) for the crash that occurred in April, then the estimation period for that crash would include the crash event window from the January crash and hence bias the estimates. To solve this problem, the first day of the estimation period for the April crash will be the eleventh trading day following the January crash, that is, the first day after the longest crash event window (ten trading days) that will be tested later in this

TABLE 2

ESTIMATES OF γ WHERE D IS {0,1} IN THIRTY-FOUR CRASHES DUE TO PILOT ERROR
MODEL: $R_{it} = \alpha_i + \beta_i R_{mt} + \gamma D_t + \epsilon_{it}$

CRASH EVENT WINDOW (Trading Days)	ESTIMATION PERIOD 50 Trading Days	100 Trading Days	150 Trading Days
1	−.01566 (−3.45)***	−.01626 (−3.63)***	−.01679 (−3.80)***
2	−.01101 (−3.39)**	−.01144 (3.58)***	−.01160 (−3.69)***
3	−.00811 (−3.03)**	−.00859 (−3.28)***	−.00864 −3.35)***
4	−.00561 (−2.40)**	−.00625 (−2.74)***	−.00631 (−2.81)***
5	−.00453 (−2.14)**	−.00522 (−2.56)***	−.00527 (−2.62)***
6	−.00253 (−1.30)	−.00312 (−1.66)*	−.00314 (−1.71)*
7	−.00150 (−.83)	−.00192 (−1.10)	−.00194 (−1.14)
8	−.00095 (−.55)	−.00134 (−.82)	−.00131 (−.81)
9	−.00151 (−.92)	−.00183 (−1.18)	−.00174 (−1.15)
10	−.00172 (−1.10)	−.00203 (−1.37)	−.00191 (−1.32)

NOTE.—t-statistics are in parentheses.
* $p \leq .10$.
** $p \leq .05$.
*** $p \leq .01$.

model, we report only the coefficient and t-statistic for the crash dummy variable.[17] The estimates, presented in Table 2, show that crashes caused by pilot error have a negative effect on the stock returns of the respective airlines. Regardless of the estimation period used (50, 100, or 150 trading days), the coefficient for the crash dummy variable is statistically significant at the 1 percent level for the event windows from one to five trading days with only two exceptions: the crash dummy-variable coefficient for the event windows of four and five trading days associated with the fifty trading days estimation period is statistically significant at the 5 percent level.

section. As discussed earlier, it is not likely that any new information concerning the crashes should develop after ten trading days (two weeks) following the crash. Adopting this procedure, the estimation period for the April 22, 1974, crash will be forty-five trading days, but will be 100 trading days for the other thirty crashes in the pilot-error category. Deleting the second Pan Am crash does not affect the results we report.

[17] The estimates of all the parameters are available upon request.

TABLE 3

% Negative Cumulative Abnormal Returns in Thirty-four Crashes due to Pilot Error

Crash Event Window (Trading Days)	Estimation Period		
	50 Trading Days	100 Trading Days	150 Trading Days
1	1.57	1.63	1.68
2	2.20	2.29	2.32
3	2.43	2.58	2.59
4	2.24	2.50	2.52
5	2.27	2.61	2.64

For the most part, the coefficients for the crash dummy variable in Table 2 decline as the event window lengthens, but the estimated effect of the crash stays approximately constant. To calculate the cumulative abnormal return, multiply the coefficient for the crash dummy variable by the number of trading days in the event window. Table 3 contains the cumulative abnormal returns corresponding to the dummy variable coefficients from Table 2 for the first five trading days.

For the crash event window of one trading day (the day of the crash if the market was open at the time of the crash), the negative abnormal returns average 1.63 percent. They increase for the two-day event window to 2.27 percent and are 2.53, 2.42,and 2.51 percent for the event windows of three, four, and five trading days, respectively. By all appearances, an airline suffers a negative abnormal return of approximately 2.5 percent due to crashes caused by pilot error.

B. *Manufacturer Error and Miscellaneous Causes*

In this section, we report the pooled, modified market model for those crashes in which passengers were killed but the airline was not directly at fault. These crashes should have a smaller effect on the respective airlines' brand names than those crashes, discussed in the previous section, that are directly the responsibility of the airline.

The pooled, modified market model was estimated for the twenty-two crashes in this category. The coefficient and *t*-statistic for the crash dummy variable from each model (estimation period—50, 100, and 150 trading days; event window—one to ten trading days) are shown in Table 4.

Unlike the results from the pilot-error category, it does not appear that crashes for which the airline is not directly responsible have much of an effect on the stock returns of the respective airlines. None of the crash

TABLE 4

ESTIMATES OF γ WHERE D IS {0,1} IN TWENTY-TWO CRASHES DUE TO MANUFACTURER ERROR AND MISCELLANEOUS CAUSES
MODEL: $R_{it} = \alpha_i + \beta_i R_{mt} + \gamma D_t + \epsilon_{it}$

CRASH EVENT WINDOW (Trading Days)	ESTIMATION PERIOD		
	50 Trading Days	100 Trading Days	150 Trading Days
1	−.00602	−.00459	−.00406
	(−.86)	(−.70)	(−.64)
2	−.00631	−.00561	−.00523
	(−1.26)	(−1.20)	(−1.17)
3	−.00231	−.00196	−.00152
	(−.56)	(−.51)	(−.41)
4	−.00288	−.00291	−.00250
	(−.81)	(−.88)	(−.78)
5	−.00231	−.00246	−.00215
	(−.79)	(−.83)	(−.75)
6	−.00091	−.00116	−.00090
	(−.31)	(−.42)	(−.34)
7	−.00281	−.00294	−.00268
	(−1.02)	(−1.16)	(−1.10)
8	−.00295	−.00312	−.00299
	(−1.14)	(−1.31)	(−1.32)
9	−.00172	−.00184	−.00185
	(−.70)	(−.82)	(−.86)
10	−.00042	−.00062	−.00060
	(−.18)	(−.29)	(−.29)

NOTE.—t-statistics are in parentheses.

dummy coefficients is statistically significant at conventional levels. This evidence suggests that airlines suffer negative abnormal returns due to crashes for which they are largely responsible but are generally immune to other types of crashes.[18]

C. Death Rate

One problem posed by the {0,1} dummy-variable technique is that it treats all crashes the same. This creates two inaccuracies: crashes differ in terms of the number of people killed and in terms of the size of the

[18] We tested one additional category that consisted of seven crashes; six occurred on training flights, the seventh on a ferry flight. The plane was destroyed in all seven crashes and in only one did any of the crew survive. None of the crash coefficients is statistically significant and the point estimates are positive.

We also estimated the pooled, modified market model for the manufacturer error and miscellaneous crash categories separately. Results from these models are not unlike those shown in Table 4 and are available on request as are any other results mentioned but not reported.

airline involved. The more people killed in an at-fault crash, the more the airline will likely suffer. That is, when the pilot misjudges the runway and goes into a ditch killing one passenger, consumers will revise their estimate of a future crash less than when the pilot takes off without clearance, hits another plane, and kills 234 people. On the other hand, the larger the airline, the more likely it is to have a crash due to any cause and the less effect an at-fault crash should have on its rate of return.

To rectify both of these shortcomings, we defined a *death-rate* variable. We modified the dummy variable to let the nonzero values become the square root of the number of passengers killed in each crash divided by the number of passengers served by the airline in the year of the crash.[19]

Employing this new crash variable, we reestimated the regressions shown in Table 2. Table 5 displays the results. In each case, the coefficients have the negative sign predicted by the theory, and the significance levels are substantially higher than the results found using the {0,1} dummy. All but eleven of the thirty coefficients are statistically significant at the 1 percent level and those eleven are significant at either the 5 percent or 10 percent level.[20] These results indicate that, when the number of people killed and the size of the airline involved are accounted for, the negative stock market performance of the negligent carriers is even more pronounced.

We also estimated death-rate model for the combined *manufacturer-error and miscellaneous causes* crash category consisting of twenty-two crashes. Results are shown in Table 6. For the first trading day event window, the estimated effect is negative and statistically significant in all specifications. However, none of the remaining death-rate dummy variable coefficients is significantly different from zero. The statistical significance of the first day is probably due to imperfect information about the cause of the crash. We interpret these results, like those shown in Table 4,

[19] Other deflators for airline size could be used. For instance, revenue-passenger-miles is a common metric in the airline business. However, because most crashes occur during the takeoff and landing phases of the flight, distance weighting seems inappropriate. In all events, we tried several deflators, including the equity value of the airline. The results are very close in every case to those found using deaths per passenger served. Similarly, employing a square root transformation of deaths per passenger served is arbitrary; this transformation maximized the goodness of fit, but the results using untransformed deaths per passenger served or higher roots of this variable are nearly identical to those reported here and are available upon request. See Table 1, Panels A and B, for the number of passenger deaths per crash. Annual passenger data comes from Airport Activity Statistics of Certified Route Air Carriers, prepared jointly by the Civil Aeronautics Board (CAB) and the FAA.

[20] All of the coefficients for the events ranging from one to six trading days are statistically significant at the 1 percent level.

TABLE 5

ESTIMATES OF γ WHERE D IS DEATH RATE IN THIRTY-FOUR CRASHES DUE TO PILOT ERROR

MODEL: $R_{it} = \alpha_i + \beta_i R_{mt} + \gamma D_t + \epsilon_{it}$

Crash Event Window (Trading Days)	Estimated Period		
	50 Trading Days	100 Trading Days	150 Trading Days
1	−6.30881	−6.23988	−6.26241
	(−5.24)***	(−5.19)***	(−5.27)***
2	−3.73167	−3.66816	−3.67762
	(−4.33)***	(−4.30)***	(−4.37)***
3	−2.93351	−2.86842	−2.84801
	(−4.14)***	(−4.09)***	(−4.13)***
4	−2.05363	−2.00388	−2.00635
	(−3.30)***	(−3.28)***	(−3.34)***
5	−1.86909	−1.83025	−1.79398
	(−3.33)***	(−3.34)***	(−3.33)***
6	−1.53917	−1.47420	−1.43356
	(−2.98)***	(−2.93)***	(−2.91)***
7	−1.26338	−1.17413	−1.07514
	(−2.62)***	(−2.51)**	(−2.34)**
8	−.90006	−.80399	−.72771
	(−1.97)**	(−1.82)*	(−1.69)*
9	−1.01744	−.91887	−.87177
	(−2.34)**	(−2.20)**	(−2.01)**
10	−.89674	−.76918	−.74794
	(−2.15)**	(−2.00)**	(−1.65)*

NOTE.—t-statistics are in parentheses.
* $p \leq .10$.
** $p \leq .05$.
*** $p \leq .01$.

to mean that carriers endure no losses as a consequence of airline crashes where the carrier is not at fault.[21]

D. *Deregulation*

To test for the effect of deregulation, we split the sample into two parts. More precisely, we included a deregulation dummy variable (zero prior to 1976 and one thereafter) interacted with the crash variable. This deregulation dummy variable is insignificant in both the at-fault and no-fault re-

[21] Borenstein & Zimmerman, *supra* note 5, at 915 n.4, take exception to this conclusion, saying that the coefficients are not statistically different. The argument is problematic. Clearly the coefficients in the at-fault regressions are statistically significant and those in the no-fault regressions are insignificant. We have already argued that the sampling errors in the no-fault category should be large and the point estimates negative because consumers will hold carriers responsible for some of these crashes. Add to this the results reported in note 18 *supra*. We stand by our conclusion.

TABLE 6

ESTIMATES OF γ WHERE D IS DEATH RATE IN TWENTY-TWO CRASHES DUE TO MANUFACTURER ERROR AND MISCELLANEOUS CAUSES

MODEL: $R_{it} = \alpha_i + \beta_i R_{mt} + \gamma D_t + \epsilon_{it}$

CRASH EVENT WINDOW (Trading Days)	ESTIMATION PERIOD		
	50 Trading Days	100 Trading Days	150 Trading Days
1	−5.30527	−4.57396	−4.41457
	(−2.02)**	(−1.85)*	(−1.86)*
2	−2.76623	−2.44749	−2.40820
	(−1.48)	(−1.39)	(−1.43)
3	−.94753	−.67739	−.55591
	(−.61)	(−.47)	(−.40)
4	−.79363	−.69778	−.56756
	(−.59)	(−.56)	(−.47)
5	−.72113	−.76665	−.67540
	(−.60)	(−.68)	(−.63)
6	−.06889	−.13051	−.05458
	(−.06)	(−.13)	(−.06)
7	−1.05332	−1.07047	−.98692
	(−1.02)	(−1.12)	(−1.08)
8	−1.20830	−1.23018	−1.18930
	(−1.24)	(−1.37)	(−1.39)
9	−.76621	−.79487	−.79161
	(−.83)	(−.94)	(−.98)
10	−.44926	−.49273	−.49139
	(−.50)	(−.61)	(−.63)

NOTE.—t-statistics are in parentheses.
* $p \leq .10$.
** $p \leq .05$.

gressions. We ran some sensitivity tests with respect to the date (1977 and 1978 were tried) and with respect to the model specification, but we uncovered no sign of a change in the pattern of stock market reactions to crashes as a result of the change in the regulatory regime.

V. INSURANCE RATING

The reaction of the stock market in the case of at-fault crashes compared to bad-luck crashes differs markedly. In the case of pilot-error crashes, airlines experience significantly negative stock market returns, whereas in crashes that are the fault of other carriers, government employees, or bad luck, no stock market effect is observed. Yet, in both cases, airplanes are destroyed and passengers are killed.[22] Since there is

[22] The average number of passengers killed is fifty-seven in at-fault crashes and sixty-four in no-fault crashes.

no evidence that liability claims for the loss of passenger lives differ between these two categories of crashes,[23] we are left with only two explanations of the difference in the stock market reaction. The stock market losses in the case of pilot-error crashes are due to a brand name effect and/or to insurance rate adjustments. The question is one of assessing the relative magnitudes.

Airlines are required by the federal government to carry liability insurance; they are required to report the amount paid for both liability and hull insurance to the U.S. Department of Transportation. In this section, we report estimates of the insurance rating formula. Our interest is in knowing if the occurrence of a crash has an effect on insurance rates. We have data on total liability and total hull insurance premiums paid annually by the airlines in our sample. The insurance data for each carrier start at least five years before its first crash and extend at least five years after its last crash, with a few exceptions.[24] The data set contains 301 observations on passenger-liability insurance and 300 observations on hull insurance. We calculate the two insurance rates by dividing total liability and total hull insurance premiums paid by each airline in each year by the revenue-passenger-miles served by the airline in that year.[25]

We hypothesize that insurance rates are a function of several things. First, there may be economies of scale. Just as two-car families typically receive lower rates than a one-car insuree, we expect big airlines to get lower rates than small airlines. Two-car families receive lower rates because the average miles driven per car declines. Bigger airlines get lower rates because they fly longer flights. Most crashes occur during takeoffs and landings. The probability of a crash declines the more the airline is engaged in the cruising phase of flight.

[23] We searched the WSJ, Business Insurance, and the aviation trade publications on this point and found no evidence of differences in settlements systematically related to the cause of the crash. Settlements appear to differ by crash based on the amount of the publicity associated with the disaster, which may or may not be related to fault on the part of the carrier.

[24] No insurance data are available for KLM because it is a foreign carrier and not required to file CAB Form 41. Pacific Southwest (PSA) was not required to file Form 41 because it operated only in California. Mohawk Airlines was purchased two years after a pilot-error crash and hence the insurance data end at that point. Insurance data for World Airlines was not consistently available due to bankruptcy.

[25] Liability insurance rates are typically expressed in this fashion. For instance, Texas Air paid fifty cents per 1,000 revenue-passenger-miles flown in 1987, whereas Frontier paid 72 cents, as reported in Texas Air Picks Hall as Aviation Broker, Bus. Ins. 1 (November 3, 1986). Hull insurance rates, on the other hand, are typically expressed as cents per $100 of insured value. The hull rate we construct approximates the industry standard in that revenue-passenger-miles are highly correlated with the value of the fleet. That is, more passengers implies more planes and longer flights means bigger planes. The data on revenue-passenger-miles were obtained from CAB Air Carrier Traffic Statistics.

Second, we expect that insurance rates for one airline are a function of the rates charged to other airlines. Obviously, there are industry-wide phenomena at play. The air traffic controllers' strike, terrorists' attacks, and general congestion are all industry-wide conditions that should affect rates.[26] Using the average rate paid by all other carriers is a convenient way to capture industry effects when estimating the rate paid by each individual carrier.

Lastly, the safety record of the carrier itself should, in an efficiently functioning insurance market, affect the rate paid by the carrier.[27] The safety record that we examine is the frequency of both at-fault and no-fault crashes. It is possible that no-fault crashes could cause insurance rates to rise; however, the absence of a significant stock market reaction reduces the probability of this.

In order to estimate the rating formula, we first regressed the liability insurance rate for each carrier in each year on the carrier's revenue-passenger-miles in that year, the average liability rates paid by all other carriers in that year, and the crash variable for both at-fault and no-fault crashes. The crash variable definition is the same as that used in the stock market analysis: using the dummy variable approach, it takes the value of one in the year of the crash and zero otherwise; similarly, the death-rate crash variable is positive in the year of the crash and zero otherwise. If there are two crashes in a year, the death rates are summed and the dummy variable takes a value of two.

We include the current value and five lags of the crash variable. This specification captures directly the continuing, but decaying, effect of idiosyncratic adjustments in the rates paid by each carrier. For instance, if a carrier is at fault in a crash, then its rates should go up and should remain high for some time thereafter. Again, like automobile insurance, the rate increases occasioned by an at-fault crash should be forgiven over time.

[26] Acording to several articles in Business Insurance, rates generally increase for all airlines following an above-normal series of crashes, such as in 1985. See Record Aviation Losses to Hike Rates for Airlines, Bus. Ins. 1 (August 19, 1985) and, likewise, following four terrorist attacks on airlines in 1985 and 1986, insurers added a "terrorist surcharge" to international carriers. See Terrorist Surcharge Adds to Growing Cost of Airlines' Coverage, Bus. Ins. 1 (June 23, 1986).

[27] For example, in 1983, while most airlines received rate reductions from 2 to 10 percent, Pan American Airlines was expected to be hit with a rate increase of about 20 percent. The rate increase for Pan Am was due to a July 1982 crash in New Orleans that killed all 146 passengers aboard and eight people on the ground. In September of 1983, Pan Am experienced another accident when one of its Boeing 747s skidded off the runway in Pakistan, resulting in several million dollars of damages. Both of these crashes combined contributed to a 90 percent rate increase from 1982 to 1984. See Increased Competition Cuts Most Aviation Rates, and Pan Am Can't Avoid Increase, Bus. Ins. 3 (July 11, 1983); Losses Force Pan Am to Take Special $10 Million Deductible, Bus. Ins. 1 (July 30, 1984).

Even though insurance rates do not necessarily formally change in the year of the crash, airlines that do not experience a crash receive a rebate.[28] Hence, a crash affects our measure of insurance rates in the calendar year of the crash. In the years after the crash, the actual rates are expected to adjust. Also, the policy date can vary through the calendar year. We estimated the insurance equations using specifications of the crash variable accounting for this effect. We weighted the crash variable based on the proportion of the calendar year remaining after the crash.

Table 7 displays the results of the liability rate estimates. All variables perform as expected. The dependent and independent variables, except for the crash variable, are in natural logs. Revenue-passenger-miles is the economy-of-scale variable and shows a small, but significant, negative effect.[29] The industry effect is similarly significant and carries the expected positive sign.

For both specifications of the crash variable (zero, one, and death-rate), the coefficients show a decaying pattern after an at-fault crash. In the dummy variable model, the coefficients represent the percentage increase in insurance premiums after the crash over what they would have been in the absence of a crash. For instance, insurance premiums are 34 percent higher in the year of a crash, 19 percent higher in the year after, 17 percent higher two years later, and so on. The total effect of a crash is the sum of these coefficients. The significance level of this sum can be investigated using a standard *F*-test. In both specifications, the significance of the sum is .007 for at-fault crashes.

In the dummy variable model, the sum of the coefficients for at-fault crashes is .88; this says that, all told, an at-fault crash causes premium increases spread over the following years that total to almost 90 percent of the premium paid in the year before the crash. In the death-rate specification, these coefficients must be multiplied by the value of this crash variable for each disaster to assess the effect of the crash on insurance premiums. We compute the discounted average dollar effect for all specifications in the next section.

There is some evidence in the liability insurance regressions that no-fault crashes have insurance rate effects. In the dummy variable model, the no-fault crash coefficients taken together are significant at the .06

[28] The airline forfeits a profit commission (as high as 20 percent of the premium paid), which it receives if no crash occurs. See American Airlines Gets Reduced Rates, Bus. Ins. 19 (September 19, 1983).

[29] We tried estimating the equation in levels and included a squared term for this variable. A U-shaped function results, but the minimum is found at the upper boundary of the data on the independent variable.

TABLE 7

PASSENGER LIABILITY INSURANCE RATES

Crash Variable Specification	{0,1}	Death Rate
Intercept	5.897	5.376
	(14.972)***	(13.419)***
Revenue-passenger-miles	−.451	−.413
	(−17.128)***	(−15.777)***
Industry liability rate	.277	.295
	(11.008)***	(11.759)***
At-fault $crash_t$	.341	105.595
	(2.616)***	(2.729)***
At-fault $crash_{t-1}$	.193	51.134
	(1.465)	(1.286)
At-fault $crash_{t-2}$	.174	44.596
	(1.274)	(1.106)
At-fault $crash_{t-3}$	.071	17.219
	(.493)	(.413)
At-fault $crash_{t-4}$	.056	3.995
	(.394)	(.096)
At-fault $crash_{t-5}$	.055	−.948
	(.139)	(−.023)
No-fault $crash_t$	.306	66.045
	(1.754)**	(.947)
No-fault $crash_{t-1}$	.067	27.944
	(.351)	(.374)
No-fault $crash_{t-2}$	.199	68.771
	(.983)	(.849)
No-fault $crash_{t-3}$	.064	22.974
	(.314)	(.289)
No-fault $crash_{t-4}$	.073	3.950
	(.369)	(.050)
No-fault $crash_{t-5}$	−.025	−5.345
	(−.130)	(−.069)
F-test on the sum of coefficients on:		
At-fault crash	7.209***	7.223***
No-fault crash	3.507*	1.853
R^2	.702	.694
Degrees of freedom for error	286	286

NOTE.—t-statistics are in parentheses; dependent variable, Passenger liability insurance rates, Revenue-passenger-miles, and Industry liability rate are expressed in logarithms.

* $p \leq .10$.

** $p \leq .05$.

*** $p \leq .01$.

level. However, the coefficients do not show the smooth decay pattern found in the at-fault category. Using the death-rate model, the sum of the coefficients is insignificant at conventional levels.

Essentially the same model is used for hull insurance rates with the substitution of industry-wide average hull rates for industry-wide liability rates. Since hull insurance covers the plane itself and not the passesngers, we substitute total miles flown instead of revenue-passenger-miles for the economy-of-scale variable. The results from the hull insurance equation, shown in Table 8, parallel those found in liability insurance. None of the dummy variable crash coefficients is significant, but the at-fault coefficients on the death-rate variable are. Their sum is significant at the .05 level. The no-fault death-rate coefficients are insignificant. The industry and economy-of-scale effects are both shown to operate in the predicted fashion.

VI. Net Brand Name Effects

The insurance results indicate that at least some of the declines in stock market value consequent to at-fault crashes can be attributed to the positive effect these crashes have on the insurance premiums paid by the airlines. In this section we compare the insurance premium adjustments to the stock market losses. To the extent that the stock market losses are greater than can be explained by the insurance adjustments, the residual can be interpreted as a brand-name loss suffered by the airlines due to at-fault crashes.

In order to compare the two effects, we first need a measure of the capitalized stock market losses resulting from at-fault crashes. For each crash we multiply the average abnormal return (−2.31 percent) on the crash variable for the five-day event window in the stock market analysis times the value of the variable (one in the dummy variable specification and the square root of deaths per passenger served in the death-rate specification) and then this times the equity value of the airline at the end of the day prior to the crash. This value is shown in Table 9 for the two specifications. Using the dummy variable model, the average value across all pilot-error crashes in 1987 dollars is $27.3 million.[30] Accounting for the number killed and the size of the airline in each crash, the estimated average stock market losses from at-fault crashes are $19.1 million.

[30] We inflated the dollar value of the lost equity to 1987 terms using the Consumer Price Index. The appropriateness of inflating equity values by the inflation rate is problematic. It measures the current purchasing power of the stock market losses. We inflated the insurance cost increases similarly.

TABLE 8

HULL INSURANCE RATES

Crash Variable Specification	{0,1}	Death Rate
Intercept	−.993	−1.135
	(−10.578)***	(−12.971)***
Revenue miles	−.713	−.740
	(−8.234)***	(−8.561)***
Industry liability rate	.337	.326
	(9.600)***	(9.422)***
At-fault crash$_t$	.055	126.636
	(.292)	(2.339)***
At-fault crash$_{t-1}$	.062	71.287
	(.324)	(1.277)
At-fault crash$_{t-2}$	−.064	33.409
	(−.323)	(.590)
At-fault crash$_{t-3}$	−.177	3.159
	(−.862)	(.053)
At-fault crash$_{t-4}$	−.196	5.817
	(−.967)	(.100)
At-fault crash$_{t-5}$	−.278	−12.152
	(−1.394)	(−.216)
No-fault crash$_t$	.222	163.932
	(.884)	(1.669)*
No-fault crash$_{t-1}$	−.030	−3.165
	(−.110)	(−.030)
No-fault crash$_{t-2}$	.248	142.162
	(.854)	(1.245)
No-fault crash$_{t-3}$	−.244	−92.627
	(−.840)	(−.830)
No-fault crash$_{t-4}$	.015	5.048
	(.054)	(.045)
No-fault crash$_{t-5}$	−.286	−116.212
	(−1.057)	(−1.078)
F-test on the sum of coefficients on:		
At-fault crash	1.597	4.022***
No-fault crash	.020	.267
R^2	.456	.465
Degrees of freedom for error	285	285

NOTE.—*t*-statistics are in parentheses; dependent variable, Revenue miles, and Industry liability rate are expressed in logarithms.

* $p \leq .10$.

*** $p \leq .01$.

TABLE 9

CAPITALIZED VALUE OF STOCK MARKET LOSSES, INSURANCE LOSSES, AND BRAND NAME LOSSES

Crash Variable Specification	{0.1}	Death Rate
Insurance cost increases ($)	8,940,097	8,055,210
Stock market losses ($)	27,275,068	19,103,226
Brand name loss ($)	18,334,971	11,048,016
% brand name loss/ stock market losses	67.0	57.8

The insurance losses are capitalized in the following fashion. The insurance premium increases occasioned by each crash are projected using the coefficients on the current and lagged values of the crash variable. Negative coefficients are set equal to zero. The projected premium percentage increases from each model are discounted back to the point of the crash.[31] In the death-rate specifications, the premium increases are found by multiplying the estimated coefficients by the square root of deaths per passenger served. The sum of these coefficients times the total insurance premium paid in the year prior to the crash gives the present value of the increase in insurance costs at the time of the crash. Hull and liability premium increases are summed, and this value is inflated to 1987 dollars and compared to the stock market losses. Table 9 reports the results. The total insurance cost increases are $8.94 million and $8.05 million for the two models.

Comparing the insurance and stock market losses yields estimates of a brand name loss of $18.3 million and $11 million. In percentage terms, the brand name loss is 67 percent in the dummy variable model and 57.8 percent using the death-rate specification.

Both specifications yield consistent results. By and large, at-fault crashes show negative abnormal stock market returns, positive insurance cost increases, and a net brand name loss. No-fault crashes produce no systematic stock market or insurance reaction. Using death-rates, there is an initial stock market blip that then recedes and there is no insurance effect following no-fault crashes. Using the dummy variable model, there

[31] To obtain a discount rate, we average the rate of return on equity for all airlines over the period 1965–86 using monthly stock market returns. This gives an estimate of the nominal discount rate. We adjust this by the inflation rate computed from the Consumer Price Index to obtain a real discount rate. The nominal return was 14.15 (in annual terms); the inflation rate was 5.95; this gives a real rate of 8.2.

is no stock market reaction and a small, erratic insurance effect. Taken together, we dismiss the no-fault effects.

VII. Conclusions

All told, the results are straightforward and support the notion that airline crashes cause consumers to reduce their demand for the services provided by negligent carriers, which is the prediction of the theory that brand names are a quality assuring mechanism. To summarize the results, in those instances where there is the greatest likelihood that the air carrier is at fault, there is a significantly negative stock market reaction to the event. However, in cases where there is less reason to suspect that the airline shirked its safety responsibilities, there is no adverse stock performance.

Together these results imply that the negative returns in the first case are not attributable to the loss of the plane or the passenger liability claims that result from the crash. In both of the categories that we have contrasted here, planes were lost and liability claims ensued. Our examination of the industry reports of liability claims for passenger deaths yields no suggestion that the awards are larger in the case of at-fault crashes as opposed to, say, cases where weather is the causal factor. Thus, the absence of stock market reaction to crashes in which the carrier is not at fault suggests that airlines purchase insurance against these perils in an amount sufficient to offset virtually all of the losses. The decline in stock market value associated with at-fault crashes must, then, represent a decline in the brand name value of the company or an expected increase in insurance rates.

To examine the magnitude of insurance rate adjustments, we estimated an insurance rating equation for both liability and hull insurance. We find that insurance rates do respond to the safety record of the airline as measured by the incidence and severity of crashes due to pilot error. The fact that insurance rates adjust as a result of these crashes implies that there is a revision of the probability of a crash. This is a necessary condition for there to be a brand name effect. When we compare the magnitude of the insurance rate increases to the stock market losses we find that, at most, 42 percent of the stock market losses can be explained by insurance cost increases. The rest, then, must be due to declines in the value of brand name.

The insurance effects, in conjunction with the analysis of brand names, provide an interesting twist in the discussion of liability claims against airlines. Consider the implication of a finding that says there is no brand name effect in at-fault airline crashes. This would mean that consumers did not care how careful the airline was and presumably this would stem from the fact that they were being overindemnified. That is, such a result would mean consumers were at least indifferent between the settlement value available to their heirs when they ride on risky airlines and the reduced probability of death when they choose a safe carrier. On the other hand, the results we have presented here suggest that consumers do, indeed, avoid risky airlines, which suggests that consumers are not overindemnified by liability awards. This, in turn, raises the question of why there appears to be no extra compensation in the liability settlements for at-fault crashes.

Finally, we find no evidence of deregulation in the pattern of brand name effects. This raises the question of whether or not we can expect deregulation to have any safety effect. Indeed, since our results suggest the market is quite efficient at punishing airlines for at-fault crashes, the need for increased airline safety regulation is not apparent.

Bibliography

Benjamin, Daniel, and Mitchell, Mark L. "Quality-Assuring Price Premium: Classic Evidence from the Real Thing." Working paper. Washington, D.C.: U.S. Securities and Exchange Commission, 1989.

Binder, John. "On the Use of the Multivariate Regression Model in Event Studies." *Journal of Accounting Research* 23 (Spring 1985): 370–83.

Borenstein, Severin, and Zimmerman, Martin B. "Market Incentives for Safe Commercial Airline Operation." *American Economic Review* 78 (December 1987): 913–35.

Cantrell, Steve; Mitchell, Mark L.; and Maloney, Michael T. "On Estimating the Variance of Abnormal Stock Market Performance." Working paper. Washington, D.C.: U.S. Securities and Exchange Commission, 1989.

Chalk, Andrew. "Market Forces and Aircraft Safety: The Case of the DC-10." *Economic Inquiry* 24 (January 1986): 43–60.

Chalk, Andrew. "Market Forces in Commercial Aircraft Safety." *Journal of Industrial Economics* 36 (September 1987): 61–82.

Gibbons, Michael R. "Multivariate Tests of Financial Models: A New Approach." *Journal of Financial Economics* 10 (Spring 1982): 3–27.

Jarrell, Gregg, and Peltzman, Sam. "The Impact of Product Recalls on the Wealth of Sellers." *Journal of Political Economy* 93 (June 1985): 512–36.

Klein, Benjamin; Crawford, Robert G.; and Alchian, Armen A. "Vertical Integration, Appropriable Rents, and the Competitive Contracting Process." *Journal of Law and Economics* 21 (October 1978): 297–326.

Klein, Benjamin, and Leffler, Keith. "The Role of Market Forces in Assuring Contractual Performance." *Journal of Political Economy* 21 (August 1981): 615–41.

Mitchell, Mark L. "The Impact of External Parties on Brand-Name Capital: The 1982 Tylenol Poisonings and Subsequent Cases." *Economic Inquiry* (in press).

Acknowledgments

Akerlof, George A. "The Market for 'Lemons': Qualitative Uncertainty and the Market Mechanism." *Quarterly Journal of Economics* 84 (1970): 488–500. Reprinted with the permission of MIT Press.

Cheung, Steven N.S. "Transaction Costs, Risk Aversion, and the Choice of Contractual Arrangements." *Journal of Law and Economics* 12 (1969): 23–42. Reprinted with the permission of the University of Chicago Press, publisher. Copyright 1969 by the University of Chicago Press.

Umbeck, John. "A Theory of Contract Choice and the California Gold Rush." *Journal of Law and Economics* 20 (1977): 421–37. Reprinted with the permission of the University of Chicago Press, publisher. Copyright 1977 by the University of Chicago Press.

Posner, Richard A., and Andrew M. Rosenfield. "Impossibility and Related Doctrines in Contract Law: An Economic Analysis." *Journal of Legal Studies* 6 (1977): 83–118. Reprinted with the permission of the University of Chicago Law School. Copyright by the University of Chicago. All rights reserved.

Hadley v. *Baxendale*, 9 Ex. 341, 156 Eng. Rep. 145 (1854). In *Cases and Problems on Contracts*, edited by John D. Calamari and Joseph M. Perillo (St. Paul: West Publishing Co., 1978): 662–65. Reprinted with the permission of the West Publishing Company.

Sherwood v. *Walker*, 66 Mich. 568 (1887). In *Law and Economics*, edited by Robert Cooter and Thomas Ulen (Glenview, Ill.: Scott, Foresman and Co., 1988): 261–63. Reprinted with the permission of Addison Wesley Longman.

Williams v. *Walker-Thomas*, 350 F.2d 445 (1965). Reprinted with the permission of the West Publishing Company.

Epstein, Richard A. "Unconscionability: A Critical Reappraisal." *Journal of Law and Economics* 18 (1975): 293–315. Reprinted with the permission of the University of Chicago Press, publisher. Copyright 1975 by the University of Chicago Press.

Brinig, Margaret F. "Rings and Promises." *Journal of Law, Economics and Organization* 6 (1990): 203–15. Reprinted with the permission of Oxford University Press.

Landes, Elisabeth M., and Richard A. Posner. "The Economics of the Baby Shortage." *Journal of Legal Studies* 7 (1978): 323–48. Reprinted with the permission of the University of Chicago Law School. Copyright by the University of Chicago. All rights reserved.

Ramseyer, J. Mark. "The Market for Children: Evidence from Early Modern Japan." *Journal of Law, Economics and Organization* 11 (1995): 127–49. Reprinted with the permission of Oxford University Press.

Paris v. *Stepney Borough Council*, 1951 A.C. 367 (H.L.). In *Tort Law: Cases and Economic Analysis*, edited by Richard A. Posner (Boston: Little, Brown and Co., 1982): 212–14. Reprinted with the permission of Little, Brown and Company, Inc.

Fishback, Price V., and Shawn Everett Kantor. "'Square Deal' or Raw Deal? Market Compensation for Workplace Disamenities, 1884–1903." *Journal of Economic History* 52 (1992): 826–48. Reprinted with the permission of Cambridge University Press.

Lehn, Kenneth. "Property Rights, Risk Sharing, and Player Disability in Major League Baseball." *Journal of Law and Economics* 25 (1982): 343–66. Reprinted with the permission of the University of Chicago Press, publisher. Copyright 1982 by the University of Chicago Press.

Coase, R.H. "The Nature of the Firm." *Economica* 4 n.s. (1937): 386–405. Reprinted with the permission of Blackwell Publishers Ltd.

Stigler, George J. "The Theory of Economic Regulation." *Bell Journal of Economics and Management Science* 2, no.1 (1971): 3–21. Reprinted with the permission of Atlantic Telephone and Telegraph.

Stigler, George J., and Claire Friedland. "What Can Regulators Regulate? The Case of Electricity." *Journal of Law and Economics* 5 (1972): 1–12. Reprinted with the permission of the University of Chicago Press, publisher. Copyright 1972 by the University of Chicago Press.

Swan, Peter L. "Alcoa: The Influence of Recycling on Monopoly Power." *Journal of Political Economy* 88 (1980): 76–99. Reprinted with the permission of the University of Chicago Press, publisher. Copyright 1980 by the University of Chicago Press.

Gallick, Edward C., and David E. Sisk. "A Reconsideration of Taxi Regulation." *Journal of Law, Economics and Organization* 3 (1987): 117–28. Reprinted with the permission of Oxford University Press.

Viscusi, W. Kip. "The Lulling Effect: The Impact of Child-Resistant Packaging on Aspirin and Analgesic Ingestions." *American Economic Review* 74 (1984): 324–27. Reprinted with the permission of the American Economic Association.

Peterson, Steven, George Hoffer, and Edward Millner. "Are Drivers of Air-Bag-Equipped Cars More Aggressive? A Test of the Offsetting Behavior Hypothesis." *Journal of Law and Economics* 38 (1995): 251–64. Reprinted with the permission of the University of Chicago Press, publisher. Copyright 1995 by the University of Chicago Press.

Mitchell, Mark L., and Michael Maloney. "Crisis in the Cockpit? The Role of Market Forces in Promoting Air Travel Safety." *Journal of Law and Economics* 32 (1989): 329–55. Reprinted with the permission of the University of Chicago Press, publisher. Copyright 1989 by the University of Chicago Press.